BABATHA'S ORCHARD

Babatha's Orchard

The Yadin Papyri and an Ancient Jewish Family Tale Retold

PHILIP F. ESLER

OXFORD
UNIVERSITY PRESS

OXFORD
UNIVERSITY PRESS

Great Clarendon Street, Oxford, OX2 6DP,
United Kingdom

Oxford University Press is a department of the University of Oxford.
It furthers the University's objective of excellence in research, scholarship,
and education by publishing worldwide. Oxford is a registered trade mark of
Oxford University Press in the UK and in certain other countries

First Edition published in 2017

Published in the United States of America by Oxford University Press
198 Madison Avenue, New York, NY 10016, United States of America

British Library Cataloguing in Publication Data
Data available

Library of Congress Control Number: 2016945505

ISBN 978–0–19–876716–9

For Patricia, Dominic, Thomas, and Sinéad

Acknowledgements

In 2013, prior to my taking up the Portland Chair in New Testament Studies at the University of Gloucestershire, I started work on two new research projects. One was Ethiopic 1st Enoch and the other was the Babatha archive of legal papyri from 94 to 132 CE. This book arises from my realization of the extraordinary and remarkably neglected riches to be found in the Babatha archive. I well remember my increasing excitement in those early months in 2013 as I worked through its thirty-five papyri one by one. Previously they had mainly attracted research on their legal dimensions. I was extremely taken, however, by the extent to which they allowed direct access to the social world of Nabatea and Judea, including the events in one Dead Sea town in 99 CE. This was the period in which some of the New Testament texts, such as the Gospel of Matthew, would have been appearing. As an erstwhile lawyer, I found myself continually caught up in the usual drama of opportunity for, or threat to, named individuals that required legal intervention in the form of commercial agreements or documents for legal proceedings. Such documents were drafted by highly competent lawyers; 'scribes', to use their own designation.

A number of people have aided me in the process that led to the completion of this book. Tom Perridge, Senior Commissioning Editor with responsibility for religion at Oxford University Press (OUP) in Oxford, initially encouraged me to submit a manuscript to OUP on this subject during a conversation at the International SBL Conference in Vienna in July 2014. When I did submit a draft manuscript in February 2015, he very expeditiously secured three anonymous reviewers to consider it. Those reviews were extremely helpful in alerting me to relevant material and in assisting me to develop the argument and I am greatly indebted to their authors. More recently, Karen Raith, Assistant Commissioning Editor, with responsibility for religion and theology at OUP, has been very efficient in assisting on certain aspects of the project, especially by arranging for high-quality reproduction of the excellent photographs that accompanied the original publication of the papyri in 2002. I am grateful to Matthew Humphrys from OUP who expertly shepherded the manuscript through the production phase, and to Nicola Sangster for her careful proof-reading. Permission to reproduce those photos (from Y. Yadin [2002] *The Documents from the Bar Kokhba Period in the Cave of Letters: Hebrew, Aramaic and Nabatean-Aramaic Papyri* [Plates]. Judean Desert Studies. Jerusalem: Israel Exploration Society, Institute of Archaeology, Hebrew University and the Shrine of the Book, Israel Museum), and the Aramaic text of P. Yadin 4 was kindly provided by the Israel Antiquities Authority (courtesy of Hillel Geva).

During the course of writing the manuscript, I profited on many occasions from relevant publications suggested (and often provided) to me by Professor Hannah Cotton. Professor Cotton also arranged for my participation at two conferences focusing on law in the ancient Mediterranean, in Oxford in May 2015 and in Saarbrücken in September 2015 (which she co-organized with Professor Tiziana Chiusi). I am very grateful to Professor Cotton for this assistance. I am also grateful for Dr Ada Yardeni's advice to me that in seeking to decipher the cursive handwriting found in the Nabatean legal papyri it is essential to complete accurate drawings of them. Observing exactly how the scribe has drawn the letters in a word or words makes one highly sensitive to the letter forms and to the order in which they were applied to the papyrus. Professor John Kloppenborg and Dr Giovanni Bazzana offered advice on a number of matters to do with papyrology and ancient contexts. Dr Mahdi (Abdelaziz) Alzoubi and Dr Kimberley Czajkowski provided me with copies of their doctoral theses, from which I learned much. My son Dominic, freshly returned from ethnographic fieldwork in northern Sri Lanka for his anthropology doctorate at University College London, rightly insisted on the importance of 'being there' in ethnography and alerted me to relevant literature. Finally, I delivered papers touching on aspects of this volume at the Saarbrücken conference, and to graduate seminars in the University of Durham and Kings College London in early 2016 and gratefully acknowledge feedback I received on those occasions. None of the scholars mentioned here, however, bears any responsibility for the views I express in this book.

My friends at the University of Gloucestershire in Cheltenham, especially Professors Gordon McConville, Andrew Lincoln, and Melissa Raphael and Drs Pekka Pitkanen, Adrian Long, and Dee Carter, welcomed me here in September 2013, were encouraging as I worked on this book, and have provided a useful sounding-board for some of the views expressed in it. I have been fully supported by

Professor Shelley Saguaro and her successor Dr David Webster in their role as Head of the School of Humanities. Library staff at the university have been extremely helpful in assisting me generally and in tracking down some of the bibliographic items (especially Anneliese Cooke and Jane Shirfield in the library at Francis Close Hall Campus and Deborah Jones-Davis and Kate Rea in relation to interlibrary loans). My daughter Sinéad read the entirety of the final manuscript, correcting typographical errors and suggesting numerous stylistic improvements. My wife Patricia and son Thomas read several sections of the manuscript, alerting me to various errors and infelicities.

Finally, over the past few years Patricia, and Dominic, Thomas, and Sinéad, have been a tower of strength (and a fount of tolerance) from early 2013 when this project began and to date, a time when they were and are busily pursuing their own lives. As a small token of my thanks and appreciation, I dedicate this book to them.

Philip F. Esler
The University of Gloucestershire

Cheltenham
October 2016

Contents

List of Figures

Prologue

Re-telling an Ancient Jewish Family Tale

This book tells a story that has gone untold for nearly two thousand years.

It is a story that—in the usual course of things—would have perished with the last person familiar with its details—the Jewish woman Babatha, daughter of Shim'on ben Menaḥem. Babatha was probably killed or enslaved by Roman soldiers at the end of Shim'on ben Kosiba's revolt in 135 CE, when they captured a cave in a wadi running into the western shores of the Dead Sea a little south of En-Gedi in which she and other Jewish fugitives had been sheltering.

But Babatha was not fated to be forgotten. On 15 March 1961, while that same cave in Wadi Ḥever was being investigated by an Israeli team led by the renowned soldier/archaeologist Yigael Yadin, a rock wobbling under the feet of a volunteer led to the discovery of a precious cache of possessions that Babatha had carefully hidden before her life or freedom was probably taken by the Romans.[1] Among them was a leather pouch containing thirty-five legal documents dated from 94 CE to 132 CE, written on papyrus in Aramaic and Greek, relating to Babatha and her family. These documents are conveniently referred to as 'the Babatha archive'. They include contracts for the purchase of property, wedding contracts, loans, the registration of land, and documents from contested legal proceedings. So much detail do these documents contain that we now know more about Babatha than any other Jewish woman from the ancient world. Also found were other items presumably belonging to Babatha, a poignant collection of the possessions that mattered to her, including a pair of sandals, a bundle of balls of yarn, remains of fine fabric, two wrappers or kerchiefs, a key, two key-rings, knives, a clasp knife, a box, a number of bowls, a sickle, and three waterskins.[2]

[1] For an account of the discovery, see Y. Yadin (1963) *The Finds from the Bar Kokhba Period in the Cave of Letters*. Jerusalem: The Israel Exploration Society.

[2] For these details, see Yadin 1963: 38–39.

The story with which this book is concerned lies hidden in the oldest four documents of the Babatha archive in chronological order, known as Papyri Yadin 1–4. The first and oldest of these dates from 94 CE and the other three from 99 CE. All are drafted in Nabatean Aramaic.[3] Although from the land and time of the Bible, the story these papyri can be coaxed to reveal is not of the sensational kind such as fills the pages of airport novels. There are no Arks of the Covenant, hidden temple vessels, Holy Grails, lost Gospels or Mary Magdalens here. Instead this is a tale of domestic life. It is the story of how, around December 99 CE, Shim'on, Babatha's father (but probably before she was born), unexpectedly came to acquire an irrigated date-palm orchard in his village of Maoza, on the southern shore of the Dead Sea, in the kingdom of Nabatea.

It is a story embedded in a complex web of events, personalities, and social relations, all intersecting with Nabatean law and agriculture. It involves a husband borrowing from his wife's dowry to finance a business venture, another husband indebted to his wife, a father's sudden death, a demand made under a guarantee, the collapse of the sale of a date-palm orchard to a high Nabatean official, and the immediate re-sale of that orchard, surprisingly enlarged, to a Jew. It involves enterprising and property-owning women, indebted Nabatean men, and people of sharply differentiated social status and ethnic identity, with one Jew among many Nabateans taking the prize.

Babatha must have received this story from her father and no doubt treasured it as part of the family's collective memory. Nearly thirty years after her father purchased the orchard at the centre of the tale, these documents, which also laid the foundation to her own title to the orchard, still mattered to her greatly. In December 127 CE she had to register her property in the Roman census. Her registration document, in Greek (P. Yadin 16), is almost perfectly preserved and among her assets are two date-palm orchards, each called 'Algiphiamma', in Aramaic meaning 'by the sea-shore'.[4] These two properties,

[3] The conventional *sigla* for these four documents are 5/6 Ḥev 1–4, and J. A. Fitzmyer (2008) *A Guide to the Dead Sea Scrolls and Related Literature*. Revised and expanded edition. Grand Rapids, MI: William B. Eerdmans: 209, notes that '(f)or some reason' Israeli scholars have added this other mode of reference: 'P. Yadin' plus a number. But the Israeli practice is useful and appropriately honours Yadin for his remarkable discoveries in the cave, so it will be employed throughout this volume.

[4] For the text, see N. Lewis (1989) *The Documents from the Bar Kokhba Period in the Cave of Letters: Greek Papyri and Aramaic and Nabatean Signatures and Subscriptions.*

which from their boundary descriptions could well be contiguous with one another, appear to comprise the property that her father purchased in 99 CE pursuant to P. Yadin 3 (but which may have been subsequently subdivided into two separate properties).[5] Babatha's father probably gave her this property when she married in 120 CE.[6] As I set out later in this book, P. Yadin 3 was necessary to establish what lawyers call 'a good root of title' for Babatha's ownership of the orchard. Further, the very presence of P. Yadin 1, 2, and 4 in the archive suggests that they also related to this transaction. That is why they formed part of the family archive that she skilfully concealed in the cave in Wadi Ḥever in 135 CE.

But this is not a story in which scholarship has shown any interest so far. Although discovered in 1961, the Greek documents from Babatha's archive were not published until 1989, while the edition of the Aramaic documents (including P. Yadin 1–4) did not appear until 2002.[7] Those editions, which benefited from significant deciphering by Yadin and his team as early as 1962,[8] were the product of an immense amount of scholarly labour, especially to transcribe scribal handwriting into printed form, to determine the meaning of certain expressions, with much of the Aramaic heavily influenced by an early form of Arabic, and to comment on numerous difficult issues. Every scholar working with these documents owes a tremendous debt to the editors of the two editions. Other writers have devoted much attention to questions of Nabatean, Jewish, and Roman law in these documents, and some have published overviews of Babatha's life.

Yet very little attention has been paid to the social world that these legal papyri reveal. In particular, the arresting story behind P. Yadin 1–4 has gone unheeded and untold. While the second and third documents obviously relate to Shim'on's purchase of a date-palm

Jerusalem: Israel Exploration Society, The Hebrew University of Jerusalem, and the Shrine of the Book: 65–68, and for a photo of the papyrus, see, ibid., Plate 13.

[5] Another, but in my view less likely, possibility is that only one of these two properties is to be identified with the property that Shim'on purchased in 99 CE, see H. M. Cotton (1997) 'Land Tenure in the Documents from the Nabataean Kingdom and the Roman Province of Arabia', *ZPE* 119: 257.

[6] See H. M. Cotton and J. C. Greenfield (1994) 'Babatha's Property and the Law of Succession in the Babatha Archive', *ZPE* 104: 217.

[7] See Lewis 1989 and Yadin et al. 2002.

[8] See Y. Yadin (1962) 'The Expedition to the Judean Desert, 1961: Expedition D—The Cave of Letters', *Israel Exploration Journal* 12: 238–249.

orchard, no one has suggested that all four documents do. No one seems to have asked why the first and fourth documents were found in the archive in the first place. The editors of P. Yadin 1–4 did not propose any connection between the first two documents, despite the fact that a party to the second deed is the son of a guarantor in the first. They also misconstrue the legal character of the fourth document and disavow any prospect of identifying the parties to it, even though, as I will argue, the two relevant names are visible in the text and one of them also appears in the attestation section at the end.

So this is a story that now needs to be told. Its telling depends upon undertaking the closest reading of P. Yadin 1–4, with frequent reference to wider contextual issues from the Dead Sea region and other parts of the ancient Mediterranean world. Probing these four legal papyri requires employing an ethnographer's concern for understanding the complex web of material conditions of life, identities, and relationships among the people present in a particular field-site, even if it is in the past, while adopting a detective's interest in what every clue may reveal.

Babatha is long dead, but part of her world and her experience has become unexpectedly available to us. So let us now honour her memory and resourcefulness in hiding the relevant documents, and indeed her father's resourcefulness in acquiring the date-palm orchard in the first place, by re-telling what her father told her about how their family came to own the orchard. The story itself will form the concluding chapter of this book. The chapters before that will contain the investigation that makes its re-telling possible.

1

Archival Ethnography

The discoveries in the Dead Sea region from the 1940s to the 1960s, especially the scrolls from Qumran, have revolutionized our understanding of ancient Israel and its religious traditions and have also illuminated aspects of the context of the early Christ-movement. The hundred or so ancient legal papyri, however, straddling the second half of the first century CE and the first half of the second and written in Aramaic, Greek, and Hebrew, which were also discovered around the Dead Sea during this period, have not had nearly as much impact.[1] They have mainly been utilized to further our understanding of Jewish, Nabatean, and Roman law.[2] This is an unfortunate limitation

[1] Most of these papyri are to be found in P. Benoit O. P. et al. (1961) *Discoveries in the Judaean Desert II: Les Grottes de Murabbaʿat. Texte*. Oxford: Clarendon Press; N. Lewis (1989) *The Documents from the Bar Kokhba Period in the Cave of Letters: Greek Papyri and Aramaic and Nabatean Signatures and Subscriptions*. Jerusalem: Israel Exploration Society, The Hebrew University of Jerusalem and the Shrine of the Book; H. M. Cotton and A. Yardeni (1997) *Discoveries in the Judaean Desert. Volume 27. Aramaic, Hebrew and Greek Documentary Texts from Naḥal Ḥever and Other Sites: With an Appendix Containing Alleged Qumran Texts* (The Seiyal Collection II). Oxford: Clarendon Press; and Y. Yadin et al. (2002) *The Documents from the Bar Kokhba Period in the Cave of Letters: Hebrew, Aramaic and Nabataean-Aramaic Papyri*. Judaean Desert Studies. Jerusalem: Israel Exploration Society, Institute of Archaeology, Hebrew University and the Shrine of the Book, Israel Museum. Also see the list in H. M. Cotton et al (1995) 'The Papyrology of the Roman Near East: A Survey', *JRS* 95: 214–235.

[2] See for example, R. Katzoff and D. Schaps (eds) (2005) *Law in the Documents of the Judaean Desert*. Leiden: E. J. Brill; J. G. Oudshoorn (2007) *The Relationship between Roman and Local Law in the Babatha and Salome Komaise Archives: General Analysis and Three Case Studies on Law of Succession, Guardianship and Marriage*. Studies on the Texts of the Desert of Judah, 69. Leiden: E. J. Brill; A. C. Hagedorn and R. G. Kratz (eds) (2013) *Law and Religion in the Eastern Mediterranean: From Antiquity to Early Islam*. Oxford: Oxford University Press; and K. Czajkowski (2017) *Localized Law: The Babatha and Salome Komaise Archives*. Oxford: Oxford University Press.

since legal documents have a pronounced capacity to reveal social context. People usually go to lawyers (and this is what the ancient scribes we will encounter in this volume were, not just 'professional writers')[3] because they have a major problem or a major opportunity in their lives, so that the legal documents that result cast light on pivotal dimensions in the experience of the parties. In addition, where the legal documentation consists of trial records, it uncovers underlying tensions in a society that suddenly burst to the surface in highly revealing displays unmediated by literary form. The warnings occasionally to be heard against deducing social contexts from literary and religious texts, whatever their merits, have little application in relation to legal documents, where the accurate representation of the actual circumstances of the parties is a *desideratum*.

When one considers that these Dead Sea legal papyri were being written fairly close in time to the composition of New Testament documents—Matthew's Gospel, for example—the case for their constituting vital evidence of context against which these biblical texts can be interpreted becomes compelling.[4] Such a process finds inspiration in Peter Oakes' innovative work *Reading Romans in Pompei,* which utilizes an in-depth examination of the archaeological evidence for certain residences and their probable inhabitants in that city as a context for assessing the original meaning of Paul's letter.[5]

In this book, however, I am not concerned to interpret New Testament texts against a social context known from the legal papyri. Rather, I am seeking to understand better that context itself, or rather a very particular aspect of it in the form of four legal transactions that date to the period 94–99 CE,[6] which are recorded in P. Yadin 1–4.

[3] For the description of scribes as 'professional writers', see C. Schams (1998) *Jewish Scribes in the Second-Temple Period.* JSOT Supp. Series, 291. Sheffield: Sheffield Academic Press. For an excellent recent discussion of scribes in the Babatha and Salome Komaise archives, see Czajkowski 2017: 60–87.

[4] See P. F. Esler (2014) 'Reading Matthew by the Dead Sea: Matthew 8:5–13 in Light of P Yadin 11', *HTS Theological Studies* 70; for an attempt to interpret Matt 8:5–13 in light of P. Yadin 11.

[5] P. Oakes (2009) *Reading Romans in Pompeii. Paul's Letter at Ground Level.* London: SPCK.

[6] Nabatean chronology is based largely on the regnal years of their kings and as the month that each king acceded to the throne is not always known, sometimes it is not possible to know precisely in which calendar year (by our calculation) an event occurred. Rather than offering cumbersome dates in the form 93/94 CE, 98/99 CE and so on, as a convention in this book I will opt for the latter year in the range.

They involve a number of Nabateans and one Judean who lived in or near Maoza on the southern shore of the Dead Sea.[7] My aim is to focus on these transactions. They were drafted in Nabatean Aramaic and represent the oldest documents in the collection known as the Babatha archive, itself part of the documents widely (and conveniently) referred to as the Yadin Papyri.[8] The Babatha archive of thirty-five legal papyri written in Aramaic (Nabatean and Judean) and Greek was discovered in 1961 in the so-called 'Cave of Letters' in Naḥal Ḥever.[9] The Greek papyri were published in 1989 and the Aramaic documents in 2002.[10] My research into these four documents has left me with considerable respect both for the sophistication of the Nabatean legal system and for the professional competence of the two scribes who drafted the four deeds under consideration. They seem to me to have been very competent lawyers, who knew Nabatean law and the necessary provisions for a range of legal documents and were able to draft documents adapted to the particular needs of the parties in question.

P. Yadin 1–4, understood in the wider context of late first-century CE Nabatea, provide rich evidence for the relationships of the people mentioned in them. We will see over the course of this volume that they reveal a story that has not been told for nearly 2,000 years concerning how Shim'on son of Menaḥem, Babatha's father, came to acquire a particular date-palm orchard in quite unusual circumstances in 99 CE. While archaeological findings were central to Oakes' book, however, my approach to unlocking the secrets of the four papyri will depend upon another methodology.

After I had begun to immerse myself in the papyri of the Babatha archive in 2013 and to reach some of the views expressed in this

[7] In Chapter 2 I will explain why 'Judean' in an ethnic sense is probably a better designator than 'Jew' in this period (but for the view we need both words, see D. R. Schwartz (2014) *Judeans and Jews: Four Faces of Dichotomy in Ancient Jewish History*. Toronto: University of Toronto Press, 91–112).

[8] For the correspondence between the enumeration of the Yadin Papyri and the more mainstream system, see J. A. Fitzmyer (2008) *A Guide to the Dead Sea Scrolls and Related Literature. Revised and Expanded Edition*. Grand Rapids, MI: William B. Eerdmans, 289.

[9] See Y. Yadin (1962) 'The Expedition to the Judean Desert, 1961: Expedition D—The Cave of the Letters', *Israel Exploration Journal* 12: 227–57 for an initial report and Y. Yadin (1963) *The Finds from the Bar Kokhba Period in the Cave of Letters*. Jerusalem: The Israel Exploration Society for a much fuller account.

[10] See Lewis 1989 and Yadin et al. 2002.

volume, the idea came to me that I was engaged in a process of 'archival ethnography'. This was probably a result of my previous interest in the usefulness of social anthropology (especially of the Mediterranean region) in the historical interpretation of biblical texts,[11] coupled with my wife and I having a son then undertaking fieldwork for a British social anthropology doctorate in Tamil-speaking northern Sri Lanka. In due course, however, I discovered that over the past few decades—in the context of the on-going dialogue between anthropology and history[12]—there has been sporadic interest shown in 'archival ethnography', construed in a variety of ways. I will return to this discussion later, but since I will be maintaining a particular position on the matter that depends on the nature of ethnographic investigation, I first must set out my understanding of ethnography itself.

THE MEANING OF ETHNOGRAPHY

At its most basic level, ethnography is the account of the everyday life of a particular group. It is an exploration of a particular world of experience.[13] Its objective 'is to describe the lives of people other than ourselves, with an accuracy and sensitivity honed by detailed observation and first-hand experience'.[14] Ethnography 'is based on direct observations of living people'.[15] One influential strand in the careful observation characteristic of ethnography is the 'thick description' that the late Clifford Geertz advocated.[16] The core of thick description

[11] See Chapter 2 in P. F. Esler (2011) *Sex, Wives, and Warriors: Reading Biblical Narrative with Its Ancient Audience*. Eugene, OR: Wipf & Stock, 35–76.

[12] On this dialogue, see J. Comaroff and J. Comaroff (1992) *Ethnography and the Historical Imagination*. Studies in the Ethnographic Imagination. Boulder, Co: Westview Press and B. K. Axel (2002a) *From the Margins: Hisorical Anthropology and Its Futures*. Durham, NC and London: Duke University Press.

[13] P. Gay y Blasco and H. Wardle (2007) *How to Read Ethnography*. London and New York: Routledge, 36.

[14] T. Ingold (2008) 'Anthropology is *Not* Ethnography', The Radcliffe-Brown Lecture in Social Anthropology at the British Academy, *Proceedings of the British Academy* 154: 69.

[15] Ingold 2008: 70.

[16] See his essay 'Thick Description: Toward an Interpretive Theory of Culture', in C. Geertz (1973) *The Interpretation of Cultures*. New York: Basic Books, 3–30. He

was to describe not only the facts of some event but also to provide commentary and interpretation of those facts and the webs of significance in which they were wrapped. Geertz indeed stated bluntly that 'ethnography is thick description'.[17]

Characteristic of ethnography at its best are 'detailed descriptions of other people's lives, informed by prolonged fieldwork'.[18] Fieldwork thus plays an important role. Paul Stoller has explained the process as follows:

> Ethnographers . . . don't visit people for a week or two or call them up on the phone and then . . . write about them; rather they live in their subject communities for long periods of time—often many years during which they establish and reinforce a network of social relationships—relationships that underscore the complex social, economic and emotional realities of contemporary social life . . . A cardinal principle of ethnographic fieldwork is this: listen to what your subjects are saying, but pay special attention to what they do.[19]

Another expression for this process is 'participant observation', which means that 'intimate coupling, in perception and action, of observer and observed'.[20] To practise participant observation 'is to join in correspondence with those with whom we learn or among whom we study'.[21]

Yet while ethnography is the product of fieldwork, it is not itself fieldwork. This is evident in the well-known phenomenon that 'the field is never experienced as such when you are actually *there* and caught up in the currents of everyday life'; indeed, 'it only stands out when you have left it far behind and begin to write about it'.[22]

The world where the fieldwork is conducted is usually (though, these days, not always) very different from that of the ethnographer. Thus ethnography also involves the twin activities of translation and hence comparison, as ethnographers strive to make sense of what they have discovered in the field in light of how they understand their

drew the expression 'thick description' from two essays by the philosopher Gilbert Ryle.

[17] Geertz 1973: 9–10. [18] Ingold 2008: 86.

[19] P. Stoller (2015) 'In Defence of Ethnography', The Huffington Post, 24 August 2015. Accessed at: <http://www.huffingtonpost.com/paul-stoller/in-defense-of-ethnography_b_8028542.html>

[20] T. Ingold (2014) 'Forum: That's Enough About Ethnography', *HAU: Journal of Ethnographic Theory* 4: 387–388.

[21] Ingold 2014: 390. [22] Ingold 2014: 386 (emphasis original).

own culture, and any others with which they are familiar, to readers 'back home'. Some ethnographers make experiential comparisons—with specific features of other cultures—while 'others rely on abstract representations or models'.[23]

To undertake such comparisons, ethnographers need to be trained in anthropology, the discipline that has been informing and theorizing ethnographic fieldwork since the late nineteenth century.[24] That is why one anthropologist has stated of the ethnographic process: 'Frankly, I cannot imagine how one proceeds without having some broad organizing topics in mind . . . '.[25] Thus, ethnographers are never aiming at 'pure description'; they need to have 'an *idea*' guiding what they choose to describe and how they choose to describe it.[26] Such an 'idea', however, might well involve a general area or areas of anthropological interest rather than a very specific hypothesis about the field-site in question in order to ensure that the ethnographer is fully open to what he or she encounters in the field and is not driven solely by an agenda conceived in advance of the experience.[27] In sum:

> Historically, ethnography finds the anthropologist telling someone else's story. The telling was, and continues to be, guided by the ethnographer's traditional set of categories and by traditional ways of relating an account that make it recognizably ethnographic. . . . What I am talking about here are accounts that from the outset are explicitly ethnographic in intent.[28]

This whole issue of comparison is inevitably charged with the ongoing dynamic relationship between ethnography and anthropology, recently the subject of two important essays by Tim Ingold.[29] Ingold argues that anthropology and ethnography are distinct but related. He strongly critiques the idea that ethnography is about empirical

[23] Gay y Blasco and Wardle 2007: 17.

[24] For a recent statement on the relationship between ethnography and anthropology, see Ingold 2008.

[25] H. F. Wolcott (1999) *Ethnography: A Way of Seeing*. Walnut Creek, CA: Alta Mira Press, 131.

[26] Wolcott 1999: 70 (italics original).

[27] For a discussion of this topic that favours the view expressed here, see A. Hegelund (2005) 'Objectivity and Subjectivity in Ethnographic Method', *Qualitative Health Research* 15: 651–652 and 660 (citing, for example, J. Lofland and L. H. Lofland (1995) *Analyzing Social Settings: A Guide to Qualitative Observation and Analysis*. Third edition. Belmont, CA: Wadsworth).

[28] Wolcott 1999: 139.

[29] Ingold 2008 and 2014.

data collection and anthropology comparative-theoretical work in the researcher's office.[30] Anthropology is 'not a study *of* at all, but a study *with*. Anthropologists work and study *with* people.' Anthropology does more than furnish us with knowledge about the world, about people and their societies, in that it 'educates our perception of the world, and opens our eyes and minds to other possibilities of being'. The questions it addresses are philosophical: about the nature of the person, of morality, of freedom, trust, and so on.[31] Anthropology is indeed comparative, but it does not compare 'bounded objects or entities but ways of being'. The 'anthropological attitude' is defined by 'the constant awareness of alternative ways of being, and of the ever-present possibility of "flipping" from one to another'. It entails that wherever 'we are, and whatever we may be doing, we are always aware that things might be done differently'. Anthropology shares with art this 'sensibility to the strange in the close-at-hand'.[32]

This systematized comparative dimension is central to the nature of ethnography as it is understood in the modern era. Accordingly, we need to distinguish ethnography in this sense from two other phenomena, which are also commonly (but in my submission wrongly) referred to as 'ethnography'. The first of these phenomena is the practice of ancient Greek and Roman authors in describing, often in considerable detail, the customs of foreign peoples. Herodotus was the pioneer of such descriptions, paradigmatically in his accounts of the Egyptians in Book 2 of his *History* and the Scythians in Book 4. Many similar accounts of ancient peoples were written by other authors after him; a recent work that exposes several Greek and Roman examples of this type of writing to illuminating analysis is entitled *Ancient Ethnography*.[33] Yet the Greco-Roman examples discussed in that book are not ethnography in the sense which is current among anthropologists and which I am applying in this volume. One reason for this is that 'ethnography was not a discipline' in the ancient world.[34] More fundamentally, however, the comparative dimension is largely absent in ancient Greco-Roman writers, and certainly not

[30] Ingold 2014: 391. [31] Ingold 2014: 82 (emphases original).

[32] Ingold 2008: 84.

[33] E. Almagor and J. Skinner (eds) (2013) *Ancient Ethnography: New Approaches*. London: Bloomsbury. Also see J. Skinner (2012) *The Invention of Greek Ethnography: From Homer to Herodotus*. New York: Oxford University Press.

[34] G. Woolf (2013) 'Ethnography and the Gods in Tacitus' *Germania*', in Almagor and Skinner 2013: 133.

systematized. I say 'largely absent' because the various scholars contributing to *Ancient Ethnography* are all very alive to the tension between 'them' and 'us' in their sources, to the ways in which Greek and Roman authors used their accounts of foreign peoples to say something about their own way of life. This discussion was ignited by Francois Hartog's 1980 publication *Le miroir d'Hérodote* and developed further in Edith Hall's work *Inventing the Barbarian: Greek Self-Definition Through Tragedy*, Jonathan Hall's *Ethnic Identity in Greek Antiquity*, and other publications.[35] Modern ethnographers do not usually focus on a direct comparison between their own culture and that of the people among whom they do fieldwork, but bring to the ethnographic task their disciplined knowledge of a wide variety of other cultures generated by ethnography and anthropology, some of which knowledge has been formulated theoretically.

The second phenomenon needing to be distinguished from ethnography is the modern use of legal documents and judicial records to create a vivid picture of a particular social world in the past when not approached from a specifically ethnographic point of view. An example of this is *Montaillou*, the celebrated account by Emmanuel Le Roy Ladurie of a village in the French Pyrenees close to the Spanish border with a strong Cathar presence, whose inner dynamics were revealed by the transcription of the Inquisition conducted between 1318 and 1325. Although Le Roy Ladurie himself occasionally describes his work as ethnography,[36] it is really social history. The reason for this is that the book does not feature the comparative situating of its findings in the wider universe of anthropological research that is integral to ethnography. It has, indeed, been observed that for all his efforts to capture the life-world of the peasants of Montaillou from within, Le Roy Ladurie was still deriving his narrative primarily from the standpoint of a contemporary inquisitor.[37]

[35] See F. Hartog (1980) *Le miroir d'Hérodote*. ET 1988 *The Mirror of Herodotus: The Interpretation of the Other in the Writing of History*. Berkeley, CA: University of California Press; E. Hall (1989) *Inventing the Barbarian: Greek Self-Definition Through Tragedy*. Oxford: Clarendon Press; and J. M. Hall (1997) *Ethnic Identity in Greek Antiquity*. Cambridge: Cambridge University Press.

[36] E. Le Roy Ladurie (1980) *Montaillou: Cathars and Catholics in a French Village 1294–1324*. ET of 1978 French original by Barbara Bray. Harmondsworth: Penguin, 30 and 103.

[37] Comaroff and Comaroff 1992: 15, citing R. Rosaldo (1980) *Ilongot Headhunting: 1883–1974: A Study in Society and History*. Stanford, CA: Stanford University Press.

Similarly, Bezalel Porten's detailed exposition of the life of Judean mercenaries in Egypt in the pay of the Persian king in the fifth century BCE, *Archives from Elephantine*,[38] is social history, not ethnography, because of its lack of developed comparisons with other settings. So much for the comparative dimension of ethnography.

The exploration characteristic of ethnography is conducted by its practitioners as they seek to set and understand the actors in view within their particular context (a word from the Latin meaning 'that which is woven together').[39] Contextualization provides 'an explanation of the scattered and sometimes puzzling details that make up human social experience by showing these details as elements of the "weave" of society or culture'.[40] Part of this contextualization entails the differentiation of the statuses of particular actors in the group and the capacities and agency attached to them.[41] All this means that ethnography inevitably combines description with interpretation. For Harry Wolcott, the 'orienting and overarching purpose' of ethnography is 'an underlying concern with cultural interpretation'.[42] Ethnography constitutes an account of a human group in which its social and cultural patterning becomes visible.

Central to ethnography is the study of relationships between the actors in the group. Ethnographers describe social roles, capacities, and statuses as 'relational' because they could not exist outside of a framework of relationships. To describe, explain, and interpret the types of personhood encountered by an ethnographer, it is necessary to situate them in the local relational framework.[43] Similarly, it is by studying roles, capacities, and statuses that the relational framework in place can be uncovered in the first place. Ethnographers often propose an abstracted, even schematic image of the central relational pattern.[44] Among British ethnographers the dominant relational pattern has been kinship.[45]

38 B. Porten (1968) *Archives from Elephantine: The Life of an Ancient Jewish Military Colony*. Berkeley, CA: University of California Press.

39 On context in anthropology, see R. Dilley (ed.) (1999) *The Problem of Context*. Methodology and History in Anthropology. Volume 4. New York and Oxford: Berghahn Books.

40 Gay y Blasco and Wardle 2007: 37.

41 Gay y Blasco and Wardle 2007: 38–41.

42 Wolcott 1999: 68.

43 Gay y Blasco and Wardle 2007: 58.

44 Gay y Blasco and Wardle 2007: 62.

45 See R. Parkin and L. Stone (eds) (2004) *Kinship and Family: An Anthropological Reader*. Oxford: Blackwell.

One aspect of the concern of ethnography with interpretation is that it involves argument. It is neither lived experience itself, nor merely one person's individual view of lived experience, but rather 'ethnographic writing argues for a particular way of understanding certain lived experiences' within the broader context of ethnographic (and anthropological) debate and the accumulated knowledge of the discipline.[46]

Finally, we must confront the fact that ethnographic research embraces elements of objectivity (the reality of the people and their world in view) and subjectivity (the inevitable involvement of a particular researcher with his or her unique perspective on the data). In parallel with the rise of postmodernist approaches to research in the 1960s, subsequent decades witnessed the emergence of various forms of ethnography that valorized the experience of the researcher in the field,[47] at times accompanied by a diminished interest in the people among whom the ethnographer was working. That postmodernist ideas had found firm traction in anthropology as early as 1986 emerges in the impact of the book along these lines published in that year and edited by James Clifford and George Marcus entitled *Writing Culture*.[48] While this work met strong criticism when it first appeared, and anthropologists continue to offer defences of objectivity and realism in ethnography from various perspectives,[49] the debate itself need not detain us here.

[46] Gay y Blasco and Wardle 2007: 96–98, at 97.

[47] As examples, see Rosaldo 1980 and R. Rosaldo (1993) *Culture and Truth: The Remaking of Social Analysis: With a New Introduction*. Boston, Mass: Beacon Press; for arguments for a connection between autobiography and anthropology, see J. Okely and H. Callaway (eds) (1992) *Anthropology and Autobiography*. ASA Monographs 29. London and New York: Routledge.

[48] J. Clifford and G. E. Marcus (eds) (1986) *Writing Culture: The Poetics and Politics of Ethnography*. Berkeley, CA: University of California Press.

[49] As examples of the critical voices, see P. S. Sangren (1988) 'Rhetoric and the Authority of Ethnography: "Postmodernism" and the Social Reproduction of Texts', *Current Anthropology* 29: 405–435; J. Spencer (1989) 'Anthropology as a Kind of Writing', *Man* n.s. 24: 145–164; H. Sidky (2003) *A Critique of Postmodern Anthropology—In Defense of Disciplinary Origins and Traditions*. Lewiston, NY: Edwin Mellen; P. Bourdieu (2004) *Science of Science and Reflexivity*. Chicago, IL: University of Chicago Press; B. Latour (2004) 'Why Has Critique Run Out of Steam? From Matters of Fact to Matters of Concern', *Critical Inquiry* 30: 225–248; and C. Toren and J. de Pina-Cabral (eds) (2011) *The Challenge of Epistemology: Anthropological Perspectives*. New York: Berghahn.

In the present volume, while eschewing a postmodernist interpretation in favour of one firmly focused on the ancient data in view and the social realities they evidence, my own subjectivity will inevitably play a role. I will, however, do all I can to avoid damaging sorts of subjectivity, such as omitting reference to data that may seem discordant to a view I am maintaining, or using knowledge I possess from other contexts to swamp data in the papyri themselves. What I cannot—and, I submit, should not—avoid is the role of my subjectivity (here embracing theories, tacit knowledge, background knowledge, experience, and so on) in relation to what counts as relevant data and to how I relate one aspect of the data to another, or how I 'draw lines between the dots'.[50] In particular, the fact that at the beginning of my career I spent some thirteen years working in the law in Sydney, Australia inevitably affects how I interpret these Nabatean legal papyri in ways I will return to later in this chapter.[51]

Ethnography of the Village

Since most of the ethnographic exploration set out in this volume will focus on the village (or perhaps small town) of Maoza on the south or south eastern shore of the Dead Sea (its exact location, however, being unknown), it is necessary to say something about the ethnography of villages. Although long popular among ethnographers, according to Diane Mines and Nicolas Yazgi, by the 1970s 'village studies' had been 'pushed to the margins of the anthropological field due to several theoretical criticisms and paradigm shifts'.[52] Ethnographers of a structuralist leaning rejected villages in favour of wider 'social facts' such as caste and kinship. Historians viewed villages as constructs or myths of colonial ethnography. More recently, attention has shifted 'to the study of non-territorially bounded and transregional issues such as politics, economy, globalization, urbanization,

[50] In this area I have profited from and drawn on the views of Hegelund 2005.

[51] My thirteen years in the law embraced one year as the Associate to a Justice of the New South Wales Supreme Court (1977), one year as a graduate articled clerk (1978), nearly five years as a commercial litigation solicitor (1979–1981 and 1984–1986) and six years as a barrister practising in equity and commercial areas (1986–1992).

[52] D. P. Mines and N. Yazgi (2010b) 'Introduction: Do Villages Matter?', in Mines and Yazgi (eds) (2010a) *Village Matters: Relocating Villages in the Contemporary Anthropology of India*. New Delhi: Oxford University Press, 1.

and transcultural flows'.[53] Mines and Yazgi, however, have argued that the pendulum has now begun to swing back in favour of ethnographies of villages, as evident in the essays they publish in their 2010 volume *Village Matters* and the research they cite therein.[54] They provide solid grounds for a shift 'from merely studying *in villages* to *studying villages* as contemporary meaningful constituents and outcomes of world shaping activities, as well as legitimate objects of anthropological conceptualization'.[55]

In taking this position, they nevertheless insist that traditional approaches to village ethnography, which tended to view each village in isolation, need to be revised given that villages conceived of as social entities and even as physical sites are always 'the outcome of multilocal processes and networks', so that multi-site research practices are necessary.[56] This is particularly important for Maoza, in as much as its inhabitants had connections of various kinds with people in other villages in Nabatea and Judea and, in one case, with the Nabatean royal court. Hence, the interest of Mines and Yazgi lies in a rigorous ethnographic study of local social institutions, relations, and networks that always move beyond bounded units. They adopt an anthropological posture that is attentive to 'the reflexive and strategic dimensions of human action and existence' in context.[57]

One of the contributors to *Village Matters*, Saurabh Dube, recalled the research his anthropologist father had conducted into a village in India in the 1950s that led to the production of a classic work in the field, *Indian Village*.[58] His father had focused upon social and economic matters, ritual, kinship, and family structures. We will see that these issues are relevant to Maoza, except that we would replace ritual (for which there is a paucity of evidence in our four papyri) with ethnic identities, which are significant. In addition to conducting a general sociological census of the village, his father had selected 120 families out of a total of 380 for intensive investigation, with 'eighty episodic and topical life-histories and eleven full biographies'.[59] It

[53] Mines and Yazgi 2010b: 1.
[54] For the latter, see Mines and Yazgi 2010b: 8–10.
[55] Mines and Yazgi 2010b: 10–11 (emphasis original).
[56] Mines and Yazgi 2010b: 10. [57] Mines and Yazgi 2010b: 12.
[58] S. C. Dube (1955) *Indian Village*. London: Routledge and Kegan Paul.
[59] S. Dube (2010) 'Lost and Found: Villages between Anthropology and History', in Mines and Yazgi 2010a: 35.

would be possible to produce a partial episodic life-history of Babatha from the papyri in her archive, but that is not the subject of this volume. Nevertheless, were it possible to do the same for her father (for which there is very much less evidence), the story of how he came to acquire a date-palm plantation on the shore of the Dead Sea in 99 CE would represent a major episode in his life-history. In this way we can see how this episode naturally falls to be investigated and explained within the larger archival ethnography of Maoza. Support for this approach is to be found in a remark by the historian Laurence Stone, that anthropology 'has taught us how a whole social system and set of values can be brilliantly illuminated by the searchlight method of recording in elaborate detail a single event, provided that it is very carefully set in its total context and very carefully analysed for its cultural meaning'.[60] He continues by noting that the 'archetypal model of this "thick description", mentioned above, is Clifford Geertz's classic account of a Balinese cock-fight'.[61]

THE NATURE OF ARCHIVAL ETHNOGRAPHY

Outlining Archival Ethnography

So much for ethnography. What then of 'archival ethnography'? There is no doubt that this endeavour is historical in the sense that it seeks an understanding of phenomena from the past. Yet it is also ethnographic, while qualified with 'archival'. In this context an archive can refer either to a place containing records, documents, or other materials of historical interest, or to a collection of such documents.[62] In this volume 'archive' has the last meaning, that of a collection of documents, especially here the thirty-five legal papyri in the Babatha archive and the first four of them, in Nabatean Aramaic, in particular. While this is admittedly a modest number, anthropologist Harry

[60] L. Stone (1979) 'The Revival of Narrative: Reflections on a New Old History', *Past and Present* 85: 13–14.

[61] Stone 1979: 14, citing Geertz 1973: 412–53.

[62] Not very useful for my purposes is the post-structuralist notion of an archive as 'a complex system of embedded rules that determines the production of knowledge' (S. Decker (2013) 'The Silence of the Archives: Business History, Post-Colonialism and Archival Ethnography', *Management and Organizational History* 8: 157).

Wolcott has made the suggestion that, in relation to this second sense of 'archive', 'for an ethnographer *any* document that proves valuable as a source of information can rightfully be considered an archive'.[63] Wolcott's view also indicates his acceptance of the fact that archives can be useful in ethnography. Indeed Wolcott has observed that, whether formally catalogued or casually handled, to a researcher 'written records can be a vital source of data. Most often such materials supplement participant observation but sometimes they are, or become, the major focus of it.' An example of the latter is *The Polish Peasant in America*, a work in five volumes by W. I. Thomas and F. Znaniecki (1918–1920), based on some 750 letters between Polish immigrants in the USA and their relatives in Poland.[64] This work, while regarded as a classic of sociology, may also be viewed as an early harbinger of archival ethnography.

By the early 1990s there were certain ethnographers explicitly working with historical materials but in a distinctively ethnographic mode. Thus John and Jean Comaroff were able to make the following observation:

> Clearly it is cultural historians, more than any other social scientists, who validate our endeavor as ethnographers . . . But eventually we must part company. Given the reluctance of historians to reflect on matters of theory, their tendency to look to empirical solutions for analytical problems, we must find our own way through the maze of conundrums that lies along the road to a principled historical anthropology.[65]

The precise expression 'archival ethnography', moreover, appears in a book entitled *Historical Ethnography* published in 1992 by no less a figure than Marshall Sahlins. In developing an integrated history of the Anahulu Valley on the Hawaian island of O'ahu, Sahlins states that he is joining together an 'archival ethnography' with archaeological surveys and excavations.[66] One might wish that Sahlins had

[63] Wolcott 1999: 59 (italics original).

[64] Wolcott 1999: 59; W. I. Thomas and F. Znaniecki, F. (1918–1920) *The Polish Peasant in Europe and America: Monograph of an Immigrant Group*. Five volumes. Chicago, IL: University of Chicago Press.

[65] Comaroff and Comaroff 1992: 18. In addition, for a discussion of 'ethnography and the archive' see B. K. Axel (ed.) (2002b) 'Introduction: Historical Anthropology and Its Vicissitudes' in Axel (2002a) *From the Margins: Historical Anthropology and Its Futures*. Durham, NC and London: Duke University Press, 12–17.

[66] M. Sahlins (1992) *Historical Ethnography, Volume One* in his work co-written with P. V. Kirch: *Anahulu: The Anthropology of History in the Kingdom of Hawaii*. Chicago and London: The University of Chicago Press, 1.

been more explicit as to the nature of this 'archival ethnography'. Nevertheless, it appears to denote his deploying his skills as one of the world's greatest anthropologists to develop a history of the island using written records, especially those of land tenure, but also accounts by traders, missionaries, and others. The project seeks to bring together history and anthropology in 'a true synthetic collaboration'.[67] Given the central role it accords to legal records in understanding the past, Sahlins' designation of his project as 'archival ethnography' represents a useful precedent for the analysis undertaken in this volume.

More recently, Swedish ethnologist Rebecka Lennartsson has employed the notion of 'archival ethnography', in research into the sex trade in seventeenth- and eighteenth-century Stockholm using the archive of legal records that are abundant from that period.[68] Lennartsson has very carefully explained what she means by 'archival ethnography' with reference to the nature of ethnography, and I will return to her explanation below.

Another scholar who has recently employed the idea of 'archival ethnography' is Stephanie Decker, in her work as a business historian.[69] In my view, however, when Decker discusses archives she is really focusing on a somewhat different subject—the ethnography of the archive. By this I mean the recent interest, exemplified in the work of Ann Laura Stoler,[70] in how an archive was put together and maintained and the extent to which the archives of colonial administrations often silenced indigenous perspectives in the process of compiling and storing records from a European point of view, at times producing epistemic confusion as a result. On Decker's view, the texts in an archive 'are not used to report on the issues that they were ostensibly written about, but rather what they tell us about

[67] P. V. Kirch (1992) *The Archaeology of History, Volume Two*, in his work co-written with M. Sahlins: *Anahulu: The Anthropology of History in the Kingdom of Hawaii*. Chicago and London: The University of Chicago Press, 1.

[68] R. Lennartsson (2011) 'Notes on "Not Being There": Ethnographic Excursions in Eighteenth-Century Stockholm, *Ethnologia Europaea* 42: 105–14 and R. Lennartsson (2012) 'Archival Ethnography: Reflections on a Lost Note', *Historische Anthropologie*. Accessed at: <http://edoc.hu-berlin.de/histfor/14/PHP/Beitraege_14-2012.php>.

[69] Decker 2013 and S. Decker (2014) 'Solid Intentions: An Archival Ethnography of Corporate Architecture and Organizational Remembering', *Organization* 21: 514–542.

[70] See A. L. Stoler (2009) *Along the Archival Grain: Epistemic Anxieties and Colonial Commonsense*. Princeton, NJ: Princeton University Press.

commonly held assumptions and intentions'.[71] She then cites, with approval, Stoler's argument to the effect that the focus should be on 'archiving-as-process rather than archives-as-things', on 'archives as condensed sites of epistemological and political anxiety rather than skewed and biased sources'.[72] This position, however, while justified for a postcolonial analysis of colonial-period archives, has little, if any, application to an archive comprising legal records such as P. Yadin 1–4. For these documents were agreed to by the parties to each transaction, were drafted by scribes at their direction, and reflect the indigenous culture and rules of law (with the latter drawing on a centuries-old Aramaic legal tradition). Documents such as these definitely do report on the issues about which they were written and are not skewed and biased sources, even though there may have been differences in negotiating power as between the parties.

One final recent use of the notion of 'archival ethnography' is worth mentioning. In an article published in 2004 Karen Gracy sought 'to propose and validate a new tradition of inquiry for the field of archival research, that of "archival ethnography"'.[73] Gracy took some pains to situate her work within the wider anthropological and ethnographic context. She helpfully noted that 'Ethnographic fieldwork is especially well-suited for studying sociocultural phenomena such as structures, processes, and interactions among members of a defined community.'[74] Yet hers was not an historical enterprise like the work of Thomas and Znaniecki, Sahlins, Lennartsson, and Decker that provides precedents for what is attempted in this volume. Gracy conducted research instead on a current group of archivists, 'the community of film preservationists who care for and preserve motion pictures'.[75] Moreover, her focus was on how this community functioned, not on the content of their archive. Accordingly, her approach is not what is needed for an archival ethnography of Dead Sea legal papyri.

For the purposes of this volume, I will operate on the basis that an archival ethnography is likely to be most productive of understanding if it captures the nature of ethnography as explained above to the fullest possible extent. Thus, I will focus on a particular field-site,

[71] Decker 2014: 520. [72] Decker 2014: 520; citing Stoler 2009, 20.
[73] K. F. Gracy (2004) 'Documenting Communities of Practice: Making the Case for Archival Ethnography', *Archival Science* 4: 335.
[74] Gracy 2004: 336. [75] Gracy 2004: 338.

Maoza, but set within the wider context of the Dead Sea region at the end of the first century CE. I will thus be subjecting to close scrutiny a particular world of experience very different from my own. Central to the investigation will be the study of the social roles, capacities, and statuses among a group of Nabateans and one Judean and the relational framework that existed among them. Supporting this approach is the circumstance that recent research has witnessed a re-assertion of the value of village ethnographies, at least where any particular village is firmly contextualized within a wider world. The investigation will be firmly comparative, with comparisons being derived from research into other cultures or from wider anthropological writing, thus reflecting the on-going dialogue between ethnography and anthropology. The outcome will be an argument that runs a particular view of the evidence and reflects my own subjectivity, including my previous career as a lawyer.

One Answer to the Problem of Not Physically 'Being There'

Yet something is obviously missing from this outline. It is that dimension of the ethnographer's work that covers the complex of activities and experience comprising fieldwork, prolonged interaction with actual subjects, participant observation, in short, 'being there'. Is the very notion of archival ethnography, in spite of its endorsement by Marshall Sahlins, a contradiction in terms? It would be if we accepted without qualification Tim Ingold's view—that 'ethnography is based on the direct observation of living people *rather than on written records or material remains attesting to the activities of people in the past*'.[76]

Rebecka Lennartsson, the pioneer in explicitly theorized archival ethnography, has provided one answer to this dilemma from her post-doctoral research into the copious seventeenth- and eighteenth-century court records in Stockholm as her basis for an 'archival ethnography' of certain darker aspects of the city's population at that time, especially its sex trade.[77] For Lennartsson, 'archive' has the first sense mentioned above, a place containing records, an

[76] Ingold 2008: 70 (emphasis added).

[77] As a foretaste of this research, see Lennartsson 2011 and 2012.

abundance of them in fact. She regards herself as a 'field-worker of the past' and argues that, although denied access to first hand data, 'the similarities outnumber the differences when comparing fieldwork in contemporary society with trying to grasp a lost world'.[78] She offers two broad reasons for this.

First, she suggests that 'being there' does not of itself 'guarantee closeness to informants, or necessarily provide a true reflection of the reality of the Other'. In this regard she cites German ethnologist Michaela Fenske:

> 'Lived life' is only to some extent accessible to cultural analysis, whether it is the life of the past or of the present, and as it is made manifest in complex relations between researcher and researched. It is always only partially reflected in historical documents or excerpts from them, only partially captured through interviews and their transcripts, and inadequately captured by either written or visual evidence.[79]

More specifically, it is worth noting that even in the field ethnographers often struggle to obtain data that they consider would enhance their understanding. Sometimes their subjects are unwilling or unable to provide information that is sought, or what they do provide is misleading or erroneous. No ethnographer in the present day operates in the possession of complete information.

Secondly, for Lennartsson ethnography is not only a genre for data gathering in contemporary society, nor 'a genre for describing or representing those experiences'. Rather, 'Ethnography comprises many different methods, all based in some way on texts of various kinds', a point for which she draws support from Norman Denzin to the effect that rather than studying lived experience, we examine lived textuality.[80] While one may well question the utility of subsuming all human experience under the banner of 'text', the prominence of texts in some versions of the ethnographic process cannot be denied. Even the ethnographer's conversations with informants are immediately 'textualized' by being summarized in field notes which are then later analysed and synthesized prior to re-textualization in various ways

[78] Lennartsson 2011: 108–109.

[79] Lennartsson 2011: 109, citing M. Fenske (2007) 'Micro, Macro, Agency: Historical Ethnography as Cultural Anthropology Practice', *Journal of Folklore Research* 44: 90.

[80] Lennartsson 2011: 109, citing N. K. Denzin (1997) *Interpretive Ethnography: Ethnographic Practices for the 21st Century*. Thousand Oaks, CA: Sage Publications.

for publication. This is not to under-estimate the importance of recorded conversations, photos, and other artefacts in the ethnographic process. These two factors probably apply with equal force to what happens when we investigate the legal papyri of the Babatha archive and other examples that survive from the Dead Sea region in the first and second centuries CE.

As she develops this second point, much of what Lennartsson suggests is also applicable to the examination conducted in this volume. She considers that ethnography is 'above all a particular approach to the field, where methods of collecting and analysing data on the one hand, and reporting it and representing it on the other are so intertwined that they cannot really be separated'. For this reason:

> Ethnography includes an awareness of detail and the heterogeneity and plurality of the field. It allows room for contradiction and for alternative stories, voices, narratives and experiences, and acknowledges that the author and interpreter is not a neutral spectator. 'Fieldwork' thus comprises numerous elements for an ethnographer of the past. [81]

We will see later that this interest in the diversity of voices is highly apposite in understanding P. Yadin 1–4.

There comes a point, however, when a different approach is needed for the Dead Sea legal papyri. In Lennartsson's view:

> Work in the archive can be regarded as fieldwork in that an archive is a physical place and a field research site . . . Archives are enchanting because they function as gateways to history.[82]

Whereas to some an archive might seem like a mausoleum, in them, she proposes, one can occasionally feel 'an overwhelming sense of closeness'. Here the archive becomes a means to an end, 'supplying documents that hold previously unknown information, allowing the researcher of the past to "walk" through a lost world' by reading the various documents it contains. She notes that we should also study paintings and drawings in addition to written records—to which we could surely add all physical remains from the historical context in question—and also visit places people inhabited and practise 'listening to their music, learning their language and codes of conduct, and

[81] Lennartsson 2011: 109. [82] Lennartsson 2011: 109.

discovering their beliefs and taste in food and clothes'.[83] After eloquently describing how she dons items of clothing similar to those in the eighteenth century and visits the places her subjects occupied, with notebook in hand, Lennartsson proposes that the 'acts of observing, documenting, analysing and otherwise performing ethnography, both as a method for collecting data and as a genre of representation, thus take place simultaneously in much the same way as when conducting fieldwork in contemporary society'.[84]

These practices are not possible for research into the papyri considered in this volume. Maoza has not been excavated and cannot be visited. While En-Gedi on the Western shore of the Dead Sea still functions as an agricultural settlement, the ancient town exists only in archaeological remains.[85] The experience of seeking access to photographs of P. Yadin 1–4 from the Israel Antiquities Authority in Jerusalem would be in no way comparable to immersing oneself in huge holdings of original documents in a legal records building in Stockholm. Much of the 'archival' work in the present case rather involves sitting over and carefully working through the photographs and published editions of the documents in their original languages in one's own office or study. The small number of legal papyri that survive from the Dead Sea region makes for a comparatively small evidentiary base,[86] as compared with the legal records in Stockholm available to Lennartsson. The distance in time means that engaging in ancient Nabatean and Judean practices in relation to cuisine, clothing, music, language, and codes of conduct is far less practical or germane.

A New Approach to Not Physically 'Being There'

Yet another response is available to the problem of not physically 'being there' that has considerable potential when the written records forming the primary evidence for the archival ethnography are legal documents drafted on the instructions of the parties to them. As already noted, these types of document do not suffer from the problems with colonial records identified by Stoler and Decker,

[83] Lennartsson 2011: 109. [84] Lennartsson 2011: 110.

[85] See Y. Hirschfeld (ed.) (2007a) *En-Gedi Excavations II. Final Report (1996–2002)*. Jerusalem: Israel Exploration Society.

[86] For a list of most of these, see Cotton et al. 1995, but also Cotton and Yardeni 1997 and Yadin et al. 2002.

especially that of their being biased from the outset in favour of the colonizing power. Legal documents such as P. Yadin 1–4 are, in fact, the best evidence we have for social life in the ancient world. With them we do not need to pierce the veil of literary or religious genre, nor interpret ambiguous archaeological remains, to arrive at conclusions on social matters. For it was in the interest of parties to the transaction in question, and to the scribe, to ensure that the document was accurate in terms of its subject matter, in relation to the rights, duties, powers, and immunities[87] of those who would sign it and in all its remaining details, details that were deeply rooted in the social and economic context of the document.

In addition, moreover, it is of the utmost importance to note that legal documents such as P. Yadin 1–4 were executed in a particular place and date and in the presence of the parties, the witnesses, and the scribe. During this process, the scribe must have read the document aloud to all those present, especially as some of them may have been illiterate. The document was then signed by the appropriate party or parties, followed by four or more witnesses, and finally the scribe. By 'appropriate party or parties' I mean, in accordance with Nabatean legal practice, the person or persons undertaking legal obligations pursuant to the transaction; in other words, the obligor or obligors. In a deed of debt (like P. Yadin 1) this was the debtor, while in a sale of land (like P. Yadin 2 and 3) the vendor signed. Anyone guaranteeing the duties of the obligor also signed (as in P. Yadin 1 and 3). If the obligor was illiterate, another person might sign after that person on his or her behalf.[88] So all these persons were present at the same time and possessed of knowledge of the legal document in question and what it meant in terms of village life. On every occasion such a legal document was executed, the local context—from its environment and agriculture, to its legal and political structures—was activated in relation to a particular set of social and monetary relationships that were being crystallized into legal rights and duties. Such a moment nicely illustrates Laurence Stone's

[87] These are the four key concepts in Wesley Hohfeld's celebrated analysis of legal obligations (W. N. Hohfeld (1978) *Fundamental Legal Conceptions*, ed. W. Wheeler Cook. Westport, Conn: Greenwood Press).

[88] This is the case in P. Yadin 2, where X, son of Zaidu, signs immediately after the name of the female vendor, and probably also in P. Yadin 3, where the man signing after her name is certainly a party (as guarantor of her obligations) but is probably also signing on her behalf, given the similarity of the handwriting.

observation, quoted above, that anthropology has shown how a searchlight method of recording a single, contextualized event in elaborate detail can illuminate a whole social system.

The distinctive nature of the execution of such a legal document allows me to propose a new approach to 'being there'. This involves imagining that one was present where and when the document was signed and, like a modern-day ethnographer, was able to observe what those present were saying and doing and to ask them to clarify any points of uncertainty. As already noted, one's own subjectivity inevitably affects the ethnographic process, in my case a subjectivity shaped in part by many years as a practising lawyer in a previous career, where I had regular interactions with clients in a variety of situations. That experience may prompt my imagination in ways different from those who lack exposure to legal practice. At times 'thinking like a lawyer' may not necessarily be the best preparation for a biblical critic, but it probably does help in seeking to get to the story that lies behind these four ancient legal documents. Yet this will not be an uncontrolled exercise of imagination. Such a process of imagining will, first, allow new questions to be put to the ancient data, but only those data can provide the answers. Secondly, it will allow 'drawing lines between the dots': in other words, it will facilitate understanding various possible answers thrown up by the data and prioritizing them in plausibility terms against the totality of the evidence so as to reach a view on what is probable, the standard of proof required of all historical research. In accordance with this approach to 'being there', I will begin my ethnographic analysis of each of the four legal papyri in view with the occasion on which it was executed. The fragmentary nature of P. Yadin 4, however, will necessitate significant emendation of the Nabatean Aramaic text in the light of the papyrus (Chapter 8) before this analysis can be undertaken (Chapter 9).

MAKING THE BEST OF THE EVIDENCE

The limited nature of the textual evidence available to re-tell the story of how Babatha's father came to acquire a particular date-palm orchard in 99 CE, P. Yadin 1–4, means that the closest possible attention must be paid to the details of these documents to ensure no relevant evidence is overlooked. In the general area of maximizing the evidentiary yield from archive documents, Lennartsson has usefully distinguished between 'traces', the documents, artefacts, and fragments that survive from the past, and 'clues', the phenomena among them that carry particular significance, having an importance extending beyond what they immediately denote. For her clues 'depend on questions set by, and ultimately from the perspective of, the researcher'.[89] In taking this approach she draws upon Carlo Ginzburg's essay 'Clues', which argues that sometimes the smallest details prove to be the indispensable clues for understanding significant relations in a culture under view.[90]

Ginzburg developed his approach initially from an examination of a series of inquisitorial trials preserved in the Modena State Archives for 1518–1520, in particular the trial of a woman called Chiara Signorini in 1519.[91] Ginzburg shows how a single legal document such as this can prove a precious source for important issues such as the connection between inquisitorial procedures and the doctrinal development of treatises on demonology, the relationship between witchcraft and popular piety, the social forces behind witchcraft, and the detailed phenomenon of actual witchcraft.[92] Ginzburg discovered a particular model for his approach in the work of Aby Warburg (1866–1929), a German art historian and theorist of culture who founded a library that later became the Warburg Institute in London. Ginzburg points out that Warburg used a very eclectic set of documents to explore the significance of Greco-Roman art in fourteenth-century Florence: 'testaments, mercantile letters, accounts of amorous adventures, tapestries, paintings, both famous and obscure'.[93] It is worth noting that the first two sets of documents were legal in nature. Ginzburg cites a remark of G. Bing that Warburg taught that 'it is possible to make human voices speak even from documents of seemingly small importance', some of which are capable of interesting only historians of everyday life.[94] Warburg's favourite saying encapsulated his focus on concrete and specific research: 'God is in the detail.'

[89] Lennartsson 2011: 112.

[90] C. Ginzburg (1989) *Clues, Myths, and the Historical Method*. ET of 1986 Italian original by J. and A. C. Tedeschi. Baltimore, IL: Johns Hopkins University Press.

[91] See the essay 'Witchcraft and Popular Piety: Notes on a Modenese Trial of 1519', originally published in Italian in 1961; now Ginzburg 1989: 1–16.

[92] Ginzburg 1989: 1–2.

[93] Ginzburg 1989: 20–21.

[94] Ginzburg 1989: 21; citing G. Bing (1960) 'Aby M. Warburg', *Rivista storica italiana* 72: 105.

Probably the fullest account of Ginzburg's views on this matter appear in his essay 'Clues: Roots of an Evidential Paradigm', first published in 1979,[95] which begins with Warburg's saying just cited. Here Ginzburg addresses the extent to which minor details may be crucial to identify and interpret a phenomenon. He begins the essay with reference to the nineteenth-century art historian Morelli, Sherlock Holmes, and Sigmund Freud, and illustrates his thesis in fields as widely separate as art history (where minor but characteristic details may reveal the work of a particular painter), criminal investigations (where apparently inconsequential features may prove determinative in solving a crime), and psychoanalysis (where inadvertent gestures may reveal character).[96] In each case:

> Infinitesimal traces permit the comprehension of a deeper, otherwise unattainable reality: traces—more precisely, symptoms (in the case of Freud), clues (in the case of Sherlock Holmes), pictorial marks (in the case of Morelli).

Equally pertinent to the investigation to be carried out in this volume is another essay by Ginzburg, 'The Inquisitor as Anthropologist', appearing for the first time in the 1986 original Italian version of the book.[97] While attending a conference on oral history where eminent anthropologists were debating the issues, Ginzburg was struck by the thought that even historians of early modern Europe sometimes use oral sources, in particular, written records of oral speech as in legal proceedings:

> For instance, the judicial proceedings of lay and ecclesiastical courts might be comparable to the notebooks of anthropologists, recording fieldwork performed centuries ago.

This consideration propelled him to the view that there was a viable analogy between inquisitors and anthropologists.[98] His further reflection on this analogy, in particular the fact that both inquisitors and anthropologists generated and then relied on *textual evidence*, led to the following statement:

> In both cases we have texts that are intrinsically *dialogic*. The dialogic structure can be explicit, as in the questions and answers that punctuate either an inquisitorial trial or a transcript of the conversations between an

[95] Ginzburg 1989: 96–125.
[96] Ginzburg 1989: 96–99.
[97] Ginzburg 1989: 156–164.
[98] Ginzburg 1989: 156.

> anthropologist and his informant. But it can also be implicit, as in ethnographic field notes describing a ritual, a myth, or a tool. The essence of what we call anthropological attitude—that is, the permanent confrontation between different cultures—rests on a dialogic disposition.[99]

Leaving aside that the practice of ethnography is often far 'messier' than Ginzburg, with his vision of the orderly questioning of informant by anthropologist, suggests, and his failure to acknowledge the necessarily comparative dimension of ethnography, this stress on dialogue represents a valuable insight. It is obviously applicable not just to inquisitorial investigations but to any judicial proceedings. But the dialogic dimension to legal documents does not emerge only in trial records. Most legal documents, every contract for example (except perhaps modern consumer contracts with their numerous standard clauses not open to negotiation), represents a collection of rights and liabilities that two or more parties have taken upon themselves, usually following dialogue *inter se* often mediated by lawyers. This is certainly the case with P. Yadin 1–4. Here the micro-historical examination of evidence is activated by the intrinsic character of legal documents to entail exploring relationships between specified individuals, which illustrate particular positions of power and articulate (or fail to articulate) particular voices. The capacity of a legal document to give vent to underlying social issues of pressing importance to the indigenous actors allows us an unusual opportunity to step into their lost world. They constitute fine 'traces' for the disclosure of 'clues' that prove indispensable in getting to the bottom of certain situations and relations.[100]

A PRELIMARY ASSUMPTION ON THE ARCHIVE

In support of the evidentiary value of the papyri in the Babatha archive, P. Yadin 1–4, it is necessary to set out here a preliminary

[99] Ginzburg 1989: 159 (emphasis original).

[100] The somewhat related field of 'ethnohistory' can involve 'the interpretative turn to a microhistorical, ethnographic concern with thickly described incidents' (P. Galloway (2006) *Practicing Ethnohistory: Mining Archives. Hearing Testimony. Constructing Narrative.* Lincoln, Nebraska and London: University of Nebraska Press, 15).

assumption, but one that must cede to the evidence if necessary. This is that any document in the Babatha archive is likely to be there because it strengthens the legal position of Shi'mon, Babatha's father, and subsequently Babatha herself—either as a positive reinforcement of that position, or defensively, as responsive to any legal attack that may be made against them or their property or has a bearing on the current legal position of cognate or affinal relatives. The alternative possibility, that they would have carefully preserved legal documents in their archive, in some cases for forty years, that were not relevant to their rights, seems far less likely. The contents of the archive suggest that Babatha, and presumably her father before her, were not in the habit of preserving stray legal documents having no connection with themselves or their family (including the affinal relatives Babatha acquired through her second marriage), of going about collecting legal papyri from their neighbours willy nilly.

In saying this I should state my view that P. Yadin 8, in Judean Aramaic and dated to 122 CE, is connected with Babatha in that the two sons of Shim'on mentioned (Yehoseph and another whose first name has not survived) are her brothers. I am also of the view that P. Yadin 9, written by same scribe as P. Yadin 8 (Yoḥanan son of Makkuta) and in the same year (the consul whose name survives being Acilius Auiola as in P. Yadin 8), but in Nabatean Aramaic, concerns this same Yehoseph (here spelt Yoseph) as a party, though now we learn that the other son is called Yehudah a son of Shim'on, who is named as a witness to the document.[101] Oudshoorn, who also identifies Yehoseph in P. Yadin 8 with Yoseph in P. Yadin 9, plausibly suggests that the first deed is in Judean Aramaic because he was contracting with his Judean brother and the second in Nabatean

[101] A certain Shim'on (presumably Babatha's father) is mentioned in these two documents. We also know that this scribe (Yoḥanan son of Makkuta) was active in Maoza in 119 CE since he drafted P. Yadin 6 in that year (as we learn from his handwriting: Yadin et al 2002: 269) and actually reappears in P. Yadin 22 (a sale of dates to defray money owed to Babatha by her deceased second husband from 130 CE) as Babatha's guardian (lines 29–30, Lewis 1989: 98). Yehudah son of Shim'on is a witness in P. Yadin 22. Given all this, it is puzzling that neither the editors (Yadin et al. 2002: 111–17) nor Oudshoorn (2007: 113) suggest that Yoseph and Yehudah, sons of Shim'on, are Babatha's brothers. It is worth noting that signing immediately before Yehudah son of Shim'on in P. Yadin 22 is one Yehoḥanan son of Menaḥem (line 37) and it is tempting to think that this is Babatha's paternal uncle, so that Babatha is ensuring that she has close relatives in her patriline attesting this important document, which was central to the restoration of her fortunes.

Aramaic because the other party, probably the obligee in the transaction and who particularly needed a copy of the document, whose name is missing, was a Nabatean.[102]

The circumstance that there are, indeed, only two documents in the archive without any *obvious* connection with Babatha's legal position or that of her cognate or affinal families, P. Yadin 1 and P. Yadin 4, strengthens the force of the assumption that they bear upon their legal position, an assumption which I will seek to show is correct in the later chapters of this volume.

CONCLUSION

Having now explained the meaning of archival ethnography, I can proceed to the next chapters of this volume. The first task is to explore Babatha's world as the necessary context within which the four papyri must be examined. In Chapter 2 I will address Nabatea and the Nabateans and in Chapter 3 life in Maoza. This exploration, like those in later chapters devoted to the texts of the four papyri, will be conducted in line with the ethnographic approach set out above. In one respect this will mean invoking comparable material from other cultures and from anthropological theory, while in another it will entail my being alive to the fact that the issues I choose to examine and the views I reach in relation to them inevitably reflect my own experience in life and my sense of what one needs to know to understand the story underlying P. Yadin 1–4.

[102] Oudshoorn 2007: 113.

2

Nabatea and the Nabateans

In Chapter 1 I noted that a characteristic of ethnography was the need for contextualization, which is the process of situating the people in view within the 'weave' of their society and culture in a way that helps us to explain their experience. In the present case, part of that process, which will occupy this chapter and the next, is to consider the highly distinctive world in which the events concerning Babatha's orchard unfolded and made sense. This distinctiveness was a product of several factors that included the unusual history and character of the Nabateans and their culture (ranging from social structures to irrigation works); the unique geography of the Dead Sea area; the hot climate that allowed the cultivation of the remarkable date-palm where irrigation water was available; the fact that an international border between the Roman province of Judea and the Kingdom of Nabatea bisected the region; the lively relationships between Judeans and Nabateans; and the relatively high income and asset levels enjoyed by many local farming families, but also the fragility to which their financial position was subject. This was the setting in which, in 99 CE, Shim'on son of Menaḥem came to purchase a date-palm orchard in Maoza on the southern shore of the Dead Sea and a few kilometres inside the Kingdom of Nabatea. It was also the world into which his daughter Babatha was to be born. Although the exact year of Babatha's birth is unknown, it was probably around 105 CE and almost certainly after her father's purchase of the date-palm orchard recorded in P. Yadin 3.[1]

[1] Babatha's first husband was Jesus son of Jesus. P. Yadin 5, from 2 June 110, is an acknowledgment that the uncle of Jesus son of Jesus holds on his behalf (as a minor, according to P. Satlow [2001] *Jewish Marriage in Antiquity*. Princeton, NJ: Princeton

In this chapter I will consider specifically Nabatean dimensions of Babatha's world, with reference where appropriate to comparable phenomena in line with the ethnographic approach set out in Chapter 1. In Chapter 3 I will complete my exploration of Babatha's world with reference to the environment, to date cultivation, and to the social and economic features of the lives of those who lived in and around Maoza.

THE HISTORY OF THE NABATEANS

The Contiguity of Nabatea and Judea

Before addressing Nabatea, we should note that the paramount political feature of the region in 98 CE was the contiguity of the Roman imperial province of Judea and the Nabatean kingdom ruled by Rabb'el II as a client king of the Romans.[2] Nabatea had become a client kingdom of Rome in 62 BCE when the Nabatean king Aretas III submitted himself to Pompey's legate Marcus Aemilius Scaurus.[3] The Dead Sea marked part of the border between the two, while at some

University Press, 97), a very considerable sum of money. We do not know when Jesus son of Jesus married Babatha but by 124 CE he had died, leaving an orphan son whose guardians, as Babatha alleged in a petition to the governor (P. Yadin 12), were providing him with insufficient maintenance. Assuming Babatha married in her early teens and Jesus was then in his early twenties (suggested by Satlow [2001: 97]), she was probably born around 105 CE.

[2] M. Sartre (2005) *The Middle East Under Rome*. ET by C. Porter and E. Rawlings. Harvard: Harvard University Press, 70. The *bet* in the name רבאל is geminated, as we know from the survival of two instances of the Greek form of the name: *Ραββηλος* (see A. Negev (1991) *Personal Names in the Nabataean Realm*. Qedem 32. Monographs of the Institute of Archaeology. Jerusalem: Hebrew University of Jerusalem, 59; citing H. Wuthnow (*Die semitischen Menschennamen in griechischen Inschriften und Papyri des vorderen Orients*. Leipzig: Dieterich'sche Verlagsbuchhandlung, 96 and 166). It is unclear to me why the name is spelt 'Rab'el' in Y. Yadin et al. (eds) (2002) *The Documents from the Bar Kokhba Period in the Cave of Letters: Hebrew, Aramaic and Nabatean-Aramaic Papyri*. Judean Desert Studies. Jerusalem: Israel Exploration Society, Institute of Archaeology, Hebrew University and the Shrine of the Book, Israel Museum.

[3] See P. Alpass (2013) *The Religious Life of Nabataea*. Religions in the Graeco-Roman World. Leiden: E. J. Brill, 25, who refers to Josephus *AJ* 14.80 and coins minted by Scaurus at Rome showing Aretas kneeling in submission.

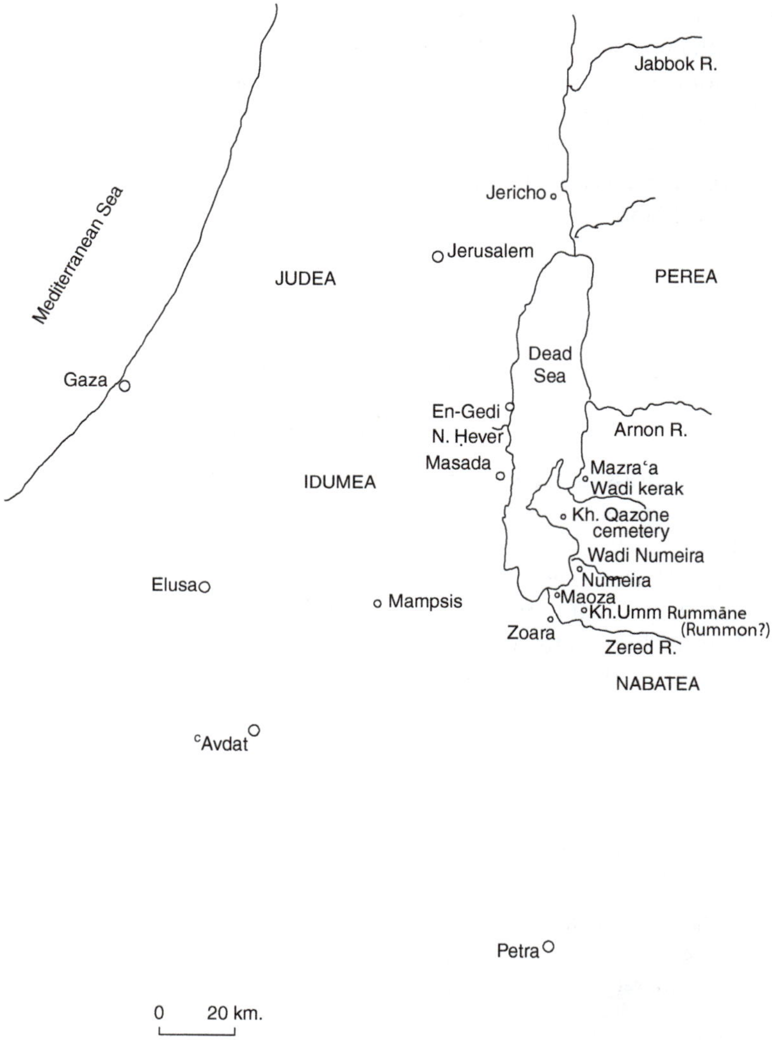

Fig. 2.1. Map of the Dead Sea region in the first century CE

point further south the border of Nabatea probably ran westwards to the Mediterranean (see Figure 2.1). But we should not make too much of the border. The Judean town of En-Gedi was only about 45 kilometres away from Maoza in Nabatea, where Shim'on lived, a journey that could be undertaken by land or by boat across the

Dead Sea.[4] It makes good sense to follow Hannah Cotton in thinking of the Judeans living in the Dead Sea region as having an identity that disregarded the boundary between Judea and Nabatea. In two days they could walk from one place in the region to most others and they entered into ties through marriage, property holding, and residence that took little or no account of the demarcation line between the two territories.[5]

A generation earlier, commencing in 66 CE, there had been a major revolt against Rome in Judea that resulted in the destruction of Jerusalem and its temple in 70 CE by legions under Titus.[6] At the beginning of the Revolt the Nabatean king Malichus II sent horsemen and infantry to support Titus.[7] Not surprisingly, therefore, after the revolt the Romans introduced several changes in the way they ruled Judea. First, the province now became independent from Syria under the name *Judaea*. Secondly, the Tenth Legion, X Fretensis, was permanently based in Jerusalem, replacing six auxiliary units that had been stationed there before 70 CE. Whereas previously the governor had been of equestrian rank, the new governor was a praetorian, the legate of the occupying legion. This imposition of direct military rule persisted up to the outbreak of the Second Revolt, led by Bar Kokhba, in 132 CE.[8] Accordingly, the Roman province adjacent to Nabatea existed in a state of heightened military readiness throughout our period.

Nabatea

But what of Nabatea itself? P. Yadin 1–4 indicate that Shim'on experienced the culture and institutions of the Nabateans in manifold ways. These four papyri reflect Nabatean agricultural practices

[4] There were harbours at various points on the Dead Sea coast. The Aramaic form of Maoza (מחוז) means 'port' and there was also a port at En-Gedi where three anchors were found in the bay (Y. Hirschfeld (2007b) 'Introduction' in Hirschfeld (ed.) (2007a) *En-Gedi Excavations II. Final Report (1996–2002)*. Jerusalem: Israel Exploration Society, 2).

[5] See H. M. Cotton (1998) 'The Rabbis and the Documents' in M. D. Goodman (ed.) (1998) *Jews in a Graeco-Roman World*. Oxford: Clarendon Press, 172–173.

[6] Some Judean garrisons held out for longer. Masada, for example, endured until 73 or 74 CE.

[7] Josephus, *BJ*, 3.68.

[8] J. Choi (2013) *Jewish Leadership in Roman Palestine from 70 C.E. to 135 C.E.* Leiden: E. J. Brill, 213–14.

and were drafted within the jurisdiction of the Nabatean kingdom, in a town in Nabatea, in Nabatean Aramaic, by Nabatean scribes, in accordance with Nabatean law and solely involved Nabateans as parties and witnesses, with the exception of Shim'on. We also know that many of his Nabatean neighbours bore names referring to Nabatean gods, since their names appear at various places in the papyri and their theophoric elements are clear. Regrettably, our knowledge of the kingdom suffers from the fact that not a single historical work or passage survives from a Nabatean author. Indeed, P. Yadin 1–4 (and two other extant Nabatean legal papyri)[9] are in fact the longest extant examples of writing in Nabatean Aramaic. Moreover, there are very few extant descriptions by Greco-Roman authors either—Nabatea's location on the remote eastern frontier of the Roman empire probably meant that fewer Greco-Roman authors were attracted to writing about it. A handful of illuminating passages have survived, however, to which we will return later.[10] For our knowledge of the kingdom, therefore, we are largely reliant on epigraphic evidence (coinage, legal papyri, and numerous inscriptions, many of the latter being graffiti of one or two words) and the surviving remains of Nabatean buildings and irrigation works.[11]

In a further complication, recent scholarship has insisted that the Nabatean kingdom embraced a number of very different geographical and cultural zones, stretching from Bosra in the north—in the Hauran

[9] P. XHev/Se Nab 1 (also known as 'P. Starcky'; see J. Starcky (1954) 'Un contrat nabatéan sur papyrus', *Revue Biblique* 61: 161–181; the document has since been re-edited by Ada Yardeni ([2001] 'The Decipherment and Restoration of Legal Texts from the Judaean Desert: A Reexamination of *Papyrus Starcky (P. Yadin 36)*', *Scripta Classica Israelica* 20: 121–137) and P. XHev/Se Nab 2 (see Ada Yardeni's drawing, transliteration into Hebrew letters and suggested date of *c.* 100 CE in A. Yardeni (2000a) *Textbook of Aramaic, Hebrew and Nabataean Texts from the Judean Desert and Related Material. A: The Documents (in Hebrew).* Jerusalem: Hebrew University, Ben-Zion Dinur Center of Research in Jewish History, 290–291 and A. Yardeni (2000b) *Textbook of Aramaic, Hebrew and Nabataean Texts from the Judaean Desert and Related Material. B: Translation. Paleography. Concordance (in Hebrew and English).* Jerusalem: Hebrew University, Ben-Zion Dinur Center of Research in Jewish History, 95).

[10] For the literary sources, see U. Hackl et al. (2003) *Quellen zur Geschichte der Nabatäer. Textsammlung mit Übersetzung und Kommentar.* NTOA 51. Fribourg: Vandenhoeck & Rupprecht.

[11] For a recent review of the inscriptional, literary, and architectural Nabatean remains, see Alpass 2013: 21–35. For the texts and discussion of Nabatean Aramaic inscriptions and papyri, see J. F. Healey (2009) *Aramaic Inscriptions and Documents from the Roman Period.* Textbook of Syrian Semitic Inscriptions, Volume IV. Oxford: Oxford University Press, 52–121.

where there was sufficient rainfall to allow settled agriculture—to Hegra in the southern desert region. For some this makes it difficult to speak of any homogeneous Nabatean culture.[12] Nevertheless, this does not mean that we cannot speak of Nabatean ethnic identity, a matter to which I will return below. In particular, it is an unsatisfactorily minimalist view of the identity of this people to suggest that all we can say that they had in common was the fact they fell under the sovereignty of the Nabatean kings, with such control being evident in any place where texts have been found that are dated by the regnal years of Nabatean kings.[13]

The Early Period

The origins of the Nabateans are obscure. A careful examination of the evidence, much of it epigraphic, has led David Graf to conclude that 'the location of the Nabataean homeland was northeast Arabia', as had previously been proposed by J. T. Milik.[14] This view is sustained in part by the essentially Arabic nature of the Nabatean onomasticon.[15] Graf also notes that 'Linguistic affinities between Nabataean Aramaic-Arabic and that of the Arab communities of Mesopotamia during the Neo-Assyrian period suggest that this was the matrix from which the Nabataean language emerged.'[16] Graf's view, with which I concur, is that it is probable that the Nabateans migrated across northern Arabia to the Levant during the Persian period and had reached Petra and Transjordan before the time of Alexander.[17] As to the language spoken by the Nabateans, there is an on-going debate as to whether they spoke Arabic in everyday life and only used Aramaic (heavily infused with Arabic) in certain contexts, such as legal documents, or whether they spoke Aramaic influenced by Arabic. John Healey has recently advised caution as to the former view; rather than assuming that all Nabateans spoke a form of Arabic

[12] Alpass 2013: 3.

[13] This is the view of Alpass 2013: 3–4.

[14] D. F. Graf (1990) 'The Origin of the Nabataeans', *Aram* 2: 67, citing J. T. Milik (1982) 'Origines des Nabatéans', in A. A. Hadidi (ed.) (1982) *Studies in the History and Archaeology of Jordan*. Jordan: Department of Antiquities. Volume 1, 261–265.

[15] Graf 1990: 45.

[16] Graf 1990: 67.

[17] Graf 1990: 67.

in everyday life, some Nabateans may well have spoken Aramaic.[18] For the purposes of this volume, however, it is not necessary to reach a conclusion on this matter.

The issues in Nabatean history requiring consideration here are those directly bearing upon the world of Shimʿon and Babatha. The earliest historical record of the Nabateans comes from the *Biblioteca historica* of the Greek historian Diodorus of Sicily, written in the decades around the middle of the first century BCE. There are two sections of this work of particular relevance for the Nabateans, a longer one from, from Book 19, sections 94.1–100.7, and a shorter one from Book 2, Section 48. The longer account describes the singularly unsuccessful campaign in 311 BCE by Antigonus *Monophthalmos* ('the One-Eyed'), one of the so-called *Diadochi* ('successors') to Alexander after his death in 323. This campaign was led by Antigonus' general Athenaeus and then by Antigonus' son Demetrius against 'the land of the Arabs who are called Nabateans' (19.94.1 and 95.2–7).[19] Into this account Diodorus interposes a description of 'these Arabs' (19.94.2–95.2). Diodorus's source for this account was Hieronymus of Cardia, an eyewitness to the events since he was one of Antigonus's commanders in the campaign.[20]

The other passage, 2.48, is an account of the people and prominent features of their territory (especially Petra and the Dead Sea). The source for this record was probably also the same Hieronymus.[21] He was the person whom Antigonus charged with leading what proved to be an unsuccessful effort to seize the valuable asphalt that occasionally floated to the surface of the Dead Sea, a sorry tale, which Hieronymus nonetheless recounts.[22]

The first account is securely dated to the late fourth century BCE and the second is probably from the same date. Notably, both attribute a

[18] J. F. Healey (2007) 'Nabataean Insriptions: Language and Script', in K. D. Politis (ed.) (2007) *The World of the Nabataeans: Volume 2 of the International Conference the World of the Herods and the Nabataeans held at the British Museum, 17–19 April 2001*. Stuttgart: Franz Steiner Verlag, 46–48.

[19] This campaign has traditionally been dated to 312 BCE, but Robert Wenning has recently stated the case for re-dating it to 311 BCE (R. Wenning [2007] 'The Nabateans in History (Before AD 106)', in Politis 2007: 28).

[20] G. W. Bowersock (1983) *Roman Arabia*. Cambridge, MT: Harvard University Press, 12, citing Diodorus Siculus, 19.100.1, where Hieronymus is mentioned as 'the writer of the history'.

[21] Hackl et al. 2003: 433.

[22] Diodorus Siculus, 19.100.1–2.

nomadic lifestyle to the Nabateans. Consider the following from the account in *Biblioteca historica* Book 19:

> They live in the open air, claiming as native land a wilderness that has neither rivers nor abundant springs from which it is possible for a hostile army to obtain water. It is their custom neither to plant grain, set out any fruit-bearing tree, use wine, nor construct any house; and if anyone is found acting contrary to this, death is his penalty.[23]

Diodorus Siculus reports that the Nabateans avoid these things lest they fall under the sway of the powerful. 'Some of them raise camels', he adds, 'others sheep, pasturing them in the desert.' While many Arab tribes use the desert as pasture, 'the Nabataeans far surpass the others in wealth although they are not much more than ten thousand in number'. Their wealth derives from the frankincense, myrrh, and other valuable spices which they bring down to the sea and which they procure from those who convey them from Arabia Felix (the southwest part of the peninsula). Bowersock explains that this statement means that the 'spice and perfume trade from southern Arabia and the East through the middlemen of the southwest corner of the Arabian peninsula depended upon the Nabataeans for the conveyance of goods to the Mediterranean by an overland route'.[24] Not only did the Nabateans make immense profit from the onward carriage of spices and perfumes from the east, they also controlled the lucrative trade in the asphalt that floated to the surface of the Dead Sea in large clumps. We know this from the report by Diodorus Siculus, later in this section of his history, which relates how, when Demetrius and his army were withdrawing in 311 BCE and some of them tried to harvest the asphalt, they were prevented from doing so by 6,000 Arabs.[25]

Diodorus Siculus also notes that the Nabateans are exceptionally fond of their freedom (φιλελεύθεροι δέ εἰσι διαφερόντως) and if a strong force of enemies approaches, they take refuge in the desert. Other armies cannot cross it for lack of water, but the Nabateans construct large subterranean reservoirs lined with stucco that are filled with rainwater but with the entries camouflaged so only they know their location. Since they water their cattle every day, they can

[23] Diodorus Siculus, 19.94.2 (ET R. M Geer [1954] *Diodorus of Sicily, with an English Translation by Russel M. Geer*. In Twelve Volumes, Volume 10. Loeb Edition. London and Cambridge: William Heinemann Ltd and Harvard University Press, 87).

[24] Bowersock 1983: 15.

[25] Diodorus Siculus, 19.100.1–2.

flee with them through waterless places if necessary. They eat flesh and milk and edible plants, including pepper and the so-called wild honey from trees, which they drink mixed with water.[26]

In our other passage, from *Biblioteca historica* Book 2, Diodorus Siculus adds that the 'Arabs', who bear the name 'Nabateans', range over a territory that is partly desert and waterless, although a small section of it is fruitful. They lead a life of brigandage and are hard to overcome in war because of their secret wells that they can access but their enemies cannot. Here mention is also made of their immensely strong rock (Petra) and the Dead Sea with its asphalt-producing propensity.[27] Of particular interest is the following:

> Yet the land is good for the growing of palms, wherever it happens to be traversed by rivers with usable water or to be supplied with springs that can irrigate it.[28]

Graf (followed by Alpass) is sceptical of Diordorus's description of the Nabateans for a number of reasons: there is no corroboration for the picture painted by Hieronymus; his reliability as an historian is unclear and he seems to have gullibly accepted tall tales elsewhere; and his account may be based on Herodotus's description of the nomadic Scythians (*History*, 4.1–82), as suggested by the fact that Hieronymus' mention of the liberty of the Nabateans is matched by the freedom of the Scythians.[29]

In my view, such scepticism is unwarranted.[30] We know from archaeological evidence (discussed below) that the Nabateans retained a nomadic dimension to their existence until the first and even second centuries CE. The freedom of the Nabateans is an inevitable reflection of their nomadic lifestyle, well known from ethnographic research (also discussed below), and not simply something that Hieronymus has borrowed from Herodotus on the Scythians. There is nothing, moreover, apparently fanciful in the Hieronymus account of the Nabateans.

[26] Diodorus Siculus, 19.94.6–10. [27] Diodorus Siculus, 2.48.1–5.

[28] Diodorus Siculus, 2.48.9 (ET C. H. Oldfather (1935) *Diodorus of Sicily, with an English Translation by C. H. Oldfather*. In Ten volumes, Volume II. Loeb Edition. London and Cambridge: William Heinnemann Ltd and Harvard University Press, 45).

[29] Graf 1990: 51–53; Alpass 2013: 27.

[30] For a less sceptical view of Diodorus Siculus (and his source, Hieronymus), see J. Taylor (2012) *The Essenes, the Scrolls, and the Dead Sea*. Oxford: Oxford University Press, 211–213.

In particular, his references to their occupancy of Petra and their skill with water storage are attested elsewhere and support the account. The reference to the Nabateans' involvement with the spice trade also accords with other evidence (some of it cited below).

Further, while Herodotus may have inaugurated the practice of including descriptions of the customs of foreign peoples in historical works, this soon became a widespread practice among Greek writers.[31] There is no reason to conclude that Hieronymus was just repeating the Herodotean account of the Scythians in relation to the Nabateans. Moreover, the details of the Nabateans that Herodotus mentions are not to be found in Diodorus Siculus's account, except for the Nabateans' love of freedom, which was and is integral to the life of all nomadic peoples. In addition, the reference to the cultivation of date-palms in the territory of the Nabateans means that some at least of these people, or other people living amongst them, must have been engaged in settled agriculture even at this early date. Finally, the fact that Hieronymus mentions the unsuccessful attempt to gather the Dead Sea asphalt even though he was leading it suggests that his account should not lightly be impugned.[32]

The Anthropology of Nomadism

The anthropology of nomadism offers valuable comparative resources with which to explore the concept of Nabatean as nomad. Tent-dwelling pastoral nomads are to be found in many parts of the world, but especially in the Middle East, Central Asia, and Africa. The main ecological factor in their lifestyles is the need to move their flocks and herds continually in the pursuit of pastures and water. A common political factor is the need to avoid other nomadic groups.[33] This lifestyle inevitably impacts upon the social structure and relations of the group. Fredrik Barth's description of one nomadic tribe is revealing:

[31] See E. Almagor and J. Skinner (eds) (2013) *Ancient Ethnography: New Approaches*. London: Bloomsbury.

[32] Diodorus Siculus, 19.100.2.

[33] As with the Basseri tribe of South Persia (F. Barth [1964] *Nomads of Southern Persia*. Oslo: Universitetsforlaget, 5).

> Unlike a sedentary community, which persists unless the members abandon their house and land and depart, a camp community of nomads can only persist through a continuous re-affirmation by all its members. Every day the members of the camp must agree in their decision on the vital question of whether to move on, or to stay camped, and if they move, by which route and how far they should move. These decisions are the very stuff of a pastoral nomad existence . . . Every household head has an opinion, and the prosperity of the household is dependent on his decision.[34]

If no such agreement is reached, the fission of the camp as a group will result. 'The maintenance of a camp as a social unit thus requires the daily unanimous agreement by all members on economically vital decisions.'[35]

This aspect of nomadic life illustrates both the freedom of the nomad (at least in terms of territory) and the power of individual family heads within a group, which is incompatible with a strongly hierarchical structure.

Yet it is rarely possible for nomads to pursue their lifestyle in the absence of relationships with other groups. More typically we observe a mutual relation between nomads and peasants, often representing different ethnic groups, of a sort that allows both to occupy specific ecological niches.[36] Thus the Pathans, who control the mountainous flanks of the valleys in the Swat region of Pakistan but cannot utilize them, allow the Gujar people to engage in transhumant pastoralism in those areas. Both benefit from this symbiotic relationship.[37] A common pattern is for nomads to sell milk, cheese, and wool to people in villages and buy from them food and products they cannot produce.[38] Archaeological research conducted in 1979 produced solid evidence that the mutualism between nomadic pastoralists and settled agriculturalists which was discovered by Barth in the

[34] Barth 1964: 25–26. [35] Barth 1964: 26.

[36] This idea was initially theorised by Fredrik Barth (1956) 'Ecologic Relations of Ethnic Groups in Swat, North Pakistan', *American Anthropologist* 58: 1079–1089. Also see F. Barth (1973) 'A General Perspective on Nomad–Sedentary Relations in the Middle East', in C. Nelson (ed.) (1973) *The Desert and the Sown*. Berkeley, CA: Institute of International Studies, 11–22.

[37] Barth 1956: 1086.

[38] See the exchanges of this kind that occur among Baggara of western Sudan (B. Michael [1997] 'Female Heads of Patriarchal Households: The Baggara', *Journal of Comparative Family Studies* 28: 171).

Swat valley was also present in the southern highlands of Jordan in Roman and Byzantine times.[39]

Sometimes, moreover, a nomadic people, or part of it, will come under pressure of various kinds to abandon their wandering life and to become sedentary.[40] Barth observed among the Basseri that 'through a constant process of sedentarization . . . , a number of camp members are sloughed off in every generation'.[41] At times, for example, a family unit will become too small to operate all the functions associated with nomadic pastoralism. A different pattern is apparent among the Baggara of western Sudan, where men frequently have one wife with them in the nomadic camp and one living in a village, which actually facilitates the maintenance of nomadism by allowing each family access to the products of both nomadic and settled forms of agricultural production. Barbara Michael refers to his process as 'tactical sedentarization'.[42] When Barth was living among the Basseri in Iran in the early 1960s, most of their current sections had both nomadic branches and also settled branches in some localities.[43]

The account Diodorus Siculus provides of the Nabateans repays consideration in the light of this comparative material. Freedom is an inevitable dimension of the nomadic life and the Nabateans would have had to reach regular decisions as to where to move their camp, a process that would have encouraged non-hierarchical social arrangements among them. The prohibitions on raising crops and building houses (probably as opposed to using tents) are a realistic means of preserving the nomadic lifestyle. The reference, however, to the fact that the land is good for growing palms indicates that, even at this early stage in their history, the Nabeteans were, just like other nomads, in contact with settled people. Possibly these were not Nabateans but some other group; yet they could also have been sedentarized Nabateans. The dates they produced would have valuably enhanced the diet of the nomadic Nabateans. Even, it seems, into the modern period some Middle Eastern nomads ate pounds of dates a day, dates that often constituted their main food for extended

[39] E. B. Banning (1986) 'Peasants, Pastoralists, and "Pax Romana": Mutualism in the Southern Highlands of Jordan', *Bulletin of the American Schools of Oriental Research* 261: 25–50.

[40] For the Basseri tribe, see Barth 1964: 3.

[41] Barth 1964: 66.

[42] Michael 1997: 171.

[43] Barth 1964: 117.

periods.[44] Nomadic Nabateans probably traded milk, milk products, animals, or meat for them.

Accordingly, this single reference to date-palm cultivation in Diodorus Siculus, another sign of his accuracy, implies a symbiotic relationship between nomadic Nabateans and others based on their occupation of different ecological niches.

The Later History of the Nabateans

The Nabateans also appear in sources that survive from later periods. Among the papyri from the Zenon archive there is one dated 259 BCE that mentions 'the Nabateans' in the context of events in the Hauran, thus providing important evidence for the Nabateans in the Hauran at that time. This is also the earliest documentary reference to the Nabateans.[45] These papyri also refer to someone who received wheat flour called Rabbelos (Rabb'el), a characteristic Nabatean name that would later be used by two of the Nabatean kings.[46] Another man, with the name Malichus (also used by later Nabatean kings) and from Moab, sold Zenon perfumes that he had received from the south,[47] thus indicating the presence of the lucrative trade mentioned above.

A very early Nabatean inscription, probably from the first half of the second century BCE, was found in Elusa in the Negev and states 'This is the (cult-) place which Notayru made for the life of Ḥaretat, king of the Nabataeans (מלך נבטו).'[48] The Greek form of Ḥaretat is Aretas. Healey notes that נבטו is a singular tribal name and that the vocalization *nabatu* is supported by the ancient Greek equivalent of the word, *Ναβαταῖοι*, and by later Arabic.[49] This inscription provides important early evidence for the institution of kingship among the

[44] P. B. Popenoe and Charles L. Bennett (1913) *Date Growing in the Old World and the New*. Los Angeles: George Rice & Sons, 203.

[45] Bowersock 1983: 17–18. For the text, translation and discussion of the Zenon papyrus mentioning Nabateans in the Hauran, see Graf 1990: 69–75.

[46] R. Wenning (1993a) 'Eine neuerstellte Liste der nabatäischen Dynastie'; *Boreas* 16: 38.

[47] Wenning 1993a: 28.

[48] See J. Cantineau (1930–1932) *Le Nabatéen*. 2 vols. Paris: Libraire Ernest Leroux, 44 and Healey 2009: 52–53 for the text, translation, and comments. Healey considers this is probably the oldest Nabatean inscription published to date (2009: 52).

[49] Healey 2009: 53.

Nabateans. In all probability, so too does the reference from 168 BCE to the former high priest Jason, in flight from the Judeans, appearing before one Aretas, 'tyrant of the Arabs', in 2 Macc. 5:8. Indeed this is the earliest datable evidence for a Nabatean king.[50] This man has come to be designated as 'Aretas I', or 'Ḥaretat I' in Aramaic. We do not know if the king just mentioned in the Elusa description is to be identified with this Aretas, of if he was an earlier king of that name. In 163 BCE the Maccabean brothers Judas and Jonathan travelled three days into the wilderness, probably in the Hauran, and encountered the Nabateans, who treated them kindly.[51]

Sometime in the second century BCE a discovery was made that would eventually sap the basis of Nabatean wealth, so that by the mid first century CE the overland route through Petra had largely ended. A Greek helmsman named Hippalus discovered the existence of the monsoon that allowed boats to sail directly between Aden and India.[52] This opened up an alternative means to bring spices and perfumes from the east to the west (Rome especially) that entailed bypassing the overland routes controlled by the Nabateans. Reports of a period when the Nabateans engaged in piracy off the coast of Egypt until they were stopped by a fleet, probably Ptolemaic, may indicate their efforts to disrupt this new alternative route between East and West because of the threat it posed to them.[53]

The next noteworthy passages from an ancient source occur in Strabo's *Geography*, written no later than 3/2 BCE.[54] At one point Strabo mentions information received from his friend Athenodorus of Tarsus, 'a philosopher and companion' of his who had been to the Nabatean kingdom,[55] which suggests that Athenodorus was the source for all of his information. Strabo describes a people who seem very different from the Nabatean nomads of Hieronymus:

> The Nabataeans are a sensible people, and are so much inclined to acquire possessions that they publicly fine anyone who has diminished

[50] On the succession of Nabatean kings, see Wenning 1993a.

[51] 1 Macc 5:25–26; see Bowersock 1983: 19.

[52] See Pliny, *Natural History*, 6.100 and *Periplus of the Red Sea*, 5. The evidence is discussed by Bowersock (1983: 21). On the spice trade between Rome and India, see J. I. Miller (1969) *The Spice Trade of the Roman Empire: 29 B.C. to A.D. 641*. Oxford: Clarendon Press and F. De Romanis and M. Maiuro (2015) *Across the Ocean: Nine Essays on Indo-Mediterranean Trade*. Leiden: E. J. Brill.

[53] Bowersock 1983: 20–21.

[54] For this date, see Bowersock 1983: 55.

[55] Strabo, *Geography*, 16.4.21.

his possessions and also confer honours on anyone who has increased them. Since they have but few slaves, they are served by their kinsfolk (συγγενεῖς) for the most part, or by one another, or by themselves; so that the custom extends even to their kings. They prepare common meals together in groups of thirteen persons; and they have two girl-singers for each banquet. The king holds many drinking-bouts in magnificent style, but no one drinks more then eleven cupfuls, each time using a different golden cup. The king is so much a man of the people (δημοτικός) that, in addition to serving himself, he sometimes even serves the rest himself in his turn. He often renders an account of his kingship to the popular assembly; and sometimes his mode of life is examined. Their homes, through the use of stone, are costly; but on account of peace, the cities are not walled.[56]

Strabo is also almost certainly reliant on Athenodorus for the following account (since he mentions him in the passage):

The metropolis of the Nabataeans is Petra, as it is called; for it lies on a site which is otherwise smooth and level, but it is fortified all round by a rock, the outside parts of the site being precipitous and sheer, and the inside parts having springs in abundance, both for domestic purposes and for watering gardens. Outside the circuit of the rock most of the territory is desert, in particular that towards Judaea . . . Petra is always ruled by some king from the royal family; and the king has as Administrator (ἐπίτροπος) one of his companions, who is called 'brother.' It is exceedingly well governed; at any rate, Athenodorus, a philosopher and companion of mine, who had been in the city of the Petraeans, used to describe their government with admiration, for he said that he found both many Romans and many other foreigners sojourning there, and that he saw that the foreigners often engaged in lawsuits, both with one another and with the local inhabitants, but that none of the local inhabitants sued one another, and that they in every way kept the peace with one another.[57]

The accuracy of the first of these two quotations from Strabo has recently been called into question. Anderson (followed by Alpass)

[56] Strabo, *Geography*, 16.4.26; ET from H. L. Jones (1930) *Strabo, Geography. Books 15–16, with an English Translation by Horace Leonard Jones*. The Loeb Edition. Cambridge, MT and London: Harvard University Press, 367–369 (but replacing Jones' 'democratic' as a translation of δημοτικός with 'a man of the people'). Note Hackl et al. 2003: 605: 'Die Passage geht auf den Augenzeugenbericht des Athenodorus . . . zurück.'

[57] Strabo, *Geography*, 16.4.21; ET Jones 1930: 351 and 353 (but replacing 'prosecuted' with 'sued' and 'natives' with 'local inhabitants').

argues that it has been affected both by literary conventions about uncivilized peoples and by the attempt to see the villain Syllaeus (vizier to the Nabatean king Obodas III) as prototypical of the Nabateans.[58] As with the accounts of Dio Siculus, however, such scepticism is in my view unjustified. That there was a tradition of writing about foreign peoples does not mean all such authors aped Herodotus on the Scythians. The details just quoted, moreover, are incidental to any attempt to tar Syllaeus (and other Nabateans) with treachery; just the contrary, in fact. As for the second passage from Strabo, the designation of the Administrator as 'brother' of the king greatly strengthens the case for the authenticity of the report, since this designation is known from the inscriptions that this very same Syllaeus commissioned on Delos and Miletus in 9 BCE, during the course of his journey to Rome mentioned by Josephus.[59] The Miletus inscription reads 'Syllaeus, brother of the king, on behalf of King Obodas, dedicated to Zeus Dusares Soter'.[60]

These passages from Strabo raise the question of what has happened to the nomadic lifestyle of the Nabateans depicted in the two passages from Diodorus Siculus. The probable answer is that powerful processes of sedentarization had occurred among the Nabateans. The huge profits they had made from controlling the overland spice routes had no doubt given them access to wealth in a manner highly unusual for nomadic peoples, so that the temptation to invest some of it in settled agriculture (including date-palms) and edifices built of stone must have been strong. In addition, they developed their earlier interest in the construction of cisterns for water into a wider range of hydraulic engineering that allowed them to supply towns and also to extend agricultural production into new areas by irrigation.[61]

Sedentarization probably started in earnest when Petra was chosen as the residency of the royal family and the nobility of the tribe.[62] As

[58] See B. Anderson (2009) 'Double-Crossing Jordan: Strabo's Portrait of Syllaeus and the Imagining of Nabataea', *SHAJ*: 10 391–397 and Alpass 2013: 27.

[59] Hackl et al. 2003: 606. Josephus, *AJ* 16.286–299 and 335–355.

[60] See J. F. Healey (2001) *The Religion of the Nabataeans: A Conspectus*. Leiden: E. J. Brill, 101. For a discussion of these inscriptions, see T. Terpstra (2015) 'Roman Trade with the Far East: Evidence for Nabataean Middlemen in Puteoli' in De Romanis and Maiuro 2015: 79–80.

[61] On the Nabateans' skill and achievements in hydraulic engineering, see J. P. Oleson (2007) 'Water Supply, Irrigation and Agriculture', in Politis 2007: 217–250.

[62] Wenning 2007: 29. In the Greek world Petra became known as the capital of the Nabateans: Josephus, *AJ*, 14.1. 4.

already noted, by 311 BCE Petra was an important gathering place for the Nabateans. Wenning has argued, however, that it was not yet the seat of the tribe at that time and not the religious centre of the Nabateans.[63] By 129 BCE, however, it must have been regarded as the place where you went to meet the king and his courtiers. We know this from an inscription from Priene in Asia Minor that praises a certain ambassador for his diplomatic efforts in various parts of the Mediterranean world, including Petra in Arabia.[64] At some point it became fixed as the royal capital and residence of the Nabatean kings. Their settlement there occurred sometime before 96 BCE when their principal god, Dushara, is mentioned in the oldest dated Nabatean inscription at Petra in the Bab-as-Siq sanctuary.[65] Nabatean coinage developed around 100 BCE.[66] These developments probably occurred during the reign of their second king, Aretas II (120/110–96 BCE).[67] Wenning has suggested that the Nabatean practice of building houses from stone (as opposed to cutting them into living rock) began in the Augustan period.[68]

We know the names and regnal years of the Nabatean kings from Aretas I, *circa* 168 BCE, to their last king, Rabb'el II, who either died or was deposed by the Romans when Nabatea became the Roman province of Nabatea in 106 CE.[69] The significance of a line of kings stretching back nearly three centuries over what was originally, and to an extent remained, a nomadic people should not be underestimated. To gain some insight into both the nature of the nomadic life and the remarkable achievement of the Nabateans in surviving as an increasingly sedentary people under a king for some three centuries, especially in light of the continuing power of a tribal tradition and lifestyle, it is helpful to consider a closely analogous case with an entirely different result.

During the pre-Islamic period (*c.* mid-fifth to mid-sixth centuries CE) northern Arabia witnessed another example of tribes from the

[63] Wenning 2007: 27. [64] Bowersock 1983: 22. [65] Wenning 2007: 30.

[66] Y. Meshorer (1975) *Nabataean Coins*. Qedem 3. Monographs of the Institute of Archaeology. Jerusalem: Hebrew University of Jerusalem, 9–14. See K. Schmitt-Korte (1990) 'Nabataean Coinage—Part II. New Coin Types and Variants', *The Numismatic Chronicle* 150: 105–133 for work on Nabatean coinage after Meshorer (and in some respects suggesting alternative interpretations of particular coins).

[67] Meshorer 1975: 85. For the regnal years of the Nabatean kings, see Wenning 1993a: 38.

[68] Wenning 2007: 25 [69] See Wenning 1993a.

region coming together under a king.[70] In the period immediately preceding Islam, central and northern Arabia became quite anarchic due to fierce wars between the tribes. Yet for a period during the mid-fifth to mid-sixth centuries CE the Bedouin tribes of northern Arabia did attempt to maintain a single political entity under a single king. The Arabian nomads of this period developed an ideology celebrating their lifestyle, which they claimed was characterized by generosity, hospitality, honour, contentment, and loyalty, as superior to all others. Loyalty to tribe coalesced around a real or imagined line of descent (*nasab*) that they staunchly defended. In particular, unquestioning loyalty was owed to descendants of the same bloodline. Nomadic genealogies played an important part in this process.[71]

At a time of increasing warfare among Bedouin tribes, the Bakr tribe launched an initiative that resulted in the establishment of the kingdom. Fractured by feuding amongst its various branches, the Bakr invited the Yemenite monarch to be their king; in reply, he delegated the position to Hijr (Akel al-Murar), the chief of the Kinda tribe.[72] Around a century later, in the middle of the sixth century CE, the kingdom disintegrated. According to Bamyeh:

> Therefore, the very development of the hierarchical and functional aspects of a monarchical system posed an unacceptable challenge to a nomad accustomed to the model of a nearly egalitarian tribe, who would submit to the tribe's unanimous decision but not to the arbitrary will of its sheikh . . .[73]

The Nabateans, however, did manage to achieve a kingship that persisted for centuries and they did this while still preserving central aspects of their nomadic lifestyle. It is of upmost importance to note that the passages from Strabo cited above contain evidence for the continuance of aspects of Nabatean social life closely connected with nomadism. The fact that their king 'was a man of the people', serving them at banquets and rendering an account of his kingship to the popular assembly, where his mode of life was examined, coheres closely with the non-hierarchical nature of Nabatean nomadic life.

[70] See M. A. Bamyeh (2006) 'The Nomads of Pre-Islamic Arabia', in D. Chatty (ed.) (2006) *Nomadic Societies in the Middle East and north Africa: Entering the 21st Century*. Leiden and Boston: E. J. Brill, 34–48.

[71] Bamyeh 2006: 36–38 (citing A. Ibn Khaldun [1961] *Al Muqaddima*. Beirut: Darab-Kitàb al Lubnani, *passim*).

[72] Bamyeh 2006: 39–40.

[73] Bamyeh 2006: 42.

Old patterns, such as the likely need for the families in each nomadic camp to agree on when to move on and where to, continued to prevail in the power that the individual members of the people held on matters of moment. Where the king led in this humble and unaffected dealing with his people, it is very reasonable to expect that other members of the elite would follow, as indeed we will see for one of them later in this volume. Nor is it unreasonable to assume that there persisted among the Nabateans the values of generosity, hospitality, honour, and loyalty—all closely tied to a nomadic lifestyle—that were valued among the Arab nomads in their region only a few centuries later.

In addition to the literary evidence from Strabo, archaeological research indicates that the nomadic lifestyle did not die out among the Nabateans. Steven Rosen has shown how recent work in the Central Negev, located south west of the Dead Sea and west of the Rift Valley, has brought to light evidence of Nabatean occupation in the first and second centuries CE, possibly extending back into the first century BCE,[74] that is to say, during the high point of Nabatean settled, agricultural culture, the period covering Shim'on and Babatha. The dominant pattern that emerged was of a system of complementary pastoral and agricultural zones of the sort discussed above.

Rectilinear architectural remains cluster in the north of the region, closer to Avdat, a town founded by the Nabateans for the spice trade and most suitable for run-off farming. These remains feature substantial buildings constructed in squares or rectangles (with one wall meeting another at, or approximately at, a right angle).[75] Construction was marked by 'the use of hewn blocks of stone, with walls occasionally preserved almost up to original roof height, two meters high.' Doorways with thresholds and lintels and windows were discovered at some sites.[76] Sites with such construction varied in size from single structures, perhaps best interpreted as lone farm houses, to large clusters with ten or more such buildings, hamlets, or even villages.[77] Such structures reflect the building style of the sedentary phase of Nabatean history mentioned earlier.

The pastoral zones, largely in the south of the region, featured camps with no architectural remains or with curvilinear architectural

[74] For the date, see S. A. Rosen (2007) 'The Nabateans as Pastoral Nomads: An Archaeological Perspective', in Politis 2007: 347 and 365.

[75] Rosen 2007: 351. [76] Rosen 2007: 354. [77] Rosen 2007: 352.

remains.[78] The latter structures are round or oval, usually between 2 and 5 metres in diameter, and often open at one end. They rarely stand more than 0.5–0.75 metres high and were probably never much higher. They are constructed of unmodified wadi cobbles or bedrock slabs. 'It seems reasonably clear that superstructures were either tents or perhaps brush.'[79] The camps that lack such features still possess signs of occupation such as hearths, stone lines, cleared areas, and other types of installations. The stone lines and cleared areas strongly suggest the one-time presence of tents, with the stones having been used to hold down tent flaps.[80]

The non-architectural or curvilinear architectural sites overlap with those featuring rectilinear structures 'in the center of the survey region',[81] suggesting that this was a system of complementary pastoral and agricultural zones. Accordingly, the archaeological remains indicate the presence of a pastoral nomadic system based on seasonal movement that was tied to a more sedentary Nabatean system that developed as a result of Nabatean trade.[82] As noticed above, ethnographic research by anthropologists such as Fredrik Barth, E. B. Banning, and Barbara Michael has revealed other examples of nomads and farmers who accommodate themselves to one another in a variety of ways.[83] Rosen concludes his survey by stating that the 'geographic overlap between the systems would be difficult to sustain given hostile relations'.[84]

But we can say more than this. Here was a population of nomadic Nabateans in the first and second centuries CE, no doubt living much as Hieronymus of Cardia had observed them four or so centuries earlier, with some of them camping in close proximity to settled Nabateans and no doubt interacting with them in activities such as trade. Such encounters would have served to remind the latter of the traditional lifestyle and values that had been theirs in recent times. The Nabatean ethnic group had not entirely shed its nomadic past but instead kept both the nomadic and sedentary options alive within its ranks. Under these circumstances it is highly probable that the style of life described by Strabo among the Nabateans around the turn of the

[78] Rosen 2007: 351. [79] Rosen 2007: 354. [80] Rosen 2007: 354.
[81] Rosen 2007: 351. [82] Rosen 2007: 345.
[83] Barth 1964 and Banning 1986, cited by Rosen 2007: 368.
[84] Rosen 2007: 368.

first century CE, where the king was a man of the people, would have continued for a century into the time of Shim'on and Babatha. Finally, some support for the continuing influence of the nomadic lifestyle among the Nabateans is found in the view of Al-Qdrah and Abdelaziz that 'Nabataean inscriptions insist on the concept of the family unit, a concept that may reflect their Bedouin background where the family ties were strong'.[85]

The End of the Nabatean Kingdom

In 99 CE, the year in which P. Yadin 2–4 were drafted and signed, Rabb'el II had been king of Nabatea for nearly thirty years. By an interesting coincidence, it was in 70/71 CE, around the time of the destruction of the Temple in Jerusalem, that he had acceded to the throne.[86] Robert Wenning has mounted an argument that Rabb'el encouraged a national and religious renewal in his kingdom. As early as 76 CE he was claiming that 'he had brought life and liberation to this people'.[87] We will encounter much the same phrase in the Nabatean legal papyri in later chapters. Rabb'el II also called himself the *σωτήρ* ('saviour') of his people.[88]

Yet a mere seven years after the events investigated in this volume, the kingdom of Nabatea was replaced by the Roman province of Arabia. Great uncertainty surrounds this transition. It is even unclear whether Rabb'el II died. There probably was an armed intervention by L. Cornelius Palma, the Roman governor of Syria, in 106 CE.[89] The evidence (in a Byzantine abridgement of Cassius Dio) suggests that the Nabateans suffered a defeat or a humiliation.[90] Nevertheless, the emperor Trajan did not take the honorific title *Arabicus* after the kingdom became a province and the province was described as *Arabia adquisita* ('acquired') not *capta* ('captured') in coins minted

[85] H. Al-Qudrah, and M. Abdelaziz, (2008) 'Kinship Terms in the Nabataean Inscriptions', *Arabian Archaeology and Epigraphy* 19: 192. Open text, accessed at: <https://eis.hu.edu.jo/deanshipfiles/pub103812316.pdf>.

[86] Wenning 1993a: 37.

[87] Wenning 1993a: 37 and R. Wenning (1993b) 'Das Ende des nabatäischen Königreichs', in A. Invernizzi and J. F. Salles (eds) (1993) *Arabia Antiqua: Hellenistic Centres Around Arabia*. Rome: Is. M. E. O.

[88] Wenning 1993a: 38.

[89] Bowersock 1983: 79–80.

[90] Bowersock 1983: 79–80.

in Rome in 111/112 CE.[91] This suggests that there was little in the way of organized opposition.

THE ETHNIC IDENTITY OF THE NABATEANS

Most of the people we encounter when reading the Yadin Papyri are either Judeans (this term is explained below) or Nabateans. A small number are Romans. Using such terms raises the issue of group identities. In P. Yadin 1–4 one Judean is named (Shim'on) and thirty-five Nabateans. We have already learned quite a lot about the Nabateans with reference to their history. By concentrating the discussion on their identity we will be able both to learn more about them and to consider how their identity may have affected their relationships with Judeans like Shim'on and Babatha.

Explaining Ethnic Identity

The whole question of identity, whether of individuals or groups, has been a very lively one across a number of disciplines for nearly three decades. Social identity theory, which was initially developed by social psychologists Henri Tajfel and John Turner at the University of Bristol in the 1970s and 1980s and flourishes now around the world as the dominant form of social psychology, has at its heart the question of how individuals derive identity from the groups to which they belong, especially in a setting of intergroup tension and conflict.[92]

Among the many types of groups to which social identity theory has application are ethnic groups, which were a concern of Henri Tajfel from the beginning of his development of social identity

[91] P. Freeman (1996) 'The Annexation of Arabia and the Grand Imperial Strategy', in D. L. Kennedy (ed.) (1996) *The Roman Army in the East.* Journal of Roman Archaeology Supp. Series, 18. Ann Arbor, MI, 112.

[92] See H. Tajfel et al. (1971) 'Social Categorization and Intergroup Behaviour', *European Journal of Social Psychology* 1: 149–178 and H. Tajfel (ed.) (1978a) *Differentiation between Social Groups: Studies in the Social Psychology of Intergroup Relations.* European Monographs in Social Psychology. London: Academic Press.

theory.[93] Conflicts that have continued or have begun in the past thirty years between Tamils and Sinhalese in Sri Lanka, Unionists and Nationalists in Northern Ireland, Hutus and Tutsis in Rwanda, Serbs and Kosovans in Kosovo, and Arabs and Kurds in Iraq have not only underlined the continuing relevance of ethnic identity in the modern world, but the potential it carries for major conflict and war. This is not to say, however, that different ethnic groups cannot live close to one another in relative peace and harmony.

What is an ethnic group? The currently most influential perspective on ethnicity originated in a 1969 essay by Norwegian anthropologist Fredrik Barth.[94] Barth was opposed to the 'primordial' approach popular at the time that treated ethnic groups as constituted by the possession of a set of cultural features. He argued, instead, that their sense of themselves as a group interacting with other groups came first and cultural *indicia* (frequently changing over time)[95] were employed, as a boundary, to express that group identity. Barth gave careful thought to the common situation where two or more ethnic groups were interacting on a regular basis (which was certainly the case in Babatha's world). He argued that the organizational feature necessary for such interaction was 'a systematic set of rules governing inter-ethnic social encounters'. In particular, he proposed that two types of arrangements were needed:

> a set of prescriptions governing situations of contact, and allowing for articulation in some sectors or domains of activity, and a set of proscriptions on social situations preventing inter-ethnic interaction in other sectors, and thus insulating parts of the cultures from confrontation and modification.[96]

In short, for Barth, ethnicity was a field of self-ascription and self-identification used by certain groups to organize their relationships with other groups.[97]

But there remained the question of what social features were typically selected to designate an *ethnic* boundary. Barth himself

[93] H. Tajfel (1978b) 'Introduction', in Tajfel 1978a: 2

[94] F. Barth (1969b) 'Introduction', in Barth (ed.) (1969a) *Ethnic Groups and Boundaries: The Social Organization of Culture Difference*. London: George Allen and Unwin, 9–38.

[95] See Barth 1969b: 14: 'ethnic categories provide an organizational vessel that may be given varying amounts and forms of content in different socio-cultural systems'.

[96] Barth 1969b: 16.

[97] Barth 1969b.

suggested that an ascription of someone to a social category was ethnic in character 'when it classifies a person in terms of his basic, most general identity, *presumptively determined by his origin and background*'.[98] John Hutchinson and Anthony Smith have suggested a list of such features, which, to accord with Barth's approach, must be regarded as diagnostic, not constitutive, of ethnic identity:

(a) a common proper name to identify the group;
(b) a myth of common ancestry;
(c) a shared history or shared memories of a common past, including heroes, events and their commemoration;
(d) a common culture, embracing such things as customs, language and religion;
(e) a link with a homeland; and
(f) a sense of communal solidarity.[99]

The best evidence for *Ioudaioi*—to use for the moment the Greek word for this ancient people—having an identity that was ethnic in character in this sense is found in the *Contra Apionem* of Josephus, written in the late first or early second century CE.[100] Josephus is defending his people against an attack on them by Apion. In so doing he refers to about fifty groups that are recognizably ethnic (although he does not happen to mention the Nabateans). He deploys the words *genos, ethnos*, and *laos* as generic descriptors for these groups, including the *Ioudaioi*. Josephus portrays his people not as unique, but as example of this type of group, as when he speaks of the *ethnê* of the Judeans, the Phoenicians, and the Syrians.[101] This does not stop him presenting them as an admirable instance of such a group. All of the six indicators of ethnic identity listed by Hutchinson and Smith appear in what Josephus says about his people, but he also attributes similar features to many other peoples. Since all of the ethnic groups are named after their homeland and since Josephus himself approves a statement attributed to Aristotle that the *Ioudaioi* were named after

[98] Barth 1969b: 13 (emphasis added).

[99] J. Hutchinson and A. Smith (1996b) 'Introduction', in Hutchinson and Smith (eds) (1996a) *Ethnicity*. Oxford: Oxford University Press, 6–7.

[100] See P. F. Esler (2009) 'Judean Ethnic Identity in Josephus' *Against Apion*', in Z. Rodgers with M. Daly-Denton and A. Fitzpatrick McKinley (eds) *A Wandering Galilean: Essays in Honour of Sean Freyne*. Leiden: E. J. Brill, 73–91.

[101] Josephus, *Contra Apionem*, 1.137.

Judea,[102] there is a good case to be made for its being more appropriate to refer to them in the first century CE as 'Judeans' than as 'Jews'.

None of this entails denying the important continuity of various kinds—religious, cultural, and in many cases biological—between these people and Jews who lived subsequently, including those alive today. As already noted, part of Fredrik Barth's approach entails that 'the cultural features that signal the boundary may change' yet the dichotomization between members of the group and outsiders continues.[103] There is no reason why this process cannot persist for a very long time indeed where the members of the group maintain their sense of its continuity, given that the fundamental observation in this area remains that 'ethnic groups are categories of ascription and identification by the actors themselves'.[104] Rather, it means recognizing the historical value of attributing to them a name they would acknowledge in the first century as according with their own understanding of themselves, which Judean, with its connection with their homeland of Judea, does and 'Jew' does not.

Nabatean Identity as Ethnic

The question of whether or not we can interpret the Nabateans as having an ethnic identity has not escaped scholarly attention. On the one hand, Peter Alpass advocates a minimalist interpretation of Nabatean identity, reducing 'Nabateans' to 'its political sense', meaning all those living in Nabatea under the control of the Nabatean king.[105] On the other hand, John Healey has suggested that it is probable that the Nabateans were 'Arabs' in an ethnic sense.[106] Approaching the matter in the light of the perspectives on ethnicity just outlined affords a firm basis for categorizing these people in terms of ethnic identity.

Granted that ethnic identity is self-ascribed, in my view Alpass nevertheless goes too far in saying 'there is no internal evidence to help us understand how being Nabataean was understood by those

[102] Josephus, *Contra Apionem*, 1.179. [103] Barth 1969b: 14.
[104] Barth 1969b: 10. [105] Alpass 2013: 3.
[106] J. F. Healey (1989) 'Were the Nabataeans Arabs?', *Aram* 1: 38–44, followed by Graf 1990: 45.

living within the kingdom'.[107] Indeed P. Yadin 1–4, the documents in scope in this volume, provide such internal evidence, as do the tomb Nabatean inscriptions from Hegra and other inscriptions and graffiti. In addition, an ethnic group inevitably makes known various dimensions of its self-ascription in its dealings with others. This is the case even though the members of a group always have a richer sense of its character and distinctiveness, in short, of the complexity of its boundary, than do outsiders, as Anthony Cohen has persuasively explained.[108]

Looking at the six Hutchinson and Smith indicators, it is clear, first of all, that this people did have a common group name: the Nabateans. As noted above, one of the Zenon papyri dated 259 BCE refers to 'the Nabateans'. This was probably a name used by this people of themselves and by others of them. The Elusa inscription, mentioned above, probably from the first half of the second century BCE, was commissioned by one Notayru in honour of Ḥaretat, king of the Nabateans' (מלך נבטו), and Notayru was certainly a member of the group calling themselves Nabatean. The expression 'king of the Nabateans' appears in several other Nabatean inscriptions.[109] Similarly, 'king of the Nabateans', not 'king of Nabatea', survives in the dating clauses of P. Yadin 1, 2, and 3.

Unfortunately, great uncertainty surrounds the origin of the name Nabateans (נבטו: *Nabatu*). Arguments formerly mounted that it was to be equated with the 'Nebaioth' who appear in Neo-Assyrian texts and the Hebrew Bible have been challenged, not least because of the incompatibility of the spellings of the two names.[110] At first it was probably the name of a particular tribe in northern Arabia, with נבטו being a singular tribal name, as noted above. That would certainly cohere with the nomadic background to this people. Perhaps the tribe was named after a real or imagined ancestor in the past.

The fact this people shared a common name, possibly a tribal one, strongly suggests that they would also have had a myth of common ancestry. A variety of evidence, such as sons inheriting their father's property and male lineage relationships being rehearsed as part of

[107] Alpass 2013: 3.
[108] See A. P. Cohen (1989) *The Symbolic Construction of Community. Key Ideas.* London and New York: Routledge, 74–75.
[109] See the inscriptions given in Healey 2009: 54, 56, 58, 60, 68, 73, and 77.
[110] Graf 1990: 45.

naming in inscriptions, shows that Nabatean society, like the cultures that surrounded it, was patrilineal in nature.[111] It is in the nature of a patrilineal society to track one's male ancestors back into the past for many generations. This pattern underlies biblical genealogies, such as in Matt 1:1–17, which was written very close in time to P. Yadin 1–4. In her recent work on the Kurds, anthropologist Diane King has explained this social form as follows:

> In patriliny, a man's generative power is cumulative, and both during his lifetime and in successive generations becomes attached to his reputation. The descendants through males of a particular man constitute a patrilineage. Some patrilineages trace their origins to particularly noteworthy men, and others to ordinary men.[112]

Although our lack of any writings on their past by the Nabateans themselves has denied us knowledge of their myths of descent, their patrilineal social structure guarantees that they existed.

The same lack of Nabatean historical sources also presents obstacles to reaching a view on the third ethnic indicator: a shared history and common memories. Nevertheless, the presence of patrilinearity in their social system presses us towards the conclusion that they must have possessed these features. Accordingly, it is highly likely that memories of the various acts of those rulers remained alive amongst them, thus continuously maintaining and renewing their collective memory, shared history, and common identity.

Perhaps more tellingly, however, Nabatean coinage inscribed in Nabatean Aramaic and bearing images of their kings (and later also queens) survives from the reign of Obodas II in the period 62–60 BCE through to that of Rabb'el II in 106 CE.[113] This means that in their everyday lives Nabateans continually had before their eyes reminders of those who had ruled them for nearly two centuries, as a review of their coinage will now reveal.

Coins were an important means by which governments communicated messages to their people, with Rome—in both Republican

[111] See H. Al-Qudrah and M. Abdelaziz (2008) 'Kinship Terms in the Nabataean Inscriptions', *Arabian Archaeology and Epigraphy* 19: 192–193 and P. Hammond (1973) *The Nabataeans: Their History, Culture and Archaeology*. Sweden: Paul Astroms Forlag.

[112] D. E. King (2013) *Kurdistan on the Global Stage: Kinship, Land and Community in Iraq*. New Brunswick: Rutgers University Press, 67.

[113] See Meshorer 1975: 87–111.

and imperial periods—being extremely active in this regard.[114] While the use of coinage for this purpose by the Nabatean kings was very modest, it did occur and was effective. Scribes, for example, when referring to current Nabatean kings in the dating formula of legal documents, adopted the royal self-designations visible on the coins. No doubt such messages seeped into the wider population. While coins abrade with use and pass out of circulation (perhaps after about thirty years), the debasement of Nabatean silver coins, especially from the reign of Malichus IV (40–70 CE) onwards meant that older coins with a higher silver content were hoarded,[115] an example of Gresham's law that bad coins drive out good. This meant that their inscriptions were likely to have been available to be read. In addition, the collective memory of the Nabatean people must have kept alive recollection of the events in Nabatea's history that I will now mention, whether or not individual Nabateans still possessed coins referring to those events.

King Ḥaretat III, or Aretas III, not only reigned over the Nabateans from *c.* 94 to 62 BCE, but was also honoured by being invited to rule over Damascus by those who held the city after the death of Antiochus XII in 84 BCE.[116] In that capacity he minted coins with his diademed head on the obverse and on the reverse the τύχη ('good fortune') of Damascus with the inscription: *ΒΑΣΙΛΕΩΣ ΑΡΕΤΟΥ ΦΙΛΕΛΛΗΝΟΣ* ('of King Aretas lover of the Greeks').[117] Schmitt-Korte has observed that it is generally accepted that 'Nabatean coinage was inaugurated by Aretas III when he held Damascus (84–71 BC)'.[118] His reign ended badly, however. Whereas Pompey had taken control of Jerusalem and Judea in 63 BCE, in 62 BCE Scaurus subdued Nabatea, requiring Ḥaretat III to submit to Rome. When he was aedile in 58 BCE, Scaurus had coins minted that showed Ḥaretat III (identified by the words *Rex Aretas*) kneeling beside a camel and holding an olive branch, an image of submission.[119]

[114] See J. Evans (1992) *The Art of Persuasion: Political Propaganda from Aeneas to Brutus*. Ann Arbor, MI: University of Michigan Press and M. Harlan (1995) *Roman Republican Moneyers and Their Coins 63 BC—49 BC*. Aspects of Ancient Classical Coins. London: Seaby for the Republic, and B. Levick (1982) 'Propaganda and the Imperial Coinage', *Antichthon* 16: 104–116 for the empire.

[115] Meshorer 1975: 67–70.

[116] Josephus, *AJ*, 13.392.

[117] Meshorer 1975: 86–87.

[118] Schmitt-Korte 1990: 125.

[119] See E. A. Sydenham (1952) *The Coinage of the Roman Republic*. London: Spink, 152, nos 913 and 914 and the discussion in Harlan 1995: 68–69.

King Obodas II reigned briefly (62–60 CE) and seemed determined to restore the prestige of the royal family,[120] and no doubt of Nabatea itself, so damaged by the events of 62 BCE. One step he took was to mint the first coins with inscriptions in Nabatean Aramaic, typically with the words 'Obodas the king, king of the Nabateans' (עבדת מלכא מלך נבטו), an expression utilized by scribes in legal documents, as we will see in later chapters. Those inscriptions were accompanied by an eagle, and although the eagle derived from the Tyrian shekel which he was imitating, eagles also had significance in Nabatean culture and religion.[121] Malichus I reigned from 60–30 BCE. His final years were marked by ferocious wars with Herod in the period 34–33 BCE and all his bronze coins were minted during this period, apparently to pay the soldiers in his army.[122] He introduced onto his coinage *cornucopiae* images, widely popular in the Seleucid and Ptolemaic periods, possibly symbolizing the Syrian goddess Atargatis. In addition, Malichus also introduced the design of the palm of the hand, a uniquely Nabatean innovation on coins, which probably had some now lost religious significance.[123]

Obodas III (reigned 30–9 BCE) took the significant step of having coins minted with a portrait of both himself and his wife on the obverse. He started this as early as the second year of his reign (29–28 BCE).[124] For some reason, however, he did not have her name inscribed on the coins. Nevertheless, the appearance of the queen on the coinage of Obodas III does appear to reflect the rising status attached to her office from the late first century BCE onwards.[125]

When Obodas III died in 9 BCE there was an internal crisis in Nabatea and the kingship did not immediately pass to his son and heir Ḥaretat IV. Instead, Syllaeus who had been influential in the court of Obodas III (see above) seized control, for which we have evidence in Josephus (*AJ* 16.16.220) and in coins minted by Syllaeus that are stamped with his name in Aramaic (שלי).[126] Schmitt-Korte has argued, however, that there is no independent coinage of Syllaeus, but only joint issues with Aretas IV dating from 9 BCE.[127] Later in the same year, Augustus had Syllaeus executed and the kingship then

[120] Meshorer 1975: 18.
[121] Meshorer 1975: 18–19.
[122] Meshorer 1975: 20–21.
[123] Meshorer 1975: 25.
[124] Meshorer 1975: 89, no. 29.
[125] Meshorer 1975: 33–34.
[126] Meshorer 1975: 93, no. 44.
[127] Schmitt-Korte 1990: 131.

passed to Ḥaretat (in Greek, Aretas) IV.[128] He reigned from 9 BCE to 40 CE and was arguably the greatest Nabatean king. He minted an enormous number of coins that testify to a flourishing economy in Nabatea at this time.[129] As early as 9/8 BCE he started minting coins that contained on the obverse his bust and the words 'Ḥaretat the king, king of the Nabateans' (חרתת מלכא מלך נבטו) and on the reverse a bust of his queen Huldu, with closely matching words, 'Huldu, queen of the Nabateans' (חלדו מלכת נבטו).[130] Later he honoured his second wife, Shuqailat, in the same way.[131] As Meshorer has observed, the addition of the queen's name to her bust indicates that the queen's status was steadily rising in the Nabatean royal house.[132] Her name was also expressed in stone inscriptions, indicating wider acceptance of this enhanced status.[133] The king's high regard for his wife and queen, publicly expressed and copied, may well have generated wider social ripples. For researchers in the area of cultural evolution have noticed a phenomenon called 'prestige bias', which means that people tend to imitate individuals of high status, presumably because similar behaviour might help them achieve social success as well.[134] Thus the appearance of the queen on Nabatean coins may have helped to create a context in which other, even non-elite, Nabatean women gained greater influence and respect, such as the two Nabatean women we will encounter in later chapters of this work. Ḥaretat IV also introduced another innovation by including on some of his coins the inscription 'Lover of his people' (רחם עמה).[135] Ḥaretat IV also showed his devotion to his family by having coins minted with the letters פצ or פצלא, in each case a reference to his son Phasael, also with a palm-leaf. These coins were probably inspired by the happy

[128] Meshorer 1975: 41–42 (reliant on Josephus, *AJ* 16. 271–299 and 335–355).

[129] Meshorer 1975: 41. [130] Meshorer 1975: 94, no. 48.

[131] See the coin from 18/19 CE (Meshorer 1975: 103, no. 96) with the inscription 'Shuqailat, queen of the Nabateans' (שקילת מלכת נבטו).

[132] Meshorer 1975: 34. [133] Meshorer 1975: 43.

[134] J. Henrich and F. J. Gil-White (2001) 'The Evolution of Prestige: Freely Conferred Deference as a Mechanism for Enhancing the Benefits of Cultural Transmission', *Evolution and Human Behavior* 22: 165–196. An example of this phenomenon from the ancient world was the practice of freedmen to erect stone reliefs with funerary portraits on the roads into Rome and other Italian towns from the first century BCE to the second century CE. These used an aristocratic visual vocabulary, in part drawn from the practice of ancestral images (*imagines maiorum*) in houses of the elite, to assert their new status as Romans (see S. Walker [1985] *Memorials to the Roman Dead*. London: British Museum Press).

[135] See Meshorer 1975: 94–95, nos. 49, 49A, 51, 52, 53, and 65 as examples.

occasion of Phasael's birth after Ḥaretat IV's accession to the throne, since the king's other sons, perhaps born before he became king, are not so honoured.[136]

The reign of Malichus II (40–70 CE) was, as noted above, marked by a debasement of this silver coinage that may well indicate a notable decline in the Nabatean kingdom.[137] He continued the practice of mentioning his wife, also called Shuqailat, on his coins, with the addition of the word אחתה, 'his sister'. The last Nabatean king was Rabb'el II, who reigned from 70 to 106 CE. After initially mentioning his mother, Shuqailat, on his coins, upon her death in 76 CE, Rabb'el began to rule with his wife, Gamilat and 'also apparently received the appellation די אחיי ושיזב עמה (who resuscitated and saved his people)'.[138] Although an inscription dated to 76 CE contains this expression,[139] no coins survive clearly containing these words. Meshorer has suggested that Rabb'el acquired this title on his mother's death in 76 CE in recognition of the fact that he was now the sovereign in his own right.[140] In 102 CE, apparently after the death Gamilat, Rabb'el took Hagru as his wife and she appears on some coins.[141]

We lack evidence on any particular rites of commemoration of heroes in the past, but the lengths to which Nabateans went to memorialize their dead in stone, most clearly seen in the epitaphs above the stone-cut tombs in Hegra,[142] raise the probability that they existed. Of particular relevance is an inscription from Madeba dated 37/38 CE that refers to the military ranks attained by the dedicators' male relatives and the combined number of years they had served in post.[143]

A richer array of evidence is available in relation to Hutchinson and Smith's fourth indicator of ethnic identity, a common culture, embracing customs, language, and religion. As mentioned earlier in this chapter, discussion continues as to whether the Nabateans spoke Aramaic (admittedly tinged with Arabic) or an early form of Arabic, while using Aramaic for formal purposes (in legal documents, for

[136] Meshorer 1975: 48–49. [137] Meshorer 1975: 69.
[138] Meshorer 1975: 72. [139] Meshorer 1975: 70–71.
[140] Meshorer 1975: 76.
[141] Meshorer 1975: 78–79 and 111, no. 164. In P. Yadin 2, from 99 CE, the scribe mentions Gamilat and Hagru as the 'sisters' of Rabb'el II.
[142] See J. E. Healey (1993) *The Nabataean Tomb Inscriptions of Mada'in Salih*. Journal of Semitic Studies, Supp. 1. Oxford: Oxford University Press.
[143] For text, translation and comments, see Healey 2009: 77–79.

example). Certainly their scribes developed a distinctive cursive script that later formed the basis for the Arabic script.[144] As far as religion is concerned, while the notion of religion as a stand-alone institution did not exist in the ancient world,[145] religious phenomena, especially in the form of cultic activity in temples and domestic dwellings most certainly did. The evidence for Nabatean religious practice is very fragmentary, consisting mainly of impressive remains of stone-cut and stone-built temples and shrines and epigraphic remains in the form of dedications in such contexts and in tombs. While insisting on the importance of local variation, Peter Alpass has argued for three phenomena of more general significance in the kingdom.[146] *First*, there was an aniconic dimension to the representation and worship of Nabatean deities, in that they were portrayed in the form of 'idol blocks' of stone. Most of these, technically referred to as 'betyls', are plain and rectangular, standing in the shallow recess of a niche, while some of them are carved with eyes, a nose, or a mouth.[147] There was thus a range from full to partial aniconicity in the carving of such deities. While Alpass provides evidence for an aniconic tendency in the religious worship of other peoples in the region and argues it was not a 'distinctly Nabataean' phenomenon,[148] it still formed part of the distinctive total package of religious practices of this people. Many of these representations were placed in sites around Petra and would have been seen by Shim'on and Babatha whenever they visited the city, for example to register land transactions or attend court.[149] In 124 CE, admittedly many years after the end of the kingdom of Nabatea, copies of minutes of the city of Petra were being displayed in the temple of Aphrodite in that city.[150] *Secondly*, ritual feasting

[144] On the link between Nabatean script and the later Arabic script, which does seem secure, see J. F. Healey (1990–1991) 'Nabataean to Arabic: Calligraphy and Script Development Among the Pre-Islamic Arabs', *Manuscripts of the Middle East* 5: 41–52 and 2009: 7.

[145] See W. C. Smith (1991[1962]) *The Meaning and End of Religion*. Minneapolis, MN: Fortress and B. J. Malina (1996) 'Mediterranean Sacrifice: Dimensions of Domestic and Political Religion', *Biblical Theology Bulletin* 26: 26–44.

[146] Alpass 2013: 229–237.

[147] J. R. Bartlett (2007) 'Nabataean Religion', in Politis 2007: 57–58.

[148] Alpass 2013: 232.

[149] For a discussion of Nabatean gods, see Healey 2001 and Bartlett 2007.

[150] See P. Yadin 12 in N. Lewis (1989) *The Documents from the Bar Kokhba Period in the Cave of Letters: Greek Papyri and Aramaic and Nabatean Signatures and Subscriptions*. Jerusalem: Israel Exploration Society, the Hebrew University of Jerusalem and the Shrine of the Book, 48–49.

seems to have been practised throughout the kingdom, as shown by the presence of rock-cut *triclinia* and chambers intended for ritual feasting. Some of these occur in the context of temples and tomb complexes (indicating devotion to ancestors). Again, similar practices are found among surrounding groups.[151] *Thirdly*, probably the most important Nabatean god, and one largely restricted to Nabatea (barring dedications and shrines set up in his honour by Nabateans elsewhere, such as in Pozzuoli, Italy, and Delos and Miletus) was Dushara.[152] Dushara is the only Nabatean god found throughout the kingdom and not elsewhere (except in the expatriate contexts mentioned). He frequently appears in connection with the king. Alpass reasonably observes that his appearance in inscriptions commissioned by Nabateans outside Nabatea suggests that 'he was perhaps thought of as representative of the kingdom and its inhabitants and acted as an expression of some kind of common Nabataean identity'.[153] The name of this god appears in the names of one of the witnesses to P. Yadin 3: Wahab-Dushara ('gift of Dushara'). Other gods revered by the Nabateans included Qos and Al-Kutba (male) and Allat and Al-'Uzza (female).[154] Baal also appeared, as in the name of another witness to P. Yadin 3: Zabad-Baal ('gift of Baal'). Foreign gods such as Atargatis, Baalshamin, Isis, Osiris, and Aphrodite were also known and venerated in Nabatea.[155]

In relation to the fifth indicator, a link with a homeland, the existence of the kingdom of Nabatea presupposes a territory with borders that fell under the jurisdiction of the king. The border with the Roman province of Judea was mentioned above. The kingdom stretched from the Hauran in southern Syria to Hegra in what is now Saudi Arabia and westwards from the oasis at Duma almost to the Nile delta.[156]

It is reasonable to consider that the sixth indicator, a sense of communal solidarity, existed because of the presence of the previous five. In addition, however, it makes sense to understand the Nabateans as an imagined *ethnic* community—'imagined' in the sense explained by Benedict Anderson in that even though most Nabateans never knew, met, or even heard of most of their co-ethnics, in the minds of each one of them lived 'the image of their communion'.[157]

[151] Alpass 2013: 232–233. [152] Alpass 2013: 234–237.
[153] Alpass 2013: 237. [154] Bartlett 2007: 62–73.
[155] Bartlett 2007: 73–75. [156] Alpass 2013: 2.
[157] B. Anderson (2006 [1983]) *Imagined Communities: Reflections on the Origins and Spread of Nationalism*. Revised edition. London and New York: Verso, 6. Anderson had in mind imagined nations.

Relationships between Nabateans and Judeans

Having considered the ethnic identity of the Nabateans, we now briefly consider their relationships with Judeans. Fredrik Barth's differentiation of areas of prescription and proscription for different ethnic groups living in proximity to one another has direct relevance for Judeans vis-à-vis Nabateans living around the Dead Sea at the end of the first century CE. On the one hand, there were very significant areas of unrestricted activity, especially in relation to commercial transactions, such as the purchase by Shimʿon of a date-palm plantation from a Nabatean woman, which is the subject of this volume.

Mention was made in Chapter 1 that P. Yadin 8 and 9 were connected with Babatha by virtue of involving her two brothers, whose names those documents revealed. But an aspect of the two papyri raised in that earlier discussion dramatically comes into its own in the present context. Here we have two documents both drafted by the same scribe (a Judean, 'Yoḥanan son of Makkuta') and in the same year (122 CE), with P. Yadin 8 in Judean Aramaic and P. Yadin 9 in Nabatean Aramaic. The likely explanation offered in Chapter 1 was that the former involved two Judeans and the latter a Judean and a Nabatean, the latter as obligee in the transaction. In other words, a Judean was clearly content to have a document drafted in Nabatean Aramaic when the other party was a Nabatean, which would have been of benefit to him as a conveniently legible record of the transaction. In addition, the scribe was quite at ease in moving between Judean and Nabatean Aramaic to effect the wishes of his clients. This all speaks of close and well-oiled commercial and legal relations between these two ethnic groups. One sees here the wisdom of Fredrik Barth's view that:

> In other words, ethnic distinctions do not depend on an absence of social interaction and acceptance, but are quite to the contrary often the very foundations on which embracing social systems are built.[158]

Funeral practice in the region also suggests another, and rather surprising area of cultural continuity between Judeans and Nabateans. During 1996 and 1997 Konstantinos Politis led a rescue excavation of a cemetery at a site known locally as Khirbet Qazone near the village of Mazraʿa at the southeastern end of the Dead Sea (now in Jordan; see

[158] Barth 1969b: 10.

Figure 2.1). This excavation has yielded further evidence of a shared culture between Nabateans and Judeans in spite of their ethnic differences. The finds from the excavations, taken with other evidence from the Dead Sea region, demonstrate that during the first and second centuries CE Judeans and Nabateans wore similar clothes and were buried in much the same way.[159] In other words, they did not use clothing or burial practices as a means to signify their ethnic boundaries vis-à-vis one another. Rather, these were areas of a broader culture that they shared.

Unfortunately, by the time Politis began excavations at Khirbet Qazone over 3,500 graves had been looted and he was only able to excavate twenty-three undisturbed graves. Nevertheless, he obtained valuable data, not least from the textiles that had been wrapped around the corpses and left discarded on the surface by the looters. The graves dated from the first to early third centuries CE.[160] Each of them held a single burial and there was no evidence of re-interment. The graves were dug about 1.5 metres deep into Lisan sediment; each of them was undercut on the eastern side and the corpse positioned in the resulting cavity, with the cavity then covered by adobe brick slabs, producing something like an *arcosolium*, before the whole grave was back-filled.[161] No evidence of Aramaic or Hebrew texts or symbols that would indicate the presence of Judeans was discovered at the site. Nevertheless, these graves bear a striking similarity to the deep shaft graves with *arcosolia*-sealed burials found at Qumran. The first such graves found at Qumran contained only adult males, but later skeletons of women and children were found in graves of this type. Moreover, similar burials have been found at Beit Safala, near Jerusalem, and attributed to Judeans.[162] From this archaeological evidence Politis concludes that 'shaft burials can neither be attributed to any particular ethnic group nor be used to identify a specific religious practice' and that they reveal cultural affinities between the different communities of the Dead Sea region.[163] It is possible that there were Judeans buried at Khirbet Qazone.[164]

[159] See K. D. Politis (2006) 'The Discovery and Excavation of the Khirbet Qazone Cemetery and Its Significance Relative to Qumran', in K. Galor et al. (eds) (2006) *Qumran, The Site of the Dead Sea Scrolls: Archaeological Interpretations and Debates*. Studies on the Texts of the Desert of Judah, Volume 57. Leiden: E. J. Brill.

[160] Politis 2006: 215. [161] Politis 2006: 213. [162] Politis 2006: 218.

[163] Politis 2006: 219.

[164] H. Granger-Taylor (2006) 'Textiles from Khirbet Qazone and the Cave of Letters', in S. Schrenk (ed.) (2006) *Textiles in Situ: Their Find Spots in Egypt and*

Clothing has proved to be another area of cultural continuity and interaction. The textiles and clothing found in the graves of Khirbet Qazone or on the surface of the site are very similar in form and colour to those found in other places with a strong Judean presence in the area, including the Cave of Letters (where Babatha's archive was discovered) and in Masada. The clothing consists principally of three major items of clothing: mantles, tunics, and women's scarves. Granger-Taylor comments as follows:

> The mantles are always of wool and are Greek in type, typically decorated with four dark *gamma-* or right-angled motifs for women and notched bands or bars for men. The tunics are mostly of wool and of the Roman type, with two shoulder stripes or *clavi* and a 'horizontal' construction. Some tunics, however, are of linen . . . The scarves are all of wool, are more open in weave than the mantles and tunics, and have long fringes at both ends.[165]

Men and boys wore a draped mantle over a knee-length tunic, while women and girls seem to have worn both a mantle and a scarf over a long tunic.[166] In both Khirbet Qazone and the Cave of Letters bright red (made from madder) was used as the ground colour for women's dress, whereas in the Greco-Roman world red was usually associated with male garments. In both sites yellow was a relatively common colour and each produced a yellow scarf, with the colour based on saffron. Blue (probably derived from woad) was also found.[167]

Yet while there were permitted areas of interaction between Judeans and Nabateans, other areas were proscribed. This fact reflects Fredrik Barth's view that ethnic boundaries mix prescription and proscription. Thus, when Yehudah son of Eleazar married Babatha he did so 'according to the laws of Moses and the Judeans' (P. Yadin 10, line 5).[168] A stricter approach is visible in the clause in a legal papyrus, probably from 111/112 CE, from Masada, whereby Yoseph son of Naqsan, in divorcing his wife, Miriam daughter of Yonatan, says that she is free to marry any *Judean* man she wants.[169] The evidence of the Yadin Papyri is that Judeans were parties to documents drafted in Nabatean Aramaic yet continued to be competent in

Neighbouring Countries in the First Millenium CE. Riggisberger Berichte 13. Riggisberg: Abegg-Stiftung, 118.

165 Granger-Taylor 2006: 113–114.

166 Granger-Taylor 2006: 114–115.

167 Granger-Taylor 2006: 115–116.

168 Yadin et al. 2002: 126–127.

169 This is P. Mur 19 in P. Benoit et al. (eds) (1961) *Discoveries in the Judaean Desert II: Les Grottes de Murabba'at. Texte.* Oxford: Clarendon Press, 104–109.

Judean Aramaic and to use the language amongst themselves even while living in Maoza.[170] Judeans and Nabateans generally had very different personal names.[171] From the abundance of the evidence from the ancient world bearing on the issue,[172] it is also unlikely that Judeans would have dined with Nabateans at the same table or where such dining involved passing around among representatives of both ethnic groups one cup or shared food.

Having now considered the role that Nabatea and the Nabateans played in Babatha's world, we will proceed to consider further aspects. This will occupy Chapter 3.

[170] See the discussion in Chapter 1 and above on P. Yadin 8 and 9. P. Yadin 6 is another document in Nabatean Aramaic involving Judeans.

[171] For Judean personal names in the period, see T. Ilan (2002) *Lexicon of Jewish Names in Late Antiquity: Part I: Palestine 330 BCE–200 CE*. Texts and Studies in Ancient Judaism, 91. Tübingen: Mohr Siebeck (although she omits names from the Babatha archive); for Nabatean names see F. H. al-Khraysheh (1986) *Die Personennamen in den nabatäischen Inschriften des Corpus Inscriptionum Semiticarum*. (Inaugural-Dissertation zur Erlangung Doktorwürde des Fachbereichs Aussereuropäische Sprachen und Kulturen der Philipps-Universität). Marburg: Lahn and A. Negev (1991) *Personal Names in the Nabataean Realm*. Qedem 32. Monographs of the Institute of Archaeology. Jerusalem: Hebrew University of Jerusalem (although the severe critique of this volume mounted by M. C. A. Macdonald [1999] '*Personal Names in the Nabataean Realm*: A Review Article', *Journal of Semitic Studies* 44: 251–289 should be noted).

[172] See P. F. Esler (1998) *Galatians*. New Testament Readings. London and New York: Routledge, 93–116 for evidence of a Judean prohibition on dining with non-Judeans during this period (meaning shared meals rather than meals in parallel). Further evidence for the prohibition (even relating to meals with 'God-fearing' non-Judeans) is found in Acts 10:28 and 11:1–3. There are also occasional references among ancient Greek and Roman authors to such a Judean disinclination to sharing meals with non-Judeans (for example, Diodorus Siculus, 34.12 [they had a law 'not to have table-fellowship with any other people'] and Tacitus, *Historiae* 5.2 [*separati epulis*; 'they sit apart at meals']). See M. Stern (ed.) (1974, 1980, and 1984) *Greek and Latin Authors on Jews and Judaism*. Three volumes. Jerusalem: The Israel Academy of Sciences and Humanities for the Greco-Roman authors on 'Jews' and 'Judaism'.

3

Life in Maoza

THE ENVIRONMENT AND THE LOCATION OF MAOZA

The locale for most of the events in this volume was a village or town bearing the Aramaic name of Maḥoz ʻEglatain, meaning 'the harbour of ʻEglatain'. This place is at times also called simply 'Mahoza', meaning 'the harbour' (since the suffixed *aleph* at the end of the word stands for the definite article in Aramaic). In the Greek form of the word, Maoza (*Μαωζα*), the definite article has become part of the name.[1] Maoza was located at the south-eastern end of the Dead Sea, as discussed below (and see Figure 2.1), and to understand life there at the end of the first century CE we have to consider the environment in which it was situated.

The Dead Sea region was characterized by a unique geography and climate that led to distinctive agricultural patterns and related social forms. The dominant feature of the region is the sea itself, which occupies most of the Jordan Rift Valley along its length. At its maximum extent the Dead Sea is about 80 kilometres long and 16 kilometres wide (although in recent years the drying out of the sea has led to a separation of the northern and southern basins). Lying 396 metres below sea level, it is the lowest place on earth.[2] The area has a hot and dry climate. In the north the mean annual temperature is

[1] For this explanation of the name, see H. M. Cotton and J. C. Greenfield (1995) 'Babatha's *Patria*: Mahoza, Maḥoz ʻEglatain, and Zoʻar', *ZPE* 107: 128. I will employ this form of the name (Maoza) in what follows.

[2] D. Baly (1974) *The Geography of the Bible*. Revised edition. New York: Harper & Row, 202.

15–17°C and in the south, 20°C.[3] The summer months are particularly hot, with a mean monthly temperature in June of 38.1°C.[4] At the southern end of the Sea the annual rainfall is about 50 mm (two inches) per annum and tends to come in heavy thunderstorms.[5] The soil in the region tends to be salty and much of the natural vegetation consists of halophytes (plants that grow in salty or alkaline soil).[6]

The lack of sufficient annual rainfall meant that agriculture was and is dependent on irrigation. The western side is in a rain shadow and no regular streams flow down into the Sea.[7] Nevertheless, strong springs above En-Gedi allow cultivation there, which today covers about 100 hectares.[8] Archaeological research has revealed much about the ancient agricultural system at En-Gedi, including a system of terraces descending the hills beneath the springs.[9] On the eastern side of the Sea, however, wadis from the plateau, which does receive rainfall, provide water even in summer.[10] Diodorus of Siculus, dependent on Hieronymus, an eyewitness to events in Nabatea (see Chapter 2), reports that 'great rivers of remarkable sweetness empty into it' (sc. the Dead Sea).[11]

The streams feeding into the Dead Sea have a direct bearing on the location of Maoza. As noted above, its name ('the harbour') means it was situated on the shore of the Dead Sea. We also know that Maoza was located 'in the vicinity of Zoara' because it is so described on nine occasions in the Greek papyri from the Babatha archive.[12] Zoara was located some kilometres south of the Dead Sea (see Figure 2.1). While the precise site of Maoza is unknown and probably now rests under many feet of sediment, it is possible to offer a likely location for it.

[3] Y. Enzel et al. (eds) (2006) *New Frontiers in Dead Sea Paleoenvironmental Research*. The Geological Society of America, Special Paper 431. Boulder, Co: The Geological Society of America, 69.

[4] H. Walter and S.-W. Breckle (1986) *Ecological Systems of the Geobiosphere: 2 Tropical and Subtropical Zonobiomes*. Berlin: Springer Verlag, 410.

[5] Enzel et al. 2006: 68; Baly 1974: 202.

[6] Walter and Breckle 1986: 410.

[7] Baly 1974: 203.

[8] See Y. Hirschfeld (2007b) 'Introduction', in Hirschfeld (2007a) *En-Gedi Excavations II. Final Report (1996–2002)*. Jerusalem: Israel Exploration Society, 1.

[9] G. Hadas (2012) 'Ancient Agricultural Irrigation Systems in the Oasis of Ein Gedi, Dead Sea, Israel', *Journal of Arid Environments* 86: 75–81.

[10] Baly 1974: 204–205.

[11] Diodorus Siculus, 2.48.7.

[12] See P. Yadin 5, lines 4–5; P. Yadin 14, line 20; P. Yadin 17, lines 2–3; P. Yadin 20, line 4; P. Yadin 22, line 5; P. Yadin 25, line 28; P. Yadin 25, line 64; P. Yadin 26, line 18; and P. Yadin 27, line 3.

P. Yadin 7, a deed dated 13 July 120 CE whereby Shim'on son of Menaḥem, Babatha's father, gave his wife, Miryam, considerable property in Maoza, mentions a large river as the western abutter of one of the properties he is giving away (line 8).[13] The editors state that it has not been identified.[14] This river could, however, be the perennial stream that flows out of Wadi Hasa, the river Zered of the Bible, marking the southern boundary of Moab with Edom, which ran from south to north as it entered the Dead Sea (see Figure 2.1). Even today the water from this stream provides irrigation for the rich farming area of Ghor as-Safi, where date-palms are still grown.[15] The water rights for properties in Maoza mentioned in the Babatha archive in P. Yadin 2, 3, and 7 are specified as a period of half an hour, one hour, or one-and-a-half hours' irrigation once or twice per week (either by day or night or both).[16] This means other farmers were also drawing the water at their allotted times and a reasonably large and continuous flow of water must have been required, such as would have been provided by the Zered. If this identification is correct, Maoza would have been situated almost due north of Zoara. Such a location is consistent with the statements in P. Yadin 2 and 3 that the property in question had the shoreline (of the Dead Sea) as its northern abutter and a road as its eastern abutter. On this view, Maoza would have served as the harbour for Zoara in relation to the movement of people and goods across the Dead Sea.

[13] Y. Yadin et al. (eds) (2002) *The Documents from the Bar Kokhba Period in the Cave of Letters: Hebrew, Aramaic and Nabatean-Aramaic Papyri*. Judean Desert Studies. Jerusalem: Israel Exploration Society, Institute of Archaeology, Hebrew University and the Shrine of the Book, 80–81 (although the editors note that the Aramaic suggested [נהרא רבא] is not entirely certain). It should be noted that in line 9 of this document another property is described that has the river on its northern boundary (along with a road). This is probably to be explained on the basis that at some point in its course from the eastern plateau the river was running from east to west in Maoza before turning north to enter the Dead Sea, perhaps before bending northwards given that there was also a road on the northern boundary.

[14] Yadin et al. 2002: 96.

[15] J. Taylor (2002) *Petra and the Lost Kingdom of the Nabataeans*. London and New York: I. B. Tauris, 177. Note that in 1995 Cotton and Greenfield had already suggested that 'The Ghor al-Safi, south of the Dead Sea, with Wadi al-Hasa nearby, would fit Mahoza/ Maḥoz 'Eglatain admirably' (H. M. Cotton and J. C. Greenfield [1995] 'Babatha's "Patria": Mahoza, Maḥoz 'Eglatain and Zo'ar', *ZPE* 107: 132).

[16] P. Yadin 7 provides several examples (see Yadin et al. 2002: 80–88 for the Judean Aramaic text and translation).

Yet while this is the likely location, one cannot be certain and two other locations have been suggested recently, each linked to a wadi from the plateau to the east containing streams flowing with reasonable amounts of water.[17] The Nabateans could have augmented the flow from such streams by constructing weirs upstream. Such works were well within the competence of Nabatean hydraulic engineering.[18] The Wadi Numeira, containing one of these streams, is roughly 10 kilometres north of Wadi Hasa and Joan Taylor has proposed situating Maoza in the vicinity of Numeira.[19] This would be consistent with the statements in P. Yadin 2 and 3 that the eastern abutter of the property was the road. Konstantinos Politis has suggested another location for Maoza. He has pointed out that modern Mazra'a is probably located over or near the ancient town of Mazraa, which is mentioned in the Babatha archive (P. Yadin 20, line 23) as the place where Besas son of Jesus, a native of En-Gedi, resided.[20] Further north of Mazra'a there are two settlement sites with adjacent ancient cemeteries: Haditha and 'Ain Sekine. These are near Wadi Kerak (see his map),[21] which could have served as a source for irrigation water. Politis takes the view that Haditha can be associated with the harbour of Maoza and 'Ain Sekine with ancient Mazra'a.[22] The problem (not necessarily insuperable) with the suggestions of Taylor and Politis is

[17] See A. Wade et al. (2011) 'Future Projections of Water Availability in a Semi-Arid Region of the Eastern Mediterranean: A Case Study of Wadi Hasa, Jordan', in S. Mithren and E. Black (eds) (2011) *Water, Life and Civilization: Climate, Environment and Society in the Jordan Valley*. Cambridge: Cambridge University Press, 178; also see N. Greenbaum et al. (2006) 'The Hydrology and Paleohydrology of the Dead Sea Tributaries', in Enzel et al. 2006: 63–93.

[18] For a treatment of the Nabateans' skill with water supply and irrigation, see J. P. Oleson (2007) 'Water Supply, Irrigation and Agriculture', in K. D. Politis (ed.) (2007) *The World of the Nabataeans: Volume 2 of the International Conference The World of the Herods and the Nabataeans held at the British Museum, 17–19 April 2001*. Stuttgart: Fran Steiner Verlag, 217–250.

[19] See Map 2 in J. Taylor (2012) *The Essenes, the Scrolls, and the Dead Sea*. Oxford: Oxford University Press.

[20] N. Lewis (1989) *The Documents from the Bar Kokhba Period in the Cave of Letters: Greek Papyri and Aramaic and Nabatean Signatures and Subscriptions*. Jerusalem: Israel Exploration Society, The Hebrew University of Jerusalem and the Shrine of the Book, 90–91.

[21] K. D. Politis (2006) 'The Discovery and Excavation of the Khirbet Qazone Cemetery and Its Significance Relative to Qumran', in K. Galor et al. (eds) (2006) *The Site of the Dead Sea Scrolls: Archaeological Interpretations and Debates*. Studies on the Texts of the Desert of Judah, Volume 57. Leiden: E. J. Brill, 213.

[22] Politis 2006: 218.

that the further north around the Dead Sea's eastern shore one postulates for Maoza, the harder it is to reconcile such a location with the frequent statements in the papyri that Maoza was 'in the vicinity of Zoara'.

DATE-PALM CULTIVATION

The Distinctive Nature of the Date-Palm and its Cultivation

There was one type of plant that was ideally suited to the desert climate of the region, as long as abundant water was available through irrigation—the date-palm (*Phoenix dactylifera*). Since the orchard that is the focus of this volume was dedicated to the cultivation of date-palms and the date crop played a major role in the local economy, we must briefly outline the distinctive character of this type of agriculture. The actual variety of date-palm that existed in the Dead Sea region ('the Judean date-palm') disappeared from the region during the Middle Ages, but there is now hope it can be resurrected. During the excavations at Masada in the mid 1960s, a number of 2,000-year-old date-palm seeds were discovered and, forty years later, in 2005, one of these was encouraged to sprout. It is growing healthily at Kibbutz Qetura. This palm has turned out to be a male tree, so that scientists now hope to perform the same feat on an ancient seed from a female tree and then begin cultivating this variety from the two trees.[23]

Valuable information about the cultivation of *Phoenix dactylifera* in the ancient world, and from the time when the Nabateans were a rising force, occurs in Theophrastus' work *Enquiry into Plants* (written in the late fourth or early third century BCE). Of great interest is that Theophrastus actually mentions the existence of date-palm cultivation in the Dead Sea region:

> However some say that the people of Syria use no cultivation (sc. in date-palm cultivation), except cutting out wood and watering, also that

[23] See T. Hanson (2015) *The Triumph of Seeds: How Grains, Nuts, Kernels, Pulses, and Pips Conquered the Plant Kingdom and Shaped Human History*. New York: Basic Books, 83–95.

> the date-palm requires flowing water (ναματιαῖον ὕδωρ) rather than water from the skies; and that such water is abundant in the valley in which are the palm-groves. And they add that the Syrians say that this valley extends through Arabia to the Red Sea, and that many profess to have visited it, and that it is in the lowest part of it that the date-palms grow.[24]

He is referring to the Jordan Rift Valley, the 'lowest part' being the Dead Sea. Here there was flowing water available from springs at En-Gedi on the western side, while on the eastern side there were and still are a handful of perennial if modest streams descending into the Dead Sea. One of these, mentioned above, is the year-round stream that flows down the Wadi Hasa into the south-eastern corner of the Dead Sea.

Theophrastus rightly remarked that the 'method of propagating date-palms is peculiar and exceptional, as also is their subsequent cultivation'.[25] By propagation (φυτεία) Threophrastus meant an unusual manner of raising young palms from seeds bundled together and buried face down. But the cultivation (θεραπεία) to which he referred was altogether more remarkable. Date trees are dioecious, meaning that a tree is either male or female, so that pollen (with its genetic material) has to be transferred from the male to the female for fertilization of the fruit to occur. Prior to human intervention, wind-borne transfer seems to have been the principal means by which fertilization occurred. At least as early as the first millennium BCE, and possibly some millennia earlier,[26] however, human beings had discovered how to pollinate the female date artificially and the process is clearly and accurately described by Theophrastus:

> With dates it is helpful to bring the male to the female . . . when the male palm is in flower, they at once cut off the spathe on which the flower is, just as it is, and shake the bloom with the flower and the dust over the fruit of the female, and, if this is done to it, it retains the fruit and does

[24] Theophrastus, *Enquiry into Plants*, 2.6.5; ET A. Hort (1916) *Theophrastus: Enquiry into Plants. Volume 1*. Loeb Edition. London and New York: William Heinemann and G. P. Putnam's Sons, 137 (except I have substituted my 'flowing' for his 'spring' for ναματιαῖον).

[25] Theophrastus, *Enquiry into Plants*, 2.6.1; ET Hort 1916: 133.

[26] See M. Tengberg (2012) 'Beginnings and Early History of Date Palm Garden Cultivation in the Middle East', *Journal of Arid Environments* 86: 139–147.

> not shed it . . . it appears that the 'male' renders aid to the 'female'—for the fruit-bearing tree is called 'female'.[27]

This process involves climbing 20 or 30 feet to the top of the tree to collect the male pollen, climbing down, then climbing up the female tree to dust the flowers with the pollen and, lastly, climbing down again.[28] This is not as difficult as it sounds. The protruberances on the trunks of date-palms, which are the woody scars where leaves have fallen away, allow a person with experience to climb the tree quickly. Sometimes modern-day cultivators practising traditional methods also tie a band of cloth around their waist and the tree, so that by leaning back against this cloth they can rely on friction to stop them slipping down the tree. Perhaps this method was also employed in the ancient world.

Useful information about traditional methods of date cultivation appears in a work by Paul Popenoe published in 1913 that draws in part on his close acquaintance with date-palm cultivation in the Middle East before the arrival of too much modern science. Popenoe recorded, for example, that it was appropriate to keep three or four male trees to every 100 female trees.[29] He also recorded that September was the principal month of the date harvest, but some fruit was picked into October and November.[30] Lewis reached a similar view when discussing P. Yadin 21: 'This contract was entered into just as the dates were beginning to ripen. Ancient sources reveal that the date harvest began in September, reached its peak in October and was over by November.'[31]

Popenoe also observed that on good soil a thorough irrigation once a week throughout the summer was sufficient, while noting that his advice did not suit all conditions.[32] P. Yadin 2 and 3, from Maoza, provide for a weekly ingress of water into the orchard lasting half an hour in duration. Popenoe also commented that date-palms had to be trimmed regularly, which meant taking off the dead or dying leaves

[27] Theophrastus, *Enquiry into Plants*, 2.8.4; ET Hort 1916: 155. Herodotus (*The Histories*, 1.193) notes that in Assyria they tie the 'fruit' of what they call the 'male' palm trees to the date-bearing (i.e. female) trees, which indicates a very similar pollination process; on this passage see L. Georgi (1982) 'Pollination Ecology of the Date Palm and Fig Tree: Herodotus 1.193.4–5', *Classical Philology* 77: 224–228.

[28] P. B. Popenoe (1913) *Date Growing in the Old World and the New*. Los Angeles: George Rice & Sons, 129.

[29] Popenoe 1913: 108.

[30] Popenoe 1913: 108–127.

[31] Lewis 1989: 94.

[32] Popenoe 1913: 90.

and cleaning the trunk of fibre and other decaying matter.[33] As noted above from Theophrastus, such trimming was carried out on date-palms in the Dead Sea region.

Over the centuries opinions have differed as to whether date-palms require manuring. In the ancient period Theophrastus noted that there was a difference of opinion as to whether manuring with dung was helpful or injurious.[34] Certainly in the early twentieth century, for example, some date growers in Oman worked into the soil around each tree a donkey-load of well-rotted manure and straw twice a year, with one application at the beginning of winter being general practice.[35] Although we do not know whether manuring was undertaken by Dead Sea date-palm cultivators, the insistence of Theophrastus (noted above) that all the date cultivators of Syria did was to trim and irrigate the trees makes one doubt it. On the other hand, when a subsidiary crop is grown between the rows of trees, the nutrition it takes from the soil needs to be replaced or the palms will be affected. Popenoe was of the view that it was usually sufficient to plough the subsidiary crop under once it had yielded its produce.[36] We know that barley was grown amongst the trees in the date-palms in Maoza, since when Babatha registered her property there in the Roman census in 127 CE she itemized the amounts of dates and barley produced by three of her date-palm orchards.[37] Perhaps her employees ploughed in the stubble after the barley harvest and provided nutrients to the soil in this way. It is also likely that fruit and vegetables were being grown in Maoza as well: this was happening at En-Gedi in the time of the Bar Kokhba revolt, as we know from two leases extant from that town,[38] and it is difficult to see why the farmers of Maoza would not also have grown vegetables to vary their diet.

In P. Yadin 46 (in Hebrew) one Yeshuâ acknowledged the lease of cropland and date-palms and made the following undertakings relating to their cultivation: 'And I will sow the cropland and I will tend the date-palms as is customary' (שאזרע תעפר הלבן ואגה תדקלים כנומס; lines 5–6).[39] The expression 'as is customary' (כנומוס) employs the Greek

[33] Popenoe 1913: 97.
[34] Theophrastus, *Enquiry into Plants*, 2.6.3; Hort 1916: 135–137.
[35] Popenoe 1913: 92. [36] Popenoe 1913: 93.
[37] P. Yadin 16; see Lewis 1989: 68.
[38] See P. Yadin 45 and 46 in Yadin et al. 2002: 60–70.
[39] For text and translation, see Yadin et al. 2002: 66. Note that the *tau* prefixed to עפר and דקלים is the *nota accusativi*.

word *νόμος*. The editors probably go astray in interpreting the rare word אגה (which they derive from הגה)[40] to mean either 'pick' or 'prune', since it plainly embraces most of the complex processes needed for successful cultivation of date-palms. The only aspect not included is the actual cultivation, since this is the subject of a separate clause concluding with another 'as is customary' provision (היך נומוס) later in the document (lines 6–8). In P. Yadin 6, a lease of farming land in Nabatean Aramaic from 120 CE, there is a reference to 'working and tilling (the land) according to the norms/customs of working (כחליקת עמל)',[41] employing the Arabic loan word in Nabatean: חליקה as equivalent to נומס/*νόμος*.[42] Here again the reference to customary practice embraces all of the agricultural practices in question.[43]

The practice in the Dead Sea area of not specifying in detail the cultivation processes that the lessee was required to undertake stands in rather stark contrast to leases that have survived from Egypt where it was quite common to itemize those duties. An example is P. Oxy XLVII, 3354, a lease relating mainly to a vineyard, though with some date-palms, from 28 October 257 CE, which specifies the works to be carried out, including fertilizing the date-palms, in minute detail.[44]

Having surveyed a variety of evidence from different parts of the world, including the Middle East, Popenoe hit upon an average yield of 100 pounds of dates per tree and fifty trees per acre. This produces a total yield of 5,000 pounds or 2.5 tons to the acre.[45] According to a computation of Michael Satlow,[46] Babatha owned six acres of land in

[40] Yadin et al. 2002: 69. [41] Yadin et al. 2002: 261.

[42] Yadin et al. 2002: 228.

[43] The word חליקה is used in reference to the customs that apply to part of a deed of sale in P. Yadin 2, line 13 and of gifts and clearances in P. Yadin 7, line 24.

[44] See the text, translation and comments in J. S. Kloppenborg (2006) *The Tenants in the Vineyard: Ideology, Economics, and Agrarian Conflict in Jewish Palestine*. WUNT 195. Tübingen: Mohr Siebeck, 528–534. For other Egyptian leases involving date cultivation see: P. Oxy 3,639 (= BASP 29 [1992] 152–163); P. Oxy 48, 3354; P. Oxy 14, 1631; and P. Col. 8, 232.

[45] Popenoe 1913: 176.

[46] See M. L. Satlow (2005) 'Marriage Payments and Succession Strategies in the Documents from the Judaean Desert', in R. Katsoff and D. Schaps (eds) (2005) *Law in the Documents of the Judaean Desert*. Leiden: E. J. Brill, 53–54, n. 11. He is relying upon Lewis's proposal that each *se'ah* of produce is equivalent to thirteen litres and each *bet se'ah* about one-fifth of an acre, and on Hannah Cotton's suggestion that a 'black' is equivalent to half a *denarius*. When he applies these amounts to the produce Babatha declared in her census registration in 127 CE (P. Yadin 16), he comes up with six acres.

Maoza. Applying in turn Popenoe's average figure for yield, Babatha could have been producing something like fifteen tons of dates per annum. Even if she paid half of that in tax, as she certainly did for the produce of one of her fields in Maoza,[47] there was a lot left for sale. Moreover, the dates from this area had a particular advantage that meant they must have been readily marketable. Theophrastus notes that only in three districts from Coele-Syria where the soil was salty (which must include the dry Dead Sea region since, as already noted, the soil is salty here) were 'dates produced that can be stored'.[48] If, as seems highly likely, the nomads of the region in the ancient period, like those in modern times,[49] carried dates as an essential food in journeys through desert lands, Babatha's were the type of dates they needed to acquire. In addition, the Dead Sea provided a means of transport of dates across the region. Maoza was a harbour and no doubt served as a shipment point for dates like the harbour at En-Gedi, which is mentioned in a letter of Bar Kokhba as a place for loading fruit (probably dates) onto a ship.[50]

Irrigation

As already noted, date-palm cultivation was only possible using irrigation from flowing water. The orchards in P. Yadin 2 and 3 were entitled to half an hour of water a week. The properties that Shim'on gave to his wife Miryam in P. Yadin 7 provide for a variety of periods per week: half an hour, one hour, and one-and-a-half hours. Presumably, the bigger the orchard the longer the time needed to inundate it. Without a guaranteed water supply, land could not be used for the lucrative cultivation of dates, or any other form of crop, in an area with so little rainfall, and it would have been worthless. The whole area devoted to date-palm orchards must have been criss-crossed with canals and channels, with apertures that could be opened and closed, which were bringing water from some reasonably major source on higher ground, such as a stream or a strong spring. As already noted, a large stream flowing through Maoza is mentioned in P. Yadin 7 (line 8). Many Nabatean aqueducts conveyed water in a channel that was usually 12 cm wide and 15 cm deep and cut

[47] See P. Yadin 16, line 23 (Lewis 1989: 68).
[48] Theophrastus, *Enquiry into Plants*, 2.6.2; ET Hort 1916: 135.
[49] Popenoe 1913: 203.
[50] P. Yadin 49 (at Yadin et al. 2002: 282).

lengthwise into blocks of sandstone, marl or limestone 60–90 cm long. These blocks were laid end to end and held in position by framing walls.[51] G. Hadas, who has conducted archaeological research into the ancient irrigation system at nearby En-Gedi, where springs in the hills supplied water through channels to agricultural terraces below, has made an observation that has equal application to Maoza: 'Undoubtedly the construction of these irrigation systems demanded an extensive and continuous investment of labour and money. Maintenance of the systems was a permanent job for generations.'[52]

Such a system reflected the remarkable degree of skill that the Nabateans had developed in the supply of water through advanced hydraulic technology. Even when they were nomads—to recall what Diodorus Siculus said of them as reported in Chapter 2—they were adept at constructing concealed reservoirs of water in desert places. By the end of the first century CE their skill in the construction of the cisterns, wells, and aqueducts needed for agriculture and domestic use had reached a high pitch of accomplishment.

Irrigation is a subject of interest to anthropologists.[53] A comment by David Mosse will resonate throughout this volume: 'water systems are not only shaped by, but also themselves shape, social and political relations'.[54] Hadas has rightly observed:

> Water rights and water control are an integral part of water management of every agricultural society. This is a social mechanism that takes care of the construction and maintenance of the water systems, and is responsible for the manner in which water is distributed among partners. This is usually based on the principle of justice.[55]

Comparative experience in modern times has repeatedly underlined the importance of ensuring equity in the distribution of water used by farmers for irrigation. 'An irrigation system that most farmers consider to be fair is more likely to be productive and efficient contrary to

[51] Oleson 2007: 230.

[52] G. Hadas (2012) 'Ancient Agricultural Irrigation Systems in the Oasis of Ein Gedi, Dead Sea, Israel', *Journal of Arid Environments* 86, 78. For a discussion (with photos) of date production in an area with traditional methods of irrigation, see C. Nesson et al. (1973) *Oasis du Sahara algérien*. Paris: Institute Géographique.

[53] See W. W. Kelly (1983) 'Concepts in the Anthropological Study of Irrigation', *American Anthropologist* 85: 880–886.

[54] D. Mosse (2008) 'Epilogue: The Cultural Politics of Water—A Comparative Study', *Journal of Southern African Studies* 34: 941.

[55] Hadas 2012: 79.

the one that farmers consider to be unfair.'[56] Inequity can occur either in accessing the resource (with people upstream taking more than they were entitled) or in its use, with provision of water modulated to socioeconomic status rather than need.[57]

What type of social mechanism relating to water supply will be adopted and how will equity and efficiency in distributing the water be achieved? The Moroccan system of irrigating fields in oases that was investigated by anthropologist Clifford Geertz in the 1970s operated without any significant superordinate political structure, although it did rely on a few minor officials. It was a low-technology system managed by the farmers themselves, who possessed rights to water (measured in periods of time as in Nabatea) that could be sold or leased separately from any land they owned (of which there is no sign in Nabatea).[58]

The importance of water and rights to water to the Nabateans and the high level of technology they had developed to bring water to their cities, homes, and farms, in a region of very low rainfall, raise the likelihood of more centralized control. The king had a direct interest in ensuring the efficient and just maintenance of water supply, not least because the crops he claimed as tax were dependent on a successful agricultural system. That the Nabateans possessed administrative systems for maintaining and regulating the flow of water (for example, by ensuring that no one took more water than they were entitled to) has been confirmed by the discovery of an inscription dated 6 BCE from the cult centre at Khirbet at-Tannu that mentions someone with the title 'Master of the spring of La'ban'. Scholars interpret this person as the government official appointed to supervise the distribution of spring water at La'ban. Water conduits can still be seen on the site.[59] It has also been suggested that the title of King Rabb'el II, 'he who brings life and deliverance to his people', drew on his enthusiastic support for agricultural development and the

[56] A. Ul-Hak (1998) *Case Study of the Punjab Irrigation Department: Consultancy Report*. Lahore: International Irrigation Management Institute, 81. For a comparison of two traditional approaches to irrigation, see C. Geertz (1972) 'The Wet and the Dry: Traditional Irrigation in Bali and Morocco', *Human Ecology* 1: 23–39.

[57] S. Chokkakula (2009) 'Interrogating Irrigation Inequalities: Canal Irrigation Systems in Injil District, Herat', Afghanistan Research and Evaluation Unit, Case Studies Series. Kabul: Afghanistan Research and Evaluation Unit, 5.

[58] Geertz 1972: 34.

[59] Oleson 2007: 225.

water supply systems that are very evident in the complex arrangements to bring water to Petra.[60]

There is a very particular reason, however, that allows us to conclude with some confidence that in the last decade of the first century CE there was both royal oversight of the irrigation system in Maoza and also that the system was kept in good working order. This was the circumstance that the king himself owned land in the form of a date-palm plantation in Maoza. We know this from the boundary descriptions of the properties sold in P. Yadin 2 and 3. In both cases the abutter to the south is the 'land' or 'plantation' of the king, meaning King Rabb'el II.[61]

PEASANT ECONOMICS

Peasant Economics and the Ancient Mediterranean World

According to Raymond Firth, 'the anthropologist economic relationships are part of an overall system of social relationships'.[62] As we will now see, this view is confirmed for Maoza by the importance of the economic factors in the life of the people who lived there, especially in view of the prominence of date crops in the local economy. Most of the people we will encounter in this book were involved in farming, date-palms especially, but also other crops like barley, and probably fruit and vegetables as well. A significant share of the date harvest was payable to the Nabatean king and, after 106 CE, to the Roman authorities. Thus in 99 CE the owner of the date orchard referred to in P. Yadin 2 had to pay ten *se'ahs* (a *se'ah* being a unit

60 Oleson 2007: 225. On the other hand, as noted in Chapter 2, Meshorer has suggested that Rabb'el II acquired this title in 76 CE when his mother died and he began to reign in his own right ([1975] *Nabataean Coins*. Qedem 3. Monographs of the Institute of Archaeology. Jerusalem: Hebrew University of Jerusalem, 76).

61 See P. Yadin 2, lines 4 and 24 and P. Yadin 3, lines 5 and 26. The text does not include the Aramaic word for 'date-palm' with the plantation in P. Yadin 3 at this point, but that is by far the most likely form of farming immediately south of an irrigated date-palm plantation.

62 R. Firth (1964) 'Capital, Savings and Credit in Peasant Societies: A Viewpoint from Economic Anthropology', in R. Firth and B. S. Yamey (eds) (1964) *Capital, Saving and Credit in Peasant Societies: Studies from Asia, Oceania, the Caribbean, and Middle America*. London and New York: Routledge, 16.

of volume, not of currency) of the harvest to the king (P. Yadin 2, line 14), and whether this is rightly classified as a tax or a lease fee[63] matters not to the fact that it was payable. What remained of the date harvest would have been sold for cash, but barley, fruit, and vegetables would have been an important source of food for the farmer and his or her family.

These two factors—the raising of food for subsistence but also for sale, and the necessity to make large contributions to the state—represent central dimensions of the accounts given of peasants in social-scientific research. In relation to the first, and looking at the matter from an economic perspective, Frank Ellis has written that while peasants have one foot in subsistence and one foot in the market, they are only partially integrated into imperfect markets.[64] As for the second factor, Eric Wolf has proposed that peasants:

> are rural cultivators whose surpluses are transferred to a dominant group of rulers that uses the surplus both to underwrite its own standard of living and to distribute the remainder to groups in society that do not farm but must be fed for their specific goods and services in turn.[65]

In short, 'it is only when a cultivator is integrated with a state—that is, when the cultivator becomes subject to the demands and sanctions of power-holders outside his social stratum—that we can appropriately speak of peasantry'.[66] This etic perspective is matched with remarkable precision by an emic one from the Hebrew Bible in the form of Samuel's warning to the Israelites of how a king will treat them if they insist on having one (1 Sam 8:11–18). The imposts payable to the Nabatean or Roman state by the farmers of Maoza demonstrate that they were peasants in this sense, by being subject to others beyond their social status.

Gerhard and Jean Lenski developed an influential macrosociological model of the development of human culture that begins with

[63] See the discussion in Yadin et al. 2002: 228–229, who suggest it is a tax and not rent because the same quantity of produce was paid on P. Yadin 3, which would have had a different yield. (They thus imply, correctly as we will see in Chapter 7, that the area conveyed pursuant to that deed was greater.)

[64] F. Ellis (1988) *Peasant Economics: Farm Households and Agrarian Development*. Cambridge: Cambridge University Press, 3–4.

[65] E. Wolf (1966) *Peasants*. Foundations of Modern Anthropology Series. Englewood Cliffs, NJ: Prentice-Hall Inc., 3–4.

[66] Wolf 1966: 11.

hunter/gatherers and proceeds to horticulturalists (who use digging sticks and produce only as much food as the family needs). The next stage is represented by the agrarian producer who, through the use of a plough, produces a surplus each year, and then the advanced agrarian producer who, now deploying an iron-tipped plough, generates an even larger surplus. As soon as families are producing surpluses, however, elites, usually living in cities, arise with armed supporters who take the surplus and erect the structure of the state. Religion often serves to legitimate the extractive processes at work.[67] The date-palm cultivators of Maoza were operating in an advanced agrarian culture and the Nabatean monarchy to 106 CE, and the Roman provincial administration thereafter, represented the inevitable entity taking their surplus.

If the 'perennial problem of the peasantry thus consists in balancing the demands of the external world against the peasants' need to provision their households',[68] as it surely does, the villagers of Maoza fell under its sway just like other peasants. In recent years there has been a lively debate among archaeologists and New Testament interpreters on socio-economic levels in the first-century CE world, both generally and also as they bear upon the Pauline communities. In 1998, Justin Meggitt argued that the society of the time was sharply dichotomized into the very rich and the very poor (early Christ-followers coming exclusively from the latter portion).[69] In 2004, Steve Friesen offered (in relation to the current state of scholarship on the apostle Paul) an astutely formulated 'poverty scale' predominantly for urban contexts in the Roman empire that differentiated seven levels: (1) imperial elites; (2) regional or provincial elites; (3) municipal elites; (4) people with moderate surplus resources (who do not include any farmers); (5) people living at stable near-subsistence (who, *inter alios*, do include 'some farm families'); (6) people living at subsistence level, and often below the level needed to sustain life (who include 'small farm families'); and (7) people living below subsistence level (such as some farm families, unattached widows, orphans, beggars, disabled, unskilled day labourers, and

[67] See P. Nolan and G. Lenski (2014) *Human Societies: An Introduction to Macrosociology*. Twelfth edition. New York: Oxford University Press.

[68] Wolf 1966: 15.

[69] J. Meggitt (1998) *Paul, Poverty and Survival*. Studies of the New Testament and Its World. Edinburgh: T. and T. Clark International.

prisoners).[70] It is clear from this that Friesen does not envisage any farm families who possessed even moderate surplus resources; farm families only enter the picture at the 'stable near-subsistence' level. As we will soon see, however, this does not accord with the picture that emerges in Maoza.

Bruce Longenecker has sought to offer a modified version of Friesen's scale, proposing a more sanguine picture of the first-century economy than Friesen (while also insisting that Paul was concerned with the poor throughout his ministry). Longenecker prefers an 'economy scale' ('E scale') to Friesen's 'poverty scale'.[71] He is also concerned with the total population, not just the urban segment.[72] Longenecker seeks to offer a more nuanced understanding of levels 5, 6, and 7. He rejects Friesen's suggestion that 'for nearly everyone in the Roman empire, poverty was a way of life'.[73] He proposes that level 4 'looks to be a significantly elongated category of wealth'.[74] When we consider the evidence from Maoza, it seems that the families like Babatha's who were involved in date-palm cultivation seem to be more closely comparable with level 4 (although perhaps its lower reaches) as being people of moderate surplus than with level 5 (stable near-subsistence). While this may have been a result of their being engaged in the rather unusual agriculture of date production, it still seems a preferable view of their economic position. Let us consider some of the evidence.

Across the world, the level of peasant capital (meaning the stock of cash, goods, and services not devoted to present consumption but retained to increase future production) is low. Since peasants tend to be poor, the conditions are not good for saving and capital

[70] S. J. Friesen (2004) 'Poverty in Pauline Studies: Beyond the So-Called New Consensus', *JSNT* 26: 341.

[71] B. Longenecker (2010) *Remember the Poor: Paul, Poverty and the Greco-Roman World*. Grand Rapids, MI: William B. Eerdmans, 45; Peter Oakes had previously questioned Friesen's use of a 'poverty' scale when the top three levels comprised elite people, who were extremely wealthy ([2004] 'Constructing Poverty Scales for Graeco-Roman Society: A Response to Steven Friesen's "Poverty in Pauline Studies"', *JSNT* 26: 368). For the purposes of the poorer sectors of the empire, Longenecker (2010: 50) also finds Friesen's original 2004 formulation more useful than the revised views Friesen subsequently published with Walter Scheidel (W. Scheidel and S. J. Friesen [2009] 'The Size of the Economy and the Distribution of Income In the Roman Empire', *JRS* 99: 61–91).

[72] Longenecker 2010: 50.

[73] Longenecker 2010: 54–55 (citing Friesen 2004: 358).

[74] Longenecker 2010: 55.

formation.[75] For the date farmers of Maoza, however, the position was different. Certain men and women possessed large amounts of cash in Maoza and surrounding areas, as can be illustrated from the following three examples.

First, the document P. XHev/Se Nab 1 (also known as P. Starcky) records that in 43 CE two (Judean) men, Nikarchos and Bannai, who were respectively the father and uncle of one 'Ele'azar, were indebted to a certain 'Isimilk son of 'Abdai in the large sum of 400 *sela's* (= 1,600 *denarii*) together with interest. They had property in Maoza approaching or equivalent to this value that 'Isimilk seized in satisfaction of his debt.[76] Some fifteen to twenty-four years later, (that is, sometime between 58 and 67 CE), according to Ada Yardeni's recent work on this papyrus,[77] 'Ele'azar, acting as heir of his now deceased father and uncle, redeemed the original writ of seizure from 'Isimilk. Presumably, therefore, he had assets to the value of 1,600 *denarii*.

Secondly, in 94 CE a Nabatean woman from a nearby village,[78] 'Amat-'Isi, possessed a dowry of 300 *sela's*, or 1,200 *denarii* available to her. She lent her husband 150 *sela's* upon entry into the loan document (which is P. Yadin 1) and the document provided for her to lend him the other 150 *sela's* as well. The husband's debt to 'Amat-'Isi was guaranteed by another Nabatean man. In 99 CE, as we know from P. Yadin 3, another Nabatean woman, 'Abi-'adan, obtained 160 *sela's*, 640 *denarii*, when she sold the date-palm orchard the subject of this volume to Shim'on, Babatha's father.

The third example is Babatha herself. When, in 125 CE, Babatha sued the two guardians of her infant son, she complained of the amount of money they were paying him for maintenance. From what she says, it is clear that 400 *denarii* had been entrusted to

[75] Firth 1964: 20.

[76] J. Starcky published P. XHev/Se. Nab 1 in 1954 (which is why it is named after him), with photographs of the then known fragments (J. Starcky [1954] 'Un contrat nabatéen sur papyrus', *revue Biblique* 61: 161–181). More recently, in 2001, Ada Yardeni published a preferable version of the text in an essay in which she rearranged the fragments (now including P. Yadin 36a and 36b) in a more convincing fashion and provided her very careful drawing of the fragments (A. Yardeni [2001] 'The Decipherment and Restoration of Legal Texts from the Judaean Desert: A Reexamination of *Papyrus Starcky (P. Yadin 36)*', *Scripta Classica Israelica* 20: 121–137).

[77] Yardeni 2001.

[78] See the argument for this in Chapter 1 of this volume.

them on his behalf.[79] She also asserts that she had property (and she probably means cash) equivalent to his,[80] so she also had 400 *denarii* available at this time. In February 128 CE Babatha's second husband borrowed 300 *denarii* in silver coins from her, although this may have come from the 400 *denarii* just mentioned.[81] But she was also owed a dowry of 400 *denarii* from her second husband.[82] On her death she claimed the 300 *denarii* she had lent him and the dowry of 400 *denarii*.[83]

These three examples indicate that these people, whose farming focused on the lucrative cultivation of dates, enjoyed moderate surpluses and are comparable with Friesen's level 4 rather than level 5.

Debt and the Fragility of Peasant Life

Yet in spite of the income to be earned from date-palm cultivation, the fortunes of the often prosperous farmers of Babatha's world were precarious and their lifestyles fragile. Central to this volatility was the existence of debt.[84] 'Even in the most primitive non-monetary economic systems', Raymond Firth noted, 'the concept of credit exists—the lending of goods or services without immediate return against the promise of a future repayment'.[85] In a monetarized society, like that of Nabatean Maoza, the existence of credit was fully to be expected. This was a setting, moreover, in which it was possible to acquire a large sum of money but also to lose it. As noted above, Nikarchos and Bannai ended up owing and being unable to repay a local Nabatean the sum of 1,600 *denarii* plus interest, so that he seized their property in satisfaction of the debt (although the men's heir was later able to redeem the property seized). I will argue in Chapter 6 that, five years after her loan to him, 'Amat-'Isi's husband was considerably in debt to her and she took action to recover the amount owing (probably

[79] The guardians were providing her son two *denarii* per month (P. Yadin 12, line 23; Lewis 1989: 52–53). Since we know that they were only obtaining 6% per annum (P. Yadin 15, line 23; Lewis 1989: 60–61), the amount vested in them was 400 *denarii*.

[80] P. Yadin 15, line 24; Lewis 1989: 60–61.

[81] P. Yadin 17, lines 25–26: Lewis 1989: 72–73.

[82] P. Yadin 10, line 8 (Yadin et al. 2002: 126–127).

[83] See P. Yadin 21, lines 11–12 (Lewis 1989: 94–95).

[84] For a recent, radical reappraisal of the nature of debt in the ancient world, see D. Graeber (2011) *Debt: The First Thousand Years*. New York: Melville House Publishing.

[85] Firth 1964: 28.

then three hundred *sela's*, or twelve hundred *denarii*, plus interest)—although not from him but from the guarantor of his debt. Babatha's second husband died owing her 700 *denarii* and she needed to seize some of his date orchards and sell their produce to recoup that debt. P. Yadin 21 and 22, from 130 CE, are two documents relating to her seizure of these orchards and sale of their crop. Her action reflects a common pattern among peasants around the world; as Firth notes: 'Sometimes land may be taken as security for a cash loan, with the right of usufruct going to the creditor so long as the loan is not repaid.'[86]

The reasons that cultivating date-palms could be a risky business and produce such fluctuations in families' capital reserves are not self-evident. Whereas the vagaries of rainfall in Judea led to the development of a diverse range of ecological niches requiring very focused farming and made agriculture that depended on unpredictable precipitation quite uncertain in its returns,[87] the farmers in Maoza relied on irrigation and there is no sign in the Babatha papyri of any interruptions to the water supply. Nevertheless, other explanations are possible. One of the factors that Frank Ellis has proposed as operative in the erosion or 'appropriation' of peasant surplus seems likely to have had major significance in relation to date-palm cultivation, namely: 'the potential for peasant incomes to be squeezed, either through falling prices or through rising prices of market inputs, or a combination of both'. Here he has in mind the concept of 'the changing *terms of trade* confronting peasant producers which measures the ratio of output prices to input prices over time'.[88] Date-palm cultivation was a labour-intensive operation and labour costs in particular were probably high; as noted above, the construction and maintenance of the water supply system was a labour-intensive and costly task. One other factor mentioned by Ellis, however—the advance of credit to peasant farmers at interest rates that do not reflect competitive market rates in the wider economy—was probably not characteristic of Maoza (see below). Popenoe was able to observe in 1913 that 'The date palm, in comparison with most other fruit trees is notably free of disease.' Yet even he adverted to the presence of the

[86] Firth 1964: 31.

[87] See E. F. Davis (2009) *Scripture, Culture, and Agriculture: An Agrarian Reading of the Bible*. Cambridge: Cambridge University Press, on the challenging nature of farming in Judea.

[88] Ellis 1988: 54 (emphasis original).

palm borer in Middle Eastern date-palms and two scale insects.[89] It is likely that pests such as these also affected date-palms in ancient times, causing fluctuations in crop yields in particular years, with serious consequences for heavily indebted producers.

No doubt central to the rising or declining circumstances of Judeans and Nabateans in Babatha's world was the availability of credit, as mentioned above, and also the existence of an effective legal system in Nabatea, as attested to by Strabo (see Chapter 2). In Nabatea, agreements relating to debt were recorded in writing, with the instruments in question containing provision for repayment of the amount loaned plus interest and rights of seizure of the debtor's property in the event of default. Such provisions had been present in legal documents for centuries, if not millennia, and occur at an earlier period of the Aramaic legal tradition, as seen in examples from the Judean settlers serving as mercenaries of the Persian king on the island of Elephantine in Egypt during the 5th century CE.[90] There is a diversity of evidence concerning credit in ancient Near Eastern societies rendering it difficult to postulate any coherent picture of the credit system diachronically or synchronically.[91]

In spite of D. N. Premnath's view that in the ancient world creditors offered loans not to earn interest on them but to get control of land,[92] it is clear that farmers in Maoza lent money precisely with the intention of earning interest. Babatha makes this clear in her dispute with her orphan son's guardians, when she complains about the interest rate they are getting on the money invested on his behalf and claims she could do better.[93] There is, moreover, no support in

[89] Popenoe 1913: 149.

[90] For the Aramaic texts and translations, see A. Cowley (1923) *Aramaic Papyri of the Fifth Century B.C. Edited, with Translation and Notes*. Oxford: Clarendon Press, and E. G. Kraeling (1953) *The Brooklyn Museum Aramaic Papyri: New Documents of the Fifth Century B.C. From the Jewish Colony of Elephantine*. New Haven: Yale University Press, and for an excellent discussion of life in the military colony, see B. Porten (1968) *Archives from Elephantine: The Life of an Ancient Jewish Military Colony*. Berkeley, CA; University of California Press.

[91] D. N. Premnath (2007) 'Loan Practices in the Hebrew Bible', in R. B. Coote and N. K. Gottwald (eds) (2007) *To Break Every Yoke: Essays in Honor of Marvin L. Chaney*. Sheffield: Sheffield Phoenix Press, 174. For the situation in ancient Athens, see P. Millett (1991) *Lending and Borrowing in Ancient Athens*. Cambridge: Cambridge University Press.

[92] Premnath 2007: 174.

[93] See P. Yadin 13, 14, and 15 for the court documentation in her dispute with her son's guardians.

this context for Premnath's assertion that in ancient societies loans in a commercial sense did not exist. More accurate, however, is his more measured next statement—that loans '*for the most part*, were not obtained to make capital investments in trade or commerce or to make improvements on one's real estate'.[94] We find precisely this sort of loan in Maoza, as with P. Yadin 1, from 94 CE, a loan by a Nabatean woman to her husband and his business partner for investment in agriculture. There is no evidence, however, that professional money-lenders were active in the town. Nor does it appear that local interest rates were excessively onerous. In P. Yadin 1 the provision for interest is expressed in this way: 'the amount specified in this deed will increase to his debit as is customary', although we are not told what the customary interest rate was. In 125 CE, however, Babatha was complaining that the guardians of her infant son were only earning (or at least paying to him) six per cent per annum on his money they had invested and she asserts, in effect, that she could earn nine per cent if she were permitted to pool her capital with that of her son.[95] Presumably this was the local customary rate, which her son's guardians were not managing to achieve.[96] In 124 CE, Babatha's second husband had borrowed 60 *denarii* for a year from the Roman centurion based in En-Gedi (a non-citizen from Thrace) at an interest rate of twelve per cent, but this was the maximum rate chargeable under Roman law.[97] The fact that there was a reasonable number of date farmers, and even Roman soldiers, with the capacity and inclination to advance loans to their neighbours at moderate interest rates would have driven any usurious money-lenders out of the market for credit. Yet even with interest at, say, nine per cent, after only a few years a debt would have grown considerably. If one borrowed 100 *denarii* at nine per cent per annum compounding over five years, by the end of the term of the loan would have increased to 154 *denarii*. This must have been a prominent factor in the rise and fall of peasant capital reserves.

94 Premnath 2007: 174 (emphasis added).

95 For the details of these figures, see P. F. Esler (2014) 'Reading Matthew by the Dead Sea: Matthew 8:5–13 in Light of P. Yadin 11', *HTS Theological Studies* 70: 6–7.

96 See Esler 2014.

97 The debt is recorded in P. Yadin 11 (Lewis 1989: 41–46); for a discussion, arguing against the notion that the centurion was engaged in a usurious squeeze, see Esler 2014.

EVERYDAY LIFE FOR MEN AND WOMEN

If we ask what everyday life was like for men and women in Maoza, we are drawn to consider the twin spheres of agricultural production and the diverse activities of the household. As the site of Maoza is not known and has not been excavated, we do not know what houses in the village were like. Nevertheless, various houses from the period in question have been excavated in Nabatea, as recently discussed by Bernhard Kolb.[98] Houses containing a courtyard together with various rooms seem to have been common. For example, a stone-built house from the first century CE has been excavated at Khirbet edh-Dharih that contains a large courtyard and two square rooms. Another first-century CE house has been discovered in Mampsis that features a paved courtyard and six to seven rooms on its three sides.[99] We will probably not go too far astray if we imagine the inhabitants of Maoza living in such houses, especially when 'houses and courtyards' are mentioned when property owned by various people in the Yadin Papyri is listed.[100]

Turning now to agricultural work, David Hopkins has recently written of the need to pay more attention to the neglected reality of 'all sorts of field work' mentioned in Exod 1:14, that is, to the immense amount of human labour in ancient Palestine (and, we might add, Nabatea) invested in the agricultural tasks 'which ultimately provisioned the larger society, satisfied the tax authorities, and secured access to international trade'.[101] While the prominence of date cultivation in Maoza meant a rather different agricultural profile than elsewhere in the region, either to the west or east of the Dead Sea, we have seen that other crops like barley were grown and much of what Hopkins describes has applicability here too. Agriculture was embedded in society and responded to a broad range of social, cultural, and political parameters. The family unit was central to production and much of the work was done by hand. For field crops the main agricultural tasks were ploughing, sowing, weeding, harvesting, threshing, and winnowing. To this one should add the

[98] See B. Kolb (2007) 'Nabataean Dwellings: Domestic Architecture and Interior Decoration' in Politis 2007: 145–172.

[99] Kolb 2007: 158–161.

[100] For example, see P. Yadin 1, line 21 and P. Yadin 2, line 12.

[101] D. C. Hopkins (2007) '"All Sorts of Work": Agricultural Labour in Ancient Palestine', in Coote and Gottwald 2007: 149.

maintenance of tools used in the various tasks and the care of livestock. Arboriculture had its own requirements, which were quite elaborate when the trees involved were date-palms: maintenance of orchards with banks along the boundaries to retain water supplied during the weekly inundations; upkeep of the canals and valves used to distribute the water; preparation of seedlings; planting; trimming of the trees of dead leaves and fibre; pollinating; harvesting and packing of the dates.

Much of this work was done by men. But what of women? Carol Meyers has written of the need to avoid interpreting the role of women in this setting on the basis of more recent human experience.[102] She has invoked research showing that women in non-Western settings and in pre-modern farming households played a far more ample social role than had previously been believed.[103] This reappraisal was in part driven by growing scepticism towards the widely accepted dichotomy between public (of the large social unit, especially villages and towns) and private realms (of the family unit), where men and women were respectively dominant.[104] In fact, in most village-based societies, including ancient Israel, the lines between such spheres are blurred. Meyers summarized this research as demonstrating that 'Public and private are thus overlapping and integrated domains in many aspects of family and community life in

[102] C. Meyers (1999) '"Women of the Neighborhood" (Ruth 4:17): Informal Female Networks in Ancient Israel', in A. Brenner (ed.) (1999) *Ruth and Esther: A Feminist Companion to the Bible (Second Series)*. Sheffield: Sheffield Academic Press, 110–127. On ancient Israelite women generally, see C. Meyers (2013) *Rediscovering Eve: Ancient Israelite Women in Context*. Oxford: Oxford University Press.

[103] See E. Friedl (1967) 'The Position of Women: Appearance and Reality', *Anthropological Quarterly* 40: 97–108; S. C. Rogers (1975) 'Female Forms of Power and the Myth of Male Dominance: A Model of Female/Male Interaction in Peasant Society', *American Ethnologist* 2: 727–756; C. Cronin (1977) 'Illusion and Reality in Sicily', in A. Schlegel (ed.), *Sexual Stratification: A Cross-Cultural View*. New York: Columbia University Press, 67–93; N. Quinn (1977) 'Anthropological Studies on Women's Status', *Annual Review of Anthropology* 6: 181–225; cited by Meyers 1999: 113–114.

[104] For the old view, see M. Z. Rosaldo (1974) 'Women, Culture, and Society: A Theoretical Overview', in M. Z. Rosaldo and L. Lamphere (eds) (1974) *Women, Culture, and Society*. Stanford, CA: Stanford University Press, 17–42. For the new view, see D. O. Helly and S. M. Reverby (eds) (1992) *Gendered Domains: Rethinking Public and Private in Women's History*. Ithaca, NY: Cornell University Press and J. Sharistanian (ed.) (1987) *Beyond the Public/Domestic Dichotomy: Contemporary Perspectives on Women's Public Lives*. Contributions to Women's Studies, 78. Westport, CT: Greenwood Press.

traditional societies.'[105] One certainly gets this impression from what we know of Nabatea. Three of the four legal documents to be investigated in this volume involved a woman as the primary party, the person either lending money or selling real estate to someone else. On one occasion the other party was a member of the Nabatean elite (P. Yadin 2), yet that was no barrier to the transaction or (as we will see in Chapter 6) its rescission. Beyond the scope of this volume, but illuminating nevertheless, is the fact that Babatha engaged in several litigious proceedings, as both plaintiff and defendant. The idea that in Nabatea women were relegated to some private, domestic sphere is flatly contradicted by the evidence.

Nevertheless, there is no reason to doubt that in the household women in Maoza played a dominant role. Meyers finds the best umbrella concept for the role of women in the phrase 'maintenance activities', a term that gained currency in the late 1990s among archaeologists who were dissatisfied with traditional accounts of household activities.[106] This concept embraces a range of practices and experiences that concern the sustenance, welfare, and long-term reproduction of the members of a group.[107] It thus includes child bearing and cultural continuity and the basic tasks that regulate and stabilize the life of the household within a particular community. This entails much more than just meeting the provision of the physical needs of the household through provision of food and clothing, though they are extremely important. It also involves (although this is not an exhaustive list): 'care of the young and the ailing, the socialization and education of children, the organization of household space, the fostering of linkages with kin and neighbors, and the performance of household rituals'.[108] Seen in this light, the activities of women emerge into their true light as essential for sustaining their households and communities.

Rare and precious empirical confirmation of the range of activities associated with women in this period actually comes from Babatha herself, in the form of the objects that were found in the same hiding-place in the cave in Naḥal Ḥever as her leather satchel of documents and presumably belonged to her. I will refer to more of these items below where they are relevant. At this point it is worth mentioning that among the objects she hid in the cave were a key and two

[105] Meyers 1999: 115.
[106] Meyers 2013: 125–126.
[107] Meyers 2013: 126.
[108] Meyers 2013: 126.

key-rings.[109] Presumably this was the key to her house, to which she apparently never returned, while the key-rings indicate that at some time she had keys for other buildings, rooms or boxes, which indicates the measure of control she had possessed in her social sphere. The change that had befallen her circumstances with the Bar Kokhba revolt of 132–135 CE, her transformation from householder to fugitive, is poignantly illustrated by her also having deposited in her hiding-spot three water-skins.[110]

Food processing was probably as central a feature of the life of women in Maoza as it tends to be in most cultures. Probably the most time-consuming and labour-intensive task was grinding grain to flour for baking. Meyers notes calculations suggesting that to prepare four pounds of flour, so as to produce enough bread for two adults and four children for a day, would have taken two or more hours of grinding the grain.[111] We know that barley was grown in Maoza, but wheat may also have been available. Once the flour had been prepared it had to be baked. The ovens were sometimes inside a single house but communal ovens serving more than one family were common in ancient Palestine.[112] Women must often have conversed with one another around these communal ovens. Women would also have been active in the preparation of other foods, such as legumes like lentils and chickpeas,[113] while dates, dried or boiled, must also have featured in the diet of the people in Maoza. Among the household items left by Babatha with her legal documents were knives, a clasp knife and a number of bowls that were probably used in food preparation.[114]

Women must also have been involved in the transformation of fibres into garments and household fabrics (for floor coverings, bags, and other items). The necessary activities were spinning, weaving, and sewing using wool or flax. Experimental archaeology has shown that it takes as many as one hundred hours spinning wool to produce

[109] Y. Yadin (1963) *The Finds from the Bar Kokhba Period in the Cave of Letters: Hebrew, Aramaic and Nabatean-Aramaic Papyri.* (Plates). *Judean Desert Studies.* Jerusalem: The Israel Exploration Society, 38–39. Also see Y. Yadin (1971) *Bar-Kokhba: The Rediscovery of the Legendary Hero of the Last Jewish Revolt against Imperial Rome.* London: Weidenfeld and Nicolson, 143–171.

[110] For these details, see Yadin 1963: 38–39.

[111] Meyers 2013: 130.

[112] Meyers 2013: 131.

[113] Meyers 2013: 132.

[114] Yadin 1963: 38–39.

enough yarn for one garment. But wool also had to be washed and the loom set. Much of the activity must have been undertaken by women working together.[115] Babatha left behind a bundle of balls of yarn which she may well have spun herself, the remains of fine fabric which were probably for clothes making and also objects that she may have made herself: two wrappers or kerchiefs, a sack-sheet and a sack that had contained the leather pouch for her papyri.

Finally, we must be open to the possibility that women were also active in areas such as the weaving of baskets, the construction of ceramic pots, the fashioning of stone tools for grinding grain, and even the manufacture of ovens for baking. Meyers has pointed out that women in other peasant societies frequently engaged in tasks such as these. Nor is the reference in Neh 3:12 to 'Shallum . . . and his daughters' helping reconstruct the walls of Jerusalem after the return from exile likely to be an error.[116] Nor is there any reason to suppose that women were not active in agricultural activities when that became necessary, at harvest time for example. Accordingly, we should not be surprised that among the personal possessions Babatha left behind was a sickle.[117]

Dowries

The experience of women in a setting like Maoza could not be adequately addressed without mentioning an important feature of the life of married women—their dowry. I noted in Chapter 2 that Nabatean society was patrilineal, with property passing down the male line. An example of this social feature in operation can be seen in P. Yadin 5. This document from 110 CE records that the man who would later become Babatha's first husband, Jesus son of Jesus (his father apparently now deceased), was entitled to a large amount of property that was being held on his behalf by Joseph, his late father's brother.[118] But where did the operation of patrilineality leave daughters? The evidence suggests that their families, their fathers in particular, took considerable care to protect their interests and, it must be added, the family honour, by providing them with dowries upon their

[115] Meyers 2013: 133. [116] Meyers 2013: 134–135.
[117] Yadin 1963: 38–39.
[118] For text, see Lewis 1989: 37–39; the arrangement is discussed by Satlow 2005: 51.

marriage. In the Dead Sea region their fathers could also make them direct gifts of property, but these were treated differently than dowry money.

Payments made between the families of bride and groom at the time of matrimony are very common and have been the subject of close attention by anthropologists. The basic distinction is between bridewealth (or bride price) and dowry. The bridewealth is a payment that passes from the kin of the groom to those of the bride.[119] It is more likely to occur in societies that are not very stratified, where agriculture is conducted by the hoe and not the plough, where population densities are low, land is not in short supply, and where men are not differentiated by their holdings of land. It is found more often in Africa than Eurasia.[120] It is quite common for the amount of the bridewealth to be the same across the society.[121]

Dowry is different; it occurs in societies that have reached what Lenski and Lensky call the agrarian or advanced agrarian phases, characterized by the use of the plough, social stratification, with higher population densities and more pressure on land which is held in plots of varying sizes. In short, the use of dowry seems to accompany a transition to more complex societal structures.[122] More specifically, however, dowry is part of a familial or conjugal fund, usually passing from the parents to the daughter. It is thus an aspect of the transfer of familial property, but one that includes women as well as men.[123] Dowry is a type of inheritance to the bride that she receives on marriage.[124] In this respect it can be seen as a means for ameliorating the effects of a patrilineal inheritance system. We know from various dowries mentioned in the Dead Sea legal papyri that the amounts in question were quite considerable. P. Yadin 10 is Babatha's wedding contract with her second husband and specifies her dowry as 400 *denarii*, which probably came from her father (although he may have been dead at this time).[125] The dowry of 'Amat-'Isi in P. Yadin 1

[119] J. Goody (1973) 'Bridewealth and Dowry in Africa and Eurasia', in J. Goody and S. J. Tambiah (1973) *Bridewealth and Dowry*. Cambridge Studies in Social Anthropology, 7. Cambridge: Cambridge University Press, 17.

[120] E. Boserup (1970) *Women's Role in Economic Development*. New York: St Martin's Press; followed by Goody 1973: 22–23 and S. Anderson (2007) 'The Economics of Dowry and Brideprice', *Journal of Economic Perspectives* 21: 156.

[121] Goody 1973: 18.

[122] Anderson 2007: 155.

[123] Goody 1973: 17.

[124] Goody 1973: 1.

[125] For the text, see Yadin et al. 2002: 126–127.

was at least three hundred *sela's* (or twelve hundred *denarii*), with Michael Satlow pointing out that the usual size of a marriage payment in the Dead Sea legal papyri (including Babatha's) was 200–400 *denarii*.[126]

Dowries are payments that are brought into a marriage which remain the property of the bride,[127] and must be returned to her under certain circumstances, typically if her husband divorces her or dies. At times, however, the husband can contribute to or even provide the dowry money. P. Yadin 18 is a marriage contract executed in En-Gedi on 5 April 128 CE between Judah (also known as Cimber) and Shelamzion the daughter of Judah son of Eleazar Khthousion by his first wife. Since this Judah was Babatha's second husband, Shelamzion was her stepdaughter. Shelamzion brought into the marriage from her father gold, silver, and clothing to the value of 200 *denarii*, while the groom promised to give her another 300 *denarii*.[128]

Jack Goody has observed that dowries are the result of a bargain with a specific intention, namely to link the daughter and hence her family with a particularly desirable son-in-law.[129] To this extent, the institution of a dowry places a premium on matching contributions between the two spouses and 'the higher the strata, the more elaborate the match'.[130] Dowries 'increase with both the wealth and the social status of both parties of the marriage bargain'.[131] In particular, where people in the local context own variable amounts of property (and this was certainly the case in Maoza and the surrounding region) and these are related to differences in status in the village, it becomes 'a strategy of utmost importance to preserve those differences for one's offspring, lest the family and its offspring decline over time'.[132] While patrilineality took care of sons and preserved family property in the male line, it was necessary to preserve the status of daughters as well. For this reason daughters had to be endowed with sufficient property to attract a husband of the same or similar rank. This often meant marrying off a daughter within the particular social group to which she belonged, for in that way her status and that of the family

[126] Satlow 2005: 54. [127] Anderson 2007: 161–162.
[128] For the text, see Lewis 1989: 77–81.
[129] Goody 1973: 17. [130] Goody 1973: 18. [131] Anderson 2007: 163.
[132] Goody 1973: 25.

investment in it could be preserved.[133] In light of this comparative material from cultures similar in many ways to that of Nabatea, it is highly likely that preceding the solemnization of any marriage contracts (such as P. Yadin 10 and 18) very serious conversations occurred within and between families on precisely issues such as these to ensure that a socially and economically appropriate match was being made.

Under Nabatean law a wife was allowed to lend from her dowry, certainly to her husband. But the deed required a separate provision indicating her consent to such as a loan (as in P. Yadin 1, lines 46–52).[134] Could a wife lend from the dowry to other people? In P. Yadin 1 (see Chapter 4) a man guarantees a loan from a husband to a wife. Although this was a collateral, and not a direct obligation, the guarantor presumably enjoyed the benefit of the loan (probably as the husband's business partner) and had a duty to repay it in the event of default. Nevertheless, it was surely the case that the most frequent borrowers from women's dowries were their husbands. Husbands themselves would hardly have welcomed their wives' dowries being denuded of funds by other men (or women) when they might need to resort to such a resource themselves. Fathers would also have been unenthusiastic about loans from their daughters' dowries to people outside the families into which they had married, since these would expose them to the potential risk of being left penniless if the loans failed and their husbands died. So there could have been considerable social disapproval of wives dipping into their dowries to lend to people apart from their husbands, even if it was legally permissible. Less stigma would have likely attached to women lending money from their cash reserves (which appear to have been unrestricted) rather than their dowries, but even here husbands might have been concerned with the potential loss of available funds for the family.

This discussion on wives lending to their husbands provides a natural point of transition to the first document for detailed consideration, P. Yadin 1.

[133] Goody 1973: 25. [134] See Yadin et al. 2002: 171.

4

Muqimu Borrows Money from his Wife (94 CE)

BEING THERE

As foreshadowed in Chapter 1, a central component of the archival ethnography undertaken in this volume is to imagine one's being present on the occasions that each of P. Yadin 1–4 was executed. To recall the view of Laurence Stone cited in Chapter 1, anthropology teaches us to train a searchlight on a single event, recording it in great detail in its cultural context and with close attention to its cultural meaning, a method akin to the 'thick description' advocated by Clifford Geertz.[1] That exercise begins here with the oldest of these four papyri, P. Yadin 1, my translation of which is provided in Appendix 2.

The document is dated the eighth of 'Elul in the twenty-third year of King Rabb'el's reign, the king 'who brings life and deliverance to his people'. This is a day in August/September of 94 CE by our modern dating conventions.[2] We do not know what time of day, but it was probably daytime, to facilitate reading the legal document aloud and the scrutiny of its terms by literate parties or witnesses present. At this time of the year the harvesting of any date-palms in the vicinity would have been under way. Since the date is computed according to Rabb'el's regnal years, we know that the document was signed in Nabatea. Yet the deed also provides the precise location in the kingdom

[1] See Chapter 1 and L. Stone (1979) 'The Revival of Narrative: Reflections on a New Old History', *Past and Present* 85: 13–14.

[2] Lewis ([1989] *The Documents from the Bar Kokhba Period in the Cave of Letters: Greek Papyri and Aramaic and Nabatean Signatures and Subsriptions*. Jerusalem: Israel Exploration Society, The Hebrew University of Jerusalem and the Shrine of the Book, 29) suggests 94 CE for the date of this document.

where events are transpiring: it was in a place, a village presumably, recorded as רמון, which I will vocalize as Rummon.[3] The deed further specifies this place to be in Moab, here spelt Maob (that part of Nabatea running eastward from the eastern shore of the Dead Sea whose southern boundary was the Wadi Hasa, the biblical Zered river).[4] Rummon must have been reasonably close to Maoza, for reasons set out at the end of this chapter.

Eight people were gathered for the occasion, the essence of which was that a man was borrowing a large sum of money from his wife, from her dowry in fact (מהר; line 18), while another man was to act as guarantor (ערב; line 35) of that debt. This transaction is redolent of the local economy outlined in Chapter 3, where date cultivation enabled some people to accumulate large cash reserves, while others fell deeply into debt. These people, some or most of whom would have lived locally, were probably engaged in active social interaction with one another. They were probably also taking part in a process, involving sophisticated legal concepts and legal drafting, with which they must have been well familiar, given the number of occasions that scribes were instructed to draft documents in this context. This was a world in which a scribe was called upon to record even quite small transactions, such as the sale of a donkey for five *sela*'s (twenty *denarii*) from one brother to another.[5]

The husband was Muqimu son of 'Awat-'Ilahi, son of Ḥalaf-'Ilahi. He is said to reside in 'Aina Shuḥaru,[6] in Moab, presumably another village close to Rummon, or even part of it. His wife was 'Amat-'Isi daughter of Kaminu (whose father was 'Ammaru). The guarantor was

[3] Other vocalizations are possible and Nabatean Aramaic does not signal geminated consonants, as with the *mem* here. Although the Aramaic could also be read דמון, because of the close similarity of *daled* and *resh* in this script, my reason for preferring the spelling with *resh* appears below. Having chosen 'Rummon' for this word, I subsequently discovered that M. Alzoubi had spelled the word 'Rammon' ([2012] *Les formules juridiques dans les inscriptions nabatéennes*. Saarbrücken: Presses Academiques Francophones, 214).

[4] Alzoubi 2012: 220.

[5] This is P. Yadin 8 (from 122 CE); see text and translation in Y. Yadin et al. (eds) (2002) *The Documents from the Bar Kokhba Period in the Cave of Letters: Hebrew, Aramaic and Nabatean-Aramaic Papyrii*. Judean Desert Studies. Jerusalem: Israel Exploration Society, Institute of Archaeology, Hebrew University and the Shrine of the Book, Israel Museum, 113. These are likely to be Babatha's brothers—see my arguments on this point at the end of Chapter 1.

[6] The name could also be spelt 'Shuḥadu' but nothing turns on this since this scribe writes *resh* and *daled* identically .

'Abad-'Amanu.[7] He is referred to in the document and designates himself in his signature without reference to his father. The husband and the guarantor were certainly present since they both signed the deed. The wife, who would not under Nabatean practice have signed a deed of loan where she was the lender, was almost certainly present. This conclusion follows from the magnitude of the transaction and because Nabatean law plainly required a wife to consent in express terms to a loan to her husband and such consent and its signatures occupy lines 46–52 of the deed.[8] Also present was Ḥuwaru son of 'Awatu, the scribe who drafted the deed (whose father was also a scribe).[9] Finally, in attendance were four other persons who witnessed the deed: Zaidu son of Shahru; Taimu son of Ḥuwaru; Wanah son of Ḥalaf-'Ilahi; and a fourth person whose name has not survived. Taimu was probably the scribe's son, thus indicating a scribal family extending over three generations. Wanah was probably Muqimu's paternal uncle.[10] Everyone present was a Nabatean. The names of six other Nabateans appear in the patronymics of these individuals, but we do not know if they were alive or dead when the deed was signed.

Let us explore in more detail what was going on in the lead-up to Ḥuwaru the scribe reading out the deed and parties and witnesses (including Ḥuwaru) signing it. My initial question for an ethnographic analysis is this: why did Muqimu need to borrow money? There are indications in the document that in the period leading up to the eighth of 'Elul in King Rabb'el's twenty-third regnal year, probably in the early to mid-summer, a business proposition had come his way. He had been offered a lease of property in one of the local villages. The principal evidence for this is that the words לאכרי, 'for the rent (*le-'ikrây*)', almost certainly appear in line 16 after mention of a sum of money in the previous line.[11] This reading is supported by

[7] The difficulties of deciphering Nabatean script mean that the second part of his name could either be spelled 'Amanu or 'Amiyu. For the sake of simplicity, I will use the first possibility throughout this book.

[8] So Yadin et al. 2002: 171.

[9] It is also possible to spell his name 'Huwadu', but nothing turns on this.

[10] A man of the same name, Ḥalaf-'Ilahi, is Muqimu's grandfather and Wanah's father.

[11] While not all letters in אכרי are certain, this is an inspired suggestion by the editors that is dependent on an Arabic word for 'leasing'. The vocalization shown here is that tentatively proposed by the editors (Yadin et al 2002: 192), although in their

the presence of the words 'two years from the date of this deed' immediately after 'for the rent'. The parties thus envisaged that the loan to cover certain rent would be repaid within two years. This expectation was likely to have been based on the term of the lease also being two years, with the profit from two harvests needed to repay the loan. Interest became chargeable on the loan only after two years, which increases the likelihood that there was a lease for two years, within which period enough profit would be made to discharge the debt.

The sums involved were very large. The amount of the loan was the sum of 150 *sela's* (Nabatean silver coins) equivalent to 600 *denarii*, plus interest at the customary rate.[12] This loan was for rent for two years. 'Amat-'Isi was additionally willing to increase the loan to 300 *sela's*, or 1,200 *denarii* (lines 49–51). This suggests that the owner of the property being leased was willing to allow a rental term of four years in all and she was willing to lend her husband and his partner the whole amount. The local customary interest rate may have been around nine per cent, which is what is was some twenty years later.[13] So a large debt would have quickly become much larger.

The eight people who gathered for the execution of P. Yadin 1 were probably all very familiar with local agricultural practices and understood the nature of leases, an important part of the local farming economy. Several of the ancient legal papyri found around the Dead Sea are leases. There are, for example, five extant among the Yadin Papyri and another six from Muraba'at.[14] Although many of the leases are fragmentary, they nevertheless shed considerable light on the nature and terms of agricultural leases in this setting. Valuable comparative information is also available from Hellenistic and Roman Egypt.[15]

transliteration they show the last letter as an *aleph* when the photo of the papyrus shows it to be a *yod* (as also in their Hebrew letter version).

[12] Line 17 states that the principal amount 'will increase to his debit as is customary'.

[13] This was the interest that Babatha believed she could obtain on money invested on her infant son's behalf: see P. F. Esler (2014) 'Reading Matthew by the Dead Sea: Matthew 8:5–13 in Light of P. Yadin 11', *HTS Theological Studies*, 70 for details.

[14] These include P. Yadin 6, 42, 44, 45, 46, and P. Mur. 24A, 24B, 24C, 24D, 24E, and 24F.

[15] See J. Rowlandson (1996) *Landowners and Tenants in Roman Egypt: The Social Relations of Agriculture in the Oxyrhynchite Nome*. Oxford Classical Monographs. Oxford: Clarendon Press, and J. S. Kloppenborg (2006) *The Tenants in the Vineyard:*

Several of the Dead Sea leases usefully preserve the date on which they were entered into, as well as the rental sum and the term of the lease (whether for one or more years). The only one of these in Nabatean Aramaic, relating to Maoza and from the Babatha archive, P. Yadin 6 (dated 119 CE, although the day and month are missing) records a lease from Yehuda son of 'El'azar Khthousion, Babatha's second husband, to another Judean, Yoḥana son of Meshullam, of land Yehuda owned in Galgala.[16] The lease was for a term of three years (line 5). The document refers to 'working [the land]' (lines 6 and 10) and to 'seed' (line 6), and the latter feature means it does not concern date-palm cultivation. Perhaps barley was the main crop. It appears that the tenant was to receive a fixed share of the crop since the expression 'one-eighth' appears on a few occasions in the document and there is no mention in it of payment in currency.[17] The fact that here we have two Judeans recording their lease in Nabatean Aramaic may suggest 'a high degree of business interaction characteristic of the southern Dead Sea region at the time', as the editors suggest,[18] or it may just mean that the only scribe available, whose name has not survived, was a Nabatean.

The six leases from Murabba'at (Mur 24A–F) are all closely connected. They are in Hebrew, executed on the twentieth of Sebat, Year 2 of the Revolt (133 CE), relate to the cultivation of wheat, and are all apparently for a term of five years. Under each lease, the rent was to be paid in a specified quantity of good quality wheat.[19]

P. Yadin 42, 44, 45, and 46 are from the archive of 'Eli'ezer son of Shemu'el. P. Yadin 42 is in Judean Aramaic.[20] It was executed on the first of Iyyar (April/May), year 1 of Revolt (132 CE), was for a term of three years, and related to the cultivation of a crop or crops requiring irrigation (line 5). The total rent was 650 *denarii* per annum, payable in three installments (on the first of Tebet [December/January], Sivan

Ideology, Economics, and Agrarian Conflict in Jewish Palestine. WUNT 195. Tübingen: Mohr Siebeck (the latter providing the Greek text, English translation and notes for fifty-eight leases or lease-related documents on pp. 359–549).

16 See Yadin et al. 2002: 260–261 for the text and a translation.

17 Yadin et al. 2002: 257.

18 Yadin et al. 2002: 257.

19 See O. P. P. Benoit et al. (eds) (1961) *Discoveries in the Judaean Desert II: Les Grottes de Murabba'at. Texte*. Oxford: Clarendon Press, 122–132. For the five-year term, see 24B, line 10; 24C, line 13, and 24E, line 10.

20 See Yadin et al. 2002: 144.

[May/June], and 'Elul [August/September]).[21] Since the lease contains the word פרין (line 4), which covers all kinds of produce, not just fruit,[22] refers to irrigation periods (line 5), has a high rental, and appears to begin in September/October (at the end of the date harvest),[23] this lease probably concerned, or at least included, the cultivation of dates. The other three leases are in Hebrew and relate to land in En-Gedi claimed by Shim'on son of Kosiba' as the *Nasi* of Israel. P. Yadin 44, which is a head-lease, was executed on the twenty-eighth of Marḥeshvan (October/November), in Year 3 of the Revolt (134 CE), for an unstated term, and related to the lease of cropland and trees.[24] P. Yadin 45 was executed on the second of Kislev (November/December), Year 3 of Revolt.[25] It related to fruits and crops and was for a term of one year ('until such time as the season of garden [plots] of En-Gedi will reach its end'; line 20). The rent was equivalent to three *sela's* (line 24). Finally, P. Yadin 46 was executed on the second of Kislev, also in Year 3 of the Revolt.[26] It related to date-palms and cropland and was also for a term of one year. But for this lease the rent was equivalent to forty *sela's*, or 160 *denarii.*

If we ask what property was being offered to Muqimu for lease at the high rental of 150 *sela's*, the likely candidate is a date-palm plantation. This was the major cash crop in this region (see Chapter 3) and serious amounts of money were going to be needed to repay the loan of 150 or even 300 *sela's* with interest. There is no other candidate for a crop likely to generate the return necessary to repay the loan. The discussion of evidence from other leases suggests that there is a direct correlation between high rents and date cultivation (whereas in P. Yadin 45, which is basically the lease of a vegetable garden, the rent is only three *sela's*, in P. Yadin 46, relating to cropland and date-palms, it is forty *sela's*). While this may reflect the different size of the plots, the disparity in rent is very

21 P. Yadin 152 (Yadin et al. 2002: 152) is a receipt for payment of 39 *denarii* on the fifth of a month that is probably 'Elul. This may have been a late payment of some of the final instalment of rent that was actually due on the first of 'Elul, as the editors suggest (Yadin et al. 2002: 150). It is curious, however, that this instalment represents exactly 6% of the total amount of rental.

22 Yadin et al. 2002: 144 for the text and translation.

23 Since the first payment of three is due in December/January.

24 See Yadin et al. 2002: 44–45 for the text and translation.

25 See Yadin et al. 2002: 58–59 for the text and translation.

26 See Yadin et al. 2002: 66 for the text and translation.

great and it would be most surprising if the nature of the date as a crop and the amount of capital and labour required for date-palm cultivation did not place a premium on the dates when they were sold, which premium would be reflected in the rental payment. It seems that Muqimu was already engaged in the business of date production, since the expression 'dates' probably appears or is implied amongst the itemization of his property (line 21 and 26).[27] All eight people present at the signing of the deed were probably aware of the nature of the land being leased and the probability that it would produce enough dates to repay the loan. Perhaps some of them were doubtful on this point. As John Kloppenborg has noted, the disadvantage to the tenant of a fixed rent payable in cash (later called *shekirut*) 'lay in the fact that it imposed the step of converting produce to its cash value and thus subjected the tenant to the vicissitudes of markets and exchange charges'.[28]

Muqimu himself may have shared any such doubts. For while he was interested in taking up this lease, he was unwilling to undertake the necessary obligations on his own. Accordingly, he enlisted a partner in this opportunity, no doubt to share the risk: 'Abad-'Amanu. It is probable that Muqimu and 'Abad-'Amanu intended leasing the property jointly and this would constitute a particular reason for the latter's providing the guarantee.[29] We learn nothing more about 'Abad-'Amanu here, but we will discover later from P. Yadin 2 that at this date he had a son high in the service of the Nabatean king. In 94 CE his son must have been holding a reasonably significant military and administrative position in the Nabatean *cursus honorum*, given the very elevated position he had attained with the king only five years later. Everyone present must have known that 'Abad-'Amanu had a son with a big future ahead of him.

Muqimu was quite a wealthy man. On the basis of his property itemized in the deed as mortgaged to secure repayment of the loan he owned, or could be expected to own: land parcels and vineyards; houses and courtyards; gardens and springs; deposits; garments;

[27] The words 'dates and harvest' appear in lines 19 and 26 and while the meaning 'harvest' is secure, some doubt attends 'dates'. Nevertheless, given the centrality of date-palm cultivation in this region at the time, it is most unlikely that a catch-all expression for 'harvest' would not include dates.

[28] Kloppenborg 2006: 293.

[29] Yadin et al. 2002: 170 (where the editors note that this suggestion originated in a private communication from Hannah Cotton).

copper vessels; wool; chains and crafted articles of silver and gold; oil, dates, and harvest; and partnership rights (lines 20–28).[30] In spite of these possessions, however, Muqimu was himself unwilling or unable from his own resources to produce the 150 *sela'*s needed to obtain the lease. It seems that 'Abad-'Amanu was equally unwilling. Nevertheless, an alternative source for this amount of money had presented itself, in the form of the dowry (*mohar*) that Muquimu's wife, 'Amat-'Isi, had brought with her to the marriage. As already noted, she was willing to lend her husband a total of 300 *sela'*s to finance his business venture with 'Abad-'Amanu.

An ethnographic approach to this transaction includes seeking to situate it within the wider contexts of Nabatea and Maoza set out in Chapters 2 and 3. At a general level, we see the extent of the process of sedentarization that had transformed the Nabateans from an originally nomadic people into one that largely engaged in settled agricultural practice (although some nomadism persisted), politically organized as a kingdom with an established dynasty that minted its own coinage (such as *sela'*s). Nabatean agriculture had from an early date included the distinctive and profitable cultivation of date-palms. Yet we have seen in Chapter 3 that growing dates was a risky business; the potential rewards were great but so were the risks. Great fortunes could be won but also lost.

In addition, seeking to generate an ethnographic 'thick description' of an event like this entails attending closely not just to what was happening but also to the cultural significance of its various features of the event, especially the prominent ones. The fact that a woman was lending to her husband, with the repayment of the loan being guaranteed by another party, calls for particular attention. Married women, possessed of considerable dowries, were often the source of credit to finance their husbands' business operations, as discussed in Chapter 3. 'Amat-'Isi's loan to Muqimu is an example of this phenomenon. The dowry system ameliorated the effects of patrilineal succession for daughters of the family and maintained the status of the family. Experience elsewhere suggests that the dowry had to be sufficient to attract a husband of the same or similar social rank.

If this pattern also characterized Nabatean society, it is somewhat surprising that we have evidence from this region of several husbands,

[30] All these details are found in the text of P. Yadin 1.

like Muqimu, who needed to borrow money from their wives. Why did they not have financial resources themselves sufficient for investing in business propositions if they had been wealthy enough to attract in marriage a woman who came with a large dowry in the first place? Perhaps the men's wealth was invested more in property, real and personal, and less in cash, so that the issue was one of liquidity, not assets as such. In the latter case, there would have been less a sense of a power differential between husband and wife and the possibility of a husband's status being diminished by too great a dependence on his wife's wealth. Moreover, the wife's dowry would be needed to support herself and her children in the event that her husband died or divorced her. A wife who lent her dowry to her husband was undertaking a significant risk in the event the investment turned sour or her husband died. That is one reason why Nabatean law required a specific acknowledgment of the wife of the provision of such a loan. The fact that the deed of loan gave her security over her husband's assets to recover the debt attenuated the risk, but only to a certain extent. Babatha encountered precisely this problem when her second husband died owing her a large amount of money and her actions to recoup it from his estate were challenged in court by his heirs from his first marriage.[31]

We may assume that the eight people present for the execution of P. Yadin 1 were well aware of the respective financial situations of 'Amat-'Isi, Muqimu and 'Abad-'Amanu. Did Muqimu have a solid reputation for sound financial dealings and everyone, his wife included, have confidence that he would repay the loan? Did he have a strong record of profit making in date cultivation? Or had his previous ventures been less than successful, which might explain why he lacked the cash needed for the lease? If everyone was confident in the prospect of his repaying the loan, why was 'Abad-'Amanu enlisted as a guarantor? After all, this was not an inevitable feature of a loan from a wife to her husband, since there was no guarantor of the loan Babatha made to her second husband from her dowry and her other liquid assets, something she may well have regretted when he died before repaying her. And was this guarantee suggested by

[31] P. Yadin 17 (Lewis 1989: 71–75) records Babatha's loan of three hundred *denarii* to her second husband and P. Yadin 21 and 22 (Lewis 1989: 94–101) show that the money had not been repaid at his death. For the litigation, see P. Yadin 23–26 (Lewis 1989: 102–115).

Muqimu, or 'Amat-'Isi to provide a greater measure of security over her dowry in the transaction? If it was 'Amat-'Isi's suggestion, had she received any advice from her cognate male relatives (father or brothers) that a guarantee would be a wise course of action? On balance, anxiety probably outweighed confidence among those present that day. The amount advanced or to be advanced was so large, Muqimu's lack of the necessary liquid capital himself and the need to introduce a guarantor together suggest that very significant risks attended the proposed investment. In Chapter 6 we will see that any such concern felt that day would prove to be well founded. Further information that will emerge about 'Amat-'Isi will strengthen the probability that she, not Muqimu, asked for a guarantor of her loan to him.

Although the deed does not, unfortunately, mention where 'Abad-'Amanu was from, three considerations render it likely that he lived in the same place as Muqimu or very close it. First, as he was probably the business partner of Muqimu in the management of the lease of a date-palm orchard, a skilled and complex agricultural operation, considerable inconvenience would have been occasioned by his not living nearby. Secondly, it would also have been more difficult, although certainly not impossible, for 'Amat-'Isi to resort to the guarantee were that to become necessary if 'Abad-'Amanu was not living in the vicinity. Thirdly, the fact that in P. Yadin 1 the scribe mentions Muqimu's village but not 'Abad-'Amanu's raises the inference that it was the same as Muqimu's. If 'Abad-'Amanu was closely associated with Muqimu and living in much the same place, there was no reason to be specific. If he had come from farther afield, however, there would have been good reason for the scribe to say where.

THE CONTRACT

In any event, on that day in August/September 94 CE the document was indeed executed in Rummon in Moab by the parties (lines 1–2; 11–12). Like many of the Dead Sea legal documents, the deed has an 'inner version' (in this case a broad summary of the provisions) and an 'outer version'.[32] That is why two line references are sometimes

[32] But note that in P. Yadin 2 and 3 the inner version is almost as detailed as the outer version. The outer version was written first, and then the inner version.

provided here. The inner version was rolled and tied with string, with the parties and witnesses signing along the knots. The outer version was left unrolled, but in the event of dispute the inner version could be opened up. In P. Yadin 1 the inner version is a brief summary of the outer version, but in some cases (P. Yadin 2 and 3 for example) the inner version is nearly as long as the outer.[33]

The provisions of the deed require noting. In the deed Muqimu acknowledged that he was indebted to his wife 'Amat-'Isi for the sum of 150 *sela's* (lines 2–3; 15–16), repayable within two years, or with interest at the customary rate if not repaid within that time, with 'Amat-'Isi having the election as to when she would seek repayment in the event of late payment (lines 16–17). This sum represented half of the 300 *sela's* that Muqimu was permitted to borrow from his wife (lines 6; 33–34). The money advanced formed part of 'Amat-'Isi's dowry (line 18). Muqimu provided security for the entire 300 *sela's* loan facility in the form of a mortgage over all his property, both realty and personalty (lines 4–6; 19–34). 'Abad-'Amanu guaranteed the entirety of Muqimu's obligations (lines 7; 35–36).

There was a clause stating that the deed has been prepared in accordance with the customary manner (line 38). There was also provision for early repayment of the loan (lines 39–42), although its precise interpretation is difficult,[34] and there is no sign that this provision was ever activated. Lines 43–44 of the document provided: 'And anyone who may acquire this deed by her assignment (of it) may seize any asset which is theirs (literally, 'to take hold of anything held by them' [למאחד כל אחד די להם] line 44, 'they' being Muqimu and 'Abad-'Amanu) in relation to everything that is (provided for) in this deed in perpetuity.' This gave any assignee of the deed from 'Amat-'Isi essentially the same powers of enforcement that she herself possessed. It was further provided 'no one may attach a condition to anything that the witnesses have signed' (line 45). A tax was payable to the king in relation to the deed (lines 9–10 and 42–43).

The document also contains, in lines 46–52, a statement by the wife, her husband's creditor, probably dated to the same day as the main contract, in which she states her agreement to the loan of 300

[33] For 'double' legal documents, see E. Koffmahn (1968) *Die Doppelurkunden aus der Wüste Juda*. Studies on the Texts of the Judean Desert, 5. Leiden: E. J. Brill, and Lewis 1989: 6–10.

[34] See the detailed discussion in Yadin et al. 2002: 197–198.

sela's and asserts her right of foreclosure against 'them', meaning her husband and his guarantor. As noted above, this was a requirement of Nabatean law.

The scribe who drafted this acknowledgement of debt—and in my ex-lawyer's view, very skilfully—was Ḥuwaru, son of 'Awatu. Muqimu and his guarantor Abad-'Amanu, but not his wife (as noted above), signed the document, as did the scribe. Four witnesses also signed it and the names of three of them survive (Zaidu son of Shahru; Taimu son of Ḥuwaru, probably the scribe's son; and Wanah son of Ḥalaf-'Ilahi, the latter probably Muqimu's uncle).

LOOKING FORWARD

One big question posed by the presence of this document in the Babatha archive, although one not usually asked, is this: what is it doing there? Why did Babatha and presumably her father before her have a copy of this document when no one connected with her, indeed no Judean whatever, is mentioned in it? Although this question may not hitherto have been asked, it is a highly significant one. Our working assumption, mentioned at the end of Chapter 1, is that if a document is present in the archive it must have some bearing upon the rights of Shim'on and later Babatha, or their cognate or affinal relations, but what? There is, as we will see in Chapter 6, a probable answer to this question and it is one that illuminates poignant aspects of the lives of these Nabateans and the legal framework in which they lived. However, a consideration of the next two documents, P. Yadin 2 and 3, which are both deeds of purchase of a date-farm orchard, is necessary before that answer can be proffered. Before moving on to consider them, it is desirable to return to the question of where P. Yadin 1 was executed. While we know that Rummon was in Moab, can we narrow down the location more precisely? Was it close to Maoza, for example, and is it possible to identify factors that might in some way link the people in P. Yadin 1 with those in P. Yadin 2 and 3 as a prelude to ethnographic analysis of those documents?

As already noted, Moab and two other place names are mentioned in P. Yadin 1: Rummon, where the deed was executed, and 'Aina Shuḥaru, where Muqimu is said to reside, both of them located in

Moab. This name means 'Shuḥaru's well' and this is perhaps the Shuḥaru mentioned as Zaidu's father or, more probably, some ancestor of his with this name. The likely explanation for two places being mentioned is that they were close to one another but that Rummon was the larger,[35] probably being the place where the witnesses resided. ʿAina Shuḥaru may even have been an area forming part of Rummon, since we know that the town of Maoza was differentiated into various areas. One of them was called Galgala and another Luḥit, while there was possibly a third called Bethphaaraia. These are mentioned in various Dead Sea legal papyri.[36]

In 1987 Robert Wenning published a comprehensive inventory of archaeological finds relating to the Nabateans.[37] In each case he related the find to the place where it was discovered. On the basis that names can persist for centuries and even millennia, these place names may go back to the Nabatean period. In this context it is of considerable interest that he notes two place-names that contain the word 'Rummâne', which is very close to Rummon (*RMWN*) mentioned in this deed.[38] One of them, Umm Rummâne lies about 30 kilometres east of the northern parts of the Dead Sea beyond the Arnon river and is about 60–70 kilometres from the likely site of Maoza.[39] But the second example, Khirbet Umm Rummâne,[40] lies north of Wadi Hasa and is only about 12 kilometres east/south-east of the likely site of Maoza (see Figure 2.1), so that it would only take about two hours to walk at a moderate speed from one place to the other. Proximity to Maoza will be relevant to the discussion of P. Yadin 2, 3, and 4, which involve property there. Khirbet Umm Rummâne is also only some 10 kilometres west of the King's Highway, the main ancient route between the south and the north in Moab. Although we cannot be

[35] The editors suggest that 'One would assume that this site (sc. *RMWN*) was not be too far from עינא שחרו] where 'Amat-'Isi's husband resided' (Yadin et al. 2002: 187).

[36] See the discussion in H. M. Cotton and A. Yardeni (1997) *Discoveries in the Judean Desert. Volume 27. Aramaic, Hebrew and Greek Documentary Texts from Naḥal Ḥever and Other Sites: With an Appendix Containing Alleged Qumran Texts (The Seiyal Collection 1): Desert*. Oxford: Clarendon Press, 164.

[37] R. Wenning (1987) *Die Nabatäer—Denkmäler und Geschichte: Eine Bestandesaufnahme des archäologischen Befundes*. Novum Testamentum et Orbis Antiquus, 3. Göttingen: Vandenhoeck & Ruprecht.

[38] Wenning lists no place names of the form 'Dumanne', however.

[39] Wenning 1987: 58 (site 3 in map section K of Map 3).

[40] Wenning 1987: 72 (site 88 in section L of Map 4).

certain that Rummon is to be identified with Khirbet Umm Rummâne, that remains an intriguing possibility.

There is, however, some other evidence that Maoza and Rummon were situated reasonably close to one another. The scribe who drafted the second, third, and fourth documents (in chronological order) from Babatha's archive (Papyri Yadin 2, 3, and 4) in 99 CE was a man called 'Azur son of 'Awatu the scribe. He is almost certainly the brother of Ḥuwaru (son of 'Awatu the scribe) who drafted P. Yadin 1 in 94 CE involving Muqimu and his wife and business partner. P. Yadin 2 and 3 were executed in Maoza and P. Yadin 4 probably was as well.[41] We thus have a scribal family whose members undertook work for clients in both Rummon and Maoza. The most likely explanation for this fact is that the two places were not too far from one another, each lying within the range, as it were, that this family of scribes were willing to travel for work or provided the only, or most highly regarded, scribal services. Given the typical cultural patterns prevailing in the eastern Mediterranean world of the time, the sons of 'Awatu (and their sons, like Taimu son of Ḥuwaru) probably lived in his house if he was still alive and perhaps continued to do even after his death. Whether they lived in Maoza or Rummon, or in some other nearby town, cannot be determined. If the family home was in one of these named places, however, and if Khirbet Umm Rummâne is to be identified with Rummon, the distance they would have had to travel to get to the other place was only about 12 kilometres.

In Chapter 1 I noted that one aspect of the recent resurgence of village ethnography was the interest in setting any village so investigated within a large social network. Within this perspective it is possible to propose an important mechanism for linkages between Maoza and nearby villages. For another dimension to the 'Awatu family of scribes undertaking work in both Rummon and Maoza is that that they represented at least one means of communication, extremely well informed communication given their profession, between the inhabitants of both places. Moving between Rummon and Maoza, 'Awatu family members must have conveyed information and gossip to those living in one place about what was going on, especially who was doing what, in the other. It is most unlikely, moreover, that this was the only link between the two places. Other

[41] See the discussion on P. Yadin 4 in Chapter 7.

sources of information flow would have come from marriages between inhabitants of Rummon and Maoza, or business relationships or friendships. The possibilities here are made manifest when we consider that about two decades later a Judean woman living in Maoza, Babatha herself, took as a second husband a Judean man dwelling in En-gedi, some 50–60 kilometres away. Later in this volume, I will mount an argument that a Nabatean called Archelaus, whom we will now meet in connection with P. Yadin 2, and a Judean, Shim'on (Babatha's father), may have been reasonably well known to one another, even though there is no evidence that they lived in the same town.

5

Archelaus Purchases a Date-Palm Orchard (99 CE)

BEING THERE

P. Yadin 2 brings us forward five years. Once again the occasion of its execution offers a suitable opportunity for archival ethnography, as, in an act of imagination, we join the parties, witnesses and scribe who gathered for that event to explore who the parties were, what was happening, and the social and cultural significance of the transaction.

The date was the third of Kislev, in the twenty-eighth year of King Rabb'el's reign; in our terms, in November/December 99 CE.[1] Dating by reference to the Nabatean king's regnal year means the events were taking place in Nabatea and the precise place is specified: Maḥoz 'Eglatain, or Maoza in the Greek version of the name. As discussed in Chapter 3, Maoza was a harbour on the Dead Sea, probably on its south-eastern shore. We know that there were seven people present, since they signed the document, and there was probably also an eighth.

Once again we encounter a woman with a major role in the transaction: 'Abi-'adan, the daughter of 'Aptaḥ, who was Manigares' son. She was selling a date-palm plantation on the shore of the Dead Sea for 112 *sela's*, equivalent to 448 *denarii*. The purchaser was a man called Archelaus, son of 'Abad-'Amanu.[2] As usual under Nabatean

[1] N. Lewis ([1989] *The Documents from the Bar Kokhba Period in the Cave of Letters: Greek Papyri and Aramaic and Nabatean Signatures and Subscriptions*. Jerusalem: Israel Exploration Society, The Hebrew University of Jerusalem and the Shrine of the Book, 29) suggests 99 CE for the date; Yadin et al. ([2002] *The Documents from the Bar Kokhba Period in the Cave of Letters: Hebrew, Aramaic and Nabatean-Aramaic Papyri*. Judean Desert Studies. Jerusalem: Israel Exploration Society, Institute of Archaeology, Hebrew University and Shrine of the Book, Israel Museum, 216) propose 97/98 CE. Nothing turns on which year it is.

[2] The spelling could either be 'Abad-'Amanu or 'Abad-'Amiyu. For the sake of simplicity, I will repeat here the practice I adopted in Chapter 4 and refer to him as 'Abad-'Amanu.

law, as the purchaser he did not sign the deed, but he was probably present. The deed acknowledges that he had paid the purchase price (lines 8 and 29) and he probably received a signed version of the deed and possession of the property at that time. For reasons to be explained later in this volume, P. Yadin 2 is almost certainly the actual document that he received.

Apart from 'Abi-'adan, there were six other people who signed the deed that day. The signature of the first of them, the son of Zaidu, whose first name is missing in the text, came immediately after the name 'Abi-'adan (although her name too is missing). The son of Zaidu was probably signing on her behalf since she was illiterate.[3] Four more people then signed the document as witnesses. Their names are all missing except for the final part of one of them: 'Ilahi, a word meaning 'god' employed in some Nabatean names. Lastly, the scribe, 'Azur son of 'Awatu, signed. He was almost certainly the brother of the scribe in P. Yadin 1, Ḥuwaru son of 'Awatu. The five people (out of eight) whose names are known in relation to this deed in whole or in part were ethnically Nabatean.

These other people who were present when the deed was signed, locals (one imagines) roped in to serve as witnesses, probably knew 'Abi-'adan and the property she was selling and understood the context (financial exigency perhaps) in which she was selling. They may also have known Archelaus and why she was selling to him and not anyone else who may have been interested in acquiring the orchard. If the witnesses did not know Archelaus before, they would (as we will see) have known him by repute and would have met him when the document was signed. If we push further and seek to understand how they would have regarded the social and cultural factors that affected this transaction, we must pay close attention to the details of P. Yadin 2. The most unusual aspect of the transaction was the social status of the purchaser—so we must begin with Archelaus.

ARCHELAUS

Three details relating to Archelaus represent valuable clues of the sort proposed by Carlo Ginzburg—and discussed in Chapter 1—that

[3] As suggested by the editors based on what survives of the signatures (Yadin et al. 2002: 205).

facilitate unexpected illumination of social situations and relationships in a micro-historical investigation—clues of the sort that if multiplied across a sufficient body of documentation facilitate the generation of an archival ethnography. First is the circumstance that Archelaus is described as *'srtg'* (אסרתגא) twice in the document, in lines 3 and 21, in its upper and lower portions.[4] The word אסרתגא is an Aramaic version of the Greek *στρατηγός* (*strategos*) but with a prosthetic *aleph* and assimilation of the first *tau*, a spelling also seen in the Nabatean tomb inscriptions edited by Healey and discussed below.[5] In Greek *strategos* meant 'general' or 'admiral' and, as we will see, was used as a loan word in Nabatea of someone with very senior military and administrative responsibilities. Second is the fact that Archelaus's father, 'Abad-'Amanu, can be none other than the man of the same name who is the guarantor of Muqimu's debt to his wife in P. Yadin 1. This link, although not mentioned by the editors,[6] will prove of critical importance in helping to unlock the story behind these documents. Third is the consideration that Archelaus's father is not described as being a *strategos* or any other sort of Nabatean official in either of the two documents where he is mentioned (P. Yadin 1 and 2).

Archelaus as a *Strategos*

What significance does it have that Archelaus is said to be a *strategos*? What do we know of such a person?[7] After a careful discussion, David

[4] The second instance of the word is virtually complete, once one adds a fragment (shown in Plate 22, Y. Yadin [2002] *The Documents from the bar Kokhba Period in the Cave of Letters: Hebrew, Aramaic and Nabatean-Aramaic Papyri.* (Plates). Judean Desert Studies. Jerusalem: Israel Exploration Society, Institute of Archaeology, Hebrew University and the Shrine of the Book, Israel Museum, in the margin, second from the top) to what is clearly the correct position (note the two ascending *lameds* from the line below in the right place) before the last four letters of the word in line 21, as is shown in Ada Yardeni's drawing in Yadin et al. 2002: 207.

[5] See Yadin et al. 2002: 213. [6] See Yadin et al. 2002: 201–219.

[7] For discussions of the Nabatean *strategos*, see H. Ingholt (1976) 'Varia Tadmorea', in *Palmyre, bilan et perspectives (Colloque de Strasbourg [18–20 octobre 1973] à la mémoire de Daniel Schlumberger et Henri Seyrig*. Travaux du Centre de recherché sur le Proche-Orient et la Grece antiques. Strasbourg: AECR, 101–137; J. Bowsher (1989) 'The Nabataean Army', in D. French and C. S. Lightfoot (eds) *The Eastern Frontier of the Roman Empire: Proceedings of a Colloquium Held at Ankara in September 1988*. BAR International Series 553, Oxford: British Archaeological Reports, 19–30; D. F. Graf (1994) 'The Nabataean Army and the *Cohortes Ulpiae Petraeorum*' in E. Dabrowa (ed.) (1994) *The Roman and Byzantine Army in the East*. Kraków: Uniwersytet Jagiellonski, 265–311; Yadin et al. 2002: 218–219; and L. Nehmé

Graf concludes that the Nabatean *strategoi* 'were charged with both the civil and military adminstration of their districts'.[8] Laia Nehmê, who has recently surveyed most of the inscriptional and literary evidence for the Nabatean *strategoi*, reaches a similar view, namely, that *strategoi* were 'characterized by a territorial based activity and had both civil and military responsibilities'. But she amplifies this by arguing that 'All the places in which a *strategos* is known to have had an authority is a central place in the Nabataean kingdom.'[9] We are able, indeed, to develop a reasonable picture of the role of the *strategos* in the Nabatean kingdom from literary and epigraphic sources.

Josephus provides much of the literary evidence, with a number of references to Nabatean *strategoi*. Sometimes they have a military function, as commanders of armies (as at *AJ* 18.5.1; *BJ* 1.19.5 [381]), and sometimes a civil or administrative one, with both functions commonly associated with this office in the wider Hellenistic world of the Ptolemaic and Seleucid kingdoms.[10] In the latter regard, Josephus records that a Nabatean princess was escorted to Petra through what appear to be the jurisdictional districts of various *strategoi* (*AJ* 18.5.1).

Illuminating epigraphic information on the nature of the Nabatean *strategos* comes from Mada'in Salih, which lies 110 kilometres south-west of Tayma and was known in ancient times as Hegra. There are thirty-eight Nabatean tomb inscriptions at Hegra dated from 1 BCE/CE to 74/75 CE, and five other closely analogous inscriptions known from elsewhere.[11] These inscriptions typically have the following elements: (a) a naming of the people who had the tomb made for themselves

(2015) '*Strategoi* in the Nabataean Kingdom: A Reflection of Central Places?' *Arabian Epigraphic Notes* 1: 103–122.

[8] Graf 1994: 278. Also see Bowsher 1989: 20.

[9] Nehmê 2015: 116.

[10] Graf 1994: 274–275.

[11] See J. F. Healey ([1993] *Nabataean Tomb Inscriptions of Mada'in Salih. Journal of Semitic Studies*, Supp. 1. Oxford: Oxford University Press), who provides the text, translations, and detailed comments on the thirty-eight inscriptions from Mada'in Salih (pp. 68–236), while helpfully supplying the text and translation of the other five, with limited notes but references to the relevant scholarship (pp. 237–248). These latter five are the Turkmaniye and Babe s-Siq Nabatean/Greek bilingual inscriptions from Petra, the Strasbourg Inscription from Al-'Ula, the tomb inscription from Al Jawf, and the Madeba Inscription in the Louvre. Inscriptions appearing in Healey's edition are cited in this volume as 'H' plus the number he assigns them. It should be noted that Healey provides transliterations of the Aramaic.

and their children and descendants; (b) a warning that they should not sell or lease the tomb to others; (c) a stipulation of an amount in which anyone who alters the inscription will incur liability; and (d) a note of the year the tomb was constructed and the mason responsible. The word *strategos* appears six times in Healey's edition of these inscriptions (6:1; 24:2; 32:1; 34:7 [*bis*]; and 38:8) and also in the Madeba inscription (in the Louvre).

The usages of *strategos* are revealing. H38:8 states that anyone who sells the tomb or claims title to it 'shall be liable to the governor (*'srtg'*) who is in Hegra in the sum of a thousand Haretite *sela's* and to our King Maliku for the same amount'.[12] Hegra was a walled town that allowed the Nabatean kingdom to impose tax on caravans moving through the area.[13] The warning just cited indicates quite clearly that the *'srtg'* was the local Nabatean commander of the town, probably with administrative and military duties, so that Healey's 'governor' is an appropriate translation.

Other inscriptions reveal that such governors were often the sons of other governors or even more highly placed officials. It was plainly a matter of considerable pride to be able to claim to be the holder of this office and to be the son of a father who held it or a higher office. In H34:7 reference is made to 'Maliku the governor (*'srtg'*), son of Rabibel the governor (*'srtg'*)'.[14] The Madeba Inscription, dated to 37/ 38 CE, is particularly interesting in this regard:

> This is the tomb and the two funeral monuments above it which 'Abd'obodat the governor (*'srtg'*) made for Itaybel the governor (*'srtg'*), his father, and for Itaybel the camp commandant (*rb mshryt'*) who is in Luḥitu and 'Abarta, son of this 'Abd'obodat the governor; in the territory of their rule which they exercised twice for thirty-six years during the time of Ḥaretat, King of the Nabataeans, lover of his people. And the above work was executed in his forty-sixth year.[15]

So we have an elite family: the grandfather (Itaybel [senior]) who was a governor; the son 'Abd'obodat (who had the tomb constructed), also a governor; and the son (Itaybel [junior]) a camp commander

[12] Healey 1993: 234. [13] Healey 1993: 11–12. [14] Healey 1993: 219.

[15] Healey, 1993: 247–248. Ḥaretat, in whose forty-sixth year the tomb was constructed, is Aretas IV Philopatris. On this inscription also see J. F. Healey (2003) 'A Nabataean Funerary Inscription from Madaba', in W. H. Hallo and K. L. Younger (eds) (2003) *Context of Scripture*, 2. Leiden: E. J. Brill, 193. Luḥitu is mentioned as a Moabite town in Isa 15:5.

(clearly a lower office than governor) in Luḥitu. Women, too, were proud to have a father who was or had been a *strategos*. Thus, in H24:2, one of the people responsible for the construction of the tomb is Arsaksah daughter of Taymu, the *strategos*.

Even higher in this military and administrative hierarchy was the position of prefect, *hprk'*, which is another borrowing from the Greek, either ὕππαρχος (or ὕππαρχης), the equivalent of the Latin *praefectus equitum* (a cavalry general) or, more likely, ὕπαρχος, used in Egypt for 'prefectus' (= *legatus*).[16] H6.1 reads:

> This is the tomb which Sullay the governor (*'srtg'*), son of 'Aydu, the prefect (*h[prk'*. . . .]), made . . . (in the year . . . of King Maliku), King of the Nabataeans.[17]

Similarly, H32 begins with the statement,

> This is the tomb which Matiyu the governor (*'srtg'*), son of Euphronios the prefect (*hprk'*) made . . . [18]

Looking at this phenomenon of children mentioning the illustrious offices held by their fathers within broader Mediterranean cultural patterns, we observe that the honour of a family and every individual it embraced was promoted by having a member who was or had been a *strategos*. All of the members enjoyed the 'ascribed honour' that came from belonging to a family such as this.[19] A fine illustration of precisely this cultural feature is found in Isaiah 22, in relation to Eliakim the son of Hilkiah, to whom God says he will give authority over Jerusalem and Judah:

> And I will fasten him like a peg in a sure place, and he will become a throne of honour to his father's house. And they will hang on him the whole honour of his father's house, the offspring and issue, every small vessel, from the cups to all the flagons (vv. 22–23; RSV modified).

[16] Healey 1993: 109.

[17] Healey 1993: 106. Healey helpfully notes there that although the inscription in its present state only shows the '*h*' of *hprk'*, a squeeze published by A. Jaussen and R. Savignac (1909) *Mission archéologique en Arabie*. Volume 1. Paris: E. Leroux, allowed *hpr[* to be read, so this emendation is secure.

[18] Healey 1993: 212.

[19] On 'ascribed honour', see B. J. Malina (2001) *The New Testament World: Insights from Cultural Anthropology*. Third edition. Louisville, KY: Westminster John Knox Press, 23–24.

Although it has sometimes been suggested that some of the higher Nabatean posts were hereditary,[20] this view appears to run against the evidence. In P. Yadin 1 the scribe does not mention that ʿAbad-ʿAmanu (the father of Archelaus) was a *strategos*, which he must have been if the position was an hereditary one. While this is admittedly an argument from silence, it is a significant one considering the extent to which the scribe of P. Yadin 2 goes to acknowledge the fact that Archelaus was a *strategos*, as discussed below, and the enthusiasm evident in the inscriptions at Hegra for recording the positions that the individuals mentioned reached in the royal service. Moreover, in the Madeba description (above), we learn that Itaybel (junior) served as a camp commander but we do not know if he ever even reached the rank of *strategos*. In addition, Laila Nehmê has recently noted an inscription of another Nabatean (ʿAnimû son of Damasippos) who was a *rb mšrytʾ* in Dûmat in 44 CE before becoming *strategos* in Hegra.[21] On the reasonable presumption, however, that Itaybel did, like ʿAnimû, become a *strategos*, the evidence mounts for the Nabateans having had something like the *cursus honorum* at Rome. The inscriptions just discussed point to a progression from camp commander (*rb mshrytʾ*) to governor (*ʾsrtg*ʾ) to prefect (*hprkʾ*). While the positions were probably not hereditary, it is likely that most of those who rose up the career path normally came from elite families. For fathers from such families would inevitably have had the connections necessary to secure their sons' entry into the *cursus* in the first place. This does not, however, exclude the possibility that a non-elite person could enter the Nabatean *cursus honorum* perhaps by meritorious action—of a military kind most likely—probably coming in at a lower rank and rising to that of *strategos*, with the speed of the elevation dependent on the character and actions of the person in question. This would be roughly equivalent to the phenomenon of the *novus homo* at Rome, a plebeian who managed to acquire admission to the Senate, perhaps one day rising as high as consul (as Cicero did). In this case, such a newcomer will be the recipient of 'acquired honour', meaning honour won in some context where he has performed at a higher level than his peers and this has been recognized

[20] See Bowsher, 1989: 21–22 for details. Nehmê also thinks the position of *strategos* may have been hereditary (2015: 116).

[21] Nehmê 2015: 116.

and rewarded by those in power.[22] I will now proceed to argue that Archelaus was precisely such a person.

Archelaus, a Nabatean *Novus Homo* and his Father

P. Yadin 2 itself raises this very issue of the *novus homo* in a Nabatean context since Archelaus is described in the document as a *strategos*, yet not as being the son of one. Although Archelaus' father, ʻAbad-ʻAmanu, is mentioned in both P. Yadin 1 and 2, he is not designated as a *strategos*. The practices relating to nomenclature in Nabatean culture just discussed, with the honour of one's family and hence of oneself enhanced by being able to record that one's father was a *strategos* or a prefect, render it highly unlikely that ʻAbad-ʻAmanu had ever attained such an office. Even if he had achieved the lesser position of 'camp commander' (*rb mshryt'*), we would expect to see that mentioned.

This does not, however, exclude the possibility that ʻAbad-ʻAmanu had served the Nabatean king in some role, for example as a soldier in his army. The factor that makes this probable rather than possible is that this would have given ʻAbad-ʻAmanu the social connections needed to secure the employment of Archelaus in the military and administrative service of the Nabatean king in the first place, and thus provide his springboard for greater advancement. Without such help when he was starting out on his career, it is hard to see how Archelaus could have reached the position he did. It is a reasonable view that when P. Yadin 1 was executed five years earlier Archelaus had already begun his rise up the Nabatean *cursus honorum*, having achieved the rank of 'camp commander' (*rb mshryt'*) if not *strategos* at that time.

That the scribe who wrote the document was very alive to the high social status of Archelaus is apparent from the beginning of the document. In the usual way, the scribe began with the date tied to the regnal year of 'Rabb'el the King, King of the Nabateans, who brings life and deliverance to his people'; as noted in Chapter 2, this phrase appeared as part of the king's honorifics in 76 CE, initially in an inscription. In addition, however, the scribe then proceeded to add an unusual feature in the Nabatean legal papyri (and one the same scribe

[22] On 'acquired honour', see Malina 2001: 33–36.

omitted in P. Yadin 3 and which his brother left out when he drafted P. Yadin 1):

> and during the lifetime of 'Obodat, son of Rabb'el the King, King of the Nabateans, who brings life and deliverance to his people, and of Gamilat and Hagru, his sisters, Queens of the Nabateans, children of Maniku the King, King of the Nabateans, son of Ḥaretat, King of the Nabateans, lover of his people . . . [23]

According to the editors, 'P. Yadin 2 has the most elaborate opening of any of the Nabatean documents in the Yadin Collection.'[24] They note that an 'elaborate opening section, almost identical to what we find in P. Yadin 2, and going back even further in time, occurs in an inscription from Petra recorded in *RÉS* no. 1434, dating from the final years of Rab'el's reign'. Yet they do not proffer an explanation for the appearance of this style of opening in P. Yadin 2.[25] In fact, although the words relating to the royal family in P. Yadin 2 appear in this inscription, its wording is actually much more elaborate than P. Yadin 2 in this respect, in that it goes on to speak about several more members of the royal family. The stone containing this inscription was probably embedded in a statue base or over a niche.[26]

The more extensive listing of the royal family in P. Yadin 2 compared with P. Yadin 1 and 3 is to be explained as the work of a scribe laying it on thick for Archelaus, a party to the transaction who happened to be a member of Nabatean elite and who probably knew the members of the royal family personally. The inscription from *RÉS* no. 1434 supports this interpretation, given its connection with the dedication of a statue, probably erected by a member of the Nabatean elite.

There is invaluable evidence for the likelihood that Archelaus would have known the Nabatean royal family and what such familiarity would have entailed in Mark 6:21–29. Here we learn that to celebrate his birthday Herod (Antipas) gave a banquet 'for his courtiers (*μεγιστᾶσιν αὐτοῦ*), senior military commanders (*τοῖς χιλιάρχοις*) and the leading men (*τοῖς πρώτοις*) of Galilee' (v. 21). Although this passage is chiefly remembered for its explanation of how John the Baptist came to be executed, it is also invaluable for its picture of one

[23] My translation; see Appendix 2.

[24] Yadin et al. 2002: 216.

[25] Yadin et al. 2002: 216.

[26] 'La pierre pouvait d'être encastrée, soit dans une base de statue, soit au-dessus d'une niche'; *Répertoire D'Épigraphie Sémitique*, Volume 3, 1918, no. 1434, 141.

way in which Near Eastern kings sought to cement good relationships between themselves and the members of their kingdom's elite.

We may be quite sure that if Herod invited his senior military commanders to his palace for a banquet, King Rabb'el II would also have invited his *strategoi* to similar events he arranged. There is, indeed, direct evidence that Nabatean kings did host such events. In Chapter 2 I quoted a passage from Strabo's *Geography* on the character of the Nabateans that is worth repeating here:

> Since they have but few slaves, they are served by their kinsfolk for the most part, or by one another, or by themselves; so that the custom extends even to their kings. They prepare common meals together in groups of thirteen persons; and they have two girl-singers for each banquet. The king holds many drinking-bouts in magnificent style, but no one drinks more then eleven cupfuls, each time using a different golden cup. The king is so much a man of the people that, in addition to serving himself, he sometimes even serves the rest himself in his turn.[27]

In such settings it is certain that Archelaus would have come to know personally the additional members of the royal family mentioned by the scribe in the date provision of P. Yadin 2. The informality and humility of the king as described by Strabo were a product of the nomadic origins of the Nabateans. With the Nabatean monarchs providing a strong lead by serving rather than being served, it is likely that such attitudes permeated through the members of the elite, such as Archelaus.

What more can be said about Archelaus and ʻAbad-ʻAmanu? The first thing is that ʻAbad-ʻAmanu, owner of the family home it seems (in the absence of any reference to his father), probably lived reasonably close to Maoza. More specifically, ʻAbad-ʻAmanu's house, where Archelaus would have been raised, was likely to have been in a nearby village or town. We have seen in Chapter 4 that the deed recording the loan by Muqimu from his wife 'Amat-'Isi (P. Yadin 1), which ʻAbad-ʻAmanu guaranteed, was executed in Rummon in Moab and that Muqimu dwelled in ʻAina Shuḥaru, possibly a part of Rummon. We have also seen in Chapter 4 why it was likely that Rummon was located reasonably near Maoza. This was possibly the location today

[27] Strabo, *Geography*, 16.4.26; ET from H. L. Jones (1930) *Strabo. Geography. Books 15–16, with an English Tranlation by Horace Leonard Jones*. Loeb Edition. Cambridge, MT and London: Harvard University Press, 367–369.

called Khirbet Umm Rummâne, about 12 kilometres east/south-east of the likely position of Maoza. In Chapter 4, moreover, I set out three reasons that together make it probable that ʻAbad-ʻAmanu lived close to Muqimu: in brief, that they were business partners and it would be inconvenient if they did not live near one another; the proximity of ʻAbad-ʻAmanu would have made it easier for ʼAmat-ʼIsi to enforce her guarantee against him if necessary; and the scribe mentions Muqimu's village but not ʻAbad-ʻAmanu's.

That ʻAbad-ʻAmanu probably lived close to Maoza also means that he and other members of his family were likely to have known people in Maoza and *vice versa*, for the reasons such as inter-marriage between members of both places, trade, and friendship. They were also likely to have heard of any news from Maoza, not least because both places were served by the same family of scribes who would have brought news of the goings on in one place to the other (in addition to anyone else who travelled between the two places). News of this kind would certainly have included the fact that property in Maoza was coming onto the market for sale or lease.

Nevetheless, whatever the location of the family home of ʻAbad-ʻAmanu, Archelaus was not living there at the time of this transaction. Lines 4 and 23 say that he is 'from ḤNH BHDRYT'' (מן חנה בהדריתא). This could either be a place, otherwise unknown, ḤNH BHDRYT', or it could be taken to mean 'the encampment at HDRYT'.[28] In the light of Laila Nehmê's argument that *strategoi* were associated with central places,[29] perhaps the former is more likely. If, however, Archelaus was in command in an important Nabatean town, where he must have lived most of the time, it would make sense to describe him in the deed as being 'from' that place. By way of contrast, in P. Yadin 1, Muqimu is described as someone 'who resides in ʻAina Shuḥaru' (line 14).

Finally, it is worth noting that there is a gap at two places in the deed where something must have been said either about Archelaus or ʻAbad-ʻAmanu. At the start of line 3, just after the words 'Archelaus, son of ʻAbad-ʻAmanu' that end line 2 there is a gap before we have 'the commander, from me'. Coincidentally, exactly the same gap occurs in corresponding place in the lower text (line 21). In line 3 the missing words begin with a *lamed* and there is another *lamed* later in the space. As we know from line 4 where Archelaus comes from,

[28] See Yadin et al. 2002: 219.

[29] Nehmê 2015: 116.

that is unlikely to figure here. Did the missing words tell us something about ʿAbad-ʿAmanu? His patronymic, for example? That seems hard to reconcile with the initiating *lamed* in v. 3 as we would expect a *bet* in *bar* ('son of'). The missing words are unlikely to have designated ʿAbad-ʿAmanu as a person of high status, however, since that would have been mentioned after his name in P. Yadin 1, where he was a party.

'ABI-ʿADAN, DAUGHTER OF 'APTAḤ, SON OF MANIGARES

What we are told, or are able to deduce, concerning 'Abi-ʿadan seems, at first sight at least, to be far more limited. From P. Yadin 2 we learn her name, and the names of her father ('Aptaḥ) and paternal grandfather (Manigares). These are both Nabatean names, as is hers.[30] She owned a valuable date-palm plantation on the southern shore of the Dead Sea, in Galgala' in Maḥoz ʿEglatain (Maoza), the sale of which is the subject of this deed. While we do not know what, if any, other property she possessed, since she had title to a well-equipped date-palm plantation, she may well have owned at least a house somewhere else. But any such dwelling was not physically adjacent to the plantation since it is not included among the properties that abut it when the boundaries of the plantation are described in the deed. Certainly, it is highly likely that she lived in Maoza. The deed was executed there and she is not described as living in any other place, of which we would expect to be told if she did.[31]

We may, however, be quite confident that 'Abi-ʿadan did not come from an elite family. Neither 'Abi-ʿadan's father 'Aptaḥ nor her grandfather Manigares had held high office in the Nabatean state. We can be confident that if they had, she (like Arsaksah daughter of Taymu, the *strategos*, mentioned above) would have ensured the scribe mentioned it.

We do not learn in this deed if 'Abi-ʿadan is married, but nor would we expect to, since even in P. Yadin 1, where 'Amat-'Isi is married, we acquire that information not from how she is described (there, as

30 Yadin et al. 2002: 218.

31 See P. Yadin 6 (from 119 CE) where a man specified to be from En-gedi leases out a property located in Maoza (Yadin et al. 2002: 257–67).

here, with respect to her father and her paternal grandfather) but from the circumstance that her husband is a party to the transaction. Nor do we discover if 'Abi-'adan (or 'Amat-'Isi for that matter) had children. While her being a mother was possible, given that it is not relevant to the terms of this deed we cannot expect it to be mentioned. Nevertheless, in P. Yadin 2 'Abi-'adan comes across very much as a woman vested, in accordance with Nabatean law, with significant legal rights, owning property on her account and entering into a contract to sell it. Whether she had a husband or not seems immaterial to her dealing with her property. In fact, analysis of P. Yadin 3 and 4 to follow in Chapters 7 and 8 will give us strong grounds to believe that she was married, and to a man whose identity we can discover. Yet the impression we gain here—of a wealthy woman exercising her rights in quite a robust and independent fashion—will be more than confirmed, even to the extent of our learning that she was financially dominant over her husband.

That this deed was signed means that at some point in the period leading up to November/December of 99 CE, a point in the year two or three months after the date harvest, 'Abi-'adan resolved to sell a date-palm plantation in her possession and found a willing buyer in the shape of Archelaus. Perhaps other people were interested in purchasing the property. But it was to Archelaus that 'Abi-'adan sold. Although we are in the dark as to how this happened, we can imagine the three main possibilities. First, she may have 'put the property on the market', as it were, by letting it be known that she was interested in selling the plantation, so that the force of rumour in the ancient world would have then ensured that potential purchasers came to hear of it. Secondly, she may have been approached by someone, Archelaus perhaps, to see if she was interested in selling the land. Or, thirdly, she might have heard that someone, like Archelaus, was interested in purchasing a date-palm plantation and approached him directly with an offer to sell. While reaching a view on this is not particularly significant with respect to the current transaction, certainly less significant than it is in relation to P. Yadin 3, the first option seems more likely. The reason for this is that Archelaus was stationed elsewhere and his father also was probably not living in Maoza, although he was reasonably close (as argued above). Whilst 'Abi-'adan and Archelaus could have been personally known to one another already (as they surely would have been if they both lived in Maoza), the fact that only 'Abi-'adan lives there lessens (though it cannot exclude) the chance that they knew one another, or knew one another well enough for either the second or third option to be more likely than the first.

THE ASSUMED PRIOR CONVERSATION BETWEEN 'ABI-'ADAN AND ARCHELAUS

By whatever means, however, at some point Archelaus and 'Abi-'adan probably met and discussed the sale of the plantation. This meeting probably occurred at the date-palm orchard itself, the subject of the transaction. It is central to the approach being taken to archival ethnography in this volume to imagine what it would have been like to be present at that meeting.

As a senior administrative and military man, with all the necessary practical skills holding the position of *strategos* must have required, we can be confident that Archelaus visited and closely inspected the property, probably in the company of 'Abi-'adan, with whom he would have discussed its various features. Did he come alone or with one or more of the men under his command in attendance? What was it like for 'Abi-'adan to be negotiating with a member of the Nabatean elite? Did she invite her husband (if she had one) or another male relative or relatives to be present on this occasion? That she would treat with someone of Archelaus' social status and power on her own seems doubtful.

We can also reasonably assume that as they walked around the orchard 'Abi-'adan would have pointed out to him, and they would have discussed, various aspects of the orchard whose existence we learn of in the deed:

> orchard and spring, and . . . and as above; and date-palms, and sycamores, and all trees, and wood, wet or dry, and arid land such as is in it, and assigned watering periods and water, and . . . and partnership and testamentary rights and . . . and courtyards inside it in every place, and everything (whatsoever), small or large, as is fitting for him in relation to these purchases, areas in sunshine and where the shade falls.[32]

[32] These details come from the upper section of the text (lines 6–8) and those in the lower section are the same (lines 26–28). Square brackets indicating reconstructed

In line 3 irrigation ditches are mentioned. So we have an orchard (probably of fruit trees) and a spring, date-palms, and other trees, including sycamores. The property carried with it the right to 'assigned watering periods, as is proper' that were essential for the date-palms, although the deed does not mention the day of the week or period of flow. Mention of the watering periods explains the presence of irrigation ditches (lines 3 and 22) that were necessary to carry the water from its source to the trees. This source was probably additional to the spring on the land since the watering periods suggest controlled irrigation from a large water supply external to the property. Archelaus no doubt paid particularly close attention to the all-important irrigation works to ensure that they were in good working order or could easily be repaired if they were not. The 'arid land' may have been used for barley production (although even barley would have required some irrigation, given the low rainfall). Reference to 'courtyards' probably also includes any buildings that went with them, as we know from P. Yadin 19, line 5 (a deed of gift from 128 CE) was sometimes the case. Reference to 'everything (whatsoever), small or large, as is fitting for him in relation to these purchases' probably includes agricultural equipment, such as the mechanism for allowing water to enter the drainage ditches and tools. Nothing is said about animals and it is hard to know if they were included or not.[33]

Did this property have a name? We know that this must frequently have been the case, given that when Babatha came to register her agricultural properties in the Roman census in 127 CE, all four of them bore a name.[34] More to the point, however, the property that 'Abi'a-dan sold to Shim'on one month after this sale did bare a name, although only three of its five consonants are clear: *GH..'* (P. Yadin 3, lines 3 and 24). For the sake of convenience I will refer to this property hereafter as Gahadiya (גהדיא), a word not attested in Aramaic but which employs an additional *daled* and *yod* reasonably consonant with the letter shapes of the word in line 3.

features of the text in Appendix 2 have been removed here to bring out meaning; but for the text with those features, see the translation of this document in Appendix 2.

[33] For a discussion of the use of animals by the Nabateans, see J. Studer (2007) 'Animal Exploitation in the Nabataean World', in K. D. Politis (ed.) (2007) *The World of the Nabataeans: Volume 2 of the International Conference The World of the Herods and the Nabataeans held at the British Museum, 17–19 April 2001*. Stuttgart: Franz Steiner Verlag, 251–72.

[34] The registration document is P. Yadin 16 (Lewis 1989: 65–70).

In fact, it is likely that the property Archelaus purchased did have a name. It is not mentioned in line 3 of P. Yadin 2 (where from the comparison with P. Yadin 3 we could expect to find it) but it is likely to occur in line 22, for reasons that I will now set out. On the plate there is little left shown of line 22 except for one *aleph* and the top strokes of a number of *lameds* and the editors have largely reconstructed this line from line 3 and, they state, 'from the tops of some letters in this damaged line'.[35] Whereas in line 3 the text runs continuously as follows: '[an orchard of d]ate palm[s, which (is) in Gal]galâ', they state that in line 22 'something additional had apparently been written in' between 'palms' and 'Galgala'. They reconstruct the missing space between 'an orchard of date-palms' ([גנ]ת תמ[ר]יא) and 'which is in Galgala' ([די בג]ל[ג]ל[א]) as follows: [גנ]ת תמ[ר]יא [ ]ל- [ ]---ל---[די בג]ל[ג]ל[א][36] But what was that addition? At exactly this point in P. Yadin 3, in both lines 3 and 23–24, between 'orchard of date-palms' and 'which is in Galgala' there are these additional words: 'which belongs to the said 'Abi-'adan which is called Gahadiya' (די לאביעדן דא די מתקריה גה--א). A similar expression may well have existed in line 22 of P. Yadin 2, with the first *lamed* in the apparent space corresponding to the *lamed* before 'Abi-'adan. The lower text was often more complete than the inner one (which was written last) and the fact that such an expression does not appear in line 3 is not a barrier to its appearance here. Yet if the name of the property was then mentioned, it cannot have been Gahadiya. The reason for this is that there is, in the editors' view, a second *lamed* at this point in line 22 of P. Yadin 2, followed by three letter spaces, which cannot be reconciled with such a reconstruction. This conclusion, that in P. Yadin 2 the property in question was either not named, or, more likely, was named but that name was not Gahadiya as in P. Yadin 3, has considerable importance for the interpretation of P. Yadin 3 and the details will be found in Chapter 7 of this volume.

It is worth noting that, while this seems to be a functioning orchard, it is unlikely that the vendor, the woman 'Abi-'adan, would have been working it herself. This view is based on comparable evidence from Egypt. Rowlandson has noted that 'The infrequency of female tenants and the concessions to women in the farming of public land are suggestive of a consensus that women could not, or should not, be directly involved in agricultural work.' In fact, no female tenants of

[35] See Plate 22 of Yadin 2002, with line 22 discussed at Yadin et al. 2002: 213.
[36] Yadin et al. 2002: 213.

private land appear in any of the Oxyrhynchus papyri in the Roman period and women tenants are also extremely uncommon elsewhere in Egypt.[37] While 'Abi-'adan was an owner, not a tenant, the rarity of women working the land over which they had control is striking. This did not mean, on the other hand, that women could not be involved in some aspects of agriculture, such as personally collecting rents and having some management roles.[38] It is also possible that 'Abi'adan had a male relative—husband, son, or brother—working the land under her direction or that she had previously leased it to someone, but no such person is mentioned. In Egypt agricultural land was not usually leased to relatives: 'it was normal for the parties to the contract to be of different origins and social status'.[39] Probably 'Abi-'adan had leased the orchard to a non-relative (pursuant to the type of contract we see in P. Yadin 6 [Nabatean Aramaic], executed in 119 CE)[40] and the lease had just expired.

These then were the matters that Archelaus and 'Abi'adan were likely to have discussed when they met prior to his agreeing to purchase the property. In any event, whoever was working in the plantation that day, Archelaus must have liked what he saw because he and 'Abi-'adan agreed that he would purchase the property for the very considerable sum of 112 *sela's* of silver (equivalent to 448 *denarii*). I will now set out the terms of their contract that 'Azur son of 'Awatu must have read out before the other seven people present: the vendor and her representative, the purchaser and the witnesses. The provisions in this deed appear in much the same order and in very similar language in P. Yadin 3 and, to an extent even in P. Yadin 4. A grasp of their character is needed to understand the course of events that lies behind the eventual purchase of the date-palm plantation by Shim'on, Babatha's father. It is instructive to observe how these papyrus documents from nearly two millennia

[37] J. Rowlandson (1996) *Landowners and Tenants in Roman Egypt: The Social Relations of Agriculture in the Oxyrhynchite Nome*. Oxford Classical Monographs. Oxford: Clarendon Press, 263. She notes, however, that a woman was one of two tenants in one fifth-century CE lease from Oxyrhynchus in which the landlord was also female (ibid.).

[38] Rowlandson 1996: 263.

[39] Rowlandson 1996: 264 (at the time this book was published there was only one known lease between relatives, P. Stras. IV 244).

[40] See Yadin et al. 2002: 257–267.

ago express sophisticated concepts of the sort still to be found in conveyances of real property in modern legal systems.

THE TERMS OF THE CONTRACT

Date and Place

Although this is a 'double document', as discussed in Chapter 4, the 'inner' version is nearly as long and detailed as the 'outer'. The deed begins with the date, as computed according to the Nabatean king's regnal year (here in an elaborate form appropriate to Archelaus), and place of execution (lines 1–2; 18–20). This arrangement is typical of Aramaic contracts, while cuneiform contracts from Mesopotamia usually include details of date and location at the end of the document.[41] The third of Kislev was after the harvest of dates and barley and a time in the year when sales and leases of agricultural land were commonly arranged (as further discussed in Chapter 8 in relation to various leases among the Dead Sea legal papyri).

The Operative Section

Then comes the operative, or dispositive, section containing various elements (lines 2–8; 20–28). First is the declaration of sale:

> On that day he purchased, he, Archelaus, son of 'Abad-'Amanu, governor, from me, I, 'Abi-'adan, daughter of 'Aptaḥ, son of Manigares, an orchard of date-palms, which is in Galgala, which is in Maḥoz 'Eglatain, together with irrigation ditches and assigned watering periods, as is fitting (lines 2–4; 20–22).

The dispositive words, 'he purchased' (זבן), come first, after 'on that day', then the name of the purchaser, then the words 'from me' followed by the name of the vendor. Finally we have a general description of the property (a date-palm orchard) in the specific

[41] A. D. Gross (2013) 'The Aramaic Law of Sale from the Papyrological and Rabbinic Evidence' in A. C. Hagedorn and R. G. Kratz (eds) (2013) *Law & Religion in the Eastern Mediterranean: From Antiquity to Early Islam*. Oxford: Oxford University Press, 135.

place, with the assurance that the (all-important) irrigation ditches and watering periods are also being conveyed. These core provisions are thus expressed as a declaration by the vendor (or alienor) referring to the purchaser (or alienee) in the third person. This is typical of Nabatean contracts of sale. In Judean deeds, however, the provision runs 'I, X, have sold to you, Y the place called . . . ', whereas in Nabatean contracts like this one the document emphasizes the actions of the purchaser. In this respect, the Nabatean deeds are like cuneiform contracts of sale.[42] After these provisions, mention is made of the place with which Archelaus was then associated, a town or a camp, as noted above (lines 4; 22–23).

The second element of the operative section is the description of the property, first with respect to 'abutters', the neighbours or neighbouring plots on the four sides of the property (lines 4–5; 23–24). Thus it was bordered on the east by a road, on the west by the houses of Taḥa, daughter of 'Abad-Ḥaretat, on the south by the land of King Rabb'el, and on the north, by the 'shallows' or 'swamp' (רקקא), almost certainly meaning the shoreline area of the Dead Sea.[43] We are not told the extent of the property in terms of area. There is, secondly, a statement that the totality of the orchard is being sold, plus a list of the constituent parts of the property (lines 5–8; 24–28).

One aspect of the boundary description deserves emphasis. The property on the southern side of the orchard purchased by Archelaus was 'land' owned by the king (lines 4 and 24). In P. Yadin 3 (lines 5 and 26) this is described as an 'orchard' owned by the king. This was probably also a date-palm plantation since irrigation water must have been readily available and dates were a valuable cash crop. The presence of royal property in Maoza must have been regarded locally as a sign of approval by the king and his officers of the quality and value of the dates that were produced there. In selling their crop the villagers neighbouring the royal plantation would have been able to claim that it equalled the quality of the royal crop. In addition, however, the question arises as to whether the fact that land owned by his master, King Rabb'el II, abutted the orchard that 'Abi-'adan wished to sell was a factor in his decision to buy it. It is easy to see how in the context of interactions at court Archelaus, probably from a

[42] Gross 2013: 136–137.

[43] See H. M. Cotton and J. C. Greenfield (1994) 'Babatha's Property and the Law of Succession in the Babatha Archive', *ZPE* 104: 214.

non-elite background but with a career on an upward trajectory, might see the benefit of being able to make it known to the king, his relatives, and other courtiers that he had purchased an orchard immediately next to the king's in Maoza.

The third and fourth elements of the operative section are the clauses specifying the price and acknowledging its receipt:

> (sc. All this) the said Archelaus has purchased with silver, (in the sum of) one hundred and twelve *sela*'s exactly. This silver, the full price of these purchases, has been received by me, I, this (same) 'Abi-'adan, the fixed price of the purchases . . . in full value, mature and non-refundable in perpetuity (lines 8–9; 29–30).[44]

M. Alzoubi accurately describes the effect of the vendor's receipt of the purchase money as follows: 'Le transfert de droit de propriété entre en application au moment de la redaction de cet acte, et restera valable jusqu'à l'éternité.'[45] In relation to the provision that the purchase price was 'non-refundable in perpetuity', we will see in Chapter 6 that, in fact, this money was probably repaid in full by 'Abi-'adan and the contract rescinded within a month or so of this deed being signed!

Confirmation of Title Clause

As a vendor of real estate, 'Abi-'adan must, above all, transfer to Archelaus unencumbered title to the property. She had already done that by the provisions of the operative section of the deed just discussed. What then are we to make of the following clause:

> (He is entitled) to buy and to sell, and to pledge and to bequeath, and to grant as a gift, and to do with these purchases everything that he elects, the said Archelaus, from the day on which this deed is executed and in perpetuity (lines 9–10; 30–31).

Andrew Gross, following Y. Muffs, refers to such a provision as an 'investiture clause'.[46] This expression suggests, however, that the

[44] For a detailed study of the acknowledgment of receipt clause in the Aramaic legal tradition, see A. D. Gross (2008) *Continuity and Innovation in the Aramaic Legal* Tradtion. Leiden: E. J. Brill, 46–91.

[45] M. Alzoubi (2012) *Les formules juridiques dans les inscriptions nabatéennes.* Saarbrücken: Presses Academiques Francophones, 242.

[46] See Gross 2013: 141, citing Y. Muffs (1969[2003]) *Studies in the Aramaic Legal Papyri from Elephantine.* Studia et Documenta ad Iura Orientis Antiqui Pertinentia, 8. Leiden: E. J. Brill, 24.

disposition occurs by virtue of this provision, whereas the disposition had already occurred and the conveyance was complete without this provision. Accordingly, a more appropriate designation for the provision is 'confirmation of title', in that it specifies particular aspects of the purchaser's title that have accrued to him by virtue of the conveyance of property that was effected by earlier provisions in the deed.[47]

Warranty and Indemnity

But there are also two sets of additional provisions, very typical of contracts for the sale of land in other settings, which provide more reassurance that this is a property that Archelaus may safely buy. The editors refer to these provisions as a 'defension clause'.[48] This expression unhelpfully lumps two rather different groups of provisions under the one heading and will probably be opaque to those familiar with the English legal system (and its offshoots in other countries), in which context the notions of 'warranty' and 'indemnity' are more useful. Andrew Gross has adopted the expression 'warranty clause' in relation to them.[49]

The first of these additional provisions are *in rem*; that is, they relate to the property itself:

> (I covenant) that (these purchases are) not (affected by) lawsuit, nor by contest, nor by oath . . . and that I, I, the said 'Abi-'adan will clear these purchases from anyone, anyone at all, distant or near, and I will leave (them) unencumbered for you, you, the said Archelaus, for you and for your sons after you in perpetuity (lines 10–11 and 32–33).

By 'clear these purchases' 'Abi-'adan warrants that she will convey the property to Archelaus with what, even today, is called 'clear' or 'clean' title, meaning that there is nothing detrimental affecting title to it. In these provisions she also clarifies that the sons of Archelaus will also benefit from such actions.

[47] There is no real equivalent to this clause in English law, since if the land is sold freehold it is inherent that the purchaser has absolute discretion to deal with the property (subject to restrictive covenants that run with the land or statutory restrictions). Accordingly, a clause like this would be redundant.

[48] Yadin et al. 2002: 226–228.

[49] See Gross 2008: 151–193 for a very thorough treatment of this feature in the Aramaic legal tradition.

The second set of more specific provisions are *in personam*; that is, they relate to Archelaus personally, freeing him from the risk of various forms of claim or litigation:

> And as well, you, the said Archelaus, are indemnified... by me, I, the said 'Abi-'adan, against all that I may claim, or that may be claimed in my name against you in relation to these purchases, pertaining to houses and courtyards, and (in relation to) requital and specification, and agreements and oath, that may still be claimed concerning thorn-bushes and... (lines 11–12 and 33–35).

After this comes a clause of uncertain effect:[50]

> And there is agreement in relation to exchanges and profits .... (concerning) purchases and clearances, as is customary for purchases and clearances as is written in perpetuity (lines 12–13; 35–36).

Apportionment, Tax, and Registration Provision

Just as modern conveyances of real estate often provide for the apportionment of moneys owed in respect of the property on an annual basis, such as taxes due to local councils, with the vendor and purchaser paying an amount proportionate to the months they respectively owned the property, so too does this deed:

> Accordingly, the said 'Abi-'adan has apportioned with respect to this orchard our lord's portion, the leasing-fee for a year, as well, in its (amount of) ten *se'ahs*, until such time as there will be a new edict and this orchard will be registered as a plot of the said Archelaus (lines 13–14 and 37–38).

This provision relates to the apportionment of the amount of crop (*se'ahs* being a unit of quantity not currency), in dates no doubt, owed to 'our lord', meaning King Rabb'el, king of the Nabateans, with respect to the annual 'leasing-fee' (אכרי). We have seen in the previous chapter that אכרי is an Arabic loan word perhaps to be vocalized as *'ikrây*. The precise legal nature of the אכרי is considered in the note on line 14 of this document that is translated in Appendix 2. In essence, it is likely to be a tax based on the king being the notional or symbolic landlord of all the land in the kingdom. The second part of

[50] See the discussion of the possibilities in Yadin et al. 2002: 228.

this clause indicates that the change of title from 'Abi-'adan to Archelaus had to be registered, as demonstrated by the new (royal) edict.[51] This was a case of registration of title, not of obtaining title by registration.[52]

Penalty Provision

The next provision of the deed, which has attracted little scholarly attention so far, perhaps because it appears only in the Nabatean documents,[53] is as follows:

> And if I, the said 'Abi-'adan will. . . . , or will deviate from this (agreement) without consent, I will owe to you, you, the said Archelaus in the entire price of these purchases and with respect to absolutely everything that I may claim or that may be claimed in my name against you regarding them, and to our Lord, Rabb'el the King as well, and claims without consent (lines 14–16 and 38–40).

This is a very draconian clause, whereby 'Abi-'adan is promising to repay to Archelaus the full purchase price of the property if she deviates from the agreement and, possibly (the meaning is obscure) other moneys that may be claimed against him, *but apparently without his having to reconvey the property to her!* So if she deviates from the agreement he could end up both with the property and the purchase price. The only exception is where such a deviation occurs by consent, and this can only mean the consent of Archelaus. This is, in fact, quite a fearsome stipulation that indicates the extent to which Nabatean law stood behind the sanctity of contracts for the sale of property. For it does not appear to entail what in English law is called 'rescission', meaning the restoration of the parties to the positions they were in before they entered into the contract. Rather, it seems to envisage, in some circumstances at least, that the purchaser keeps the

[51] For a fuller discussion on this point, see the note to line 14 of P. Yadin 2 in Appendix 2.

[52] The latter being the view of J. Taylor ([2002] *Petra and the Lost Kingdom of the Nabataeans*. London and New York: I. B. Tauris, 178), who errs in thinking that the deed itself did not transfer ownership. Passing of title in the deed is effected by the clear words of the document and if such transfer depended on any condition subsequent, that would have been mentioned by the scribe.

[53] '(T)his formula is peculiar to the Nabatean documents' (Yadin et al. 2002: 230). It is not covered by Gross, for example (2008: 2013).

property *and* gets back the purchase price, the vendor being left with worse than nothing, since he or she would have lost a property and received nothing in return. It is worth noting that the Aramaic papyri from Elephantine relating to the conveyances of real estate do not contain such a provision; that is, one requiring repayment of the purchase price in the event of the vendor breaching the contract. Instead, the vendor in the Elephantine conveyances offers various kinds of recompense in the event of subsequent claims against the purchaser by the vendor or his/her heirs or by third parties.[54] I will say more on this clause in Chapter 8, in relation to P. Yadin 4, where its presence in that document will provide the key to identifying the two parties to it.

Confirmation of Title for the Purchaser, his Heirs, and Assignees

The last operative provision is as follows:

> And empowered and clean and . . . is the said Archelaus and his sons after him, and anyone else who may acquire this deed by his assignment (of it)[55] regarding these purchases as (provided) in it in perpetuity (lines 16 and 40–41).

This provision has been designated a 'reaffirmation of investiture clause'.[56] Yet such a description is beset with the same problem as describing the earlier clause as one of 'investiture'. This clause does not operate to convey title; it rather re-asserts that the purchaser has title and confirms that title will also vest in his heirs and assignees.

Following this (re-)confirmation of title, it is provided that 'no one may attach a condition to anything that the witnesses have signed' (lines 17 and 41–2).

[54] See, for example, Papyrus 3 in E. G. Kraeling (1953) *The Brooklyn Museum Aramaic Papyri: New Documents of the Fifth Century* B.C. *from the Jewish Colony of Elephantine*. New Haven: Yale University Press, 153–164.

[55] See my note on P. Yadin 1, line 44.

[56] By Gross 2008: 205 and 2013: 142–143, following B. Porten and A. Yardeni (1986–1999) *Textbook of Aramaic Documents from Ancient Egypt*. Jerusalem: The Hebrew University.

The Attestation Clause

According to John Healey, P. Yadin 2 is 'a discarded draft of the sale of the same property referred to in P. Yadin 3'.[57] This view is mistaken, however, since P. Yadin 2 is a signed original document, not a draft, discarded or otherwise. The remains of the signatures were discussed at the start of this chapter. Although the name 'Abi-'adan has not survived in the document, there is space for it and the document is witnessed, which it would not have been if she had not signed it. Four names are partly legible.[58] One person, who probably signed for 'Abi-'adan is called '. . . son of Zaidu'. The name of another witness survives in part: '. . . -'Ilahi'. Also identifiable is the scribe, 'Azur, son of 'Awatu.

CONCLUSION

On the basis of this discussion, we may now return to our starting-point: the occasion when, on the third of Kislev in Rabb'el's twenty-eighth regnal year, the deed was executed. Everyone present must have been very aware of the unusual character of this transaction. Here was a *strategos*, a very senior officer in the king's service, buying land in their village of Maoza. Even if his father lived in a nearby village, so that those present may have known Archelaus growing up and possibly followed news of his career in the royal service with interest, to have him actually buying a date-palm orchard in their village was a very significant event. They could not have considered it otherwise than as a happy circumstance that a member of the Nabatean elite should have chosen to invest in Maoza, an unambiguous sign of favour.

Had 'Abi-'adan agreed to sell the property for something less than its market value with a view to receiving favours from Archelaus in the years ahead? Since, as argued above, neither her father nor grandfather had held a senior position in the kingdom, we must

[57] J. F. Healey (2013) 'Fines and Curses: Law and Religion among the Nabataeans and their Neighbours', in Hagedorn and Kratz 2013: 176.

[58] Yadin et al. 2002: 205.

reckon with the fact that she was someone of much lower social status than Archelaus and probably of negligible political influence. It is hardly likely that she would have risked his disapproval by driving a very hard commercial bargain. Subsequent analysis in this volume will give grounds to submit that she did agree a favourable price for Archelaus. Nevertheless, it will emerge that any discount offered to Archelaus was only a modest one. There is no sense that 'Abi-'adan was overawed by Archelaus as she proceeded to sell him the property.

There are, moreover, factors that may have somewhat lessened the social distance between her and Archelaus. We would not expect Archelaus, as a member of the Nabatean elite still affected by nomadic culture as expressed in its unusually humble monarchs, to be so preoccupied with his own status and importance that he acted in an overbearing way towards non-elite Nabateans like 'Abi-'adan. In this respect, he would have exhibited attitudes very different from those of a member of the Roman senate to the *plebs*. Moreover, even granted the elevated social status of Archelaus, the fact that he was probably the first member of his family to become *strategos* must have impacted on how he interacted with 'Abi-'adan. It is likely, for example, that any disparity in wealth between her and him would have been attenuated by the circumstance that Archelaus was the first *strategos* in his family. If he had only recently attained that position, the opportunities for his personal enrichment that it certainly presented over the long term would have been necessarily limited.

Accordingly, while the disparity between Archelaus and 'Abi-'adan in terms of social status and political power was no doubt pronounced, it is not possible to reach the same view in relation to their respective real and personal assets. Indeed, that the financial position of Archelaus was surprisingly insecure emerges through an investigation of the events that transpired very soon after he had signed this deed. That enquiry will also allow an answer to be given to the puzzling question of what this document, concerning only Nabateans, is doing in the Babatha archive. While we will see that the answer is more straightforward than for P. Yadin 1, it is necessary to consider the main features of the next deed, P. Yadin 3, to solve the puzzle for both documents. To the events that occurred less than a month after Archelaus and 'Abi-'adan executed this deed of sale, and which must have provoked quite a stir in Maoza and in neighbouring towns and villages, we now proceed.

6

Archelaus Rescinds his Purchase

The preceding Chapters 4 and 5 in this volume have begun with a discussion of the execution on a particular date of a Nabatean legal agreement that documented a transaction set in a distinctive context and within a web of personal relationships. This process provided the focus for an archival ethnography that sought to rise to the challenge of not actually 'being there', as contemporary ethnographers are, by imagining that one was present and then developing an argument based on all available evidence as to the nature and meaning of what was happening. By analysing in detail a single event with its cast of characters and what led up to it, it has proven possible to cast light on the social microcosm of the inhabitants of date-producing villages in the Dead Sea region of Nabatea and the social, economic, and political realities that formed part of their everyday experience. All of this has relevance for the story of how Shim'on, Babatha's father, came to buy a date-palm plantation that he subsequently transferred to her.

In the present chapter, while the approach will be the same, a different starting point is needed. This is because no document exists that directly and unequivocally refers to the legal arrangement that must have been entered into if we are to make sense of the information that is to be found in P. Yadin 1, 3, and 4. What was this arrangement? I will argue that it was an agreement reached between Archelaus and 'Abi-'adan that the former's purchase of the date-palm orchard as documented in P. Yadin 2 would be rescinded, that is, annulled *ab initio*, with the purchase price of 112 *sela's* being refunded to him and ownership of the orchard restored to her. There are two dimensions to this agreement; first, the fact that it was reached between Archelaus and 'Abi-'adan and, secondly, the reason for it.

Looking at the matter ethnographically, I will argue that at some point very soon after Archelaus had purchased the orchard there was a discussion between him and 'Abi-'adan about rescission of the purchase. Reasons must have been given during the conversation for that surprising step. They probably also discussed a sale to someone else, since this would be necessary if 'Abi-'adan was to receive money in lieu of what she would have to pay back to Archelaus in the event of rescission. Later in this chapter I will return to the dynamics of their relationship. First, however, I will summon evidence for the fact of the rescission and then explain why the purchase to Archelaus was rescinded and what this meant for his relationship with 'Abi-'adan.

THE FACT OF THE RESCISSION OF ARCHELAUS' PURCHASE

The primary consideration driving the argument that the purchase by Archelaus was rescinded is this: one month less one day after 'Abi-'adan sold the orchard to Archelaus, we find a contract dated the second of Tebet (December/January) in which she is selling a very similar property, though with somewhat different abutters and with a price increase of fifty per cent (from 112 to 168 *sela's*), to Shim'on, of Maḥoz 'Eglatain. This contract is P. Yadin 3 in the Babatha archive. So how do we explain the curiosity of two sales of much the same property to two different purchasers in the space of one month? While Chapter 7 of this volume will be devoted to a detailed consideration of P. Yadin 3, it is necessary to set out here basic aspects of the agreement it records in order to demonstrate that P. Yadin 2 was rescinded.

One preliminary issue must be dealt with first. Some commentators have suggested that P. Yadin 2 never came into effect. If so, it would never have needed to be rescinded. In Chapter 5, for example, we noted John Healey's view that P. Yadin 2 is 'a discarded draft of the sale of the same property' referred to in P. Yadin 3.'[1] I submit this

[1] J. F. Healey (2013) 'Fines and Curses: Law and Religion among the Nabataeans and their Neighbours', in A. C. Hagedorn and R. G. Kratz (eds) (2013) *Law and Religion in the Eastern Mediterranean: From Antiquity to Early Islam*. Oxford: Oxford University Press, 176.

view is mistaken, however, since P. Yadin 2 is a signed original document, not a draft, discarded or otherwise. Nor, as we will see, does P. Yadin 3 refer to 'the same property'. In addition, Jacobine Oudshoorn has suggested that 'if the sale of P. Yadin 2 had been immediately effected the sale of P. Yadin 3 would not have been possible'.[2] This view is problematic for two reasons. First, P. Yadin 2 provides on its face evidence that it was put into effect immediately, in that the dispositive words were provided and 'Abi-'adan expressly acknowledged receipt of the purchase price. Secondly, even if P. Yadin 2 had come immediately into effect (as it did), the parties were always free to annul it by agreement. Accordingly, I reiterate that P. Yadin 2 is a signed original contract recording the purchase of a date-palm orchard that came into effect, with title passing to the purchaser, on the date it was executed.

Although there are a number of differences between P. Yadin 2 and P. Yadin 3 that will be discussed in Chapter 7, two significant discrepancies bear directly on the question of rescission. The first of these is the way the properties are described with reference to abutters. In P. Yadin 2 we have the following boundary description:

> To the east, the road; and to the west, the houses of Taḥa, the daughter of 'Abad-Ḥaretat; and to the south, the land of our Lord, Rabb'el, the King, King of the Nabateans, who brings life and deliverance to his people; and to the north, the swamp (lines 4–5).

In P. Yadin 3 the boundaries are similar but not identical:

> To the east, the road; and to the west, the houses of Ḥunainu, son of Tayim-'llahi, and the houses of Taḥa, the daughter of 'Abad-Ḥaretat; and to the south, the orchard of our Lord, Rabb'el, the King, King of the Nabateans, who brings life and deliverance to his people; and to the north, the swamp (lines 4–5).

The eastern, southern, and northern boundaries remain the same. The difference here is that the boundary on the west has been enlarged by the addition of 'the houses of Ḥunainu, son of Tayim-'llahi'. As the southern side is mentioned first, this suggests that the

[2] J. G. Oudshoorn (2007) *The Relationship between Roman and Local Law in the Babatha and Salome Komaise Archives: General Analysis and Three Case Studies on Law of Succession, Guardianship and Marriage*. Studies on the Texts of the Desert of Judah, 69. Leiden: E. J. Brill, 108.

houses of Ḥunainu lay south of those of Taḥa, that is, away from the sea. The best explanation for this (with the detailed argument deferred to Chapter 7) is that Shim'on bought a larger property and paid more for it (fifty per cent more in fact). Since Shim'on purchased from 'Abi-'adan the same property that Archelaus had purchased from her only one month before, although augmented by some additional land, the purchase by Archelaus must have been rescinded by the time Shim'on acquired ownership.

A curious feature of this conclusion, however, is that there is no indication on the face of P. Yadin 2 that it has been rescinded. In modern legal systems it is common for documents, or parts thereof, that have been superseded to be 'scored out', that is to have lines drawn across their face with some language stating that fact, which lines the parties have signed or initialed. Some commentators have observed that there are no such markings on P. Yadin 2. Before that becomes significant, however, we need to assure ourselves that ancient lawyers also had their clients in some way indicate on the face of the documents that they had been superseded.

Evidence does exist in the papyri from the Dead Sea and from Egypt for a practice something like this.[3] The marriage contract P. Ḥever 69, which was originally executed in Judea in 130 CE, has crossed diagonal strokes over it.[4] Cotton and Yardeni comment that the strokes themselves do not invalidate the document; they merely provide a visual representation that the document is no longer in force, either through death or divorce.[5] An Egyptian papyrus, P. Col 10.249, dated 9–10 CE, recording a loan of money, also has crosses written over its surface. This presumably indicates that the money was repaid. Possibly a receipt was issued to the debtor. K. Maresch and Z. M. Packman, in discussing a cancelled papyrus from the Walshington University collection, provide a useful discussion and

[3] In this area I register my gratitude to assistance provided to me by Dr Giovanni Bazzana of Harvard University.

[4] On this document, see H. M. Cotton (1994) 'A Cancelled Marriage Contract from the Judaean Desert (XHev/Se Gr.2)', *JRELS* 84: 64–86, Plates I–II and H. M. Cotton and A. Yardeni (1997) *Discoveries in the Judean Desert. Volume 27. Aramaic, Hebrew and Greek Documentary Texts from Naḥal Ḥever and Other Sites: With an Appendix Containing Alleged Qumran Texts (The Seiyal Collection I): Desert.* Oxford: Clarendon Press, 250–274 and Plates XLV and XLVI.

[5] Cotton and Yardeni 1997: 250.

list of cancelled papyri in that collection.[6] If this was a practice known to scribes and their clients in the Dead Sea region, as well as in Egypt, why was P. Yadin 2 not subject to the same treatment? The fact that it was not may be what led John Healey (as noted in Chapter 5) to suggest that it was 'a discarded draft of the sale of the same property' referred to in P. Yadin 3,[7] even though it is an executed original document.

Nevertheless, even if P. Yadin 2 had been scored across its face with crosses, the point made by Cotton and Yardeni in relation to P. Ḥever 69—and also probably applicable to P. Col 10.249—is relevant: such marking itself would not constitute the rescission of the purchase. Presumably, 'Abi-'adan and Archelaus both had originals of P. Yadin 2. Archelaus would not have signed either copy, since the transferees in these Nabatean documents did not sign them. It also possible that 'Abi-'adan only signed one copy and gave it to Archelaus. After all, he was the party who would need a signed document to prove his ownership of the property, in legal proceedings for example by him or his heirs, whereas she only needed what today we call 'a file copy'. When they decided to rescind the transaction, how did they put that decision into effect? The fundamental requirement was that 'Abi-'adan would have repaid the purchase price to Archelaus. Further, if he had already assumed occupation of the orchard, probably with agricultural labourers, he would have had to vacate the property. Yet they would probably also have needed documentation. The most useful document for both of them would have been one specifically undoing the transaction, which would also conveniently record the receipt by Archelaus of the price he had paid. Such a document was the best protection 'Abi-'adan could have to block any subsequent claim to ownership of the property by Archelaus or his heirs. Whether the deed of purchase by Archelaus was scored out or not was largely irrelevant to this process, as it would merely be a visual sign that rescission had occurred. In Chapter 7 we will consider the interest that Shim'on had in getting into his possession Archelaus's signed original of P. Yadin 2, and also P. Yadin 1.

[6] K. Maresch and Z. M. Packman (eds) (1990) *Papyri from the Washington University Library Collection, Part 2*. Papyrologica Coloniensia 18. Opladen: Westdeutscher Verlag GmbH, 75–78.

[7] Healey 2013: 176.

WHY WAS THE PURCHASE BY ARCHELAUS RESCINDED?

This rescission of P. Yadin 2 so soon after it had been executed was quite a dramatic turn of events requiring an explanation. Why did this happen? What is going on here? Does the presence of P. Yadin 1 in the archive have any bearing on this big issue? Let us begin considering this question with some explanations that have been proposed.

Current Explanations

Jane Taylor, realizing the significance of the question, suggests that we 'can only guess at an answer' as to why the property was sold to Shim'on a month later. She speculates that 'perhaps Archelaus backed out of the deal; but what seems more likely, in view of the increased price, is that 'Abi-'adan high-handedly rescinded her agreement with Archelaus when she received a better offer from Simon'.[8] Yet Taylor's first option is the far more likely. As noted in Chapter 5, 'Abi-'adan's contract with Archelaus was complete and title passed to him when she took his money in payment; she could not simply have reneged on the transaction. He had significant rights under the contract, including the heavy penalty clause in P. Yadin 2 discussed in Chapter 5. In addition, it is highly unlikely that a non-elite woman would act in such a high-handed way toward a Nabatean *strategos*. Yet that still leaves hanging the question of why Archelaus would have sought to have the contract rescinded and why Shim'on bought a similar property at a price increased by fifty per cent.

Mahdi Alzoubi has made another suggestion for why the orchard was resold to someone else. He proposes that Archelaus had not honoured one of his promises. He then concedes that any such failure could not have concerned payment, because 'Abi-'adan had confirmed that she had received the total amount of the purchase price.[9] The problem with this suggestion is that the only promise that Archelaus made in the deed on a substantive matter and likely to be relevant in

[8] J. Taylor (2002) *Petra and the Lost Kingdom of the Nabateans*. London and New York: I. B. Tauris, 178.

[9] M. Alzoubi (2012) *Les formules juridiques dans les inscriptions nabatéennes*. Saarbrücken: Presses Academiques Francophones, 242.

the circumstances was to pay the purchase price. The two other areas where Archelaus did enter into undertakings, such as his 'agreement in relation to exchanges and profits' (lines 12 and 35) and his undertaking not to add to the deed (lines 17 and 42), were comparatively trivial (in the first case) and highly unlikely to have occurred so soon after execution of the deed or at all (in the second case). Accordingly, it is difficult to see a promise in the deed that was of such a nature that if Archelaus broke that promise 'Abi-ʿadan would have been entitled to rescind her contract with him and enter into a new one with Shimʿon. In addition, it seems unlikely that so senior an officer in the royal service, and someone who was purchasing a date-palm orchard contiguous with one owned by the king himself, would have risked his reputation by a major breach of contract within one month of entering into it.

P. Yadin 1 and the Rescission of P. Yadin 2

Having ruled out the suggestions of Taylor and Alzoubi, what other explanation for the rescission might there be? In particular, although neither Taylor nor Alzoubi mentions P. Yadin 1 in relation to this issue, does that document have a bearing on why Archelaus might have 'backed out of the deal'? The critical observation is that Archelaus, the first purchaser from 'Abi-ʿadan, was very likely the son of ʿAbad-ʿAmanu, the guarantor in P. Yadin 1. A consideration of the known Nabatean names listed by Negev reveals the following: that there is no other instance of ʿAbad-ʿAmanu (or, in its alternative spelling, ʿAbad-ʿAmiyu); that there are indeed only two words in the Nabatean onomasticon beginning with ʿAbad; and that ʿAmanu and ʿAmiyu are both rare, with only one known instance in each case.[10] Accordingly, it would be simply too much of a coincidence if the ʿAbad-ʿAmiyu who is the guarantor in P. Yadin 1 were anyone other than the person of the same name specified as the father of Archelaus in P. Yadin 2. This is especially the case when both deeds were written only five years apart and by scribes who were brothers. It is surprising that nowhere in their discussion of P. Yadin 2, where they discuss the parties to that transaction, do the editors mention the likelihood that

[10] See A. Negev (1991) *Personal Names in the Nabataean Realm*. Qedem 32. Monographs of the Institute of Archaeology. Jerusalem: Hebrew University of Jerusalem.

the purchaser Archelaus was the son of the guarantor in P. Yadin 1.[11] Admittedly, in discussing P. Yadin 1, the editors do state that 'In P. Yadin 2, the purchaser Archelaus' father bears this name.'[12] Yet they make nothing of this. It is not clear, indeed, whether they recognize that this is the father of Archelaus or just a man with the same name. Further, in discussing P. Yadin 2 they also note that 'The name Archelaus is borne by a witness to the transaction recorded in P. Yadin 3 (line 51), but the name of the father of that Archelaus is comprised of only three letters',[13] without making anything of that issue. Jacobine Oudshoorn also misses the connection between P. Yadin 1 and the later documents when she observes as follows:

> P. Yadin 1, a debenture, is drawn up between two Nabataeans, who do not seem to have any connection with the other persons mentioned in the documents, that is, they were probably not related to Babatha's family. Why the document was included in Babatha's archive is not clear . . . [14]

Here she wrongly characterizes P. Yadin 1 as having two parties, when it has three, and also overlooks the fact that the third Nabatean is the father of the purchaser in P. Yadin 2.

Yet the fact that the guarantor in P. Yadin 1 is the father of the purchaser in P.Yadin 2 is the only aspect of P. Yadin 1 that has any connection with the later documents in the archive. Unless it was significant in some way, the very fact that P. Yadin 1 was kept by Babatha's father and then by herself as part of the family archive is entirely inexplicable. That Babatha's father and then Babatha retained possession of P. Yadin 1, a document establishing an obligation of guarantor upon the father of the first purchaser of the orchard, cannot be a coincidence. The question of how a Judean villager came to have and retain in his possession a deed of loan signed by a guarantor who was the father of a Nabatean *strategos* no less demands an explanation.

Indeed, it is this very father–son relationship that, in the light of a feature of the ancient law of succession, provides the probable

[11] See Y. Yadin et al. (eds) (2002) *The Documents from the Bar Kokhba Period in the Cave of Letters: Hebrew, Aramaic and Nabatean-Aramaic Papyri*. Judean Desert Studies. Jerusalem: Israel Exploration Society, institute of Archaeology, Hebrew University and the Shrine of the Book, Israel Museum, 218–219.

[12] Yadin et al. 2002: 188. [13] Yadin et al. 2002: 218.

[14] Oudshoorn 2007: 9, fn 10 (and she makes the same point on p. 55, fn. 30: 'P. Yadin 1 is an act between two Nabataeans who do not seem to have any relation to Babatha or her family.')

solution to the whole situation. This is that Nabatean law provided for what is called 'universal succession', meaning that an heir acquired not just the assets of his parent but also the debts and that Archelaus found himself in such a position when his father, 'Abad-'Amanu, died shortly after Archelaus had purchased the property. It is submitted that it is the death of his father and the operation of the law of universal succession that explain Archelaus's precipitate withdrawal from a purchase less than one month after he had made it.

The Law of Universal Succession

Universal succession is best known in connection with Roman law; indeed it was the fundamental principal upon which the whole structure of the Roman law of succession rested.[15] 'Universal succession' means that an heir succeeds to the entirety of the estate, which includes all the rights and obligations, the assets and liabilities, of the deceased, the totality of which was called the *hereditas* in Roman law. Sir Henry Maine quotes the Latin version of this principle from the Roman jurist Julian: *hereditas est successio in universum jus quod defunctus habuit* ('An inheritance is a succession to the entire legal position of the deceased').[16] Universal succession took place both under a will and upon intestacy. Its origin probably lay in the area of Roman religious beliefs, since it 'was necessary that some one would replace the deceased in performing the duties of the family worship'. At a later date another reason came to assert itself: that creditors of the deceased 'should know who to look to for payment of debts'.[17] Francis de Zulueta explained this principle as follows:

> It was the natural expression of the continuity and solidarity of the early patriarchal family and involved the identification of the *heres* with the deceased for religious as much as for economic purposes.[18]

[15] B. Nicholas (1962) *An Introduction to Roman Law*. Oxford: Clarendon Press, 234.

[16] Justinian, *Digest* 50.17.62; H. S. Maine (1930) *Ancient Law: Its Connection with the Early History of the Family, and Its Relation to Modern Ideas*, ed. Frederick Pollock. London: Oxford University Press, 203.

[17] R. W. Lee (1956) *The Elements of Roman Law, with a Translation of the Institutes of Justinian*. Fourth edition. London: Sweet & Maxwell, 185.

[18] F. de Zulueta (1953) *The Institutes of Gaius. Part II. Commentary*. Oxford: Clarendon Press, 83.

Since the situation often arose that the estate was insolvent, with liabilities exceeding assets, it could be something of a poison chalice for the heir, or to use the Latin expression frequent among Roman jurists, a *damnosa hereditas.*[19]

But did this principle apply in Nabatean law? Here we have a major problem in that the Nabateans have left us very few written records containing their laws. As Mahdi Abdelaziz has noted, we have two direct resources: first, the tomb inscriptions, since they contain many legal expressions, and, secondly, the written papyri from the Dead Sea, such as those in the Babatha archive itself, and an indirect resource in the form of comparative studies of legal systems from the ancient Mediterranean world.[20] Roman law represents one such legal system. Hannah Cotton has recently proposed another resource, in the form of the early Byzantine papyri recently found in Petra and written in Greek that nonetheless provide evidence of Nabatean law.[21] Nothing in what survives of Nabatean law expressly mentions the principle of universal succession. Accordingly, we must come at this issue by an indirect route.

That route consists of situating the Nabatean legal documents in the wider context of the Mesopotamian and, more specifically, the Aramaic legal tradition. John Healey has suggested that the overall impact of the Nabatean legal documents in the Babatha archive:

> shows that the Nabataeans followed the Aramaic customary law tradition which is known from the non-Nabataean texts in the same archive, from the Samaria Papyri and from the Elephantine Papyri. This Aramaic tradition of legal documents is influenced by Assyrian and Neo-Babylonian habits, but nonetheless is very well established.[22]

Andrew Gross has also pointed to Akkadian precursors to Aramaic contracts of sale, while highlighting distinctive features of such documents in Nabatean and Judean Aramaic.[23]

[19] Nicholas 1962: 236.

[20] M. Abdelaziz (2005) 'Notes on the Nabataean Legal System', *Dirasat: Human and Social Sicences* 32: 189–199. Also see Alzoubi (= Abdelaziz) 2012.

[21] H. M. Cotton (2009) 'The Continuity of Nabataean Law in the Petra Papyri: A Methodological Exercise' in H. M. Cotton et al. (eds) *From Hellenism to Islam: Cultural and Linguistic Change in the Roman Near East.* Cambridge: Cambridge University Press, 154–174.

[22] Healey 2013: 172.

[23] A. D. Gross (2013) 'the Aramaic Law of Sale from the Papyrological and Rabbinic Evidence' in Hagedorn and Kratz 2013: 129–164, and also A. D. Gross (2008) *Continuity and Innovation in the Aramaic Legal Tradition.* Leiden: E. J. Brill for the broader picture.

Turning to the law of succession in Mesopotamia, Karen Radner has noted that in the neo-Assyrian period in the event of the death of the head of the house, the heir was responsible for the deceased's debt.[24] This is an example of universal succession. In the neo-Babylonian period as well children inherited the debts of their fathers, not just as creditors but also as debtors, as can be seen in several trial records.[25] Perhaps most relevant for current purposes, however, are the legal documents that survive from the colony of Judean mercenaries in the pay of the Persian king on the island of Elephantine in Egypt in the fifth century BCE. Cotton and Yardeni have noted that the legal documents in the Babatha and Salome Komaise archives all bear 'a striking resemblance to their Egyptian counterparts'.[26] This provokes the thought that perhaps there was also a similarity in the law of succession beween Elephantine and Nabatea.

In this context, it is a matter of considerable moment that Reuven Yaron has noted, with reference to the provisions of two particular documents, that in the Aramaic papyri from Elephantine the 'children of a debtor are liable to pay his debts and their property is liable to seizure'.[27] In the first of these documents, from 456 BCE, a woman expressly acknowledges that she is indebted to a man for a certain sum and if she dies without repaying the loan 'my children are to pay you this money and interest thereon'. If they do not, 'you Meshullam have a right to take for yourself any food or security that you may find of theirs until you have full payment'.[28] The second document is an acknowledgment of loan dated 402 BCE in which the debtor says that if he dies without repaying the loan, then his children and relatives must repay it, and, if they do not, the creditor can seize their personal property from their house to cover the debt.[29] Yaron notes, however, that in the Aramaic documents (unlike the demotic ones) the creditor

[24] K. Radner (2001) 'Neo-Assyrian Period' in R. Westbrook and R. Jasnow (eds) (2001) *Security for Debt in Ancient Near Eastern Law*. Culture and History of the Ancient Near East. Leiden: E. J. Brill, 266.

[25] See S. E. Holtz (2014) *Neo-Babylonian Trial Records. Writings from the Ancient World*. Atlanta, GA: SBL, nos. 13, 32, 33.

[26] Cotton and Yardeni 1997: 159.

[27] R. Yaron (1961) *Introduction to the Law of the Aramaic Papyri*. Oxford: Clarendon Press, 41.

[28] A. Cowley (1923) *Aramaic Papyri of the Fifth Century* B.C. *Edited, with Translation and Notes*. Oxford: Clarendon Press, 30–31.

[29] E. G. Kraeling (1953) *The Brooklyn Museum Aramaic Papyri: New Documents of the Fifth Century* B.C. *From the Jewish Colony of Elephantine*. New Haven: Yale University Press, 260–261.

cannot seize the children of the deceased. According to Yaron, the rule that the children of a deceased debtor were bound to pay his debts 'has its basis in the rules of succession' and is not connected with the *potestas* of the father.[30] Further on Yaron repeats that 'the sons of a debtor are bound to pay his debts'.[31] To the suggestion that is prompted by the express statement of these provisions in the two contracts just mentioned, that perhaps there was no general duty on the part of heirs to pay their father's debts, Yaron makes this response:

> The duty cannot simply be a creation of the contract, since this would imply imposing a burden upon a person not party to it (nor always under the authority of the debtor), and this is not plausible.[32]

On this highly plausible view, the express statements in the contracts are merely assertions of the prevailing law, not attempts to create such obligations.

While we have no direct evidence of a Nabatean law of universal succession, therefore, the existence of such law in the legal systems of Mesopotamia, Rome, and the Aramaic-speaking Judeans of Elephantine makes it likely that this was the case. Once we assume that Nabatean law provided for universal succession—that is, for the heir to inherit the debts as well as the assets of his father—everything seems to fall into place and an explanation for the presence of P. Yadin 1 in the Babatha archive emerges. This explanation is that, after Archelaus had entered into the contract to purchase the date-palm plantation from 'Abi-'adan, his father, 'Abad-'Amanu, unexpectedly died. At this point, 'Amat-'Isi was still owed money under the loan agreement with her husband, Muqimu, and 'Abad-'Amanu, his guarantor. This loan agreement was executed four or five years earlier, but it provided for an initial term of two years capable of extension with her agreement (see Chapter 4 on P. Yadin 1). If the initial lease had been extended by a further term of two years, that would have required another 150 *sela's* rent and also meant that the total repayment would have fallen due not too long before December/

[30] Yaron 1961: 41. [31] Yaron 1961: 66.

[32] Yaron 1961: 66. A further piece of evidence from Egypt merits attention. In *P. Oxy.* LXI 2973 (CE, 103) a debt owed to a tenant by the deceased father of the landowner was still outstanding. While this is relevant, the situation is not quite the same in P. Yadin 1, where the debt is (on my assumption of the death 'Abad-'Amanu) owed by the guarantor of a loan, a loan advanced by a wife to her husband.

January of 99 CE. While we do not know how much 'Amat-'Isi was owed at this point, on this reasoning it could well have been the maximum amount of 300 *sela'*s. There would also have been interest thereon, perhaps at nine per cent per annum, which was probably the local interest rate in this area.[33]

So 'Amat-'Isi turned to Archelaus as his father's heir to repay the outstanding sum under the law of universal succession. In my view, this is far more likely than that she would have acted in accordance with the supposition of the editors that: 'Since she was the debtor's wife, there is the implication that 'Amat-'Isi might forgive the debt at some future date.'[34] This move had the advantage for 'Amat-'Isi that she was able to rely on a third-party external to the family to replenish her dowry. The alternative course, asking her husband repay the debt, would have produced no net increase in the entirety of the assets available to him and her. Turning to Archelaus to repay the outstanding amount meant a net increase in the resource of wife and husband. On the other hand, Archelaus was a *strategos*, so she was risking getting offside with one of the Nabatean elite. But she probably reasoned that Archelaus was not yet firmly established in this position and also had his reputation to maintain in Maoza. If she knew him from the proximity between his father's village and Maoza, she may also have been on good personal relations with him. Her bedrock consideration, however, was no doubt the fact that at stake was a very considerable sum of money that she needed to replenish her dowry, which was the key to financial security for herself and her children were her husband to die or to divorce her.

If, on the other hand, 'Amat-'Isi's husband, Muqimu, had died before the events of 99 ce discussed in this volume had transpired, with the debt still owed to her,[35] Archelaus would have represented her only means to secure its repayment once his father had died after Archelaus had purchased the orchard from 'Abi-'adan. 'Amat-'Isi's would still have faced the same issues of a non-elite person requesting a large sum from a member of the elite, but in this case sheer necessity would have made this an easier course of action for her. It was also one that Archelaus would have well understood.

[33] See P. F. Esler (2014) 'Reading Matthew by the Dead Sea: Matthew 8:5–13 in Light of P. Yadin 11', *HTS Theological Studies* 70.

[34] Yadin et al. 2002: 193.

[35] My lawyer daughter, Sinéad, raised this possibility with me.

As far as Archelaus was concerned, the whole situation must have been a threat to his honour as a *strategos*. He had purchased a date-palm orchard right next to one owned by his king (knowledge of which might already have reached the court in Petra) and now he needed to have the transaction nullified. Nevertheless, it was important for him to maintain his reputation as best he could in the circumstances, and this meant repaying his father's debt. Making life difficult for 'Amat-'Isi, a commoner, as his creditor, a course that would have been attractive to the elites of many Mediterranean societies of the time, would probably have been of little interest to him in view of the Nabatean disdain for such attitudes as discussed in Chapter 2. Moreover, as Raymond Firth has noted, in peasant societies failure to repay a loan does not just trigger economic and legal sanctions, since 'a social, moral and even ritual order may be invoked'.[36]

Since Archelaus was now required to pay off what was likely to have been quite a large amount, the sum of 112 *sela's* he had paid 'Abi-'adan for the date-palm plantation would have been very useful. That Archelaus was the first *strategos* in his family, a *nouveau*, would have meant that he did not have available to him the substantial resources that would have been amassed in a family that had had a succession of members holding such high office. Since the contract records that Archelaus had already paid the purchase price in silver, it cannot have been the case that he simply chose not to proceed with the transaction. Instead, he needed to persuade 'Abi-'adan to rescind the transaction and give him his money back. The fact that it was a *strategos* making the request for a refund must have weighed heavily with her, but she would also no doubt have wanted to find another purchaser. So rescind she did.

One final point to mention is the question of why Archelaus, on becoming liable for his father's debt, did not simply sell the property directly to Shim'on. The main reason for this must have been that the property had not yet been listed in the royal register under his name, as would happen in due course (see Chapter 5). Since the property was still listed on the register under 'Abi-'adan's name, it was clearly

[36] R. Firth (1964) 'Capital, Savings and Credit in Peasant Societies: A Viewpoint from Economic Anthropology', in R. Firth and B. S. Yamey (eds) (1964) *Capital, Savings and Credit in Peasant Societies: Studies from Asia, Oceania, the Caribbean, and Middle America*. London and New York: Routledge, 32.

much more expeditious if she rescinded her sale to Archelaus and sold on the property to Shim'on. Yet this is not likely to have been the only reason for the rescission. Shim'on wanted more property than Archelaus had purchased and he needed to get this via 'Abi-'adan. This brings us to Shim'on's purchase.

7

Shim'on Purchases a Date-Palm Orchard (99 CE)

On the second of Tebet, in Rabb'el II's twenty-eighth regnal year, or December/January 99 CE), one month after Archelaus's purchase of a date-palm orchard from 'Abi-'adan, another group gathered in Maoza to sign as parties and to witness the purchase of a date orchard from her by a different purchaser. As in earlier chapters, let us begin by imagining we are there with them and taking an ethnographic interest in what is being said and done. We will be exploring the actions, roles, and experience of those present and seeking to understand the relationships between them and to reveal the various voices in the material.

First, who was present? Even though in accord with Nabatean practice, the purchaser of the orchard did not sign the deed, he was no doubt there, since he had to pay the purchase price and needed to obtain a signed deed evidencing his purchase. This was Shim'on, a Judean to judge from his name. Although his patronymic has disappeared in lacunas in the papyrus, he is certainly to be identified with Shim'on, the son of Menaḥem, Babatha's father, who is mentioned in other documents in her collection.[1] Then there was the vendor, 'Abi-'adan, the first signatory. Third comes someone who signed immediately after her who also, to judge by the handwriting, signed on her behalf. It is likely he did so because of her illiteracy. In the body of the deed he is called 'the son of LTY',[2] which for convenience I will vocalize as 'Lutay'. His first name appears at one place in the text (see below) and he included it in his signature, although the word has not

[1] P. Yadin 7 is a deed of gift from Shim'on son of Menaḥem to his wife Miryam.

[2] He signs as 'son of LTH' but the difference is explicable in terms of a drift in orthography between *yod* and *he*.

survived there. He is both a party to this transaction—broadly speaking a guarantor (as described below)—and probably a party to another. After him four witnesses signed the document. The first of them is one Archelaus. Of the other three, two did not attest P. Yadin 2 (Wahab-'Ilahi son of Mushalimu and Zabad-ba'al son of Zabadion) and one of them (Wahab-Dushara son of Shulay) may or may not have done so. Finally, the scribe signed; he was 'Azur son of 'Awatu, the same scribe as for P. Yadin 2.

Everyone present on that occasion was a Nabatean except for Shim'on. As we know that there had been Judeans living in Maoza for some fifty years previously,[3] that is a significant *datum* that indicates a high level of tolerance of inter-ethnic commercial transactions on everyone's part that we also deduced from P. Starcky in Chapter 3. Given the power of gossip in the ancient world and the inevitable interest in the doings of the elite,[4] it is likely that all present were aware that the very recent sale to the *strategos* Archelaus had been rescinded. They must have been struck by the curious business in which they were engaged.

In many respects, such as the order of the various clauses and their content, this deed is very similar and at times *verbatim* identical to P. Yadin 2, a fact no doubt explicable on the basis that the same scribe was responsible for both. Yet there are a number of differences. Four of these are major: the purchaser is different; more property is being conveyed; the price for the property is fifty per cent higher (168 rather than 112 *sela's*) and we have an additional party, the son of Lutay. There are also a number of minor, but revealing differences that I will raise where relevant below. I will now discuss the major differences. Little more can be said about Shim'on and his interactions with 'Abi-'adan and (as we will see) Archelaus until the document has been analysed in respect of these other issues, to which I will now proceed. At the end of this chapter, however, I will return to these interactions.

[3] Because three Judeans appear in P. Starcky: see Chapter 3 above. For the text of P. Starcky, see J. Starcky (1954) 'Un contrat nabatéen sur papyrus', *Revue Biblique* 61: 161–181 and A. Yardeni (2001) 'The Decipherment and Restoration of Legal Texts from the Judaean Desert: A Reexamination of Papyrus Starcky (P. Yadin 36)', *Scripta Classica Israelica* 20: 121–137.

[4] See R. L. Rohrbaugh (2001) 'Gossip in the New Testament' in J. J. Pilch (ed.) (2001) *Social Scientific Models for Interpreting the Bible: Essays by the Context Group in honor of Brice J. Malina*. Leiden: E. J. Brill, 239–259 and M. B. Kartzow (2009) *Gossip and Gender: Othering of Speech in the Pastoral Epistles*. Berlin and New York: Walter de Gruyter.

A LARGER PROPERTY WITH A DIFFERENT NAME

The fact that the abutters in this deed differ in a significant respect from those in Archelaus's deed of purchase, indicating that a larger orchard was sold here, was mentioned in Chapter 6. Whereas in the case of both sales the abutters on the east, south, and north are the same (the road, land owned by king, and the swamp), the western boundary of the orchard that Shim'on purchased in P. Yadin 3 encompasses not just the houses of Taḥa daughter of 'Abad-Ḥaretat but also those of Ḥunainu son of Tayim-'Ilahi. This means not only that an extra piece of land has been added but that it is also one contiguous with the orchard that 'Abi-'adan previously sold to Archelaus. Such contiguity is necessary since P. Yadin 3, like P. Yadin 2, still envisages just one orchard, not two. Furthermore, I argued in Chapter 5 that the orchard sold in P. Yadin 2 bore a name that has not survived, but which was not the name of the orchard purchased by Shim'on in P. Yadin 3: Gahadiya.

The plot adjacent to the houses of Ḥunainu lay either north or south of the houses of Taḥa. The usual order of mentioning abutters is east, west, south, and north. The priority thus given to south over north in describing abutting properties would suggest that Ḥunainu's houses lay south, since his houses are mentioned first. Whether Ḥunainu's houses lay to the north or south, however, we have the problem that this new area of land is not described in P. Yadin 2 as the abutter to the south (rather than the king's land) or to the north (rather than the swamp). Yardeni has suggested two solutions, either that 'the borders of the grove and of its additional area were not rectangular', or that some of Taḥa's houses had been sold off to Ḥunainu in the meantime.[5] The latter option can be discounted for two reasons. First, Taḥa's houses are described in the same way in both deeds and we would expect a boundary description that made this point to be expressed more clearly. Secondly, it would offer no explanation for the considerably increased purchase price.[6] This issue is best resolved by suggesting a modified version of Yardeni's astute former suggestion.

[5] A. Yardeni (2000a) *Textbook of Aramaic, Hebrew and Nabataean Texts for the Judaean Desert and Related Material. A: The Documents (in Hebrew).* Jerusalem: Hebrew University, Ben-Zion Dinur Center of Research in Jewish History, 864.

[6] Yardeni suggests the increase in price as 'a third more than that paid by Archelaus' (2000a: 864); at 50% it was significantly higher than this.

The likely answer is that the section adjacent to Ḥunainu's houses did not extend the entirety of the distance to the road on the east (whether it lay south or north of the land adjacent to the houses of Taḥa). If it only stretched part of that distance, the specification of the northern abutter as the swamp and the southern as the king's land would still be reasonable, especially in view of the complexity of also referring to the plot next to Ḥunainu's houses which must have projected somewhat into the southern (or northern) reaches of 'Abi-'adan's land. On this view, it should be noted, it is likely that the extra piece of land was considerably smaller than the parcel that 'Abi-'adan sold to Archelaus. Once we introduce the need for the additional plot not to stretch all the way from the houses to the road and only to occupy a proportion of the western boundary, the result suggests a property roughly one-quarter to one-third of the size of the orchard sold to Archelaus, unless its shape was very strange indeed. This only roughly correlates to the additional 56 *sela's* (a fifty per cent increase) Shim'on was paying for the whole property (see below).

For the probable shape and boundaries of the orchards sold in P. Yadin 2 and 3, see Figures 7.1 and 7.2.

In P. Yadin 3 this enlarged property is named Gahadiya (lines 3 and 24), which is different from the name of the smaller property sold to Archelaus (see Chapter 5). How are we to explain this curious phenomenon?

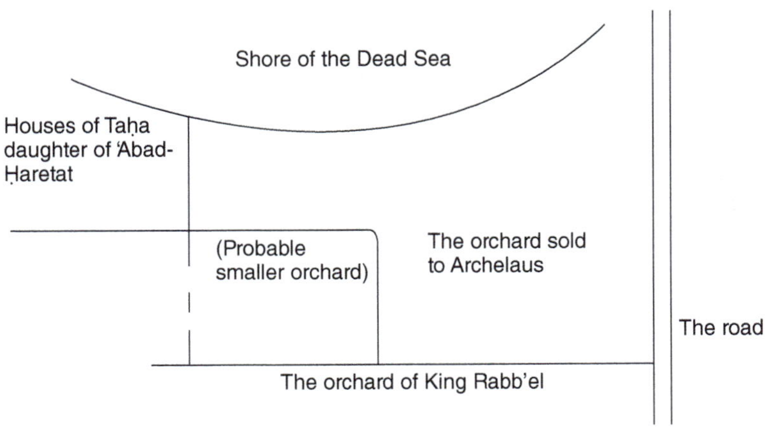

Fig. 7.1. The orchard sold in P. Yadin 2

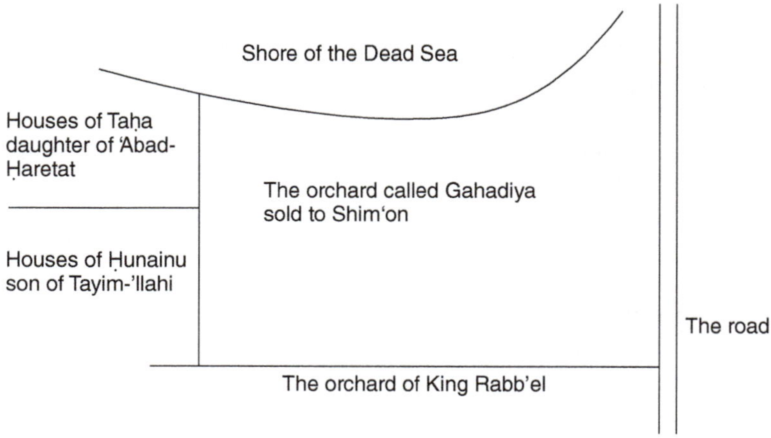

Fig. 7.2. The orchard sold in P. Yadin 3

First of all, this is a name by which the property was known by 'Abi-'adan: she is selling a date-palm orchard belonging to her called Gahadiya, which is in Galgala, etc. (lines 3 and 24). The names that properties bear when they are sold have either been previously attached to them by the vendors or have been retained by those vendors from the time when they themselves purchased the properties. Then, presumably as now, the name of a property aids in its identification (for land registration and tax purposes for example) and even carries a certain cachet that enhances its attractiveness in the marketplace. Confirmation of this common practice in this case is found in the fact that in due course Shim'on (possibly Babatha, but that seems less likely) renamed the orchard *Algiphiamma* ('By the Sea-shore'). For that is the name the orchard bears when Babatha includes it in the registration document of her property for the Roman census in 127 CE (P. Yadin 16).[7] Yet it is hardly likely that 'Abi-'adan would bestow a name on a newly enlarged orchard only to sell it immediately to another purchaser. It is difficult to imagine a reason why a vendor would do that. This analysis leaves one likely explanation: that Gahadiya was the name of the full extent of the

[7] See N. Lewis (1989) *The Documents from the Bar Kokhba Period in the Cave of Letters: Greek Papyri and Aramaic and Nabatean Signatures and Subscriptions.* Jerusalem: Israel Exploration Society, The Hebrew University of Jerusalem and the Shrine of the Book, 66–68 for the text of this document.

orchard *before* it was reduced in size by the excision of a section of land on its south-western boundary that is now being re-attached to the property for sale to Shim'on. As argued in Chapter 5, the smaller property sold to Archelaus probably had a name but it was not Gahadiya. That name was probably attached to it after the excision of the parcel on the south-western boundary, such appellation assisting in relation to its registration in the Nabatean land registry.

One other issue with some bearing on the larger property purchased by Shim'on deserves some consideration: that of water rights. Whereas P. Yadin 2 states that the sale of the property includes 'assigned watering periods, as is fitting' (lines 3–4), P. Yadin 3 stipulates that the property includes 'assigned watering periods; half of one hour on the first day of the week, every single week in perpetuity' (lines 24–25). Why the greater specification? Jacobine Oudshoorn has suggested that it reflects the sentiments of Shim'on, a Judean, who wants it made clear on the face of the document that he will not be doing any work in relation to irrigation on the Sabbath (in breach of the law of Moses).[8] John Healey offers some support to this view, seeing it as evidence of 'willingness on the part of a Nabataean vendor and scribe to accommodate the specific wishes of the purchaser'.[9] Yet Healey also plausibly notes that 'the specification of the day of the week must be simply making explicit what was in any case the fixed irrigation arrangements for the plot of land in question'. He suggests that a rearrangement of the irrigation schedule for the benefit of an observant Jewish purchaser was extremely unlikely, as this would affect other landowners who were also part of the irrigation system.[10] The principal motivation for the change, therefore, is that Shim'on considered the question of water rights too important for them not to be precisely specified. It is his care as a purchaser perhaps more than his ethnic identity (with its religious component) that explains the alteration. At the same time, Shim'on's concern to have his water

[8] J. G. Oudshoorn (2007) *The Relationship between Roman and Local Law in the Babatha and Salome Komaise Archives: General Analysis and Three Case Studies on Law of Succession, Guardianship and Marriage*. Studies on the Texts of the Desert of Judah, 69. Leiden: E. J. Brill, 95.

[9] J. F. Healey (2013) 'Fines and Curses: Law and Religion among the Nabataeans and their Neighbours', in A. C. Hagedorn and R. G. Kratz (eds) (2013) *Law and Religion in the Eastern Mediterranean: From Antiquity to Early Islam*. Oxford: Oxford University Press, 176.

[10] Healey 2013: 177.

rights specified precisely reflects the wider care of agriculturalists reliant on irrigation to ensure reliability of flow and equity in distribution of the water. This issue is still of lively interest to anthropologists, as discussed in Chapter 3.

Perhaps more significant than the possible issue of Shim'on's Judean sensitivity to the Sabbath is the fact that only one watering period is specified for what is now a re-amalgamated property. This means that the smaller plot that I have argued above was re-attached to the orchard for the sale to Shim'on must have been reliant on the same period and time of water supply that served the rest of the orchard. Otherwise there would have been two watering periods mentioned in P. Yadin 3. Geography helps us understand this: the water probably flowed down the Wadi Hasa (or possibly Wadi Numeira or Wadi Kerak [see Chapter 3]) from the plateau to the east and when the sluices were opened for half an hour on the first day of the week into the large orchard, the sluices were also opened for the smaller plot on the south-west. This is a further factor supporting the idea that at some stage in the past there was an orchard, called Gahadiya, that was at some point subdivided and then re-consolidated for on-sale to Shim'on. Additionally, 'Abi-'adan must have been on good relations with the owner of the smaller plot for this arrangement to have worked. I will set out proposals as to the nature of their relationship in Chapter 9.

A HIGHER PURCHASE PRICE

As already noted, the purchase price in P. Yadin 3 compared to P. Yadin 2 has been increased by exactly fifty per cent, from 112 *sela's* to 168 *sela's*. It is difficult to see how Gahadiya could have been fifty per cent larger in size to match a fifty per cent increase in price. In addition, fifty per cent looks very much like a deliberately rounded figure. After all, the chance of the enlarged plot having been exactly fifty per cent larger or more valuable than the property purchased by Archelaus is small. This suggests that while the increased price reflects the larger plot of land sold, there were other elements in the discussions that 'Abi-'adan had first with Archelaus and then Shim'on that explain the respective prices of 112 *sela's* and 168 *sela's*. It is unfortunate that we do not know the absolute basis for the sale price of a date-palm orchard. Presumably it was related to some multiple of the value of the dates and other produce harvested from it each year. It is possible, however, that the price Shim'on paid for the combined property included a modest premium and/or that 'Abi-'adan may have given Archelaus a discount in order to build a good relationship with him in the future. In addition, as we will see in Chapter 9, the whole transaction with Shim'on had implications for the honour of 'Abi-'adan (and indeed for the son of Lutay) in Maoza and charging a small premium helped her in this regard.

THE ROLE OF THE SON OF LUTAY

The Son of Lutay's First Name

Prior to looking at the role of the son of Lutay in the transaction, we should seek to determine his first name. Hitherto the son of Lutay's first name has been thought irrecoverable. Reaching a view on this matter is not essential for the argument that is maintained in this book. Nevertheless, whereas in modern ethnography the actual names of the subjects are disguised by pseudonyms, for an ancient text it is appropriate to give people being discussed their actual names whenever possible. Accordingly, in order to stimulate further discussion and to avoid this person appearing in this volume only under his patronymic, I will now mount an argument as to his first name.

Although the son of Lutay's first name was written in line 44 of P. Yadin 3 and its letter-forms are visible on the papyrus (see Figure 7.3), the editors have not been able to discover a name in them.

Figure 7.3 is a photo of the beginning of line 44 of P. Yadin 3. Lines 43–46 form the onerous penalty provision from P. Yadin 2 mentioned in Chapter 5, whereby breach of a contract of sale by the vendor meant repayment of the purchase price. The previous line (line 43) ended with the beginning of this penalty, namely, the words 'And if we' (והן אנחנה), and the editors rightly propose 'Abi-'adan as the first word in line 44. They also rightly detect the word 'these (אלה; sc. 'persons')' a little further on in line 44. Clearly another name between 'Abi-'adan and 'these' is needed and that name can only be the first name of the son of Lutay mentioned in the previous provisions of the deed as a co-obligor with 'Abi-'adan. In many cases, and

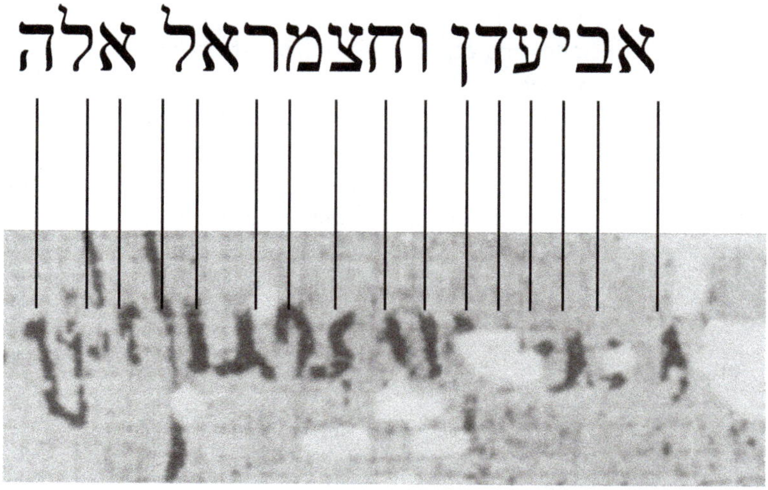

Fig. 7.3. The name Ḥaṣmar'il in P. Yadin 3, line 44

this is clearly one of them, certainty is impossible in deciphering the cursive hand of this scribe. Nevertheless, it is submitted that an Aramaic name is discernible in these letters.

The editors have commented upon the letters that form the son of Lutay's first name as follows:

> ... although all of its letters are preserved their readings are uncertain. The final *lamed* is preceded by five letters, the first of which is a short, vertical down-stroke, which may be *waw*, *zayin*, *daleth*, or *resh*. The second may perhaps be *beth* or *yod*; the third is either *pe'* or *qoph*, and the fourth may be *beth*, *kaph*, or *nun*. The fifth letter is again a short, vertical down-stroke, resembling the first letter. None of these alternatives has yielded an identifiable name.[11]

This description matches their transliteration of the document which reads as follows: אביע[ד]ן ר־פ/ק־־ל; that is, Abi-'adan followed, on their view, by five letters between the *lamed* at the end of the word that must be the son of Lutay's first name and the *nun* at the end of Abi-'adan.[12] It is evident, however, from the photograph of the papyrus

[11] Y. Yadin et al. (eds) (2002) *The Documents from the Bar Kokhba Period in the Cave of Letters: Hebrew, Aramaic and Nabatean-Aramaic Papyri*. Judean Desert Studies. Jerusalem: Israel Exploration Society, Institute of Archaeology, Hebrew University and the Shrine of the Book, Israel Museum, 242.

[12] Yadin et al. 2002: 240.

(see Figure 7.3) that there are six letters between the final *nun* of Abi-'adan and the final *lamed* of the word that constitutes the son of Lutay's first name.

From inspection of the word in the papyrus we learn the following. Although the first of the six letters is almost certainly a *waw* (a possibility the editors themselves suggest), this is not part of the son of Lutay's name. In fact, I submit that it is merely a conjunctive *waw*: ''Abi-'adan *and*...' The conjunctive is appropriate since the two of them together are referred to as אנחנה ('we') at the end of the previous line and as אלה ('these [persons]') immediately after the name we are seeking to decipher.

So we have a name of six letters ending in *lamed*. There is a measure of uncertainty about the first letter of the name, but a probable solution suggests itself. After the *waw*, which is fairly close to perpendicular from the line, the straight stroke of this first letter of the name has a pronounced lean to the left. In addition, the top point of the stroke has just begun to move back downward at an acute angle to the first line, but with the left stroke starting just a little below the top of the stroke on the right, thus producing an imperfectly formed inverted 'v' shape. Yet in my view this is not a *beth* or a *yod* as the editors seem to suggest. This is the letter *het*, of which there are numerous examples in other parts of this document.[13]

The second letter is also not *beth* or *yod* but probably a *sade*, as is supported by comparison with instances of this letter elsewhere in the text. For example, a very similar shape can be seen in the terminal *sade* in the last word of P. Yadin 3, line 32 (חרץ), with the long downward stroke for the terminal form not obscuring the resemblance.[14] Other examples occur elsewhere,[15] although in line 44 the letter is more upright in form. *Het* followed by *sade* produces the Aramaic word for 'arrow'. While there are examples of a different

[13] Examples appear in P. Yadin 3, lines 23 (מחות), 25 (חדה), 26 (חנינו), 28 (תחומיה), and 29 (חדד), to name just a few. Also see A. Yardeni (2000b) *Textbook of Aramaic, Hebrew and Nabataean Texts from the Judaean Desert and Related Material. B: Translation, Paleography, Concordance (in Hebrew and English)*. Jerusalem: Hebrew University, Ben-Zion Dinur Center of Research in Jewish History, 245–246 for a discussion of the development of *het* in Nabatean script, with examples from first century CE cursive calligraphic script in ink on p. 246 showing the form of the letter apparent in the name under discussion.

[14] Yardeni lacks this precise form for *sade* in her discussion of the letter's development in Nabatean (2000b: 259).

[15] For example, in צדק in line 28 and אצפא in line 35.

letter, *tau*, that are close to this shape,[16] reading a *tau* would mean we had a name starting with the Aramaic word for 'sackcloth' or 'plank', which seems unlikely.

Then comes the third letter which, from comparison with other examples in the document, is probably not *pe* or *qoph*, but medial *mem* that is, admittedly, in an incompletely rounded form that nevertheless occasionally appears elsewhere in the writing of this scribe.[17]

The fourth letter is not *beth*, *kaph*, or *nun*, but I submit is either *resh* or *daled* in a shape quite common in these papyri for medial *resh* or *daled*.[18] In my view it is more likely to be a *resh*. By reading *resh* as the fourth letter instead of *daled*, we produce the word מר, or 'Lord', whereas reading *daled* would produce מד, for which the only possible meaning in Aramaic as a common noun would be 'priest's cloak', which makes no sense in this context; that is, coming after the Aramaic word for 'arrow'. The penultimate letter, a short stroke with a very slight expansion at the bottom, is undoubtedly *aleph*. There are numerous instances of this form of *aleph* in the document. The sixth and last letter is the *lamed*. Negev lists thirty-nine Nabatean names ending in *lamed* and thirty (or seventy-seven per cent) of them are preceded by *aleph*.[19] That is to say, the *aleph–daled* combination, meaning אל (*'il*) or God, is very common in the Nabatean onomasticon.

Accordingly, this scrutiny of what remains of the letter-shapes of this name makes probable the following word: חצמראל ('Ḥaṣmar'il'). This is recognizable Aramaic and also produces the magnificent name: 'Arrow of the Lord God', the word *ḥaṣ* (חצ) being a common Aramaic word for 'arrow',[20] *mar* (מר) meaning 'lord' and *'il* (אל) meaning 'god'.

[16] For example, the second letter in the first word in P. Yadin 2, line 6 (ותבת) and in וש]ותפו in line 7.

[17] For example in גמרין in line 9 of P. Yadin 2, in תחומיה in line 25 of P. Yadin 2 (unless the letter is damaged), and in קדמיכי in line 14 of P. Yadin 4 (perhaps the clearest example), while the *mem* in שמאלא in line 27 of P. Yadin 3 is rather similar. Although Yardeni has not quite this particular shape for *mem* (2000b: 252–254), some of her examples come close.

[18] For examples see the *resh* in ולמרהן in P. Yadin 3, line 33, or אחריך in P. Yadin 3, line 36. Yardeni does not include this particular shape for *resh* in her discussion (2000b: 261).

[19] A. Negev (1991) *Personal Names in the Nabataean Realm*. Qedem 32. Monographs of the Institute of Archaeology. Jerusalem: Hebrew University of Jerusalem.

[20] See the numerous instances cited by J. Hoftijzer and K. Jongeling (1995) *Dictionary of the North-West Semitic Inscriptions*. With appendices by R. C. Steiner, A. Mosak Moshavi, and B. Porten. Two volumes. *Handbuch der Orientalistik* 1/21. (Part 1). Leiden: E. J. Brill, 397–398.

If we may now proceed on the assumption that the name is Ḥaṣ-mar'il, the next hurdle to be overcome is that this is an unusual name among the Nabateans. No other Nabatean name so far discovered begins with *ḥaṣ-* (*'arrow of'*). In addition, whereas most Nabatean personal names have two elements, this one has, or seems to have, three (or two if Lord-God counts as one element). Most Nabatean names ending in *'il* or *'Ilahi* are composed of a triliteral word followed by the divine name, where the lack of vocalization renders it difficult to know if the triliteral is verbal or nominal in form. Thus, the name of one of the witnesses to P. Yadin 3, והבאלהי, vocalized by the editors as *Wahab-'Ilahi*, could mean 'God gives' or 'gift of God'. There is also an Aramaic verbal form חצץ, 'to shoot arrows', but that word has not yet shown up in Nabatean. This suggests that we should accept that here the word is nominal in meaning, 'arrow', not 'shoot arrows'. Yet that we have four letters in the name before the divine element indicates that this name is different in form from the usual pattern in any event. Nevertheless, there are some Nabatean names that do have four letters before the word 'god'.[21] This brings us to the מראל– (*-mar'il*) part of the name.

On one view, this expression is already found in Aramaic onomastics—in the name מראלמלכו.[22] Although this could be interpreted 'The Lord God is his king', it might also be interpreted as Mar-al-Maliku ('Lord the King') or 'Our Lord Malik' with Littmann.[23] Nevertheless, there are other grounds for regarding מראל– ('Lord God') as an acceptable ending for a Nabatean name. Hoftijzer and Jongeling note, in a section covering instances where the word 'is further defined by another substantive or a name, used to indicate a deity', one such use of מרא ('lord') is in the expression מרא אל,[24] meaning 'Lord of the gods'. It is not a big step from this to מראל (*mar'il*', 'Lord God').

The Central Aspects of the Role of the Son of Lutay in the Transaction

The central aspects of the role of Ḥaṣmar'il in the transaction, although not yet adequately explained in scholarship, can be deduced

[21] For examples, see Negev 1991, nos 708, 830, 1052, and 1228.

[22] Negev 1991: 41 (no. 686).

[23] See E. Littmann (1913) 'Semitic Inscriptions' in *Syria. Publications of the Princeton Archaeological Expeditions to Syria* (Div. IV, Sect. A, Leyden) 59, no. 72 and RES 2093. Leiden: E. J. Brill, 1–93.

[24] Hoftijzer and Jongeling 1995 (Part 2): 686.

from the terms of P. Yadin 3 (within the wider context of P. Yadin 3 and 4). In lines 42–43 we find the following critical provision (the corresponding part of the inner text, line 16, being lacunate):

וכל די כתיב במתנא בה בר לתי דנה ----ן ועלה די אביעדן דא עליך

The editors translate this as follows:

> And everything that is written in it as a condition (**or**: gift), this (same) son of LTY . . . , and regarding what [this] (same) 'Abi-'adan (has stipulated) pertaining [to] you.[25]

The word missing after Lutay, with five letters the last of which is *nun*, has hitherto defied attempts to decipher it. But it must mean something like 'confirms' or 'agrees to'. The editors remain silent on what the word might have been and finding an Aramaic expression with five letters ending in 'n' that can be reconciled with the physical remains on the papyrus has proved very challenging. I have not been able to find an appropriate candidate: a word like מהימן ('trustworthy') carries a suitable meaning but the remains of the Nabatean Aramaic letters (in this scribe's hand) on the papyrus do not match the required letters. Nevertheless, it is not difficult to deduce the general sense of the missing word—something like 'agrees to' or 'is legally responsible for' is needed.

Unfortunately, the editors' translation of the first section of the provision above ('And everything that is written in it as a condition (**or**: gift),') is, in my view, a misinterpretation of the Aramaic in three respects, and this has the consequence of rendering difficult their efforts to make sense of this deed (or indeed of P. Yadin 4). First, although the editors prioritize 'condition' over 'gift' as a translation of מתנא, as soon as we replace 'as' with 'in' (the common meaning of ב) the expression 'in a condition' makes little sense—for the reason that a (legal) condition normally deals with one matter and to interpret it as a container for 'everything written' is a very unnatural reading. The words 'everything written' make better sense in reference to a deed, with its multiplicity of provisions. This impression finds further support in the emphatic word בה, 'in it', that appears after מתנא and makes better sense in relation to a deed than a condition. Therefore, we may exclude 'condition' and suggest that the words וכל די כתיב במתנא בה בר לתי דנה ----ן should be translated, 'and

[25] Yadin et al. 2002: 240.

everything that is written in a grant (מתנא), in it, the said son of Lutay . . . '.

Secondly, this translation drives a wedge between whatever 'it' might refer to in the word 'in it' (בה) and 'condition' or 'gift'. This is unfortunate, since the 'it' here is a grant (מתנא). This expression, literally and correctly, means, 'And everything that (is) written in מתנא, in it, the said (literally, 'this same') son of Lutay . . . ' It is strained Aramaic to read במתנא as '*as* a condition (**or**: gift)', since prefixed ב normally means 'in'.

Thirdly, the following consideration also pushes one towards translating מתנא as 'a grant' or 'a gift' rather than 'a condition'. The editors suggest two possible translations for מתנא.[26] The first is that the word is derived from נתן, meaning, 'he gave, granted'. In this case it would mean 'a gift' or 'a grant'. They even note that if the word meant 'gift' it 'might refer to some additional part of the parcel contributed by the guarantor, which could be the reason for the higher sale price, or to pay-off of some debt owed to 'Abi-'adan by the guarantor'.[27] Having thus come tantalizingly close to what I will argue in this chapter and Chapter 8 was the truth of the matter, the editors then proceed to their second proposal, namely, that מתנא could represent a variation of תנא, meaning 'condition, authorization'. They prefer this latter option since 'condition' is the translation they offer for the word in their translation of the line, with 'gift' appearing as an alternative in brackets after it (as noted above). Although תנא is a known Aramaic word and, according to the online Aramaic Lexicon, includes among its various meanings 'contract', it has no certain appearance in the Nabatean or Judean Aramaic documents in the Babatha archive.[28] A verbal form of the word, which the editors surmise derives from the root *t-n-y/t-n-'*, 'to make a condition', possibly occurs in P. Yadin 2, line 17 (מתנו), although it could also be another word altogether.[29] Nor does it appear among the Aramaic in the collection of Dead Sea papyri edited by Cotton and Yardeni.[30] Nor do the editors offer any other instance of מתנו meaning 'condition'. They do cite the word meaning 'condition, authorization' ('permission'

[26] Yadin et al. 2002: 243–244. [27] Yadin et al. 2002: 244.

[28] See Yadin et al. 2002: 398–404 (Judean Aramaic wordlist) and 405–410 (Nabatean Aramaic wordlist). These helpful lists having been prepared by Andrew Gross (personal communication).

[29] Yadin et al. 2002: 243–244 and 230 (on P. Yadin 2, line 17).

[30] Cotton and Yardeni 1997: 349–359 (Aramaic wordlist).

being another possible translation) in a Nabatean-Aramaic sepulchral inscription from Arabia,[31] but in my view there the word means 'authorization' or 'permission', not 'condition', so this evidence does not support their preferred translation 'condition'.[32]

Unlike the difficult task involved in translating מתנא as 'condition', which is the editors' preference, the case for it meaning 'grant' or 'gift' is very strong. The word actually appears in this sense, in various forms, twenty-five times in P. Yadin 7 (a deed of gift from 120 CE that covers realty and personalty). It also appears quite frequently with this meaning elsewhere in Aramaic and it has a close Hebrew equivalent in מתנה. Accordingly, I submit that it is far preferable to interpret מתנא as 'a grant' or 'a gift' in line with its established usage in P. Yadin 7 (and elsewhere) than to adopt a postulated connection with an otherwise unattested word תנא. Moreover, the verbal form למנתן ('to grant' or 'to give') is one of the standard rights regularly included in a sale of land to a purchaser; it appears not only in P. Yadin 2, lines 9 and 31 but also in this very document at lines 10 and 33. Since it contains writing, the מתנא must be envisaged as a document, most likely (given the context) a legal document, a deed, which provides for a disposition of property in the form of a grant or gift.

It is submitted that while this evidence alone makes a good case for translating מתנא as 'a grant' or 'a gift', further evidence for this view will emerge from an analysis of further provisions of this deed and of P. Yadin 4. Accordingly, I translate the critical words in lines 42 and 43 as follows:

> And everything that is written in a grant, in it, the said son of Lutay, (is responsible for) and (also) concerning what the said 'Abi-'adan (has agreed) pertaining to you (sc. Shim'on).

Ḥaṣmar'il the son of Lutay, is thus assuming responsibility for the terms of 'Abi-'adan's sale to Shim'on and also for everything written in a legal document taking the form of a grant. While we will return to the question of the parties to the grant in Chapter 8 (in relation to P. Yadin 4), the son of Lutay was very likely to have been one of them, otherwise why would we find him in P. Yadin 3 confirming its terms? Moreover, the obligations in the envisaged grant shouldered by the

[31] Yadin et al. 2002: 230–231.

[32] Thus they quote the text as, 'No person at all may be buried in this sepulcher except the one for whom authorization of burial is written in these deeds of consecration, forever' (Yadin et al. 2002: 231).

son of Lutay must be directly owed to someone, and that someone must either be 'Abi-'adan or Shim'on (or, conceivably, both)—a matter upon which P. Yadin 4 will provide the answer—while the second set of obligations represents the son of Lutay guaranteeing 'Abi-'adan's obligations to Shim'on.

Yet what substance was there to the guarantee provided by the son of Lutay? How does one guarantee a sale of land? After all, only the owner of a property can convey title to it, as expressed in the Latin maxim *nemo dat quod non habet* ('No one gives what he/she does not have').[33] So if 'Abi-'adan did not convey title to her property, the son of Lutay could not do it for her. Yet that this was a guarantee with real force emerges in the penalty provision discussed in Chapter 6. For P. Yadin 3 provides that in the event that 'Abi-'adan *and the son of Lutay* alter or deviate from the agreement, *they* shall owe the entire purchase price to Shim'on and everything that they may claim or that may be claimed against him in their name regarding the purchase (lines 16–18 and 43–45).

Since P. Yadin 3 provides for the son of Lutay to be responsible for 'everything that is written in a grant' and for 'what the said 'Abi-'adan (has agreed) pertaining to' Shim'on, meaning in P. Yadin 3, it is clear that Shim'on regarded both deeds as necessary for his acquisition of the plantation. Yet the language used does not necessarily indicate that both documents would be in binding force at the same time. The reference to 'everything written in *a* grant', rather than '*the* grant', suggests that it did not exist at the time P. Yadin 3 was executed, but was rather a document that the parties contemplated would be brought into existence at some future date. If so, Shim'on must have had a high level of trust in his Nabatean neighbours that they would have the grant drafted and put into effect so as to satisfy the requirements of this provision. That there was a future dimension to the grant will find confirmation in the terms of P. Yadin 4 (see Chapter 8).

The Son of Lutay, 'Abi-'adan, Shim'on, and the Grant

We must now enquire what is going on here. What is the grant that the parties have in view and why is the son of Lutay acting as a

[33] The maxim is more precisely expressed in the alternative form: *Nemo plus iuris ad alium transferre potest quam ipse habet* ('No one has the capacity to transfer more title to another than he himself possesses').

guarantor for 'Abi-'adan in her sale to Shim'on? At this point we should note the legal significance of a 'gift' or a 'grant', especially the need to distinguish them from a sale. In a sale what lawyers call 'valuable consideration' in the form of the purchase price passes from the purchaser to the vendor in return for title to the property. In a gift no such valuable consideration passes; the donor provides the property to the donee *gratis*. The word 'grant' appears to offer something of a position midway between gift and sale. It certainly refers to a transfer of property, yet it is not a sale, so that the use of 'purchase price' would not usually be appropriate in relation to it. On the other hand, it could be used in a context where the transferor was getting something of value in return even if that something was not a 'purchase price' in the strict sense, in which case 'purchase price' might not be entirely inappropriate. As the course of my argument in the next chapter of this volume will indicate that the meaning of מתנא in line 43 is a grant in this sense and not a 'gift' provided *gratis*, I will henceforward generally use the word 'grant' in relation to it.

As to the identity of the grantor, this is very likely to have been the son of Lutay. This conclusion flows from the fact that it is he who stands behind the grant, by asserting his legal responsibilities in relation to it, as argued above. The only other possible role available is that of grantee, yet it would make little sense for such a person to assume responsibilities for the transfer as the son of Lutay does here. It is upon the person who has owned and possessed property that the duty falls to ensure that his or her gift or grant of it occurs without any problems attached, as can be seen in the detailed provisions in the deed of gift dated 120 CE from Shim'on the son of Menaḥem to his wife Miryam (P. Yadin 7).

The very fact that the son of Lutay, probably the grantor of the grant that is envisaged, enters the scene in a transaction in which the major change is that the area of orchard being conveyed has been enlarged sufficiently to justify, at least in part, a fifty per cent price increase, strongly suggests that the two issues are connected. To be more precise, the combination of these two additional features in the sale to Shim'on raises the possibility that the grant was the source of the extra piece of orchard he purchased, as compared with Archelaus. This would suggest that 'Abi-'adan was to acquire the extra piece of orchard from the son of Lutay, who was its owner, and then amalgamate it with her existing holding and sell on the enlarged orchard, called Gahadiya, to Shim'on. Further argument will be required to strengthen this view, by proving that 'Abi-'adan was to receive property from the son of Lutay, in particular with respect to P. Yadin 4 in Chapter 8. There we will need to assess what light that document sheds on the identities of the grantor and the grantee and on the subject matter of the grant. For the moment I repeat a point made earlier, that the deed of grant was probably not in existence at the time P. Yadin 3 was executed (and, if so, no grant could yet have occurred). This would mean that 'Abi-'adan was selling to Shim'on, and he was agreeing to buy and paying for, a property part of which she did not yet own when P. Yadin 3 was signed. Shim'on was able to rely on the fact that the son of Lutay was not only promising to abide by a grant but also guaranteeing all of the provisions in 'Abi-'adan's sale to Shim'on that included title passing in the whole property, including that in the south-west corner apparently owned by Ḥaṣmar'il. Analysis of P. Yadin 4 will set out further argument in support of this.

Again, at this point I will raise, though defer answering until after analysis of P. Yadin 4, certain intriguing questions that arise from the fact that the son of Lutay was assuming responsibility not only for the grant but also for 'Abi-'adan's obligations to Shim'on. These questions are: what is the basis for his undertaking the role of guarantor of her contractual promises to the Judean purchaser? More particularly, was some relationship needed between them for him to do so and, if there was, what was the nature of that relationship? Relevant to that discussion is the fact that in the attestation clause at the end of P. Yadin 3 the same handwriting appears for the son of Lutay and for 'Abi-'adan. It is for this reason that the editors observe the son of Lutay 'presumably signed for her'.[34] A detailed examination of the relationship between the son of Lutay and for 'Abi-'adan, however, must await analysis of P. Yadin 4. But before proceeding to P. Yadin 4, let us first consider one particular aspect of the attestation clause in P. Yadin 3 and how it illuminates the personal dimensions underlying this deed.

ARCHELAUS AS SIGNATORY TO P. YADIN 3

As previously noted, in the Nabatean legal papyri the order of people who sign is, first, the obligors (such as those transferring title to

[34] Yadin et al. 2002: 233.

someone else), followed by the witnesses and, finally, the scribe. The obligee, the person receiving the property, does not sign. Thus in P. Yadin 3, 'Abi-'adan signs, as does Ḥaṣmar'il the son of Lutay. Then, as noted above, come four witnesses, the first of whom is Archelaus, son of . . . (a name of three letters). The circumstance that a man named Archelaus had pulled out of the purchase of the orchard only a month before obliges us to ask the question of whether this is the same Archelaus who now witnesses the second purchase of this property (albeit somewhat enlarged) to Shim'on. The editors do not ask this question, but they do note that the name of Archelaus's father is here written with three letters that are indecipherable except for a possible medial *aleph*. Since the father of the Archelaus who first purchased the property in 99 CE was 'Abad-'Amanu, a name having many more than three letters, that may seem to be the end of the matter—the two men, one might well conclude, can hardly be the same person. Yet I submit that there are a number of factors that cast serious doubt over that conclusion.

First of all, it is worth noting how rare is the name Archelaus in Nabatean onomastics. This particular Archelaus is, in fact, the only instance among the 1,249 Nabatean names listed by Negev.[35] Moreover, among nearly thirty Nabateans who appear in P. Yadin 1–4, either as parties, witnesses, scribes, or the fathers or mothers, or grandparents of any of these, Archelaus is the only one to bear a Greek name. It is possible that his having been given a Greek name by his father or mother was to assist his eventual entry into the king's service, in light of the fact that one of the Nabatean kings, Aretas III in the mid first century BCE, had referred to himself on his coinage as 'philhellene' (see Chapter 2) and this attitude may have persisted among the royal family. If Archelaus's parents were motivated by such a consideration in giving him that name, it would be another example of the phenomenon of 'prestige bias' mentioned in Chapter 2. Given the uniqueness of Archelaus in the Nabatean onomasticon and the highly unusual nature of a Greek name at all among this group of Nabateans, one really has to wonder at the extremely low odds of another Archelaus turning up. This seems even more improbable when this Archelaus is the first person to witness P. Yadin

[35] Negev 1991: 15 (No. 144). He learned of this person from Y. Yadin (1962) 'The Expedition to the Judean Desert, 1961: Expedition D—The Cave of the Letters', *Israel Exploration Journal* 12: 240.

3 after 'Abi-'adan and the son of Lutay, which gives him the place of honour among the witnesses to the transaction, as would be appropriate for a member of the Nabatean elite.

But the position of Shim'on is also relevant to this question. He faced the potential problem that one day Archelaus (or his heirs or assignees) might arrive in Maoza waving a signed copy of P. Yadin 2 and claiming that he (or they) had title to the orchard by prior acquisition and not Shim'on.[36] While I will discuss this risk and the steps Shim'on took to mitigate it in more detail later in this chapter, one solution was to ask the previous purchaser of the property, Archelaus, to witness his purchase of the property. This is what most likely happened here and it represents a further reason for it being Archelaus, the son of 'Abad-'Amanu, who witnessed this document.

The question is how can this view be reconciled with the fact that Archelaus's father's name in P. Yadin 3 only has three letters, the middle one of them probably an *aleph*? To begin with, there is something rather unusual about this name. In Negev's list of Nabatean names, only 127 out of 1,249, or about ten per cent, comprise three letters.[37] And only one of these names features a medial *aleph*. The likely solution to the problem rests in the solution that this is not a name in the usual course, but a nickname, a popular phenomenon in this world.

In an important article Joseph Naveh has proffered abundant evidence that 'Informal names and nicknames were commonly used in Semitic society.'[38] A man had a personal name and a patronymic ('X son of Y') that were used outside his family and circle of friends and commonly in legal documents, in inscriptions designating ownership, seals, and burial inscriptions. This was his formal and official name. Yet 'people spent most of their lives in informal and familiar surroundings, such as military units, working groups, or among friends, where there was a tendency to abbreviate and drop one of the elements of the "X son of Y" formula'.[39] More particularly, Naveh showed that:

[36] The legal principle expressing the risk to Shim'on is encapsulated in the phrase *prior tempore potior iure* ('The one who is earlier in time is stronger in law').

[37] Negev 1991.

[38] J. Naveh (1990) 'Nameless People', *Israel Exploration Journal* 40: 122.

[39] Naveh 1990: 116–117.

> ... whatever his status, a person might be called by his personal name, his nickname or the form 'son of X.' In this combination X may be the name of the father or the nickname of the father, but sometimes 'son of X' is a nickname in itself.[40]

For example, there survive epigraphic finds from the end of the Second Temple period testifying to the fact 'that within a particular social group people often called each other "*ben X*"(X could be either a proper name or a nickname), or by a personal name or a nickname alone'.[41] Bringing the picture forward to the first century CE and to the Dead Sea area, among the Aramaic and Hebrew *ostraca* left behind by the defenders of Masada in 73 CE, there are name-lists and sherds bearing a single name or nickname.[42] Many of them are patronymics where the operative name is probably the father's normal name. But, more relevant to Archelaus (where the possibility that he was simply calling himself בר עבד ['son of *'Abad*'], the first part of his father's name, is excluded by the initial *aleph*), there are examples where the word after 'son of' was a common noun. Relevant examples in patronymic form include 'Son of the Baker' (בן הנחתם) and 'Son of Round-cake' (בן כנבון).[43] In addition, in a deed included by Cotton and Yardeni in their 1997 collection, a man is referred to as Shim'on son of דקנה (perhaps meaning 'the beard'), which the editors suggest was his 'by-name'.[44] Similarly, in an article published in the early twentieth century, Klein collected from the Mishnah, Talmud, and Midrashim nearly 100 nicknames beginning with בן or בר, including 'son of the murderer', 'son of the star', 'son of the sated dog', and 'son of the smith'.[45] From the New Testament we have James and John, the sons of Zebedee, also described as the 'sons of Thunder' (*Boanerges*; Mark 3:17).

All this has application to Archelaus. It would not have been surprising if Archelaus's father had acquired a nickname, especially as his name is quite a mouthful. This could have happened among his family or friends or among military comrades, since we have already argued above Archelaus's father had served in the Nabatean army. This nickname could then have found further use in Archelaus's

40 Naveh 1990: 116. 41 Naveh 1990: 113.

42 Naveh 1990: 113–114. 43 Naveh 1990: 113–115.

44 The deed is XHev/Se papDeed of Sale D ar: See Cotton and Yardeni 1997: 39–44, at 44.

45 S. Klein (1929) '"לחקר השמות והכינויים"', *Leshonenu* 1: 341; cited by Naveh 1990: 116.

patronymic: Son of X. Alternatively Archelaus could have gained a nickname 'Son of X' on his own account, without any reference to his father. In either case, when the scribe wrote his name in P. Yadin 2, in a formal legal context, mentioning also his status of *strategos*, and embellishing the date clause with several other members of the royal family, he inevitably spelled out the full and correct patronymic for Archelaus. But when Archelaus himself, under fewer professional constraints and also exhibiting the social informality of the Nabatean elite, signed his own name at the end of P. Yadin 3, he opted for a nickname form of patronymic. Presumably, this word, of three letters with the middle one an *aleph*, consisted of a common noun like the nicknames described by Naveh.

We thus have a number of factors that bear on the identity of the first witness to P. Yadin 3: the rarity of Archelaus in the Nabatean onomasticon; its uniqueness as a Greek name among the Nabateans mentioned in P. Yadin 1–4; the practical need for Shim'on to have Archelaus, as the first purchaser of the property, witness his purchase; and the common use of nicknames in patronymics. Putting all these together, it is reasonable to conclude that the Archelaus, who was the first witness on Shim'on's deed, is to be identified with the Archelaus who purchased the property one month earlier.

THE PERSONAL DIMENSIONS

Shim'on and 'Abi-'adan

It is now possible to return to the roles of the various parties in this transaction and the interactions between them. Events must have begun with the rescission of Archelaus's contract with 'Abi-'adan. As mentioned in Chapter 6, perhaps his withdrawal from the purchase was sweetened for 'Abi-'adan by the knowledge that there was another willing purchaser waiting in the wings. This is rendered probable by a consideration of Shim'on's situation. It can hardly have escaped his attention, living in the same village as her, that 'Abi-'adan had decided to sell a date-palm orchard she owned on the shore of the Dead Sea. Moreover, since he purchased such a property from her in Tebet of Rabb'el's twenty-eighth regnal year, he was presumably also willing to do so a month earlier. This introduces the likelihood that Shim'on had previously met with 'Abi-'adan to see if she would sell the orchard to him. During that meeting it is possible that she said to him in words to the effect, 'I'm sorry, Shim'on, but I have decided to sell it to Archelaus.' Such a decision on her part would have made good sense in view of the social and political prominence of Archelaus stemming from his position as *strategos*. 'Abi-'adan would have wanted to avoid making an enemy of Archelaus by selling an orchard he wanted to someone else, someone not even a Nabatean. She also no doubt considered it likely that she would thus put herself in a position to benefit from this sale to Archelaus in the years ahead by being able to rely on her relationship with him. Once Shim'on knew that Archelaus wanted to buy the property he too would probably have stepped aside for the same two reasons: to avoid incurring the enmity of Archelaus and to enjoy his good favour. Both 'Abi-'adan and Shim'on had more to gain if Archelaus knew that Shim'on wanted the orchard but had dropped his interest in favour of Archelaus and that her preferred purchaser was Archelaus. To secure such advantages for both herself and Shim'on, 'Abi-'adan probably told Archelaus about Shim'on's interest.

There must have been a second meeting between Shim'on and 'Abi-'adan after the purchase by Archelaus was rescinded but before the second of Tebet (when P. Yadin 3 was executed). At that meeting Shim'on, surely aware of the rescission, expressed his willingness to purchase the orchard that Archelaus had bought. But the conversation must also have included discussion of his purchasing an orchard enlarged by the addition of the section in the south-west corner adjacent to the houses of Ḥunainu (see Figures 7.1 and 7.2 above), with the two parcels together comprising a total plot previously called Gahadiya. It is not easy to decide whether Shim'on or 'Abi-'adan suggested his purchase of the enlarged property. In any event, it involved a complication. She did not own the smaller plot. It was owned by Ḥaṣmar'il the son of Lutay. Accordingly, 'Abi-'adan had to acquire title to this extra plot to sell the enlarged orchard to Shim'on. She would ultimately do so via a grant, not by a purchase, and the corroborating evidence for this and the means by which that result was achieved must await discussion of P. Yadin 4 in Chapter 8.

At some point 'Abi-'adan must have raised with the son of Lutay his transferring the smaller plot to her for sale to Shim'on and he agreed. There is no way of determining whether he was actually present at the conversation between 'Abi-'adan and Shim'on and agreed there and then, or whether she raised the matter with him later, he agreed, and she reported his agreement to Shim'on. 'Abi-'adan must then have instructed the scribe, 'Azur son of 'Awatu, to draft an appropriate deed. Kimberley Czajkowski rightly suggests that the same scribe was employed because the 'principals found someone competent, possibly a competent family, whom they trusted to write their documents and so simply returned to them whenever they needed a new contract drawn up'.[46] And the scribe would no doubt have been happy to be paid twice in the same month for deeds of purchase over much the same property! But on the second occasion the transaction was more complicated. 'Azur was required to give legal effect to a staggered transaction; that is, that the parties wanted Shim'on to obtain possession of the orchard sold to Archelaus immediately on his paying the purchase price and the deed being signed, whereas the extra parcel of land was to be handed over later. His elegant lawyer's solution was to draft the deed to ensure that the son of Lutay assumed contractual responsibility not just for the future grant but also for the entirety of 'Abi-'adan obligations under the sale to Shim'on.

I mentioned in Chapter 6 that a sale of the orchard directly from Archelaus to Shim'on was probably ruled out by reason of the fact that this would first require the property to be listed in the king's property register under the name of Archelaus and he needed the money quickly. In addition, however, Shim'on wanted to purchase the extra orchard owned by the son of Lutay and his purchasing from 'Abi-'adan gave him extra leverage in relation to the total sale. Especially important in this regard was that the son of Lutay guaranteed the obligations of 'Abi-'adan in relation to her sale to Shim'on (P. Yadin 3, line 43).

Shim'on and Archelaus

We now arrive at the occasion when the deed of purchase was executed, the second of Tebet, with all those present as described at the start of this chapter, including (as argued above) Archelaus son of 'Abad-'Amanu, the *strategos*, who was the first witness to attest the signatures of 'Abi-'adan and Ḥaṣmar'il the son of Lutay. The parties,

[46] K. Czajkowski (2017) *Localized Law: The Babatha and Salome Komaise Archives*. Oxford: Oxford University Press, 73.

the scribe, and probably Shim'on knew the background to the document. Whether the other witnesses were also aware of the circumstances before the scribe read out the document cannot be determined with certainty, but seems likely. There must have been intense local interest in a situation where a *strategos* had had to back out of a transaction and the manner in which closure had been obtained.

Was this the first time that Shim'on had met Archelaus or did they already know one another? Since the father of Archelaus lived reasonably close to Maoza and Archelaus had probably been to the village recently to inspect the property before he purchased it, the latter seems the more likely option. Strengthening this likelihood are three points in particular, all of which are related to the fact that Shim'on must have been anxious lest Archelaus or an heir or assignee of his would some day turn up claiming ownership of the property that Archelaus had purchased only a month previously in that very year.

The first point, mentioned earlier in this chapter, is that Shim'on asked Archelaus to witness his purchase of the enlarged orchard. Archelaus duly obliged by witnessing the document immediately after the two parties, 'Abi-'adan and the son of Lutay, in the place of honour at the head of the list of witnesses, as befitted his status as a member of the Nabatean elite. This may have meant Archelaus paying a special visit to Maoza from wherever in the kingdom he was then based in his official role.

The second point is this. Shim'on was buying a property one month after a very similar property had been sold to Archelaus, a *strategos* no less, a member of the Nabatean elite with very high administrative and military authority. The problem, noted above, is what would happen if, once Shim'on had paid the purchase price and taken possession of the date-palm orchard, Archelaus (or his heirs or assignees) claimed that he (or they) had prior title to the property? After all, there was no legal relationship between Archelaus and Shim'on that could be undone by an appropriate document. One way for Shim'on to assure himself on this point was to get into his possession the version of P. Yadin 2, signed by 'Abi-'adan, that Archelaus had received when he paid the purchase price, which established the latter's title to the property at that time. This he achieved. In my view P. Yadin 2 is almost certainly Archelaus' signed original of the deed (as noted in Chapter 6, 'Abi-'adan may not even have possessed a signed copy). Even though 'Abi-'adan arguably did not strictly need Archelaus's signed copy of P. Yadin 2 if she had a signed deed of rescission, the fact that it came into Shim'on's possession indicates reasonably good relations between the parties. This is not to deny, however, that Shim'on would probably have been unwilling to purchase the orchard at all if Archelaus had been unwilling to hand over to him his original deed of purchase.

If one were to ask, why did Shim'on not ask for a copy of the rescission document signed by Archelaus that we suggested in Chapter 6 was probably entered into between Archelaus and 'Abi-'adan, the answer in my view is that this was, after all, a Nabatean *strategos* he was dealing with. There may well have been a point beyond which Archelaus was not willing to be pushed by someone who was not his social equal and not even a Nabatean, especially if it might have involved the nuisance and (perhaps minor) cost of the scribe drafting another copy. Shim'on, accordingly, did well to get his hands on Archelaus's copy of P. Yadin 2. Perhaps when the issue was raised, Archelaus replied to Shim'on (or to 'Abi-'adan, if she was asking on Shim'on's behalf): 'Why don't you just take my copy of the deed that 'Abi-'adan has signed?' In fact, Shim'on asked for and received one other document from Archelaus.

This brings us to the third point and arguably the most surprising piece of evidence. Shim'on must have raised the following issue to Archelaus in words to this effect: 'I know you have given me your deed of purchase and witnessed my purchase, but these are still very unusual events. How will I explain the course of events in future if challenged? Say people ask me why a *strategos* like you would pull out of his purchase so soon after entering into it. To avoid any future problems for me, would it possible for you to let me have your deceased father's copy of the loan from 'Amat-'Isi that he guaranteed?' This request Archelaus also granted, which, I submit, is how the deed of loan that is P. Yadin 1 came to be in the possession of Shim'on and his daughter after him. That it did so is eloquent testimony to the fact that a member of the Nabatean elite, true to their nomadic heritage as discussed in Chapter 3, did not stand on ceremony and could deal with members of the non-elite in a manner not fixated upon status consciousness. But it is also a sign of good ethnic relations between Nabatean and Judean in the kingdom of Rabb'el II.

8

P. Yadin 4: Its Character and Parties

At first sight it is not at all obvious what role, if any, P. Yadin 4 played in Shimʿon's acquisition of the date-palm orchard called Gahadiya, or how it might contribute to an ethnographic discussion of the people involved in that transaction and the relationships between them. Although P. Yadin 4 is a typical Nabatean double legal document, its fragmentary state means that only parts of the outer version and some fragments of the signatures have survived.[1] The editors suggest that the body of the outer text (that is, excluding the signatures) probably contained nineteen lines.[2] This number is confirmed by scrutiny of the digital photo of the papyrus.[3] The editors present about thirty per cent of it as extant on the papyrus, seven lines being reasonably complete. They have not, however, been able to detect any names in the document. Nevertheless, they note that 'the identity of the handwriting of P. Yadin 2, 3 and 4 allows us to

[1] For the Nabatean Aramaic text, translation and discussion, see Y. Yadin et al. (eds) (2002) *The Documents from the Bar Kokhba Period in the Cave of Letters: Hebrew, Aramaic and Nabatean-Aramaic Papyri*. Judean Desert Studies. Jerusalem: Israel Exploration Society, Institute of Archaeology, Hebrew University and the Shrine of the Book, 245–256. For photos of the papyrus, see Y. Yadin (2002) *The Documents from the Bar Kokhba Period in the Cave of Letters: Hebrew, Aramaic and Nabatean-Aramaic Papyri*. Judean Desert Studies. Jerusalem: Israel Exploration Society, Institute of Archaeology, Hebrew University and the Shrine of the Book, Israel Museum, Plates 25 and 26 and the enlargeable, colour digital photos in the Leon Levy Dead Sea Scrolls Digital Library: recto of outer text (accessed at: <http://www.deadseascrolls.org.il/explore-the-archive/image/B-513109>, and verso of outer text (accessed at: <http://www.deadseascrolls.org.il/explore-the-archive/image/B-513111>).

[2] Yadin et al. 2002: 251–252.

[3] See, on <http://www.deadseascrolls.org.il/explore-the-archive/image/B-513109>, that letter remains are visible on two lines above the first group of largely distinct if not easily legible letters on the right side of the document.

conclude that all three deeds were written by the same scribe'.[4] This was ʿAzur the son of ʿAwatu. The editors acknowledge the difficulties in the interpretation of P. Yadin 4 when they state: 'Whether or not it was related in substance to P. Yadin 2 and/or P. Yadin 3, which is possible, remains unclear because of the extent of the missing information.'[5]

In my submission, however, the visible remains on the papyrus permit the restoration of more of the text than the editors have realized. The reasons for my principal emendations are set out in this chapter. These include the names of the two parties. Appendix 1 provides the Nabatean Aramaic text of P. Yadin 4 as I reconstruct it with my full set of emendations, including the reasons for those not provided in this chapter (where they are not central to the argument). My English translation of this emended text appears in Appendix 2.

Given its fragmentary nature, discussion of P. Yadin 4 must begin with the identification of its legal character and the parties to it, and that task occupies this chapter. Only then, in Chapter 9, will I proceed to an ethnographic analysis of the information thus yielded by P. Yadin 4 and its relationship with P. Yadin 3.

P. YADIN 4 AS A GRANT, NOT A GUARANTEE

There is as yet no decided view on the nature of this document. The editors identify it as 'a possible guarantor's agreement in Nabatean Aramaic' based on their proposed reading of ערב ('guarantor') in line 12. They note, however, that this reading 'is decidedly uncertain, and yet it is virtually the only explicit basis for characterizing this document as a guarantor's agreement'.[6] Beyer describes it as a guarantee.[7] Jacobine Oudshoorn also considers that it is probably a guarantor's agreement.[8] One of the standard *sigla* for this papyrus

[4] Yadin et al. 2002: 253. [5] Yadin et al. 2002: 245.

[6] Yadin et al. 2002: 245.

[7] K. Beyer (2004) *Die aramäischen Texte vom Toten Meer. Band II.* Göttingen: Vandenhoeck & Rupprecht, 215.

[8] J. G. Oudshoorn (2007) *The Relationship between Roman and Local Law in the Babatha and Salome Komaise Archives: General Analysis and Three Case Studies on Law of Succession. Guardianship and Marriage.* Studies on the Texts of the Desert of Judah, 69. Leiden: E. J. Brill, 55, fn. 30.

is P. 5/6HevGuarantee nab.[9] It is likely that this is the currently dominant interpretation.

It is interesting to note, however, that when Naphthali Lewis published his edition of the Greek papyri from the Yadin collection in 1989 he described this document as a 'Sale' and dated it *circa* 2 Tebet 99, while describing P. Yadin 3 as a 'Sale of Property' dated 2 Tebet 99.[10] Another voice dissenting from the guarantor explanation is that of Baruch Levine, who stated in 2000 that P. Yadin 4 is 'a Nabatean document involving the purchase of land'. Levine hindered himself from developing a satisfactory explanation of the document by discovering in the transaction a party (non-existent, as is argued below) called 'Yehoseph'.[11] He was also one of the editors of the collection that appeared two years later with the 'guarantee' explanation.[12]

A preliminary yet major objection to characterizing P. Yadin 4 as a guarantee comes from the general practice of Nabatean law, where the available evidence reveals that a guarantee was provided *not in the form of a separate contract* by guarantor A with one of two parties, B and C, in a contract between B and C, *but as a clause in that contract*. This is what we find in P. Yadin 1, where 'Abad-ʿAmanu guaranteed the obligations of Muqimu to his wife 'Amat-'Isi (line 16), where the word ערב is used of the guarantor.[13] Yet we also see this pattern in P. Yadin 3, line 43, where the son of Lutay offers Shimʿon a guarantee of 'Abi-ʿadan's obligations using some word (ending in *nun*) meaning 'is legally responsible for' that serves the same purpose in this context as ערב. As a matter of legal convenience, and to reduce the scribal costs of any transaction, it is obviously better to have a simple statement that A (the guarantor) is guaranteeing the obligations of party C to party B in the very document recording the

[9] J. A. Fitzmyer (2008) *A Guide to the Dead Sea Scrolls and Related Literature. Revised and Expanded Edition*. Grand Rapids, MI: William B. Eerdmans, 121.

[10] N. Lewis (1989) *The Documents from the Bar Kokhba Period in the Cave of Letters: Greek Papyri and Aramaic and Nabatean Signatures and Subscriptions*. Jerusalem: Israel Exploration Society, The Hebrew University of Jerusalem and the Shrine of the Book, 29.

[11] B. A. Levine (2000) 'The Various Workings of the Aramaic Legal Tradition: Jews and Nabateans in the Naḥal Ḥever Archive', in L. H. Schiffmann, E. Tov, and J. C. Vander Kan (eds) (2000) *The Dead Sea Scrolls Fifty Years After Their Discovery: Proceedings of the Jerusalem Conference, July 20–25, 1997*. Jerusalem: Israel Exploration Society and the Shrine of the Book, 837.

[12] Yadin et al. 2002.

[13] Although it is possible that the word ערב was also used of Muqimu himself in line 35 of P. Yadin 1, as the editors assume (Yadin et al. 2002: 180–181). See my note on this line in Appendix 2.

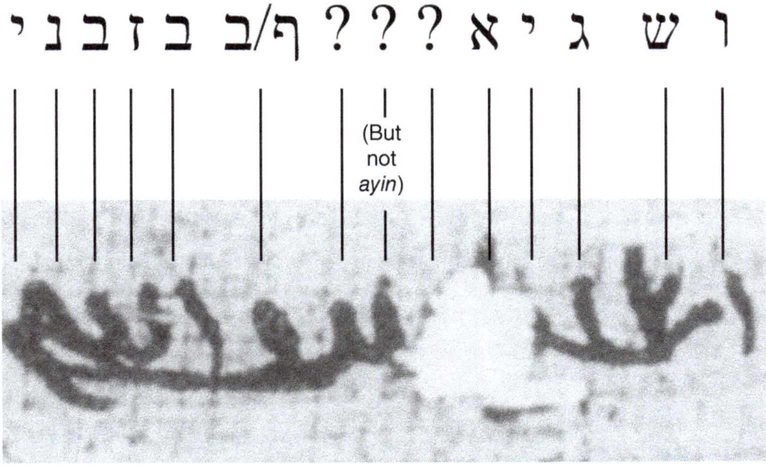

Fig. 8.1. Detail of P. Yadin 4, line 12

contract between B and C than to have a separate and quite unnecessary contract of guarantee. This is especially the case in a deed like P. Yadin 4, where the extant outer version is nineteen lines long. This is almost as long as contracts for the sale of land, such as P. Yadin 2 and P. Yadin 3, where the outer versions are twenty-four and twenty-seven lines long, respectively.

The editors' postulation of the word ערב ('guarantor') in line 12—the only possible evidence for the document being a guarantee—is not just 'decidedly uncertain' but in my view highly unlikely (See Figure 8.1).

The editors postulate that a word appeared in the space between the words 'and large' (ושגיא) and 'in the purchases' (בזבני). There was indeed a word in that location. After 'and large' there is a space that probably contained one letter (as shown here), but maybe two. Then we have the remains of three letters, the first of which, on the editors' reconstruction, must be an *ayin*. The second is a *resh*, *daled*, *beth*, or *zayin*. Thirdly, there is a terminal *pe* or *beth*, with its long tale running to the left under 'in the purchases' (בזבני). The shape of other examples of *ayin* in this document, however, for example in lines 14 and 16 (in עקרנא), the latter of which is Figure 8.2, and 18 (in יתערב), is so unlike the letter proposed here by the editors as *ayin* as to exclude that possibility.

By comparison with these examples of *ayin*, in Figure 8.1 we observe that the necessary stroke branching diagonally to the right about one-third to one-half way down from the vertical stroke is missing.

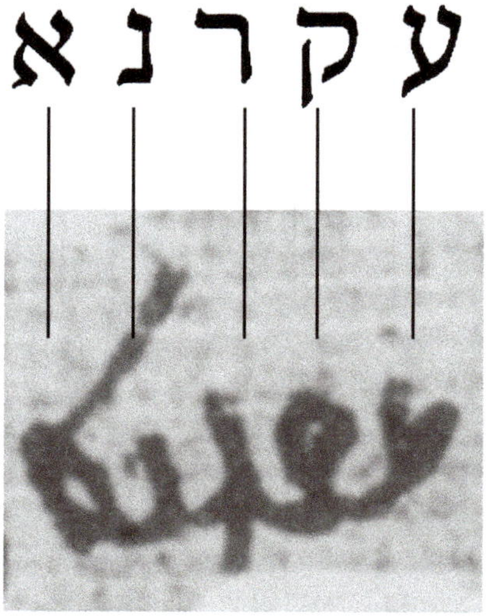

Fig. 8.2. Detail of P. Yadin 4, line 16

There are further difficulties in reading the editors' proposal of ערב ('guarantor'), namely, the middle letter (as noted above) is not necessarily a *resh* and the last letter could be *pe* rather than *bet*. Also problematic is that there is no name or pronoun in proximity to the word that is supposedly ערב that would be needed here.

The main objection to the editors' view of the document, however, is that the evidence of its character that we can derive from a consideration of its terms indicates that it is not a guarantee. Several aspects of P. Yadin 4, taken together, disclose its nature. Line 9, although fragmentary, mentions 'the orchard that (is described) above' (גנתא די עלא). This means that earlier in the document, probably in lines 6–7 (see Appendix 1), an orchard was described with reference to its abutters, which we have seen in P. Yadin 2 and 3 was a feature of Nabatean deeds of sale of real estate. In line 12 there is reference to 'the said orchard' (גנתא הי), literally 'that orchard', without doubt to be identified with the same orchard previously described. Most pertinently, in line 14, we find the principal evidence for the nature of the transaction: 'I will grant to you the real property that (is described) above' (אנתן לכי עקרנא די עלא),[14] meaning the

[14] An alternative reading for עקרנא, עקדנא, meaning 'contract' (Yadin et al. 2002: 255), makes little sense in this context. Both of these words are from Arabic.

orchard, where the 'you' in 'to you' (לכי) is in the feminine singular. This means that the deed has the legal character of a grant or gift (מתנא) but one in which the actual transfer of title (of ownership in the orchard) is delayed for some period of time. This statement is consistent with a document that contains a clause that speaks of 'the entire price of those *purchases*' (line 16),[15] in a provision to which I will return below, that indicates a change of title to or ownership in property, here an orchard. As mentioned in Chapter 7, only the owner of a property can convey title to it, so that the 'I-voice' in this provision, and in the document generally, is the owner of the orchard. According to the editors, however, by the words 'I will grant to you the real property that (is described) above',[16] 'the guarantor pledges that he will . . . convey "clear" title to the said real property . . . as delimited above, should the vendor fail to do so'.[17] But that would be legally impossible, since a guarantor has no title to convey. There are only two parties to this deed, a grantor and a grantee (who is a single female), and there is no guarantor.

Aligning this conclusion with my previous discussion of the role of Ḥaṣmar'il the son of Lutay in 'Abi-'adan's sale to Shim'on takes us a long way to understanding how P. Yadin 3 and 4 are related. In Chapter 7 I argued that the son of Lutay was going to be the grantor in a grant (מתנא), a written document, of a plot of property to 'Abi-'adan that she would consolidate with the orchard sold to Archelaus for on-sale of the whole to Shim'on. This grant was to occur in the future. Now in P. Yadin 4 we have a person saying 'I *will* grant' (אנתן) an orchard to a single female. Moreover, P. Yadin 4 mentions the twenty-eighth regnal year of Rabb'el (lines 10–11), the same year in which P. Yadin 3 was executed, while the same scribe ('Azur son of 'Awatu) produced P. Yadin 2, 3, and 4.

In my view these considerations point unerringly to the likelihood that P. Yadin 4 is the grant envisaged in P. Yadin 3, with the son of Lutay being the grantor and 'Abi-'adan the grantee.

It was only some time after reaching this view that I realized, following scrutiny of magnified photographs of the P. Yadin 4 papyrus, that the text itself provided further support for this

[15] Note that these documents use the plural 'purchases' where a modern lawyer would prefer 'purchase'.

[16] Their translation is different but the meaning is the same.

[17] Yadin et al. 2002: 255.

interpretation. I will now proceed immediately to that issue. Furthermore, given the formulaic nature of the documents drafted by this scribe, addressing these issues will then allow us to propose solutions to a number of lacunas in the text that will assist in understanding the roles and relationships of the parties to it in the context of the sale of an orchard to Shim'on.

THE PENALTY CLAUSE IN P. YADIN 2 AND 3

The key to both the nature of P. Yadin 4 and the parties to that deed arises from the circumstance that it contains a provision which matches one found in both P. Yadin 2 and P. Yadin 3, the onerous penalty clause mentioned in Chapter 5 and now requiring close consideration.

Here, for example, is the relevant section from P. Yadin 2, lines 14–15. I have broken up the quotation to highlight its various elements:

1 והן
2 אנה אביעדן דא א---- ואשנא מן דנה
3 די לא ברשא
4 אחוב לך אנת ארכלס דנה
5 בכל דמי זבניא אלה

1. And if
2. I, the said 'Abi-'adan, will . . . or will deviate from this (agreement)
3. without consent,[18]
4. I will owe to you, you, the said Archelaus[19]
5. in the entire price of these purchases.[20]

[18] Literally, 'which (is) not with consent'. I have restored די at the beginning of this expression by reference to P. Yadin 3, line 44; there is a *vacat* of two letter spaces at this place in P. Yadin 2.

[19] Literally, 'this Archelaus'.

[20] There could well be a ב before כל in both P. Yadin 2 and 3 but the relevant sections of these texts are too indistinct in each instance to be sure. The appearance of the ב here in P. Yadin 4, line 15 (see below), however, makes its appearance in these same provisions in the other two papyri likely (and I have included the ב in the translations in Appendix 2 in these locations).

Unfortunately, although the Nabatean Aramaic letter-forms of the first verb after ’Abi-‘adan are reasonably clear, no one has yet been able to propose a word that fits. But the meaning must have involved breaching the contract. The next expression, referring to a deviation from the contract (literally מן דנה [‘from this’]), is reasonably clear. In this set of provisions, therefore, we have a protasis beginning with ‘And if’ (והן) and an apodosis beginning with ‘I will owe’ (אחוב), where the speaker is the vendor and the person addressed the purchaser. In the event that the vendor breaches or deviates from the contract, except by consent, she will owe the purchaser the entire purchase price of the property (expressed in these two documents as ‘the entire price of these purchases’). The corresponding provision is found in P. Yadin 3, lines 44–45,[21] and it is, *mutatis mutandis* (especially in relation to the son of Lutay sharing the liability), the same.

Two observations should be made relating to this clause that will feature in the discussion below. First, this is a provision that pertains solely to a contract for the sale of property (that is, where title passes), since that is the only type of transaction where there is a ‘purchase price’. Thus the provision appears in P. Yadin 2 and 3, contracts for the sale of realty, but also in P. Yadin 8 (lines 8–9) in relation to the sale of personalty (there a donkey or donkeys).[22] Secondly, the provision is subject to an exception: an alteration or deviation is allowed with ‘consent’ (רשא),[23] which can only mean with the consent *of the purchaser*. This exception envisages a situation in which the vendor requests some alteration of or deviation from the terms of the contract and the purchaser agrees, thus providing the necessary ‘consent’.

THE CORRESPONDING PROVISION IN P. YADIN 4: ITS INITIAL SIMILARITY AND THE CHARACTER OF THE DEED

Figure 8.3 is a reproduction of lines 14, 15, and 16 of P. Yadin 4. My interest here lies mainly in lines 15 and 16, but adding line 14 allows one to see the long upward tail of any *lamed* from line 15 where the

[21] The parallel passage on the inner text, lines 16–17, is not quite so complete.

[22] For the text, see Yadin et al. 2002: 112–113.

[23] The root רשי means ‘to have authority’; see Yadin et al. 2002: 230.

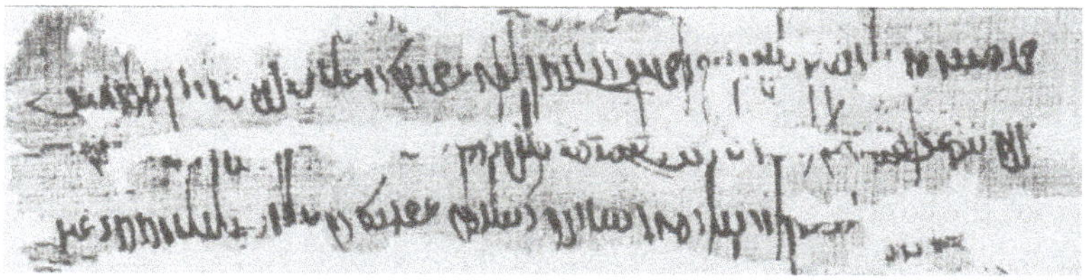

Fig. 8.3. P. Yadin 4, lines 14–16

Fig. 8.4. Detail of P. Yadin 4, line 16

rest of the letter has not survived. It is of utmost importance for the interpretation of P. Yadin 4 that following certain other words on line 15, and just beyond its mid-point and before the long lacuna, we have: 'And if . . .' (והן). This is the same as Element 1 of P. Yadin 2, lines 14–15 above. When we next move to the first part of line 16 where the text has survived intact we find 'in the entire price of those purchases' (בכל דמי זבניא אנו; see Figure 8.4) which is identical to what we have in P. Yadin 2 and 3 above (Element 5), except that in P. Yadin 4 we find 'those' (אנו) instead of 'these' (אלה). We will see below, however, that the change from 'these' to 'those' is explicable in the circumstances of P. Yadin 4.

All of this is to say that lines 15 and 16 of P. Yadin 4 contain a contractual provision that begins with 'And if . . .' and ends with the expression 'in the entire price of those purchases', with the words in Aramaic quoted above being the same as those in Elements 1 and 5 from P. Yadin 2 and 3. The presence of the same words in the same positions in P. Yadin 4, drafted by the scribe responsible for P. Yadin 2 and 3, necessarily signifies that this deed also concerned a transaction of purchase (or something very like one, for example a grant), with an obligation to repay the purchase price upon fulfilment of whatever condition was specified in the protasis. This is so even though the words specifying the nature of the breach of contract or deviation from its terms that would trigger this clause have not survived in the lacuna.

This conclusion is strengthened when we factor into the discussion the words that appear immediately after 'in the entire price of those purchases' in line 16 of P. Yadin 4: 'and in the entire price of the real property' (ובכל דמי עקרנא). Although these words do not appear in the corresponding places in P. Yadin 2 and 3, their addition does not create a substantial difference and are likely added *ex abundanti cautela*, presumably in recognition of the fact that this was not technically a 'purchase' where money would be passed over when the deed was signed. As noted above, in this deed 'the real property' (עקרנא) is an orchard that must have been described by reference to its boundaries early in the document. The legal character of P. Yadin 4, therefore, like that of P. Yadin 2 and 3, was one involving the transfer of title to property, in this case most probably real property in the form of an orchard (of date-palms, for example).

The editors, perhaps under the influence of their guarantee idea, have misunderstood the effect of this provision. They fail to notice the similarity of this 'and if' (והן) penalty clause to those in P. Yadin 2 and 3 and instead suggest that it means 'that in the event that the vendor does not clear the property of encumbrances, he, the guarantor, agrees to repay the purchaser the full cost'.[24] I submit that this view, however, misunderstands Nabatean conveyancing law, in as much as while both P. Yadin 2 and 3 contain provisions obligating the vendor to clear the property of encumbrances,[25] none of those provisions requires repayment of the purchase price in the event of breach. This is limited to what must have been major breaches of or deviations from a contract that related to the transfer of title to

[24] Yadin et al. 2002: 255.

[25] See P. Yadin 2, lines 10–12 and 32–35 and P. Yadin 3, lines 11–14 and 35–39.

property by the party with legal capacity to do so, in this case real property in the form of an orchard.

THE PARTIES TO P. YADIN 4

The Grantor

When during the research for this book I realized that P. Yadin 4 contained a penalty clause like that in P. Yadin 2 and 3, I was intrigued by the prospect that close inspection of it might yield the names of the parties to the deed. For the penalty clauses in P. Yadin 2 and 3 contain the parties' names and my hope was that the corresponding provision in P. Yadin 4 might disclose the names of its parties, given that the first few lines of the text, where they would have appeared, are missing. From my previous investigation of P. Yadin 3, I was expecting the parties to be the son of Lutay as grantor and 'Abi-'adan as grantee.

My first inspection of the photo of the papyrus was disappointing. The precedents in P. Yadin 2 and 3 lead us to expect to find the name of the party undertaking not to deviate from or change the contract immediately after the expression 'and if' (והן). This would mean that, although the body of the text in line 15 of P. Yadin 4 is missing after the 'and if', we would expect to see the ascender of the *lamed* in Lutay (or Ḥaṣmar'il or both) poking up towards or touching the letters in line 14. But we see no such *lamed*.

Returning to the photograph from Yadin's 2002 edition of the photos the next day, however, I cast my eyes leftwards towards the final, fragmentary words of line 15 and there discerned the name Lutay (לתי), with the ascender of the *lamed*, the *tau* and a faint *yod* clearly visible in the photograph (see Figure 8.5), where I have also indicated the clear 'this' (דנה) to the left of the name.

The shape of the letters here is virtually identical to the instance of these two words written by the same scribe in P. Yadin 3, line 43 (see Figure 8.6).[26] The usual practice of this scribe also necessitates that Lutay was preceded by 'son of' (בר) and there is space consistent

[26] This is a case where the online colour digital photograph of the word is better than the photo (Yadin 2002) and there is no doubt it is דנה, virtually identical to the word in Figure 8.6 (accessed at: <http://www.deadseascrolls.org.il/explore-the-archive/image/B-513109>).

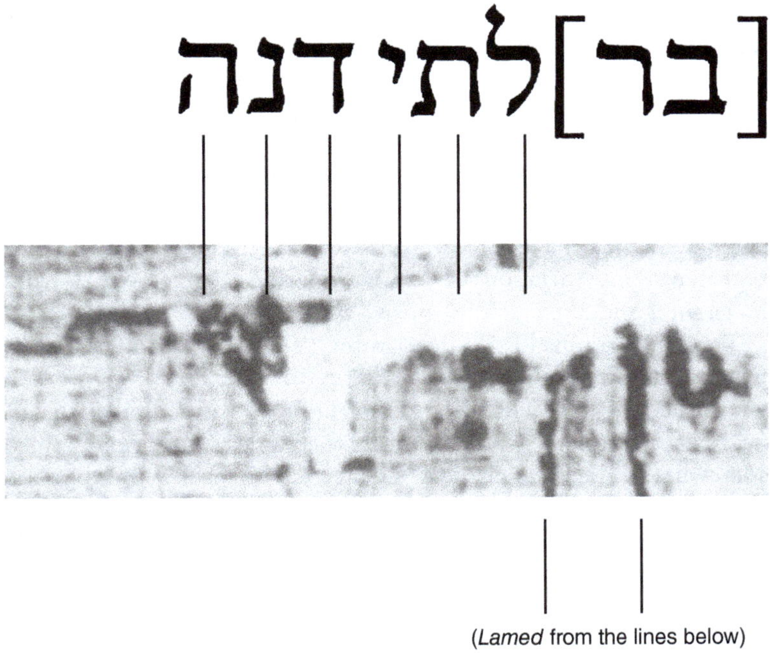

Fig. 8.5. Detail of P. Yadin 4, line 15

Fig. 8.6. Detail of P. Yadin 3, line 43

with this solution, although the ascenders of two *lameds* from the line below make the section of the papyrus very crowded and indistinct. The name Ḥaṣmar'il does not appear in this section of the text, however, for there is no sign of the ascender of the necessary *lamed* in the line above. The presence of the name of 'this son of Lutay' at the end of the line indicates that the verb or verbs (in the first person singular) designating breach of or variation from the agreement must have appeared just or shortly after 'and if', thus representing a variation of the word order of Element 2 from P. Yadin 2 and 3.

The photographs of this deed in the Leon Levy Dead Sea Scrolls Digital Library, unlike the photos in the 2002 edition, do not show the *tau* very clearly and the faint *yod* has almost disappeared.[27] Presumably, over the years the papyrus has been abraded somewhat or the letters have faded. We have Yigael Yadin to thank for the survival of the word Lutay (לתי) in line 15 for the care he took over the original photographs of the papyri in the early 1960s.[28]

There is a second area of physical evidence in the deed for the word 'Lutay'—in the signatures section on the verso. Although the signatures have largely disappeared from the papyrus, some remains are visible. The editors discern seven signatures, a number that is justified against the photograph when one resorts to maximum magnification.[29] Figure 8.7 is my drawing of the first three lines of this section.

The signatures on lines 20 and 21 are very close together and then there is a long break to the signature on line 22. The signature on line 20 is in much larger letters than that on line 21. It is difficult in one respect to reconcile the transcription offered by the editors with the photo (especially the digital colour photo on the Leon Levy Dead

[27] Accessed at <http://www.deadseascrolls.org.il/explore-the-archive/image/B-513109>.

[28] Yadin 2002.

[29] For an enlargeable black and photo of the verso of the document (although it is displayed upside down), see <http://www.deadseascrolls.org.il/explore-the-archive/image/B-300430>. For an enlargeable colour photo, see <http://www.deadseascrolls.org.il/explore-the-archive/image/B-513111>. Rotating the image 90 degrees anticlockwise produces a version with the photos running down from the top.

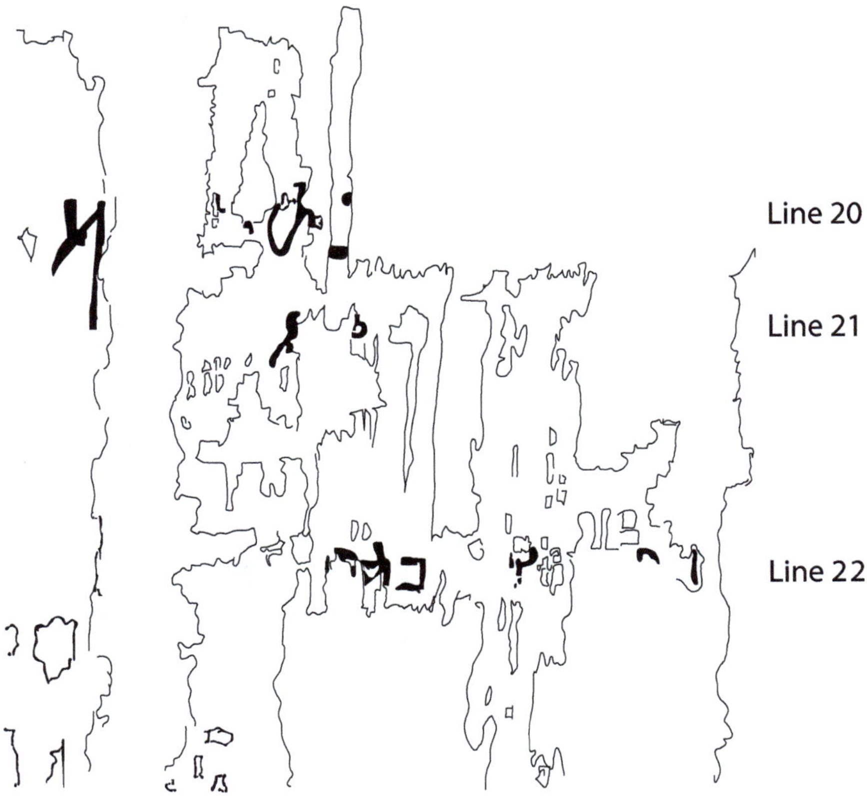

Fig. 8.7. Author's drawing of P. Yadin 4, lines 20–22 (the first three signatures)

Sea Scrolls Digital Library), or with the drawings by Ada Yardeni and myself.[30] For lines 20 and 21 they read the following (while expressing some doubt about the last three letters in the word on line 21):[31]

[?]ת[	]20
מ]מרה	]21

[30] See Yadin et al. 2002: 248 (Yardeni's drawing) and 250 (the editors' transcription). The colour photo on the Leon Levy Dead Sea Scrolls Digital Library is accessed at: <http://www.deadseascrolls.org.il/explore-the-archive/image/B-513111>. The black and white photo is accessed at: <http://www.deadseascrolls.org.il/explore-the-archive/image/B-513112>.

[31] Yadin et al. 2002: 250.

Yet this transcription does not include the large letter appearing on the far left of line 20. This is surprising, since the word they tentatively (and, as we will see, probably correctly) identify as a *he* at the end of the word visible in line 21 is very similar in shape to the letter at the end of line 20, a feature I will return to below.

On the basis that the son of Lutay is the grantor in the deed, in accordance with usual Nabatean practice we expect to find him signing first, then the witnesses and scribe, with the grantee not signing at all. This is the case with P. Yadin 7, Shim'on's gift to his wife, Miryam, of property in Maoza from 120 CE (although by then Nabatea had become the Roman province of Arabia): first Shim'on signs, then five witnesses, and then the scribe.[32]

Let us now consider the details. Figure 8.8 is my drawing of the first line of signatures (line 20) with suggested emendations to the latter part of the signature.

Fig. 8.8. Author's drawing of the surviving part of the first signature on P. Yadin, with emendations

[32] See Yadin et al. 2002: 80–88 for the Aramaic text and translation.

Note that, from the right, we have the remains of two letters that end a word (the second of them a reasonably well formed, roughly heart-shaped letter, which the clear space after it shows is a terminal letter), then some letter fragments and, finally, a large well-shaped terminal letter. The first partially extant letter (the second last in a word) is a *tau*. It is encouraging that the editors identify the second last letter of the first name (which is likely to be the name of the principal party's father) as a *tau* (see their transcription above). This, after all, is precisely what we need for Lutay, or rather, as the man himself (unlike the scribe) spelt his father's name (see Chapter 7), Lutah (לתה). Nor is this an insignificant feature. Avraham Negev's work *Personal Names in the Nabataean Realm* lists 1,249 Nabatean names. Of them, only fifty-six, or 4.48 per cent, have *taw* as their second last letter. So it is reasonably uncommon to have a name with this feature.

It is likely that the letter to the left of the *tau* is a *he*. The editors have not made this identification, but it is reasonably secure. In the photograph one can see a space that could have been a stroke we expect across the top of a *he*, the remains of the right end of which remain. Moreover, the photo also reveals the remains of the little upstroke on the right hand 'corner' of the letter. This is a *he*. The only letter that is even remotely similar, *mem*, is not drawn with a line above its top or with a slight upward projection on the top right side. Admittedly, the bulk of the letter is pear- or heart-shaped rather than rhomboid in form, which may be more common in these documents. Nevertheless, the Nabateans did sometimes write a *he* in a rounded form. After all, the scribe himself has written small and rounded *hes* in places in these documents (for example P. Yadin 2, line 16 [בה] [see Figure 8.9] and P. Yadin 3, line 47 [בה]).

Accordingly, in my view we have a name ending *tau-he* (-תה).

We are expecting the son of Lutay (spelt 'Lutah') to be the first party to sign and here he is, even though no sign remains of the initial *lamed* in his name. It is probable that his first name appeared as well, requiring the emendation (as appearing in Appendix 1): [חצמראל בר ל]תה ('Ḥaṣmar'il the son of Lutah'). The gaps in the papyrus, however, mean that there is no sign of the necessary two *lameds*.

Returning to Figure 8.8, the letter at the far left of the line is a terminal *he*. It is written in a large form and differently from the previous *he*, but such exuberance is often seen in a word at the end of a line in the Dead Sea legal papyri where there is plenty of remaining space. A terminal *he* is often written in these papyri as an elongated

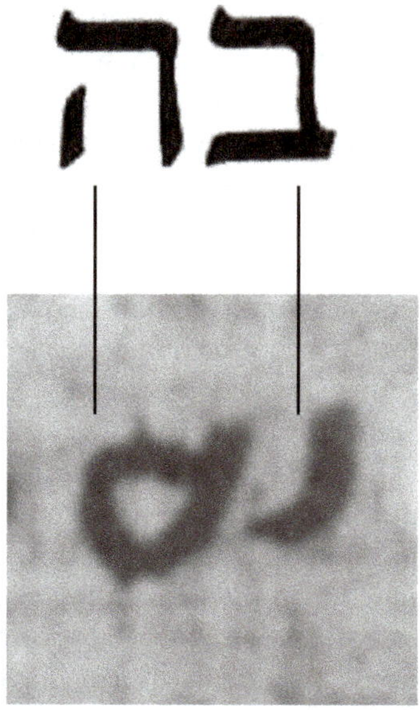

Fig. 8.9. Detail of P. Yadin 2, line 16

rectangle, sometimes with the angles not at 90 degrees. With this *he* the person responsible has drawn, first, a vertical upstroke on the right and then, in a continuous movement, the angled stroke downwards and to the left. But then, rather than continuing to draw the long vertical down stroke and the bottom stroke across to the right, he has returned to the top stroke and bisected it with a small stroke that bends towards the right underneath that top stroke. This produces a miniature version of the form he would have produced if he had completed the rectangle, so the logic of this variation on more common forms of terminal *he* is evident. This bent stroke bisecting the top stroke is clearly visible in Yadin's black-and-white photograph and in the colour photographs in the Leon Levy Dead Sea Scrolls Digital Library.[33]

The word כתבה has been restored to the end of line 21 by comparison with other Dead Sea legal papyri. There is only room

[33] The colour photo is accessed at: <http://www.deadseascrolls.org.il/explore-the-archive/image/B-513111>. The black and white photo is accessed at: <http://www.deadseascrolls.org.il/explore-the-archive/image/B-513112>.

for three letters after the final *he* in Lutah and this word appears frequently in the Dead Sea legal papyri adjacent to signatures, as we will now see. There are two possible meanings of כתבה after the son of Lutay's name and the distinction between them is an important one, in general terms and in relation to the son of Lutay's signature on P. Yadin 4. It was usual for the parties to the Dead Sea legal papyri to insert a form of words after their name. The simplest was כתב (*ketab*), meaning 'he signed' or 'he wrote'. Another approach was to add a *he* as a prepositional suffix: כתבה, meaning 'he signed/wrote it' (as in Wahab-'Ilahi in witnessing P. Yadin 3). Another variation was כתבידה, meaning 'signed/written in his own hand' (as in three of the signatures on P. Yadin 3). Often, however, the expression על נפשה (either *'al nepsheh* in the masculine or *'al nepshah* in the feminine) appears. Cotton and Yardeni have shown that the expression על נפשה indicates that a person was present in person at the signing.[34] When Shim'on, the son of Menaḥem (Babatha's father) signed at the end of P. Yadin 7 (a deed of gift to his wife), he wrote כתבה על נפשה, meaning 'he signed/wrote it for himself/in person'.[35] But the expression על נפשה was used even when the person who was present did not actually sign him- or herself,[36] typically because of his or her illiteracy. We see this in P. X Hev/Se 89 (in Aramaic and from 134 or 135 CE), where the name 'Shalom daughter of Shim'on' is followed first by the words על נפשה meaning 'in her presence' and then by 'Ele'azar son of *Mtt*' 'signed at her direction (ממרה)'.[37]

Hannah Cotton and Ada Yardeni have plausibly argued that sometimes כתב (or, we might add, כתבה) had a factitive meaning, 'he had it signed/written/issued'.[38] Another person would be delegated to write someone else's signature where that person was unable to sign the document,[39] for example because he or she was illiterate, sick, or simply absent. The practice of using an agent to sign was common.[40] In P. Yadin 44, a Hebrew legal text from En-Gedi from the third year

[34] See H. M. Cotton and A. Yardeni (1997) *Discoveries in the Judaean Desert. Volume 27. Aramaic, Hebrew and Greek Documentary Texts from Naḥal Ḥever and Other Sites: With an Appendix Containing Alleged Qumran Texts (The Seiyal Collection II)*. Oxford: Clarendon Press, 220 and the other scholarship that they cite.

[35] See Yadin et al. 2002: 73.

[36] Cotton and Yardeni 1997: 220.

[37] See Cotton and Yardeni 1997: 34–37 for this document.

[38] On this factitive sense of כתב, see Yadin et al. 2002: 12–13.

[39] See Yadin et al. 2002: 13.

[40] See the evidence cited in Yadin et al. 2002: 11–12.

Fig. 8.10. Signature of the son of Lutay, P. Yadin 3, line 50

of the Bar Kokhba revolt, three of four principals employed someone else to sign on their behalf (a different person in each case), although without using the precise formula under discussion here.[41]

From this discussion the question arises as to whether כתבה here means 'he signed/wrote it' or 'he had it issued' (the factitive sense). The reason for doubt in this case is that there are dissimilarities in appearance between what remains of his signature here (in both the letters *tau* and *he*) and its form in the one other place where it occurs, at the end of P. Yadin 3 (see Figure 8.10).

It is possible that the signatures appearing in Figures 8.8 and 8.10 were written by the same person; the fact that in signing the name in P. Yadin 4 the son of Lutay then continued with כתבה might explain some of the difference. And there may have been some variation in the way people drew their signatures, but this seems unlikely as it would rather defeat the purpose. Yet if this is an instance of the same name written by two different people, the factitive use of כתבה in P. Yadin 4, with someone else signing on behalf of the son of Lutay would provide the explanation. It is significant that there is no room of after 'Lutah' for the words על נפשה, which, as noted above, indicate the personal presence of the person.

[41] See Yadin et al. 2002: 44–45.

There is evidence on the papyrus to support the suggestion that someone signed on behalf of the son of Lutay. From Figure 8.7, as noted above, we observe that the second of the seven signatures is written in smaller letters and just under the first. The editors suggest that the 'small space between the first and second letters of the signatures may indicate that the second line belongs to a person who signed in the name of the first party, the latter being illiterate'.[42] Yet we know from his signature at the end of P. Yadin 3 that the son of Lutay was not illiterate. Nevertheless, another reason why a person can sign on someone else's behalf is when the latter is unable to sign, for example, through absence, illness, or injury. The last letter appears to be a *he*, very similar to that at the end of the writing on the line above, both because it features the top and right half of a rectangle and because of the short curved line bisecting the top stroke. This bisection is just visible on the digital photograph at high magnification,[43] and I have sought to reproduce it in Figure 8.7. The letter visible to the right of this *he* is almost certainly a *mem* (as the editors also propose). Accordingly, in my view the editors' tentative suggestion of ממרה (*m-m-r-h*; 'by his order') is almost certainly correct (see Figure 8.11).

This would mean someone signed on behalf of the son of Lutay, because he was absent, sick, or injured. In Chapter 9 I will suggest a possible reason for his absence.

On this view, the son of Lutay issued the document, but someone else actually signed it on his behalf. This would mean P. Yadin 4 was signed by the principal party (though his agent), four witnesses (the same number as in P. Yadin 1, 2, and 3) and the scribe. Strongly supporting this view is the pronounced similarity in the (unusual) form of the two instances of *he*; this indicates that the same person wrote both and means that someone else signed for the son of Lutay. In my view this is probably what happened. On the less likely scenario, that the second signatory is the first witness (meaning the son of Lutay signed himself), there would have been five witnesses to the deed. This is the same number as in Shim'on's deed of gift to his wife (P. Yadin 7) and it may have been thought that where no money was actually being handed to the donor on the occasion the document was executed having an extra witness was a sensible precaution.

42 Yadin et al. 2002: 247.

43 See <http://www.deadseascrolls.org.il/explore-the-archive/image/B-513109>.

Fig. 8.11. Author's drawing of detail of P. Yadin 4, lines 20–21, with emendations

The Grantee

What now of the other party? Comparison with the penalty provision in P. Yadin 2 and 3 requires that, immediately before the words 'in the entire price of these purchases' (Element 5) in line 16, we expect to see an expression along to the lines of 'I will owe to you, you, this X . . . ' (Element 5). We may expect such a statement would have been in the first person singular since it comes after two first person singular statements in lines 14 and 15, including 'I will give/grant to you' (feminine singular; line 14) and the words 'Accordingly, I acknowledge liability, I, in the (amount of) the said silver' (כדנה מודא ומתחיב אנה בכסף דנה; lines 14–15), which latter clause is discussed below. The reference to 'the said silver' (in addition to the discovery of the actual two parties to the deed) rules out interpreting --סף ד[נ]ה in line 12 as the name 'this Yehosef' as postulated by the editors.[44] It is just another instance of 'in the (amount of) the said silver' (בכסף דנה).

When we move to line 16 of P. Yadin 4 we discover that a name is discernible at the right location and it is the name we have been expecting: 'Abi-'adan. Consider Figure 8.12.

This shows the beginning of line 16, ignoring the third letter from the left side, which is the down-stroke of a terminal *nun* (in דין) from the line above. One need only compare, for example, these words with Figure 8.13.

Here we have the words אנה אביעדן דא ('I, this 'Abi-'adan') from line 35 of P. Yadin 3 and the similarity of letter-forms is apparent. The forms are essentially identical. As in Figure 8.13, there is a ligature joining the *bet* and the *yod* in אביעדן in P. Yadin 4, line 16, but it is clearer on the digital colour photograph.

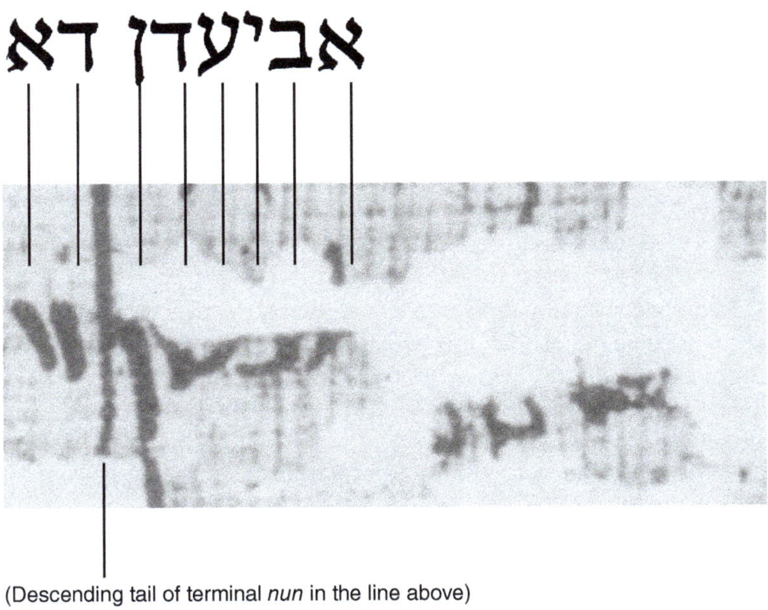

Fig. 8.12. Detail of P. Yadin 4, line 16, with emendations

[44] Yadin et al. 2002: 251.

Fig. 8.13. Detail of P. Yadin 3, line 35

In my view we can also reach a position on the three words before אביעדן דא. The pattern for this provision evident in P. Yadin 2 and 3 suggests that before mention of the purchaser should come a statement 'I will owe' (אחוב). This is very probable here since we have already encountered an 'I-voice' in the document (line 14) making a very significant promise to transfer property to 'you', where the 'you' is a single female, whom we now submit is ʼAbi-ʻadan. With this in mind and in view of the similar situations in P. Yadin 2 and 3, where at this point we have the expression to 'to you, you X', we are expecting to find 'to you, you' (לכי אנתי). While nothing remains of the expression 'I will owe' (אחוב), revealing remnants of these two words are visible.

Consider the way that לכי has been drawn by this scribe in line 14 of this same deed (see Figure 8.14).

Moreover, we observe in line 15 (see Figure 8.3) that the letter *samek* in the words בכסף ('in silver') above, the second word in the

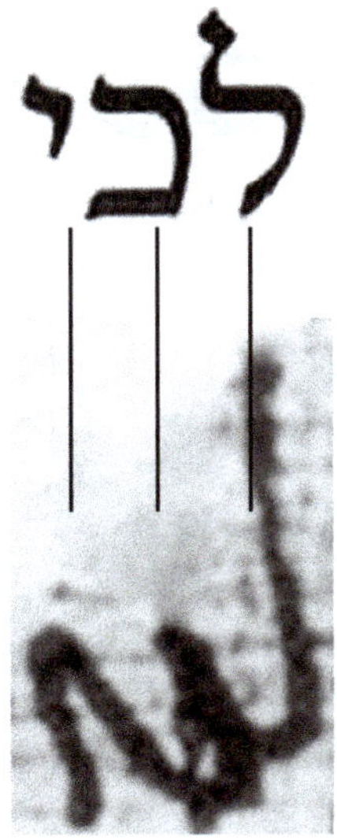

Fig. 8.14. Detail of P. Yadin 4, line 14

line, has touching its lower curve the top part of a vertical upstroke from below, certainly of a *lamed*. Although this *lamed* does not appear in the editors' transcription,[45] it is visible when one enlarges the photo of this papyrus in the Leon Levy Dead Sea Scrolls Digital Library (and see Figure 8.15).[46] In short, it is a *samek* touched by a *lamed* from below, the *lamed* in לכי ('to you').

Reverting now to Figure 8.3, we see that the top of the *lamed* touching the *samek* in line 15 (as just discussed) is situated approximately above the start of the first visible remains in line 16. Figure 8.12 reveals that these remains are compatible with the lower parts of a *kappa* and then a *yod* (joined by a ligature). On the basis of the frequent use of the formula, 'to you, you, X', we can be almost certain that the word that appeared in the gap between לכי and אביעדן was אנתי (the feminine singular form of 'you'). Physical evidence supporting this view can be seen in the way that the letters אנת in the word אנתן ('I will grant') are drawn in P. Yadin 4, line 14 (see Figure 8.16).

In line 16 of P. Yadin 4 the *nu* (see Figure 8.12 above), the bottom of the *tau* and the characteristic ligature between them in אנתי) can be

[45] See Yadin et al. 2002: 250 where no *lamed* is shown near the start of line 15.
[46] See http://www.deadseascrolls.org.il/explore-the-archive/image/B-513109>.

Fig. 8.15. Detail of P. Yadin 4, line 15

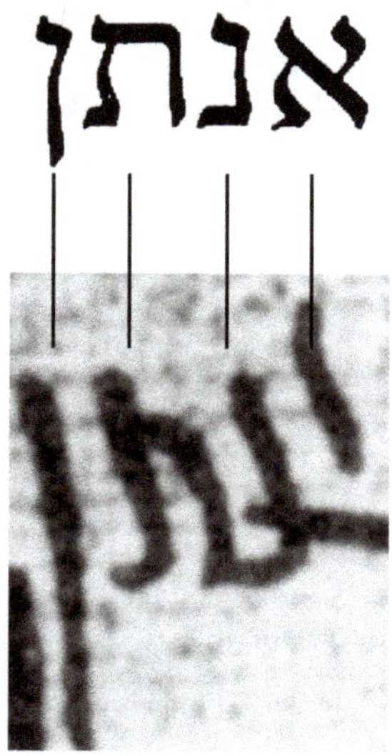

Fig. 8.16. Detail of P. Yadin 4, line 14

לכי אנתי אביעדן דא

Fig. 8.17. Author's drawing of words near the start of P. Yadin 4, line 16, with emendations

clearly seen and there is room on the papyrus for the preceding *aleph* and *yod* that follows.[47] Accordingly, my reconstruction of what appeared in this space is Figure 8.17.

Immediately after 'this (or 'the said') 'Abi-'adan' we have: בכל, meaning 'in/with respect to everything'. Thus we can restore this section of line 16 as follows: ... אביעדן דא בכל דמי, as opposed to the editors' reading for this part of line 16: ... די כול דמי, which is explicable on the basis of their failure to recognize the words 'this 'Abi-'adan' (אביעדן דא) immediately before בכל דמי. Accordingly, we have emended line 17 by adding 'I will owe to you, you, the said 'Abi-'adan, in the entire price . . .' (... אחוב לכי אנתי אביעדן דא בכל דמי).

Before moving on, however, it is important to note the likelihood that the word 'I' (אנה) also appeared in line 14 of P. Yadin 4, either immediately before 'the son of Lutay', thus producing the phrase 'I', this son of Lutay' (אנה בר לתי דנה), or earlier in the line after the words

[47] A very similar form of אנת occurs in P. Yadin 3, line 14.

'and if'. The principal reason for assuming an אנה before the son of Lutay, is that we have one continuous statement that contains both the statement of the indebtedness of the 'I-voice' and the repayment of purchase price provision:

> Accordingly, (I) acknowledge liability, I, in (the amount of) the said silver, which is not subject to any suit, or contest, or oath, in any respect, and if . . . . (I) the said son Lutay (I) will owe to you, you, the said 'Abi-'adan, in the entire price of those purchases . . . (lines 14–16).

This is a long sentence with only one name (before we get to 'Abi-'adan) and only room for one name.[48] The invariable practice of this scribe in P. Yadin 2 and 3, moreover, is that where he has a sentence in the first person he always includes, at least once, the name of the speaker, in the form 'I, this X' or 'we, these X and Y'. Thus, his usual practice requires 'I' (אנה) to occur with the son of Lutay and the invariable order is אנה בר לתי דנה.

This discussion confirms the status of the son of Lutay as the 'I-voice' in the deed and that there are only two parties to it, he and 'Abi-'adan. If there was another party to the grant, moreover, Shim'on would surely have required him or her also to be a party to P. Yadin 3, just like the son of Lutay.

P. YADIN 4 AS THE GRANT MENTIONED IN P. YADIN 3: FURTHER EVIDENCE

The identification of the son of Lutay as the 'I-voice' and grantor in P. Yadin 4 and 'Abi-'adan as the grantee confirms, in my view, that this document is indeed the grant (מתנא) referred to P. Yadin 3. As argued previously, it also provides for the future grant of an orchard, which is, I submit, the additional plot on the south-western corner of the larger orchard previously sold to Archelaus that Shim'on also wished to purchase. Three other pieces of evidence further corroborate this view.

First, towards the end of P. Yadin 4 there is a notable omission in comparison to P. Yadin 2 and 3. Both of them contain a penultimate clause, which is as follows in P. Yadin 2:

[48] The word ending in -סף in line 12 is simply כסף ('silver'), not the partial form of the personal name Yehoseph, as occasionally discovered in this document, such as by B. Levine (2000: 837) as mentioned above.

> And empowered and clean and . . . is the said Archelaus and his sons after him, and anyone else who may acquire this deed by his assignment (of it) regarding these purchases as (provided) in it in perpetuity (lines 16–17 and 40–41; cf. P. Yadin 3, lines 18–19 and 46–47).

This is a very important provision, as it assures legal capacity and clean title to the purchaser *and his sons and any assignees* relating to the transaction in perpetuity. The place for this provision, if P. Yadin 4 was following P. Yadin 2 and 3 in this respect, was in line 18, before the provision beginning 'And no one may attach a condition . . . '. But it does not appear there. Why did 'Abi'adan, who was about to receive title to an orchard, not have the scribe insert such a provision so as to provide similar protection for any sons she might have or for subsequent assignees of the deed? This is not a document, after all, which is parsimonious in the legal protection it accords to her. In the context of the relationship between P. Yadin 3 and 4, however, a very likely answer to this question suggests itself. It is this. 'Abi-'adan knew that the orchard she was going to acquire from the son of Lutay would immediately pass to Shim'on pursuant to the provisions of P. Yadin 3. There was, therefore, no need for a term to the effect that there was no impediment on 'Abi-'adan's sons inheriting the orchard or any other persons taking an assignment of P. Yadin 4. There was never going to be any such a bequest or assignment since she had agreed that the property in question would be acquired by Shim'on. This is also a sign of very careful draftsmanship by the Nabatean scribe.

The other two items of evidence can be dealt with more briefly. The second is that P. Yadin 4 contains a reference, in lines 10–11 (discussed below), to the twenty-eighth regnal year of Rabb'el II and this was the year in which P. Yadin 2 and 3 were executed, which represents an important connection. Thirdly, Babatha and her father before her show no signs of having been collectors of Nabatean legal documents not related to their property, so P. Yadin 4 must have some bearing on their assets.

EXPLAINING THE FUTURE TRANSFER OF THE ORCHARD

The fact that transfer of title would not occur until some future date explains an interesting variation in the P. Yadin 4 version of the penalty clause discussed above. Whereas in P. Yadin 2 and 3 the relevant clause reads 'in the entire price of *these* (אלה) purchases', the corresponding provision in line 16 of P. Yadin 4 reads 'in the entire price of *those* (אנו) purchases'. Why the change from 'these' to 'those'? The answer is that in both P. Yadin 2 and 3 the transfer of title was achieved in and by the deed itself. For that reason it was appropriate to speak of 'these purchases', meaning the purchases achieved by the deed. But in P. Yadin 4 the transfer of title, and hence the 'purchase' or more precisely 'the grant', will only occur in the future. The scribe, in a drafting alteration that nicely illustrates his skill and precision, alters 'these' to 'those' so as to refer to the deferred nature of the transaction: the parties are looking forward to a transfer of title in the future, in which perspective the grant must be designated by 'that' not 'this'.

But why was transfer of the orchard deferred to the future? Why did the son of Lutay not just transfer the property immediately? There is no suggestion in the deed, after all, that he lacks title to it. It is extremely difficult to think of any reason for this except one: that on the date that P. Yadin 4 was executed the orchard in question was leased to another party. Rendering this solution probable is not merely the difficulty of coming up with any other explanation but the common occurrence of leases of agricultural land in the Dead Sea region during this period.

Certain leases among the Dead Sea legal papyri were discussed in Chapter 3. The local practice in relation to leases bears upon P. Yadin 4 in two respects. First, the term of the leases varied considerably: from a minimum of one year (P. Yadin 46), to three (P. Yadin 42), and even to five years (P. Mur 24A-F). Thus we have the likely limits for the term of the lease that the son of Lutay entered into over the orchard referred to in P. Yadin 4. Secondly, the leases were, by and large, executed towards the end of the agricultural year, in the months of Marshevan (roughly equivalent to October/November; P. Yadin 44), Kislev (roughly equivalent to November/December; P. Yadin 45 and 46), and Sebat (roughly equivalent to January/February; P. Mur 24A-F). Tebet, not mentioned in these leases, falls between Kislev and Sebet (and roughly equals December/January). The only exception is P. Yadin 42, executed on the first of Iyyar (a month roughly equivalent to April/May). The reason for most of them being dated to these months was no doubt that the harvest needed to be complete so that the tenant could pay his rent to the landlord—a factor expressly mentioned with respect to vegetables in P. Yadin 45. For present purposes, P. Yadin 46, which includes date-palm cultivation, is a significant document, since it provides evidence that in the southern Dead Sea area, where similar climatic conditions would have been experienced in Maoza as well as En-Gedi, the date-palm and crop harvest was complete by Kislev (November/December), although the harvest for any other crops growing among the date-palms might have occurred a little later in the year.

P. Yadin 2 was executed on the third of Kislev in the twenty-eighth year of Rabb'el II's reign, who acceded to the Nabatean throne in 70 CE,[49] and P. Yadin 3 one day less than a month later, on the second of Tebet, in the same regnal year. Since P. Yadin 3 includes a promise by the son Lutay to perform his obligations under the grant (which we now know is P. Yadin 4) and since that document provides for a *future* transfer of property to 'Abi-'adan, we have—on the basis of the practice relating to agricultural leases just discussed—two possibilities with regard to the lease. First, it would expire very soon, say later in Tebet, or Shebet, or Adar (the latter being the last month in the calendar) of that year, or, secondly, it would not expire until the winter of the next year, or even a year or more after that. In the latter case, however, it is likely that the lease would expire and the transfer take place in the twenty-ninth regnal year of Rabb'el II, since although we appear not to know the day or month in 70 CE when he came to the throne, it cannot have been later than the third of Kislev (that is, November/December), which is the date P. Yadin 2 was executed, in his twenty-eighth regnal year (line 1).

Given that Shim'on was paying fifty per cent more for the orchard than Archelaus had agreed to pay (possibly somewhat more than its market value, as argued above), whereas it is unlikely that he was getting fifty per cent more orchard, it seems unlikely that he would have been willing to wait too long to receive the extra piece of land into his possession and begin earning an income from it. Even if the extra land he was purchasing was equal to fifty per cent of the area of the plot sold to Archelaus, commercial reality suggests that he would still want to get his hands on the extra portion as soon as possible. For this reason, it is probable that the lease from the son of Lutay to some unknown tenant would expire and he would transfer the plot to 'Abi-'adan within the next three months, or, at the latest and very unlikely,

[49] G. W. Bowersock (1983) *Roman Arabia*. Cambridge, MT: Harvard University Press, 71.

during the winter of the next year. It is very difficult to imagine a purchaser in Shim'on's position being willing to wait much more than a year to receive the land for which he had already paid.

Fortunately, data is available allowing us to pin down the possibilities relating to the expiration of the lease and the subsequent transfer to 'Abi-'adan. It is highly unlikely, if not inconceivable, that P. Yadin 4 failed to mention the date on which or by which transfer of title was due to take place. From a legal and a practical point of view, someone ('Abi-'adan in this case) who was going to receive the transfer of property in the future would insist that a date was fixed in the deed for that event. We will see in Chapter 9 that the grant was to be in return for the extinguishing of some debt owed to her by the transferor (here the son of Lutay). If no date were fixed for the transfer, the promise to transfer would be practically worthless. Nor would Shim'on have ensured that the son of Lutay promised to perform the obligations of the grant (as he did in P. Yadin 3) if the deed of grant itself (P. Yadin 4) did not or was not to contain a date for the transfer to 'Abi-'adan, on which he, Shim'on, was dependent to secure the remaining piece of land for which he had paid a considerable sum of money. Accordingly, we confidently expect to find such a date in the body of this deed.

By a happy circumstance, in spite of its fragmentary character, a date does occur in P. Yadin 4. Although the text is incomplete, since the last two letters of line 10 are ־ין and line 11 begins with ותמנא מראנא בשלמא ('and eight [of] our lord in well-being'), the editors have produced the following reading, which is plainly correct: שנת עשרין ותמונא מראנא בשלמא ('year twenty and eight [of] our lord in well-being'). A lacuna in the text makes it impossible to restore the day and month. The reference is to the twenty-eighth year of the reign of King Rabb'el II who, as noted above, became king in 70/71 CE. The twenty-eighth year is the same year in which the sales from 'Abi-'adan to Archelaus and then Shim'on were executed.

The editors rightly note that the fact that this date appears in the middle of the document and not at its beginning means that it is not the date on which the document was executed. They then suggest that it refers 'to some other action, or rental payment, that took place at that time'.[50] While it does refer to some other action, that action is

50 Yadin et al. 2002: 254.

most unlikely to be a rental payment. In raising this possibility the editors seem to have been overly influenced by their postulation of the word אכרי, meaning 'leasing fee', at the start of line 9,[51] and their failure to appreciate the nature of P. Yadin 4 as a grant. In my view this is a very insecure emendation. While the first letter of אכרי is probably *aleph*, the next two letters are short, downward strokes that could represent a number of letters in Nabatean Aramaic, while the fourth letter has not survived. It is certainly not impossible that a lease was mentioned in this document—as we have just seen, this is likely to have been the reason why the transfer of property was delayed. Nevertheless, given that the principal legal result of this deed is the agreement to transfer title to real property in the future and that it is virtually certain that the date for such transfer appeared in the deed, we are on firm ground in relating the reference to the twenty-eighth year of King Rabb'el's reign to the date on which that transfer was stipulated to occur, or (possibly but less likely) the date on which the lease would end. Since, however, termination of the lease would trigger the transfer, these two events were likely to have occurred on the same date. Although we do not know the month in Rabb'el's twenty-eighth regnal year in which the transfer was to take place, it must have been after the date of execution of P. Yadin 3, the second day of Tebet in the king's twenty-eighth year, since the grant lay in the future at the time of that transaction.

The number of months after the date of execution of P. Yadin 3 that still lay within the twenty-eighth year of Rabb'el's reign depends on the month of the year in which he acceded to the throne. It would be helpful if we knew that from another source.[52] Nevertheless, it is reasonable to conclude that the lease was probably coming to an end, with the transfer to occur, in the very near future, within a month or so. For if the lease was longer than this it would probably extend to the harvest at the end of the next calendar year, which was likely to be in the king's twenty-ninth regnal year. It is very difficult to see Shim'on waiting a whole year to receive the additional plot he had paid for.

When, finally, was P. Yadin 4 executed? This certainly happened before the grant itself (which speaks of it in future terms). Although P. Yadin 4 had not been drawn up or signed at the time the parties

[51] Yadin et al. 2002: 254.
[52] I have not yet found a reliable reference for this.

signed P. Yadin 3, on the second of Tebet, it is most unlikely that Shim'on would have accepted much delay in its preparation. Accordingly it is reasonable to suggest that this occurred in the month of Tebet.

With the character and parties to P. Yadin 4 and its link to P. Yadin 3 thus considered, it is now necessary, in Chapter 9, to explore the implications of the transaction, and in so doing present an ethnographic account of the interactions between Shim'on, 'Abi-'adan, and the son of Lutay.

9

P. Yadin 4 and Shim'on's Purchase of the Orchard

Using the character of P. Yadin 4 and the parties to that deed as explained in Chapter 8, it is possible to undertake the ethnographic exercise attempted with P. Yadin 1, 2, and 3, namely to imagine oneself present on the occasion the document was executed and to consider, within the distinctive social and cultural context that was Maoza, what was happening and how this sheds light on the parties and the relationships between them. All of this is germane to the over-arching question of how it was that Shim'on came to purchase a date-palm orchard in 99 CE.

The people we know were present on this occasion were the person signing on behalf of the son of Lutay (or, less likely, he in person) and the scribe. It is likely that 'Abi-'adan was also present, even though she was not to receive payment in cash, given her direct interest in the outcome. There were also four (or, less likely, five witnesses). It is also likely that Shim'on was present, because he would have been concerned to see that this outstanding aspect of his contract with 'Abi'-adan and the son of Lutay was brought to a successful conclusion and he obtained title to the entirety of the property he was purchasing. It is tempting to think that he was one of the witnesses to the execution of P. Yadin 4. This would have suited 'Abi-'adan and the son of Lutay, since Shim'on would thereafter have found it difficult to impugn execution of the deed, and it would not have put him at any disadvantage.

THE RELATIONSHIP BETWEEN ḤATṢMAR'IL, THE SON OF LUTAY, AND 'ABI-'ADAN

The Financial Dimension of their Relationship

In Chapter 3 of this volume I discussed the financial risks accompanying date cultivation, with its propensity to generate large profits and large losses, to be a cause of fortunes won and fortunes lost. Further reflection on the reason for the grant in P. Yadin 4 illustrates the extent to which the son of Lutay was subject to those pressures.

I explained the difference between a grant and a gift in Chapter 7, noting that while there is nothing in the nature of valuable consideration in relation to a gift, a grant can cover a situation where the transferor was getting something of value in return, even if that something was not a 'purchase price' in the strict sense. So in P. Yadin 4 are we dealing with a gift, one made gratuitously and not for valuable consideration, or a grant, one in which consideration was involved in some way? P. Yadin 4 provides strong evidence in favour of the latter alternative, such as the following provisions spoken by the son of Lutay:

> . . . I will grant to you the real property that (is described) above.
>
> Accordingly, (I) acknowledge liability, I in the (amount of) the said silver, which is not subject to any suit, or contest, or oath, in any respect, and if. . . . . I, the said son of Lutay, I will owe to you, you, the said 'Abi-'adan in the entire price of those purchases and the entire price of the real property (lines 14–16).

Here the son of Lutay is acknowledging that he is in debt to 'Abi-'adan, with the reference to 'the said (literally 'this') silver' meaning that the specific amount in question was mentioned earlier in the deed. The only scenario that accounts for the proximity of one statement by the son of Lutay promising the future transfer of real property and another acknowledging indebtedness to 'Abi-'adan in some previously specified amount of silver is that *the transfer will be in satisfaction of some or all of his indebtedness to her*. That is, the son of Lutay would be reducing some or all of the debt he owed to 'Abi-'adan in return for transferring the property to her. As noted in Chapter 7, since Shim'on paid 56 *sela's* (224 *denarii*) more than Archelaus for the enlarged property, the extra plot covered by the grant was probably worth that amount on the market and the debt was to be reduced by that amount.

This means that the transfer was to be made for valuable consideration, which makes the transaction a grant and not a gift. It is not a simple purchase (such as in P. Yadin 2 and 3) where the agreed price in silver was handed over in return for title to the property, with receipt of the money acknowledged by the vendor in the deed itself. Nevertheless, the grantee, 'Abi-'adan, is obtaining, or rather will obtain, title to an orchard *for value*, not by actually receiving money when the deed is signed but by the reduction or extinguishing of a debt in an agreed amount of silver owed to her, probably around 56 *sela's*. That the son of Lutay is receiving value for the property he has agreed to convey to her justifies the scribe continuing to refer to this transaction as a 'purchase' in line 16 (as discussed above). In such a context, if the son of Lutay breaches the agreement, he will pay 'Abi-'adan the value of the property that he is conveying, 56 *sela's*. Yet why did the son of Lutay not have sufficient cash to repay 'Abi'adan? Presumably because he was experiencing strained finances.

Another feature of P. Yadin 4 supports the suggestion that the son of Lutay was in a difficult financial position. This consists of one further difference between the penalty clause in P. Yadin 2 (and 3) and P. Yadin 4, namely that the expression די לא ברשא ('without consent'), which is Element 3, did not feature in the gap in line 15 of P. Yadin 4. The reason for this is that, although the words are missing, there is no sign of the long stroke of the necessary *lamed* in לא protruding into the line above. Lending support to this view is that with this expression included we would need about twenty-six or twenty-seven letters between והן and בר and there is only room for about fourteen to sixteen. Accordingly, this is a deed of grant that does not permit the grantor (the son of Lutay) to ask the grantee ('Abi-'adan) to agree to a variation from its terms. Although words to the effect 'without consent' were also omitted by the scribe responsible for the (comparatively uncomplicated) sale of a donkey or donkeys in P. Yadin 8 (lines 8–9), there are two particular reasons for their non-appearance in P. Yadin 4. First, since this exception softens the overall effect of the clause, by allowing alterations of the contract where the purchaser—here the transferee—agrees, its omission represents a tightening of the clause. The transferee, 'Abi-'adan, is saying, in effect, that no alterations to this contract will be allowed under any circumstances whatever. She can do so because she holds all the cards; the son of Lutay is indebted to her and has to relinquish possession of property to her in consequence. His position is weak. In such a context, her insisting that she would permit no alterations to the contract whatsoever is readily explicable. Secondly, Shim'on may have requested the omission of this provision to prevent the two of them varying the terms of the grant in a manner contrary to his interests. Asking why he might worry about such a possibility brings us to another aspect of the relationship between the son of Lutay and 'Abi-'adan.

The Son of Lutay and 'Abi-'adan as Husband and Wife

At least four pieces of evidence bear upon the question of the fundamental nature of the relationship between the son of Lutay and 'Abi-'adan. First, in 'Abi-'adan's sale to Shim'on (P. Yadin 3), the son of Lutay not only undertook to honour the terms of the grant but also guaranteed her obligations to Shim'on under that deed. This was a guarantee with teeth since by its terms the son of Lutay made himself jointly liable with 'Abi-'adan to repay the purchase price if the contract was breached (see Chapter 7). Why would the son of Lutay agree to this? This is very different from the situation in P. Yadin 1, where 'Abad-'Amanu guarantees Muqimu's loan from his (Muqimu's) wife 'Amat-'Isi. There the two men intended to invest the money in an agricultural lease, so that thereafter they would have an on-going relationship with a view to profit, that is a partnership. But in P. Yadin 3 'Abi-'adan owns, in her own right, the bulk of the date-palm orchard she is selling to Shim'on, even though a transfer (from the son of Lutay to her) has been agreed to provide the extra portion. Apart from the fact that he owes her money, there is no sign that the son of Lutay and 'Abi-'adan have any on-going commercial relationship. How then could Shim'on ask, or even insist, as he most surely did, that the son of Lutay act as guarantor? The fact that the son of Lutay was a debtor of 'Abi-'adan would not be a reason for him to become a guarantor of her obligations—just the contrary in fact. As a general principle, guarantors are chosen because they have available capital. More particularly, by incurring a possible liability to Shim'on the son of Lutay would have been less able to repay 'Abi-'adan. Accordingly, by far the most likely explanation for his guarantee (and it is not easy to think of any other) is that he was married to 'Abi-'adan. Given the close relationship between the two by virtue of their marriage (including their capacity to move assets between one another and the family honour that they shared), Shim'on wanted the son of Lutay to stand behind his wife's obligations. It is an interesting sign of Shim'on's power in this transaction, to which we will return later in this chapter, that the son of Lutay and 'Abi-'adan agreed!

Secondly, the son of Lutay was indebted to 'Abi-'adan in the considerable sum of approximately 56 *sela's*, or 224 *denarii*. How did such indebtedness come about? I suggested in Chapter 3 that while women could lend from their dowries (with specific acknowledgment of this fact in the deed) and from general cash reserves, their husbands were the main recipients. Social pressures from their cognate kin (who would wish their female relatives to protect their dowries) and from their husbands (who would have preferred such a source of capital to be restricted to themselves) would have reduced the incidence of loans by wives to anyone else. In my view, it is therefore probable that in lending money to the son of Lutay, 'Abi-'adan was lending to her husband.

Thirdly, the son of Lutay signed P. Yadin 3 on behalf of 'Abi-'adan. Her name, 'Abi-'adan (without her patronymic) appears first, together with the words 'in person'. Directly underneath her name appears '. . . . .]l the son of Lutah.' But both names are in the same handwriting. In my submission this is the handwriting of the son of Lutay.[1]

The fourth area of evidence is this. At one point in P. Yadin 3 'Abi-'adan and the son of Lutay are referred to together solely by reference to their first names: ''Abi-'adan and Ḥaṣmar'il' (line 44), a notably familiar manner of designation, given that their patronymics also appear earlier in the deed. For the scribe to include this description without the use of patronymics conveys a strong impression that these two are, to cite a modern idiom, 'an item'. That is, the expression is redolent of a situation where the two are a married couple, well known to the witnesses to, and the scribe of, the deed and are thus appropriately mentioned together with respect to their first names alone.

[1] 'He probably signed in her name' (Y. Yadin et al. (eds) (2002) *The Documents from the Bar Kokhba period in the Cave of Letters: Hebrew, Aramaic and Nabatean-Aramaic Papyri*. Judean Desert Studies. Jerusalem: Israel Exploration Society, Institute of Archaeology, Hebrew University and the Shrine of the Book, Israel Museum, 244).

On the basis of these points, I submit that the son of Lutay and 'Abi-'adan were husband and wife. I will now utilize this view in probing further the nature of their relationship.

The Son of Lutay and 'Abi-'adan: Further Aspects of their Relationship

At the heart of the reason for the existence of P. Yadin 4 was the personal situation of the son of Lutay. He was indebted to 'Abi-'adan, his wife, and the transfer of an orchard plot he owned was necessary to discharge some or all of this indebtedness. The precedent of P. Yadin 1 shows that there must have been a signed deed wherein he acknowledged his debt to 'Abi-'adan, probably containing the clauses evident in P. Yadin 1. That document has not survived, however, presumably because there was no need for Shim'on to acquire it. The debt of the son of Lutay to his wife was certain to be increasing, and increasing fast, since we know from P. Yadin 1 that even when a wife was lending money to her husband, the loan amount increased 'as is customary' (line 17), that is, by the application of interest at the local customary rate. This was probably around 9 per cent per annum, which was the rate in 125 CE (see Chapter 3) and perhaps also the customary rate in the 90s of the first century CE. P. Yadin 1 gives the creditor-wife the power both to elect when the principal and interest must be repaid (line 18) and also to seize property of the debtor in satisfaction of the debt. These provisions were probably a regular feature of loans.

The indebtedness of the son of Lutay requires consideration in the context of the discussion of dowries in Chapter 3. As noted there, in other social settings where dowries occur it is common to find the fathers of young women seeking to match them to men of roughly similar social status and economic position. If that was the case in Nabatea as well (and it is difficult to see why it would not have been), it is clear that things went badly awry for 'Abi-'adan, just as they would later for Babatha herself, both of whom married men who fell into debt. In Babatha's case it was a large debt that was not repaid before her husband died. In such a situation, we must assume that the son of Lutay and Babatha's second husband were the subject of significant disapproval by the cognate relatives of the two women and that their honour (and that of their cognate relatives) must have been diminished in the wider community as well.

It is probable that when the son of Lutay entered into the lease of his orchard with the unknown tenant, he was either not in debt to 'Abi-'adan or, if he was, the debt was not on such a scale that it caused her any due concern. If it had worried her, she would have acted at that point to exercise her rights under the loan document and to take possession of property he owned in satisfaction of the debt, lest the rights of an incoming tenant interfere with her capacity to have her debt repaid. This argument assumes (it is submitted reasonably given their relationship and the close-knit nature of village life) that it would not have been possible for the son of Lutay to keep any proposed tenancy of the orchard plot secret from 'Abi-'adan.

These considerations suggest that having entered into the lease when his position was sound, the son of Lutay then found that his financial circumstances deteriorated, so that he either fell into debt to 'Abi-'adan, or a pre-existing debt he owed her grew, in either case resulting in a situation that she was no longer willing to tolerate, even when the debtor was her husband. While I have discussed the economics of date cultivation in Chapter 3, we have no way of knowing what particular issues led to the son Lutay finding himself in this position. In addition to the lease, he may well have had a number of financial ventures in play at that time. We gain a vivid picture of the nature and possible intensity of the commercial activities in which men in this world engaged from P. Yadin 5. This document, written in Greek and signed in 2 June 110 CE, is a deed of deposit in which Joseph son of Joseph surnamed Zaboudos of Maoza acknowledges that he holds on behalf of Jesus son of Jesus (the latter Jesus being Joseph's now deceased brother), a sum of money as a deposit in relation to all (a) assets of silver, (b) contracts of debt, (c) investment in factory, (d) value of figs, (e) value of wine, (f) value of dates, (g) value of oil, and of everything else which belonged to Joseph and the late Jesus. There is also mention of three other loans, presumably to close friends or relatives.[2]

[2] See N. Lewis (1989) *The Documents from the Bar Kokhba Period in the Cave of Letters: Greek Papyri and Aramaic and Nabatean Signatures and Subscriptions.* Jerusalem: Israel Exploration Society, The Hebrew University of Jerusalem and the Shrine of the Book, 35–40. The beneficiary of this deed, Jesus (minor), later became Babatha's first husband (P. Yadin 10 is her *ketubba*).

It may only have taken one or more of any such ventures in which the son of Lutay was engaging to turn sour for him to sustain losses on such a scale that he became unable to repay his debt to 'Abi-'adan. Essential to my argument in Chapter 6 of this volume is that Muqimu and his guarantor 'Abad-'Amanu had fallen into debt to 'Amat-'Isi, having borrowed money from her for a business venture (probably an agricultural lease). Upon the death of the latter, she turned to 'Abad-'Amanu's son and heir, Archelaus, to discharge the debt. This illustrates the capacity for business ventures in this context to fail and for a creditor (here a woman) to seek repayment of money owed to him or her. In this setting the fact that the son of Lutay fell into trouble so that his debt to wife 'Abi-'adan became a matter of concern to her is readily explicable.

It is difficult to reach a view on whether the son of Lutay suffered a progressive or a sudden deterioration in his financial circumstances. Whereas, however, the death of Archelaus's father led to Archelaus suddenly having to expend some of his financial assets to pay out 'Amat-'Isi, we have no evidence of such an emergency affecting the son of Lutay. Perhaps a progressive deterioration was more common than a sudden catastrophe, but we have no way of knowing in this case. All we have is his indebtedness to 'Abi-'adan and the fact that they had agreed he would repay some or all of that debt by transferring title of an orchard plot he owned to her.

In the light of the difficult financial situation of the son of Lutay, the probability (discussed in Chapter 8) that someone else signed P. Yadin 4 on his behalf raises an interesting possibility. Did he absent himself deliberately from Maoza on the occasion that P. Yadin 4 was executed, whatever ostensible excuse he offered, to avoid the dishonour of being present when his lack of success would be so evident to everyone who was present on that occasion? No doubt in a small farming community word that it had been necessary to extinguish some or all of the debt he owed to his wife by transferring title of an orchard to her would soon have become widely known. But actually to be present on that occasion in the presence of his neighbours would only have compounded his embarrassment. Did 'Abi'adan and maybe even Shim'on concur that such a course would be desirable? While the evidence is lacking to conclude that this was what probably happened, it remains an intriguing possibility.

SHIM'ON'S RELATIONSHIP WITH 'ABI-'ADAN AND THE SON OF LUTAY

The issues raised in this discussion are all deeply relevant to the overall question of how Shim'on came to acquire a date-palm plantation in 99 CE. The argument so far entails that Shim'on had decided both to purchase the property included in the sale to Archelaus and also to ask 'Abi-'adan to add to the property to be transferred the smaller plot of land then owned by the son of Lutay. It is highly likely, bordering on certain, that Shim'on had (from village gossip or first-hand knowledge) considerable awareness of their personal circumstances; otherwise, he would not have been in a position to make this request. He must have known that they were husband and wife, that the son of Lutay owned the smaller plot, its market value, that it was currently leased, and that he was indebted to 'Abi-'adan. He was probably aware of the reason for that indebtedness and maybe even of its extent. He would have been familiar with the range of the business interests of the son of Lutay in Maoza and in neighbouring villages and his lack of overall success with them.

Yet Shim'on was not merely in possession of information concerning the son of Lutay and 'Abi-'dadan; he also had a relationship with them that plainly included his trust. That there were mutual good relations between the three of them, in spite of their differing ethnic identities (as discussed in Chapter 2), is evident from the fact that the grant (P. Yadin 4) had not been drafted and executed at the time that Shim'on's purchase (P. Yadin 3) was concluded and he handed over the full purchase price. As noted in Chapter 7, this conclusion flows from the reference in P. Yadin 3 to the terms of '*a* grant' not '*the* grant' (lines 16 and 43) and the fact that 'Abi-'adan acknowledged receipt of the whole purchase price in the deed (lines 9 and 32–33). On the other hand, as argued above, Shim'on—a willing purchaser with a large amount of cash at his disposal—would have been disinclined to wait too long to receive the remaining portion of the orchard land he had paid for, and the evidence of P. Yadin 4 suggests no more than a month or two was necessary.

That P. Yadin 4 was entered into for no other reason than the request of Shim'on, when Archelaus, after all, had not wished to purchase this extra plot, raises another interesting prospect. Although P. Yadin 4 was not in existence when P. Yadin 3 was concluded, so that Shim'on was placing considerable trust in 'Abi-'adan and the son of Lutay, he probably discussed the sort of provisions that it would contain. It is most unlikely that he would have paid 168 *sela's* for the property, fifty per cent more than Archelaus had paid, if he was not aware of the provisions that they intended inserting into P. Yadin 4. Perhaps the scribe gave him reassurances on this score.

But Shim'on appears to have gone even further, by intervening in relation to the actual drafting of P. Yadin 4. Two features of the deed suggest this quite strongly. First, it was in his direct interest to request that 'Abi-'adan and the son of Lutay omit the provision that would have allowed them to agree on a fundamental variation of the contract (via the 'except with consent' [די לא ברשא]) clause present in P. Yadin 2 and 3 but absent in P. Yadin 4 and mentioned above). Omitting the clause prevented collusion between husband and wife that might have denied him possession of the extra plot. He may well have specifically requested this amendment of Abi-'adan. Secondly, as we saw in Chapter 8, also missing from P. Yadin 4 is a provision that assures 'Abi-'adan as transferee that she and her sons and any assignees of the deed have capacity and clean title in relation to the transfer of title. The only plausible explanation for that omission is that it was irrelevant in a context where the property the subject of the deed was going to pass to Shim'on pursuant to P. Yadin 3. Yet, again, it was in Shim'on's direct interest for this clause not to appear in the deed and it was presumably omitted on his request. Ultimately, it is worth noting, Shim'on received (no doubt at his request) a signed original copy of P. Yadin 4; otherwise it would not form part of the archive.

Having reached these conclusions we must note that they demand a remarkable degree of intrusion by Shim'on into the lives of 'Abi-'adan and the son of Lutay. Wives must at times have exercised their legal rights against husbands indebted to them, including the right of foreclosure on hypothecated realty, but the least painful route to achieve this, in relation to the reputation of those concerned, was for the wife to take action on her account and not at the bidding of someone else, especially not some other adult male. Even if 'Abi-'adan and the son of Lutay had no relationship other than as creditor and debtor, for Shim'on to persuade 'Abi-'adan to foreclose on her loan to him with respect to the plot of land that the son of Lutay owned would have been shameful for him. It would have represented a public and humiliating demonstration of his commercial weakness vis-à-vis 'Abi-'adan. Yet on the basis, for the reasons set out above, that the two were married, the shame would have been enhanced, for Shim'on would also have demonstrated the incompetence of a husband in relation to his wife. Nevertheless, this is what seems to have happened.

Here is the likely course of events. Archelaus must have approached 'Abi-'adan with his debt travails—caused by his father's sudden death—requesting that she rescind the sale to him. News of this surprising turn of events reached Shim'on. A discussion then occurred between 'Abi-'adan and Shim'on, most probably at her instigation, about his buying the orchard that Archelaus had purchased. Shim'on must have extended the ambit of the negotiation by requesting his purchase of the extra orchard plot owned by her debtor husband, but under lease. Next, 'Abi-'adan must have broached the subject with her husband. This would have been a difficult conversation as it was being driven by Shim'on's wish to acquire both orchards and would have exposed the son of Lutay's financial weakness, causing him shame. Yet the son of Lutay did agree to this idea. P. Yadin 3 was drafted and executed and so, shortly afterwards (probably in the same month), was P. Yadin 4. Finally, the transfer of the orchard to 'Abi-'adan provided for in P. Yadin 4 occurred, with title to that property immediately passing to Shim'on pursuant to the provisions of P. Yadin 3. Thus he acquired the entirety of the orchard she called Gahadiya.

CONCLUSION

At some stage, probably in Tebet in Rabb'el II's twenty-eighth regnal year, and in Maoza, a group of people gathered for the reading and signing of the deed we call P. Yadin 4. Certainly the son of Lutay (but probably through his authorized representative) was there and so was the scribe, 'Azur son of 'Awatu. Also present were four or maybe five witnesses. It seems likely that 'Abi-'adan and also Shim'on were present, given their interest in this event.

This must have been a poignant moment for Ḥatṣmar'il the son of Lutay, and for his wife. While the infusion of cash beyond what they had received from Archelaus must have been welcome, there was no getting away from the fact that underlying the transaction was the son of Lutay's lack of commercial success. This was known to Shim'on and the scribe, and perhaps also to the witnesses. In a culture where personal and family honour mattered, the process must have caused the son of Lutay and 'Abi-'adan some pain. On the other hand, it is hard to imagine Shim'on revelling in their discomfort. He was on friendly and trusting terms with them and while he had sought that extra plot, he may have wished there had been some other way to acquire it. He already had the bulk of the orchard in his possession via P. Yadin 3. All that was now required was for the lease over the smaller plot to expire and the entire grove would be his, a possession that he would one day pass on to his daughter Babatha, along with the intriguing tale of how he had come to acquire it.

10

An Ancient Jewish Family Tale

While Babatha was growing up her father Shim'on, son of Menaḥem, told her several times the story of how he came to acquire the date-palm orchard, which he re-named *'Al-giph-yamma*, Aramaic for 'on the seashore'. He was proud of himself for having acquired it at all, especially as he was the sole Judean among many Nabateans, one of whom, a high official, had wanted it for himself. Moreover, it was a productive orchard in a good location and contiguous on its southern side with an orchard owned by King Rabb'el himself. This is the tale he told Babatha.

It was early winter in the twenty-eighth year of King Rabb'el's reign. The king had ascended the throne of the Nabateans in the very year in which the Roman legions under Titus had captured Jerusalem and destroyed the Judeans' temple. Throughout Shim'on's village of Maoza on the southern shores of the Dead Sea men were busy—getting in the last of the date harvest, working in the vegetable plots, tending the land to be sown with barley, and carrying out maintenance on the irrigation ditches and sluice-gates.

News travels fast in Maoza and word reached Shim'on that his near neighbour, the Nabatean woman, 'Abi-'adan daughter of 'Aptaḥ, son of Manigares, was planning to sell a date-palm orchard she owned in the village. It had the Dead Sea on its northern boundary and the royal lands to the south, while its eastern boundary was a road running north/south. The houses of Taḥa daughter of 'Abad-Ḥaretat, occupied part of its western boundary. It was an awkwardly shaped orchard, however, since there was another plot forming an intrusion occupying its south-western corner. This plot had the houses of Ḥunainu, Tayim-'Ilahi's son, on its western side, but only stretched part of the distance eastward to where the road lay. The plot, about one-quarter of the size of 'Abi-'adan's, was owned by Ḥaṣmar'il the son of Lutay. Shim'on had always been quite taken with Ḥaṣmar'il's impressive name, given its meaning in Aramaic, 'Arrow of the Lord God'.

Ḥaṣmar'il was 'Abi-'adan's husband. Some years before, 'Abi-'adan had owned both the larger portion and the smaller part in the south-western corner. They had formed one orchard called Gahadiya. When the orchard was subdivided, each part was given its own name. Ḥaṣmar'il had acquired possession of the smaller part. The larger orchard was supplied with irrigation water for the date-palms from the stream emerging from the hills to the east. When it received the usual thirty minutes' flow of irrigation water on the first day of the week, with the sluices being opened on the eastern side of 'Abi-'adan's property, similar sluices were opened onto Ḥaṣmar'il's land so that his date-palms could be irrigated at the same time.

Ḥaṣmar'il was quite successful in his business ventures at the time he obtained the orchard and one of them consisted of his leasing it out to a tenant. As the years passed, however, for various reasons Ḥaṣmar'il's financial position deteriorated and Shim'on knew that he was now considerably in debt to his wife. She had lent him money, possibly from her dowry, and, as required under Nabatean law, that loan was recorded in a legal document that provided 'Abi-'adan could seize any of Ḥaṣmar'il's property in the event of his failure to repay the loan.

Shim'on, who already owned land in the village and had money to invest, was very interested in purchasing the orchard that he had heard 'Abi-'adan was selling. So he visited 'Abi-'adan to ascertain the truth of what he had heard and to see if she might be willing to sell the orchard to him. He was disappointed to learn that she already had another interested purchaser, in the shape of Archelaus, the son of 'Abad-'Amanu. Everyone in Maoza knew Archelaus, since he came from a nearby village, Rummon. The whole area bathed in the honour he had brought to it, for Archelaus was a local boy made good. He had recently been appointed to a high position in the service of the king, as a *strategos* no less. At that time he was exercising the high military and administrative responsibilities the position entailed in another part of the kingdom. Yet he had grown up in nearby Rummon and his father still lived there. 'Abad-'Amanu had served in the king's army and, while never achieving a position as lofty as that of his son, had tapped into his old military connections to help his son get launched on a successful career in the king's service. Archelaus had become interested in buying an orchard near his hometown and increasing his family's property in the area. He was particularly interested in purchasing the date-palm orchard 'Abi-'adan was selling because on its southern boundary was an orchard owned by the king himself. This was evidence of its productivity, but owning it would also bring him closer to the royal family, whose members he knew from the dinners and other events arranged by the king.

Shim'on was not surprised when 'Abi-'adan told him that, although she appreciated his interest, she was minded to sell the orchard to Archelaus. She said that he was already a big figure in the realm, with influential friends, including the royal family, in the Nabatean court, and he had a bright future ahead of him. She did not want to get on the wrong side of him and hoped, indeed, that he might prove a useful friend in the future. Shim'on understood her position. He asked her whether Archelaus was also interested in purchasing her husband's plot of land in the south-west corner of the orchard and she said no. So Shim'on left her, asking her as he did so that, if Archelaus decided not to proceed with the sale, to bear him in mind. Shortly afterwards, Shim'on was disappointed to hear that Archelaus had indeed purchased the orchard from 'Abi-'adan, for a price of 112 *sela's*, equivalent to 448 *denarii*. The Nabatean scribe who drafted the deed of sale was very sensitive to the high social status of Archelaus and embellished the date of execution provision at the start of the document by adding to the king's name those of several other members of the royal family, all of whom Archelaus knew. The deed of sale was executed by the parties and witnesses on the third day of Kislev in the twenty-eighth year of King Rabb'el's reign.

Almost before the ink had dried on the deed of sale for the orchard, however, surprising events began to occur. The first was that 'Abad-'Amanu, Archelaus' father, died unexpectedly. The second came about because of a business partnership in which 'Abad-'Amanu had been involved with Muqimu, son of 'Awat-'Ilahi and grandson of Ḥalaf-'Ilahi. Five years earlier Muqimu and 'Abad-'Amanu had the opportunity of becoming lessees of some agricultural land. But neither of them had the 150 *sela's* (600 *denarii*) the landlord required as the initial lease fee. So Muqimu had borrowed the money from the dowry of his wife 'Amat-'Isi. She consented to this in writing as required by the law of the Nabatean kingdom, but insisted that 'Abad-'Amanu provide a guarantee for her husband's debt. All parties envisaged that a further 150 *sela's* might be added to the original 150, to cover further lease fees, with the whole of the amount advanced to bear interest at the customary rate of nine per cent per annum. Muqimu and ʻAbad-ʻAmanu proved not very successful lessees. They borrowed the further 150 *sela*ʻs from ʼAmat-ʼIsi but were not able to repay the loan from the produce of the land they had leased. So when Abad-ʻAmanu died there was a very sizeable debt owing to ʼAmat-ʼIsi. She needed the money to replenish her precious dowry, upon which she and her children might need to rely if her husband Muqimu died.

It was at this point that a third surprising event occurred. Rather than asking her husband to repay the loan, ʼAmat-ʼIsi activated the guarantee in the deed of loan. But with ʻAbad-ʻAmanu dead, she could hardly ask him for the money. Instead she turned to Archelaus as his father's son and heir and therefore—under Nabatean law that was aligned with the centuries-old Aramaic legal tradition—responsible for the payment of his father's debts. Her husband was either unable to repay the loan, or ʼAmat-ʼIsi simply preferred to bring in money from outside the family when she had the tempting opportunity provided by the guarantee.

Yet this was still a bold manoeuvre on the part of ʼAmat-ʼIsi, given the social position and political influence of Archelaus by virtue of his office of *strategos*. Why chance incurring his anger? A number of factors led this enterprising woman to conclude that the benefit outweighed the risks. If she did not require Archelaus to repay the loan, she was facing a serious depletion of her dowry that meant she was risking poverty if her husband died or divorced her. Alternatively, if her husband could repay, she would have lost a chance to increase their joint wealth by asking Archelaus for the money. She also judged that the honour of Archelaus and his family was at stake in the local area—where he was known to virtually everyone—if he did not stand by his father's debt. Influenced by the nomadic traditions still operative among the Nabatean elite, Archelaus was not someone filled with his own sense of importance and was not likely to hold it against ʼAmat-ʼIsi in the future that she had asked him for the money. Finally, she was confident that he must have been enriching himself from his official position and could easily afford to repay the debt.

Then came the fourth surprise, and the biggest of all. Archelaus proved not to have the resources that ʼAmat-ʼIsi and the local population thought he did. He was too recently appointed a *strategos* to have acquired the wealth that normally flowed to those in that position. This meant he was put in a difficult position by ’Amat-’Isi’s request that he repay his father’s debt, since he did not have all the *sela‘s* he needed to do so. He thus found it necessary to ask ’Abi-‘adan to rescind her very recent sale of the orchard to him and repay him the purchase so that he could give the money to ’Amat-’Isi in partial satisfaction of his deceased father’s debt to her. He did not want to sell directly to Shim‘on, because to do this he would have first needed to have his property listed in the king’s land register under his name and that would have taken time. ’Abi-‘adan knew Shim‘on had also been interested in buying the orchard and thought that it would be a simple matter to sell it to him instead. So the sale to Archelaus was rescinded, allowing him to pass on 112 *sela‘s* to ’Amat-’Isi as a part-payment of the total debt he owed her.

This time Shim‘on waited for ’Abi-‘adan to approach him and it did not take her long to do so. It turned out that he was the only other potential purchaser of the land, which put him in a strong position in the negotiation since ’Abi-‘adan needed the money she would get from the sale. He agreed to buy the orchard that Archelaus had bought from her but he had one major condition. The orchard had to be enlarged by consolidation with the plot in its south-west corner owned by Ḥaṣmar’il. Shim‘on was only interested in purchasing the whole orchard that had previously been called Gahadiya. Shim‘on was happy with the fact that Archelaus, to save time, did not want to sell to him directly, because this allowed him to bind ’Abi-‘adan and her husband, Ḥaṣmar’il the son of Lutay, together in relation to the overall transaction. So he suggested that she take the smaller plot back into her possession, either with the agreement of her husband, or pursuant to the provisions of the deed of loan she had with her husband, and sell the combined area to him.

Shim‘on thought that he was on solid ground in asking for this. He knew that Ḥaṣmar’il was a husband, not unusually among local farmers, indebted to his wife, and that the loan document allowed her to seize any property he owned, including the plot in the south-west corner of the orchard. Accordingly, Ḥaṣmar’il was in a weak position and Shim‘on considered it likely that ’Abi-‘adan would persuade him to transfer the plot to her in return for a reduction in the money he owed her. Yet there was a downside as far as ’Abi-‘adan and Ḥaṣmar’il were concerned. They had their honour to think of. What Shim‘on was proposing meant making very public the fact of the failure of Ḥaṣmar'il in business and his indebtedness to his wife. From her point of view, any dishonour her husband suffered necessarily reflected on her. In the event, when it came time to sign the deed of grant, Ḥaṣmar'il absented himself, and had an agent sign on his behalf, perhaps to avoid the embarrassment of his presence at an occasion that made all too evident his commercial failure.

Nevertheless, both 'Abi-'adan and Ḥaṣmar'il agreed. To salvage his and their honour somewhat, 'Abi-'adan did not proceed to enforce the foreclosure provision in her deed of loan with him. Instead, she and he agreed that he would voluntarily grant the property to her in satisfaction of money he owed her. This was scheduled to happen within a month or so, and still in the twenty-eighth year of King Rabb'el's reign, when the lease to which the orchard was subject came to and end.

'Abi-'adan also persuaded Shim'on to pay a premium for the combined property. 'Abi-'adan and Shim'on agreed a price for the reconsolidated orchard, now under its original name Gahadiya, of 168 *sela's*, equivalent to 672 *denarii.* This was exactly fifty per cent higher than the price paid by Archelaus for the large section of it, although Ḥaṣmar'il's plot was not fifty per cent of the size of the principal section of the orchard. There were two reasons for this. First, whilst 'Abi-'adan had given Archelaus a reduction in price for the portion he was purchasing—so she might keep in the good favour of someone in such a high position—she was unwilling to give Shim'on a discount. Secondly, she aimed to salvage the family honour somewhat by securing a price above market value.

Shim'on was very careful to protect his position. He was on excellent terms with his Nabatean neighbours, yet he was still the only Judean amidst a number of Nabateans. Even the scribe was a Nabatean and the language and script of the document were both in Nabatean, not Judean, Aramaic. So he took a number of precautions.

One of the provisions on which Shim'on insisted was that Ḥaṣmar'il not only sign a transfer to his wife but also guarantee her sale to him. Shim'on also requested when the document recording the grant was being drafted that it not contain the usual provision allowing the two parties to change its terms by mutual agreement and 'Abi-'adan and Ḥaṣmar'il had agreed to this (which suited her personal interests as well). Nor did it contain the usual clause allowing future transfers to her heirs and assigns.

Once the transaction had been agreed, 'Abi-'adan approached the scribe who had drafted the sale to Archelaus to draft both a new deed of sale to Shim'on and also the deed of grant from Ḥaṣmar'il to her. Shim'on familiarized himself with the terms of the deed of sale before it was signed on the second of Tebet and was happy with them. The deed of grant was not available on that date, but Shim'on had discussed its likely terms with 'Abi-'adan. In relation to the deed of sale, he ensured that the orchard was now described as having as its western abutters not just 'the houses of Taḥa, daughter of 'Abad-Ḥaretat', but rather 'the houses of Ḥunainu, son of Tayim-'Ilahi and the houses of Taḥa, daughter of 'Abad-Ḥaretat'. To make certain that there could be no mistake as to which orchard was being sold, he also required that 'Abi-'adan's orchard be referred to in the deed by the name she used for it, a name that formed part of its registration in the Nabatean land register. He sought and obtained specificity as to the day of the week and the time that the irrigation sluice gates would be opened. In relation to Ḥaṣmar'il's deed of grant to 'Abi-'adan, Shim'on requested that the scribe omit some of the standard Nabatean clauses found in deeds of sale, noted above, to protect his position. In any event, once Ḥaṣmar'il's property had been transferred to 'Abi-'adan when the lease expired, both plots would be covered by provisions in the deed of sale of Gahadiya from 'Abi-'adan to Shim'on.

Yet Shim'on's concern with the transaction did not end with his ensuring that the clauses in the deed of sale and the deed of grant matched his interests. For he also sought to protect his legal position by obtaining three other documents, in addition to the deed of sale from 'Abi-'adan to him. First of all, he requested and obtained a signed original of the deed of transfer from Ḥaṣmar'il to her when it had it been drafted and signed, an event he attended. But Shim'on was most concerned about Archelaus. While he had known him as a boy growing up in a nearby village, Archelaus was now a senior official in the service of the king. Shim'on was on good terms with him but he was also nervous. The thing he feared most was that Archelaus, or an heir of his, might later claim that he and not Shim'on owned the orchard by virtue of the prior sale. Shim'on wanted written reassurance concerning three issues and, as it turned out, Archelaus proved very reasonable in respect of all of them.

First, Archelaus agreed to Shim'on's request to give him the signed original of the deed of loan from 'Amat-'Isi to Muqimu that Archelaus's father had signed as guarantor five years previously. Shim'on needed this, coupled with the additional factor of Abad-'Amanu's death, to explain what lay behind the sudden and highly unusual rescission of the sale from 'Abi-'adan to Archelaus. Secondly, he obtained from Archelaus his own signed original of his purchase from 'Abi-'adan a month before. Thirdly, he asked Archelaus to witness 'Abi-'adan's deed of sale of the enlarged orchard to him. Archelaus did so, signing just after 'Abi-'adan and Ḥaṣmar'il and referring to his father in his signature with his old army nickname. So Shim'on ended up possessing four Nabatean legal documents proving his title to the orchard and kept them safe before passing them onto Babatha.

Such is the story Shim'on told Babatha of how, on the second day of Tebet in the twenty-eighth year of King Rabb'el's reign, he came to purchase the date-palm orchard in Maoza called *'Al-giph-yamma* that he later gave to her.

APPENDIX 1

Emended Nabatean Aramaic Text of P. Yadin 4 (with Annotations)

Lower Version

Recto

1. [ב   בטבת שנת עשרין ותמונא לרבאל מלכא מלך נבטו די אחיי ושיזב עמה במחוז עגלתין
2. יומא הו איתי לכי אנתי אביעדן ברת אפתח בר מניגרס עמי אנה חצמראל בר לתי בעלה בכסף סלעי]ן
3. ....]טמא ..ה[
4. ....
5. ....גנת תמר]יא די[לבר לתי די מתקריה ... די בגלגלא די במחז עגלתין על שקיא ועני מיה כדי חזא
6. ואלה תחומיה למדנחא גנת שמעון די מתקריה .....ולמערבא בתי חנינו בר תימאלהי ולימינא
7. גנת מראנא רבאל מלכא מלך נבטו די אחיי ושיזב עמה ולשמאלא[
....
8. ....
9. ....גנתא די עלא .... עלא
10. ....[.......שנת עשר]ין
11. ותמונא מראנא בשלמא ....די אנוש כלא[ ]כל מ[נדע]ם[זעיר]
12. ושג[יא]... בזבני גנתא הי קדם זמנא די עלא כתיב ...קים ....[בכ]סף דנה
13. ....
14. קדמיכי מן[כ]ל אנוש כלה רחיק וקריב די אנתן לכי עקרנא די עלא כדנה מודא ומתחיב
15. אנה בכסף דנה די לא דין ולא דבב ולא מומא כלה והן .... אנה בר לתי דנה
16. אחוב לכי אנתי אביעדן דא בכל דמי זבניא אנו וכול דמי עקרנא די עלא וכלכל די תתרעין
17. בצבות..]מראנ
18. רבאל מלכא כות ועררין לא ברשא ..די בשטרא דנה יתעבד ולא מתנו בכל שהיה
19. יתנו.

20. [חצמרא בר ל]תה[כתב]ה
21. מ[מר]ה
22.
23.
24.
25.
26.

Emendments to P. Yadin 4, Lines 1–9 (Emendments to Lines 12–20 are discussed in Chapter 8)

The words underlined are my reconstruction. Because of the paucity of remains for the first ten lines, the attribution of words to particular lines is not certain (although see note on the remaining letters יא די. . . in line 5 below). But gauging from the two reasonably complete lines, 14 and 18, and his practice in P. Yadin 2 and 3 this scribe was managing about 55–65 letters per line and I have used that as a rough guide in allocating words to lines.

The Date and Place of Execution Clause (Line 1)

The conventions governing Nabatean legal papyri, the conclusions reached concerning the nature of P. Yadin 4 in Chapter 8, and the fact that the scribe responsible for P. Yadin 4 also drafted P. Yadin 2 and 3 mean we can be confident that the first line of the document contained its date of execution with respect to the twenty-eighth year of the reign of King Rabb'el. It is also likely to have been in the month of Tebet, since Shim'on would have insisted on the deed being drafted and executed within a short time of the execution of P. Yadin 3, on the second of Tebet in that year. Only the day of the month is unknown. More particularly, since neither the son of Lutay nor 'Abi-'adan were members of the Nabatean elite such as to require the elaborate date of execution clause the scribe drafted for Archelaus (P. Yadin 2), there are solid grounds for the view that the date of execution clause took the same form as in P. Yadin 3. We can be equally confident that the place of execution, 'in Maḥoz 'Eglatain', appeared after the date.

The Disposition Clause (Lines 2–4)

It is clear from both P. Yadin 2 and 3 that after the date and place of execution clause in P. Yadin 4 there would have followed a clause relating to the disposition of real property effected by or referred to in the deed. As in those other deeds, this provision would have begun with the expression 'on that day' (יומא הו), meaning the date of execution just stated, and then would have provided the full names of the two parties and specified the legal disposition effected by the document. We know that the three people directly affected (Shim'on, 'Abi-'adan, and the son of Lutay) characterized the document as a 'grant' (מתנא; P. Yadin 3, line 43), albeit one to occur at some future time. From Chapter 8 we also know that this was a grant in partial or complete satisfaction of a debt owed by the son of Lutay to 'Abi-'adan. The disposition clause is likely to have referred to both dimensions of the arrangement, even though the parties regarded the grant dimension as dominant.

First, it needed to contain an acknowledgment of indebtedness, no doubt in a designated amount, by the son of Lutay. Mentioning the debt was essential, not least because it explained why 'Abi-'adan would not be handing over a purchase price to the son of Lutay on the occasion that the deed was signed, since a debt owed by him to her would be reduced or extinguished instead. The manner in which the Nabateans expressed indebtedness is clear from P. Yadin 1, lines 2–3 and 13–14 (drafted by the brother of the scribe here).

Secondly, and the core of the transaction, it must also have contained (in line 3) a promise by him to transfer the property, a date-palm orchard, to 'Abi-'adan, by a certain date. That date may well have been expressed in relation to the (probably imminent) termination of an existing lease over the property (see Chapter 8), possibly even mentioning the name of the lessee. We can be reasonably sure that the central dispositive provision was expressed as 'I will grant' (אנתן), an expression that appears later in the document (line 14). Probably the operative statement in relation to the future grant was something like this: 'I (the son of Lutay) promise that in discharge of the said X *sela's* I will grant to you (using אנתן as appears in line 14)... by... in year twenty-eight of our Lord in well-being an orchard ...'.

The Orchard and its Boundary Description Clause (Lines 5–7, possibly to 9)

At this point in the deed there would have been a brief description of the property to be granted by its owner pursuant to the provisions of the deed. We can be confident of its broad nature, a plantation, because in line 9 reference is made to 'the orchard that is (written) above' (גנתא די עלה). Moreover, this was almost certainly a date-palm orchard. Dates were clearly an important local crop and Shim'on would probably not have wanted this parcel of land included in his purchase if it did not contain date-palms. So this part of the deed of grant probably made reference (as in P. Yadin 2 and 3) to a 'date-palm orchard' (גנת תמריא). That the word for dates (תמריא) does not actually appear in 'the orchard that is (written) above' (גנתא די עלה) in line 9 does not affect this result since its absence is paralleled frequently elsewhere in the practice of this scribe to include the whole phrase גנת תמריא the first time it appears, in the disposition clause (so P. Yadin 2, lines 3 and 22, and P. Yadin 3, lines 2 and 23), but thereafter to refer to it as 'this' or 'that orchard',[1] expressions which are a close equivalent of 'the orchard that is (written) above' (גנתא די עלה) in P. Yadin 4, line 9.

To judge by the precedents from this very scribe in P. Yadin 2 and 3, the brief description of the orchard would have been in this form: 'a date-palm orchard, belonging to the son of Lutay,[2] which is in Galgala, which is in

[1] So P. Yadin 2, lines 5, 13, 14, 24, and 38, and P. Yadin 3, lines 5, 15, 27, 41, and 42.

[2] I have proposed 'the son of Lutay' rather than 'Ḥaṣmar'il' because in P. Yadin 3 the former is used (as here) when he is mentioned on his own, whereas the latter is used when linked to ''Abi-'adan' by 'and'.

Maḥoz 'Eglatain'. I have included these words in line 5 since there survive (early in the line) the letters ...יא די which helpfully correlate with the necessary words 'a date-palm plantation which (גנת תמריא די) (belongs) to the son of Lutay'. After this I have added 'which is called' (די מתקריה), on the basis that distinct plots had their own names to assist registration for tax-paying purposes, although the name itself is not known. Following this would have come the location in Galgala in Maḥoz 'Eglatain, followed by the important statement 'together with irrigation ditches and assigned watering periods'. There are two options for words that came after this assertion of watering rights: either the general statement we find in P. Yadin 2 ('as is fitting') or the more specific statement in relating to watering periods P. Yadin 3 (by mentioning 'half of one hour on the first day of the week'; lines 24–25). The latter formulation is likely to reflect the great care Shim'on, a Judean among Nabateans, took with all aspects of this transaction. Shim'on, who may have discussed P. Yadin 4 with 'Abi- 'adan and the son of Lutay before it was executed, may have wanted the wording to reflect what he required in his purchase. On the other hand, if, as suggested in Chapter 7, the smaller orchard would necessarily receive its water (from the stream flowing from the hills to the east, presumably), from and contemporaneous with the supply to the larger part of the plot, it may not have mattered much to him. On balance, the P. Yadin 2 formulation, 'as is fitting', seems more likely and I have included this.

Just as with P. Yadin 2 and 3 and as required by the words 'the orchard that is (written) above' (גנתא די עלה) in line 9, this provision in the deed would also have contained immediately after these words (line 6) a description of the property that was to be the subject of the grant in the future beginning with words 'and these are its boundaries' (ואלה תחומיה). Then would have followed a list of abutters in the order east, west, south, and north, commencing with the words 'To the east' (למדנחא). What can we say about the abutters in the case of P. Yadin 4 in relation to the likely layout of the area as proposed in Figure 7.1? The eastern and western boundaries seem reasonably secure. The property to the east must have been something very like 'The orchard of' (גנת ....), since we know that property devoted to date cultivation lay along the eastern boundary and the genitive construction ('the orchard of') rather than the other possible formula ('the orchard which [belongs] to... [גנתא די ל...]) is used of Rabb'el's land/orchard to the south in the boundary descriptions in P. Yadin 2 and 3. Furthermore, since the grant was completed after P. Yadin 3 was executed, and property passed to Shim'on, this orchard belonged to him, not 'Abi-'adan.

As argued in Chapter 5, the orchard (as sold to Archelaus in P. Yadin 2 and prior to its reconsolidation with that covered by the grant) probably had a name, that is likely to have appeared here as well, preceded by the formula 'which is called' (די מתקריה). So the likely words were: 'the orchard of Shim'on which is called . . . ' (גנת שמעון די מחקריה . . .). On the western side the property was abutted by the houses of Ḥunainu son of Tayim-'Ilahi. We know this because whereas the property that 'Abi-'adan sold to Archelaus had as its western abutter the houses of Taḥa daughter of 'Abad-Ḥaretat, the western abutters in the sale to Shim'on were these houses and those of Ḥunainu. Thus, it is this parcel of land abutting the houses of Ḥunainu that is to be provided by the grant from the son of Lutay to 'Abi-'adan. This means that at some point in this section of the deed would have appeared the words: 'and to the west, the houses of Ḥunainu, son of Tayim-'Ilahi' (ולמערבא בתי חנינו בר תימאלהי). Moreover, in Chapter 7 of this volume we argued that Ḥunainu's houses were probably to the south of Taḥa's. From this it follows that the southern abutter must have been the royal plantation, and this section would have come immediately after the specification of the western boundary in continuous text. Accordingly we can add still more language to this section of the document: 'and to the south: the orchard of our Lord, Rabb'el, the King, King of the Nabateans, who brings life and salvation to his people' (ולימינא גנת מראנא רבאל מלכא מלך נבטו די אחיי ושיזב עמה). This follows the language of P. Yadin 3; it is equally possible that rather than 'orchard of our Lord' it read 'land of our Lord' as in P. Yadin 2. A more difficult question is what lay to the north (לשמאלא). If it was precisely as in Figure 7.1, we might expect to see further reference to Shim'on's orchard. Sufficient doubt attends the question of how the scribe would have handled this to render it difficult to reach even a probable view on this. Nevertheless, this section would certainly have begun with the words 'and to the north' (ולשמאל א). It is possible that further aspects of the property being granted were supplied in lines 7, 8, and perhaps the early part of 9, as occur in P. Yadin 2 and 3.

APPENDIX 2

Translations of P. Yadin 1–4 (with Annotations)

General Notes

1. The four deeds translated below constitute what are called 'double documents'. This means that there were actually two versions of the agreement (both written on the one piece of papyrus): the 'upper' one, which was rolled up and tied and sealed (hence also the 'inner' copy), and the 'lower' (or 'outer') copy that was left unsealed and hence easily accessible.[1] The upper version was generally written after the lower version had been completed and could either be an abbreviation of the lower version (as with the upper version of P. Yadin 1, a severely abbreviated version indeed) or an almost complete version (as with P. Yadin 2 and 3). In the latter case, much the same text appears in both versions and this assists with filling in absent or damaged sections of the text. The editors of P. Yadin 1–4 are regularly able to reconstruct *vacats* in the text of one deed by reference to its more complete upper or lower version.[2] Accordingly, their Aramaic transcriptions contain passages in square brackets that they have been able to reconstruct in this way. They also provide square brackets around the English translations of Aramaic text so amended. In the translations below, since I accept their Aramaic (with one or two exceptions noted below and adding substantially to the Aramaic text of P. Yadin 4) and to avoid a rather rebarbative text I have not adopted their practice of adopting such square brackets for the English translations.

2. Round brackets indicate that words are added to the translation to produce a better sense in English, especially in view of the fact that

[1] On this type of legal document, see E. Koffmahn (1968) *Die Doppelurkunden aus der Wüste Juda*. Studies on the Texts of the Judean Desert, 5. Leiden: E. J. Brill and N. Lewis (1989) *The Documents from the Bar Kokhba Period in the Cave of Letters: Greek Papyri and Aramaic and Nabatean Signatures and Suscriptions*. Jerusalem: Israel Exploration Society, The Hebrew University of Jerusalem and the Shrine of the Book, 6–10.

[2] See Y. Yadin et al. (eds) (2002) *The Documents from the Bar Kokhba Period in the Cave of Letters: Hebrew, Aramaic and Nabatean-Aramaic Papyri*. Judean Desert Studies. Jerusalem: Israel Exploration Society, Institute of Archaeology, Hebrew University and Shrine of the Book, Israel Museum. In this Appendix page references to this work will appear in round brackets in the text where needed.

Nabatean Aramaic is parsimonious in its use of language, verbal forms in particular.

3. In this version of the Nabatean Aramaic script the same letter-form, a small, reasonably straight vertical line going up from the line, often joined by ligature to the preceding or following letter, is used for both *daled* and *resh*. The letters *zayin, yod* and *nun* are written in a similar way and can also be indistinguishable. As a result, when the word is otherwise unknown, it is difficult, although sometimes possible, to determine which is meant. In this case, I have opted for one of the forms in the translation, while mentioning the possibility of an alternative in the notes.

4. There is considerable uncertainty as to how Aramaic names of persons and places should be vocalized. In some cases, the existence of a version in Greek from the period provides invaluable assistance. In the translations below, the vocalizations suggested by the editors have been generally adopted. Occasionally, I have ventured to vocalize a word that they have not, for reasons already explained or set out in the notes below.

P. Yadin 1

Upper Version

1. On the eighth of 'Elul, in the twenty-third year of Rabb'el the King, King of the Nabateans, who (brings) life and salvation to his people in Rummon,
2. which is in Moab. On that day, I owe you, you, 'Amat-'Isi, daughter of Kaminu, son of ʿAmmaru, I, Muqimu, her husband,
3. .... silver (in the sum of) one hundred and fifty *selaʿs* ....
4. .... and garden .... and everything whatsoever,
5. small or large, which is fitting for her, and the sunny areas and (where) shade falls. The ban ....
6. the amount (in) silver (of) three hundred *selaʿs* and the entire mortgage ... are trustworthy for this (amount). The ban ....
7. And the said ʿAbad-ʿAmanu is a guarantor in relation to everything that (is) written above. And we, the said Muqimu and ʿAbad-ʿAmanu, except for roots and fruit ...
8. ... by the ban of heaven ... that is in them ... is sufficient ... are ripened. And the manner of preparation of this deed ...
9. .... such as for you, you, the said 'Amat-'Isi, in relation to everything that (is provided for) in this deed of yours and for our Lord, Rabb'el the King
10. as well .... And no one may attach a condition to anything that the witnesses have signed.

Lower Version

11. On the eighth of 'Elul, in the twenty-third year of Rabb'el the King, King of the
12. Nabateans, who (brings) life and salvation to his people in Rummon, which is in Moab. On that day,
13. I owe you, you, 'Amat-'Isi, daughter of Kaminu, son of ʿAmmaru, I,
14. Muqimu, her husband, son of ʿAwat-'Ilahi, son of Ḥalaf-'Ilahi, who lives in ʿAina-Shuḥaru, which
15. (is) in Moab, silver (in the sum of) one hundred and fifty *sela*ʿs exactly, the principal (sum) of the contract,
16. which (is) for the rent, two years from the date of this deed. And if he will not make payment before the arrival of
17. the date which is written above . . . . (the amount specified in) this deed will increase to his debit as is customary until the date which
18. she elects, the said 'Amat-'Isi. And this silver from the provisions of the dowry of the said 'Amat-'Isi
19. and this mortgage of the properties and the interest on it, all that belongs to the said Muqimu from . . .
20. . . . . person . . . And the manner of preparation
21. . . . and encumbrance, and dates and harvest, and plots of land and vineyards and houses and courtyards and gardens and . . . s,
22. and repayments and (rights of) purchase, everything that (there is), roots and branches, and gardens and springs, and . . . . as above,
23. . . . . and record and valid document, all of it, and (and without) public notices of
24. seizure relating to it, deposits and penalties . . . and garments, copper vessels,
25. . . . . wool, necklaces and jewellery in silver and gold,
26. . . . . oil and dates and harvest,
27. and improvements and the original property, ... and he is able . . .
28. . . . . and rights of partnership, gift, pledge, security, requital and specifications, and agreements,
29. and oaths . . . .
30. And he will also have from this time (onwards) . . . . and in every place whatsoever
31. . . . and everything whatsoever small or large, which is fitting or will be fitting for him, the sunny areas,
32. and (where) shade falls . . . . and requital and specifications,
33. and agreements, and oaths that relate to it, on the face of the earth and under the heavens. The price in silver (in the sum of)
34. three hundred *sela*ʿs, the entire mortgage, ... are trustworthy for this (amount).

35. . . . and liable (for this amount) is the said Muqimu, son of ʿAwat-ʿIlahi, and guarantor for this amount is the said ʿAbad-ʿAmanu,
36. in relation to everything that is written above. And we, the said Muqimu and ʿAbad-ʿAmanu, except for roots and fruit
37. . . . . or is sufficient
38. these . . . ripened. And the manner of preparation of this deed by them is in accordance with the customary manner of preparation.
39. . . . . three. And if she elects for payment (in advance),
40. advance payment will be made to the extent of one third of the assets. And all income and expenditure that is received and expended
41. . . . . that is not . . . . . .
42. to you, you, the said ʾAmat-ʾIsi, in relation to everything that (is provided for) in this deed of yours and to our Lord, Rabbʾel, the King
43. as well . . . . and after her. And anyone who
44. may acquire this deed by her assignment (of it) may seize any asset which is theirs in relation to everything that is (provided for) in this deed
45. in perpetuity. And no one may attach a condition to anything that the witnesses have signed.
46. On the eighth of ʾElul, in the twenty-third year of Rabbʾel the King, King of the Nabateans,
47. who (brings) life and salvation to his people, on that day she (had) prepared, she, ʾAmat-ʾIsi, daughter of
48. Kaminu, son of ʿAmmaru . . . . and all that
49. . . . requital and specifications and agreements which they have. The amount in silver of three hundred *selaʿs*,
50. the entire mortgage . . . . by them, one hundred
51. and fifty *selaʿs*, which, if they do not repay according to its provisions, you solemnly undertake that
52. . . . . [in relation to everything that is (provided for) in this deed] in perpetuity.

53. Muqimu, in person; he signed it.
54. ʿAbad-ʿAmanu, in person; he signed it.
55. Zaidu, son of Shahru, witness; his signature.
56. Taimu, son of Ḥuwaru; his signature.
57. . . . . . ; his signature.
58. Wanah, son of Ḥalaf-ʾIlahi, witness; his signature.
59. Ḥuwaru, son of ʿAwatu, the scribe, he drafted it.

60. Muqimu, in person; he signed it.
61. ʿAbad-ʿAmanu, in person; he signed it.
62. Zaidu, son of Shahru, witness; his signature.

63. Taimu, son of Ḥuwaru; his signature.
64. . . . . . . his signature.
65. Wanah, son fo Ḥalaf-'Ilahi, witness; his signature.
66. Ḥuwaru, son of ʿAwatu, the scribe, he drafted it.

Notes to P. Yadin 1

Line 1: The place mentioned could either be RMWN or DMWN, as in this form of Nabatean Aramaic *resh* and *daled* are written indistinguishably (see General Note 3 above). I have chosen a vocalized form of the former alternative in view of the existence of the modern place name, Umm Rummâne, for the reasons advanced in Chapter 4.

Line 2: For 'I owe you' the Aramaic literally reads, 'There is for you, you X, . . . with me.' The Aramaic word 'her husband' appears here, rather than that for 'your husband'. Given the meticulous work of this scribe, this is likely to be a deliberate choice, not an error.

Line 7: Two comments are needed for 'the said ʿAbad-ʿAmanu'. First, the words 'the said' translate the Aramaic word for 'this' (singular masculine: דנה). This expression captures the usage for previously mentioned parties in English legal documents right up to the current period, when parties are now generally defined at the outset and such a technique is not necessary. Although the man has not actually been mentioned in the inner text so far, he is mentioned in the outer text, which would have been written before the inner text, thus making the use of דנה explicable. In the translations that follow, 'the said' will regularly represent a 'this' (masculine or feminine) or 'these' (as with 'the said Muqimu and ʿAbad-ʿAmanu' in this line) appearing in the Aramaic. Secondly, the name that I have spelt here (and throughout the text of this volume) as ʿAbad-ʿAmanu could also be spelt ʿAbad-ʿAmiyu (see General Note 3). The editors note that 'roots and fruit' in this line probably means 'capital and revenue' or 'principal and interest' (188–189).

Line 9: As with 'the said ʿAbad-ʿAmanu' in line 7, the words 'the said (literally, 'this', דא) 'Amat-'Isi' appear even though she has not yet been mentioned in the inner text, because she was mentioned in the outer text that was written before this.

Line 10: The editors note that the difficult Aramaic word translated here as 'attach a condition' (מתנו) has a (less likely) alternative translation: 'And no one has delayed anything to which the witnesses have signed' (230–231).

Line 15: 'Exactly', or 'precisely', is the most likely translation for the difficult Aramaic word פרס, as explained by the editors (190–191). Since it is very difficult to distinguish *daled* and *resh* in Nabatean Aramaic (see General Note 3), the Aramaic word here translated 'contract' could either be עקרן or עקדן. The editors plausibly relate both words to Arabic originals (191–192). The former word, meaning 'real property' (from the Arabic word *'aqârun*) appears in this sense in P. Yadin 4.14. The latter word would mean 'contract' (from the Arabic word having that sense, *'aqdun*). As it makes no sense in the context of this document to speak of the 'principal of the real property', since we are talking about the principal and interest on a deed of loan, it is best to read עקדן here.

Line 16: 'Rent' translates the word אכרי. The editors discuss the word and translate it as 'leasing fee' (192).

Line 17: The words 'the amount specified in' (or something very like them) are added here as necessary to make sense of the words that follow. The editors propose that line 17 relates to the interest payable on the principal amount (192–193).

Line 18: 'She elects' is literally 'she wants', or 'she desires' (תצבא), but here in relation to the date on which, in legal language, 'Amat-'Isi, elects to stop letting interest on the principal accrue and to call instead for payment of principal and interest. The Aramaic word for 'the provisions' is עדי, which is a 'singular construct form, with collective force: "treaty, treaty provisions, agreement"'(193). The Aramaic word for 'dowry' is *mohar* (מהר).

Line 19: The Aramaic for 'the interest on it' is 'its interest'.

Line 21: The editors reasonably propose 'dates and harvest' as the best translation for two difficult words (וחרף ועללהי), which are most likely from Arabic, with 'harvest' marginally more secure than 'dates' (193–194).

Line 22: The editors propose that 'roots and branches' probably mean 'capital and revenue' or 'principal and interest' (188–189). Note that 'roots and fruit' occurs with this meaning in line 7. The two Aramaic words for 'gardens and springs' can also be translated 'concealed and open', in which case referring to the two different types of legal documents (222). It is also possible to read 'as above' as Arabic meaning 'public' (222).

Line 24: The words 'and without' are required by the sense, as the deed here lists a number of possible problems (culminating in 'penalties') that could affect the property Muqimu is putting up as security for the loan, but in fact do not. An alternative, proposed by the editors (195), but less likely, translation for 'relating to it' is 'by him'. Probably the meaning is that there are no writs of enforcement against any of the properties Muqimu has put forward as security for the loan from his wife. 'Garments' (לבשין) is the first (or at least the first extant) in a list of assets that comprise part of the property Muqimu is providing as security for the loan.

Line 27: The other possible translation for 'he is able' is 'it is sufficient'.

Line 28: The word translated as 'agreements' here could also be 'accounts' if a *daled* is read as a *resh*.

Line 29: The Aramaic word מותו ('oaths', 'promises') is plausibly restored here by the editors (180) since this word follows the preceding two in P. Yadin 2:12, so that the three of them together seem to constitute a formulaic expression.

Line 35: In this verse we have a statement that both Muqimu and 'Abad-'Amanu are liable for the obligations in the deed. The word translated here as 'guarantor' is ערב, in line with the editors' emendation (181). Yet they also restore this word of Muqimu and translate using 'guarantor' in relation to him. Since the word 'guarantor' is not appropriate in English for someone carrying the principal obligation, as Muqimu is here, I have used the word 'liable' in relation to him. While a different Aramaic word was perhaps used of his obligation, it was possible in Aramaic to describe the vendor and all his property, in a contract for the sale of land, as אחראין וערבין, meaning 'responsible and liable' (as in P. XHev 9:8).[3]

Line 38: In the Aramaic 'by them' is literally 'by their hands'.

Line 39: Literally, 'if her payment is desired'. This is preferable to the alternative translation, 'its payment'. See the editors' discussion (197–198).

Line 40: The editors helpfully suggest (199) that the remainder of this clause made provision for the *pro rata* allocation of income and expenditure to the parties in the event of 'Amat-'Isi opting for early repayment.

Line 43: Here 'as well' is restored from line 10. The translation 'after her' of the Aramaic word here, אחריה, favoured by the editors (199), possibly represents the conclusion of the phrase 'her descendants after her'. The editors note that another way to translate the word is 'responsible' in the Nabatean legal formula 'accountable and responsible'.

Line 44: The Aramaic expression translated as 'by assignment' here (מן מלמיה) is probably based on the Arabic word *lama'a*, meaning 'to get possession of', 'take away', as noted by the editors (199). Although they translate these words 'by right of possession', the legal notion of assignment of a debt is what is in view and the *he* at the end of the word requires 'her' or 'its'. 'Assignment' is a very appropriate translation of the nominal form of the Arabic word in a legal context.

Line 45: The Aramiaic translated as 'in perpetuity' here and elsewhere in these translations is literally 'for ever'.

[3] See H. M. Cotton and A. Yardeni [1997] *Discoveries in the Judean Desert. Volume 27. Aramaic. Hebrew and Greek Documentary Texts from Naḥal Ḥever and Other Sites: With an Appendix Containing Alleged Qumran Texts (The Seiyal Collection I):* Desert. Oxford: Clarendon Press, 42–43.

Line 46: Here begins a new section of the document, proceeding to line 52, in which 'Amat-'Isi expressly consents to the loan from her dowry. Such a provision must have been a requirement of Nabatean law.

Line 50: The words 'the entire mortgage' are restored by the editors by reference to lines 6 and 34, probably correctly.

Line 51: 'According to its provisions' translates the Aramaic 'as is in it' (כדי בה). 'You solemnly undertake' translates the Aramaic 'you are alive and trustworthy'.

Line 52: The added words in square brackets (which the editors do not supply) are based on lines 44–45 and are precisely what is required at this point. 'Amat-'Isi is promising to strictly enforce the terms of agreement. At this point, however, the editors comment (200): 'Perhaps with some poignancy, we read here that 'Amat-'Isi can be relied on to foreclose if the debtors defaulted!' But the whole point of the Nabatean law that required her express consent in this situation was to ensure that her interests (and those of her family who might be reliant on her) were protected in the event that she lent money from her dowry, so that an undertaking of this kind was quite important. It was aimed at preventing collusion between a wife and her husband to the detriment of her cognate kin.

Lines 53–66: There are two versions of the list of signatories to the document. Lines 53–59 are from the recto, but the list on the verso (see p. 174, the drawing by Ada Yardeni[4]) has the names in a more complete form and this list has been used to complete the names on the recto.

P. Yadin 2

Upper Version

Verso

1. On the third of Kislev, in the twenty-eighth year of Rabb'el the King, King of the Nabateans, who (brings) life and salvation to his people, and during the lifetime of 'Obodat, son of Rabb'el the King, King of the Nabateans, who (brings) life and salvation to his people,
2. and of Gamilat and Hagru, his sisters, Queens of the Nabateans, children of Maniku the King, King of the Nabateans, son of Ḥaretat, King of the Nabateans, lover of his people, in Maḥoz 'Eglatain. On that day he purchased, he, Archelaus, son of 'Abad-'Amanu,
3. . . . . the governor, from me, I, 'Abi-'adan, daughter of 'Aptaḥ, son of Manigares, an orchard of date-palms, which (is) in Galgala, which (is) in Maḥoz 'Eglatain, together with irrigation ditches and assigned watering periods, as

[4] Yadin et al. 2002: 174.

4. is fitting. That . . . . . Archelaus, from ḤNH BHDRYT' . . . . . . And these are its boundaries: to the east, the road; and to the west, the houses of Taha, the daughter of ʿAbad-Ḥaretat; and to the south, the land of our Lord, Rabb'el, the King, King
5. of the Nabateans, who (brings) life and salvation to his people; and to the north, the swamp. That orchard, in its entirety, within all its boundaries, and everything that belongs to the said 'Abi-ʿadan within it, by entitlement and permission, (by) boundary and portion, and (by) valid document
6. and sound registration and parcelling and entitlement; and (including) orchard and spring, and . . . and as above; and date-palms, and sycamores, and all trees, and wood, wet or dry, and arid land such as is in it, and assigned watering periods,
7. and water, and . . . . and partnership and testamentary rights and . . . and courtyards inside (it) in every place, and everything whatsoever, small or large, as is fitting for him
8. in relation to these purchases, the sunny areas and (where) shade falls—the said Archelaus has purchased with silver, (in the sum of) one hundred and twelve *selaʿs* exactly. This silver, the full price of these purchases, has been received by me, I,
9. the said 'Abi-ʿadan, the fixed price of the purchases . . . . . . in full value, mature and non-refundable in perpetuity. (He is entitled) to buy and to sell, and to pledge and to bequeath, and to grant as a gift, and to do with these purchases everything that he elects,
10. the said Archelaus, from the day on which this deed is executed and in perpetuity. (I covenant) that (these purchases are) not (affected by) lawsuit, nor by contest, nor by oath . . . . . . and that I, the said 'Abi-ʿadan will clear these purchases from anyone,
11. anyone at all, distant or near, and I will leave (them) unencumbered for you, you, the said Archelaus, for you and for your sons after you in perpetuity. And as well, you, the said Archelaus, are indemnified . . . by me, I, the said 'Abi-ʿadan, against
12. all that I may claim, or that may be claimed in my name against you in relation to these purchases, pertaining to houses and courtyards, and (in relation to) requital and specification, and agreements and oath, that may still be claimed concerning thorn bushes and . . . . And there is agreement in relation to exchanges and profits . . .
13. . . . . (concerning) purchases and clearances, as is customary for purchases and clearances as is written in perpetuity. Accordingly, the said 'Abi-ʿadan has apportioned with respect to this orchard
14. our Lord's portion, the leasing-fee for a year, as well, in its (amount of) ten *se'ahs*, until such time as there will be a new edict and this

orchard will be registered as a plot of the said Archelaus. And if I, the said 'Abi- 'adan will . . . , or will deviate from this (agreement)

15. without consent, I will owe to you, you, the said Archelaus in the entire price of these purchases and with respect to absolutely everything that I may claim or that may be claimed in my name against you regarding them, and to our Lord, Rabb'el the King as well, and claims
16. without consent. And empowered and clean and . . . is the said Archelaus and his sons after him, and anyone else who may acquire this deed by his assignment (of it) regarding these purchases as (provided) in it in perpetuity.
17. And no one may attach a condition to anything that the witnesses have signed.

Lower Version

18. On the third of Kislev, in the twenty-eighth year of Rabb'el the King, King of the Nabateans, who (brings) life and salvation to his people, and during
19. the lifetime of 'Obodat, son of Rabb'el the King, King of the Nabateans, who brings life and salvation to his people, and of Gamilat and Hagru, his sisters, Queens of the
20. Nabateans, children of Maniku the King, King of the Nabateans, son of Ḥaretat, King of the Nabateans, lover of his people, in Maḥoz 'Eglatain. On that day he purchased,
21. he, Archelaus, son of 'Abad-'Amanu, ... governor, from me, I, 'Abi-'adan, daughter of 'Aptaḥ, son of Manigares,
22. an orchard of date-palms, ... which (is) in Galgala which (is) in Maḥoz 'Eglatain, together with irrigation ditches and assigned watering periods, as is fitting. That . . . Archelaus,
23. from ḤNH BHDRYT' . . . . . . And these are its boundaries: to the east, the road; and to the west, the houses of Taha, the daughter of 'Abad-Ḥaretat;
24. and to the south, the land of our Lord, Rabb'el, the King, King of the Nabeteans, who (brings) life and salvation to his people; and to the north: the swamp. That orchard,
25. in its entirety, within all its boundaries, and everything that belongs to the said 'Abi-'adan within it, by entitlement and permission, (by) boundary and portion, and (by) valid document and sound registration and parcelling
26. and entitlement; and orchard and spring, and . . . . and as above; and date-palms, and sycamores, and all trees, and wood, wet or dry, and arid land
27. such as is in it, and assigned watering periods, and water, and . . . . and partnership and testamentary rights and . . . and courtyards

28. . . . inside (it) in every place, and everything whatsoever, small or large, as is fitting for him in relation to these purchases, the sunny areas and (where) shade falls—
29. the said Archelaus has purchased with silver, (in the sum of) one hundred and twelve *sela's* exactly. This silver, the full price of these purchases,
30. has been received by me, I, the said 'Abi-'adan, the fixed price of the purchases . . . in full value, mature and non-refundable in perpetuity. (He is entitled) to buy and to sell,
31. and to pledge and to bequeath, and to grant as a gift, and to do with these purchases everything that he elects, the said Archelaus, from the day on which this deed is executed
32. and in perpetuity. (I covenant) that (these purchases are) not (affected by) lawsuit, nor by contest, nor by oath . . . and that I, I the said 'Abi-'adan will clear these purchases from anyone,
33. anyone at all, distant or near, and I will leave (them) unencumbered for you, you, the said Archelaus, for you and for your sons after you in perpetuity. And as well,
34. you, the said Archelaus, are indemnified . . . by me, I, the said 'Abi-'adan, against all that I may claim, or that may be claimed in my name against you in relation to these purchases,
35. pertaining to houses and courtyards, and (in relation to) requital and specification, and . . . . . . and oath, that may still be claimed concerning . . . . . . And there is agreement in relation to exchanges and profits
36. . . . . (concerning) purchases and clearances, as is customary for purchases and clearances as
37. is written in perpetuity. Accordingly, the said 'Abi-'adan has apportioned with respect to this orchard our Lord's portion, the leasing-fee for a year, as well, in its (amount of) ten *se'ahs*,
38. until such time as there will be a new edict and this orchard will be registered as a plot of the said Archelaus. And if I, the said 'Abi-'adan will . . . , or will deviate from
39. this (agreement) without consent, I will owe to you, you, the said Archelaus in the entire price of these purchases and with respect to absolutely everything that I may claim or that may be claimed in my name
40. against you regarding them, and to our Lord, Rabb'el the King, as well, and claims without consent. And empowered and clean and . . . is the said Archelaus
41. and his sons after him, and anyone else who may acquire this deed by his assignment (of it) regarding these purchases as (provided) in it in perpetuity. And no one
42. may attach a condition to anything that the witnesses have signed.

43. . . . .

44. . . . . son of Zaidu
45. . . . .
46. . . . .
47. . . . .
48.
49. ʿ Azur, son of ʿAwatu, the scribe . . . .

Notes to P. Yadin 2

Line 3: 'Governor' is a translation of the word אסרתגא, a Greek loanword (*stratêgos*) in Nabatean, which was used of a senior military/administrative leader (as discussed in Chapter 5).

Line 6: The word here translated as 'entitlement' can either be read חרר or חדד and in either case, the editors note, it represents an Arabic legal word being added to the previous list for more abundant caution, with the former meaning something like 'entitlement' and the second something like 'boundary' (221–222).

Line 8: The Nabatean translated 'has been received by me' is literally 'has come to me'.

Line 9: The Aramaic here for 'non-refundable in perpetuity' is חלטין לעלמין; ironically, the money was probably repaid in full by 'Abi-ʿadan to Archelaus within a month of this statement being made: see the argument in Chapter 6.

Line 10: To 'clear (sc. 'purify') the purchases' is very similar to the modern legal notion of providing 'clear title' to real estate someone is buying, meaning that there are no claims by others on the owner's title and no history of past claims that might affect the vendor's ownership. 'Abi-ʿadan is promising Archelaus that this will be case with the property she is selling to him.

Line 11: The Aramaic word translated here as 'leave unencumbered' is שבק (literally, 'leave, release'). The words translated here as 'indemnified . . . against' (in line with modern legal parlance) are literally 'clean . . . from'.

Line 12: As the editors point out (227–228), the meaning of the Aramaic word here (הגין) is uncertain; 'thorn bushes', a possible translation, may have been used to mark boundaries.

Line 14: There are two major points worthy of note in this line. *First*, the Aramaic word translated 'leasing-fee' here is אכרי, which appeared in P. Yadin 1 (line 16) with the meaning 'rent'. Although little of practical significance turns on the point, it is worth considering whether this payment should be understood as a lease payment ('ground rent' in

English law) on the basis that the king owned the land and all that Archelaus was purchasing was a perpetual lease and not freehold in the property, or whether Archelaus is purchasing freehold and this is a tax to the king. The latter option is far more likely. There is no sign in P. Yadin 2 and 3 that the purchasers were acquiring anything other than freehold. Moreover, the payments that Babatha made on this orchard thirty years later look like tax payments (P. Yadin 16). Hannah Cotton's suggestion is a useful one: 'Was all land in the Nabataean kingdom, unless said to belong to the king, . . . conceived to be on lease from him? If so, then lease-rent could be considered as equivalent to tax.'[5] This is possible, but probably the notion of the land being on lease to the king existed in a symbolical rather than a legally binding sense. After all, in this very deed there is a reference to 'the land of our lord, the king' (lines 4 and 24) which indicates a clear division of land owned by the king from other land owned by others but, it would appear, notionally liable to a 'leasing-fee' to him. *Secondly*, 'new edict' represents the Aramaic אסר חדת, a 'new אסר'. This word can mean either 'a binding agreement' or an edict (of a king for example) that 'binds' his subjects, as on several occasions in Daniel 6 (see the editors' discussion of this word in P. Yadin 44, line 16 (50–51). Here it has the latter meaning (in spite of the editors opting for the former) and refers to the royal confirmation of the property transfer to Archelaus. The deed itself was binding and there was no other agreement, binding or otherwise, needed (which excludes the former meaning of the word). Accordingly, we are probably dealing with the registration of title, not with title by registration. Registration of title was of interest to the king, especially in relation to the collection of tax. This interest remained after the Roman takeover of Nabatea in 106 CE, as can be seen in the document Babatha later filed at Rabbath (about 40 kilometres from Maoza)[6] in the census of 127 CE declaring (*ἀπογράφεσθαι*; line 15) the properties she owned and the tax she had to pay on each. This document is P. Yadin 16.[7] Hannah Cotton offers two explanations: first, a contract between the king and the new owner; or, secondly, and more likely she believes, a 'new order', 'i.e. a periodic reorganization of all land leased from the king which was likely to be accompanied by a readjustment of the terms of the lease'.[8] But the former seems the simpler and more likely option and is close to the solution favoured by the editors, namely that 'the new agreement'

[5] H. M. Cotton (1997) 'Land Tenure in the Documents from the Nabataean Kingdom and the Roman Province of Arabia', *ZPE* 119: 256.
[6] Lewis 1989: 69.
[7] For text, translation, and commentary, see Lewis 1989: 65–70.
[8] Cotton 1997: 256.

referred to the confirmation by the royal administration of the purchase by Archelaus (229).

Line 15: The consent referred to can only be the consent of Archelaus.

Line 16: An alternative translation for a difficult Aramaic expression, rendered here as 'and claims without consent', suggested by the editors (229–230), is 'deceptive actions are not permitted'. On 'by his assignment (of it)', see my note above on P. Yadin 1, line 44.

Line 17: As noted above, in relation to P. Yadin 1, line 10, an alternative translation (of the difficult verb מתנו) discussed by the editors (230–231) is 'And no one has delayed anything to which the witnesses have signed.'

Line 22: For my argument that there was likely to be a name of the orchard in the space after 'date-palms', but that it was not Gahadiya, see Chapter 5.

P. Yadin 3

Upper Version

Verso

1. On the second of Tebet, in the twenty-eighth year of Rabb'el the King, King of the Nabateans, who (brings) life and salvation to his people, in Maḥoz 'Eglatain. On that day
2. he purchased, he, Shim'on, son of . . . . of Maḥoz 'Eglatain, from me, I, 'Abi-'adan, daughter of 'Aptaḥ, son of Manigares, an orchard of date-palms
3. that belongs to 'Abi-'adan (and) that is called Gahadiya which (is) in Galgala, which is in Maḥoz 'Eglatain, together with irrigation ditches and assigned watering periods; half of one hour on the first day of the week,
4. every single week in perpetuity. And these are its boundaries: to the east, the road; and to the west, the houses of Ḥunainu, son of Tayim-'llahi, and the houses of Taha, the daughter of 'Abad-Ḥaretat;
5. and to the south, the orchard of our Lord, Rabb'el, the King, King of the Nabateans, who (brings) life and salvation to his people; and to the north, the swamp. That orchard, in its entirety, within all its boundaries,
6. and everything that belongs to the said 'Abi-'adan within it, by entitlement and permission, (by) boundary and portion, and (by) valid document and sound registration and parcelling and entitlement; and (including) orchard and spring, and . . . and as above; and wood,

Recto

7. wet or dry, and arid land such as is in it, and . . . and . . . and . . . and partnership and testamentary rights, and . . . and courtyards inside it in every place, and everything (whatsoever),

8. small or large, as is fitting for him in relation to these purchases, the sunny areas and (where) shade falls—the said Shim'on has purchased with silver, (in the sum of) one hundred and sixty-
9. eight *sela's* exactly. This silver, the full price of these purchases, has been received by me, I, the said 'Abi-'adan, the fixed price of the purchases . . . . in full value, mature
10. and non-refundable in perpetuity. (He is entitled) to buy and to sell, and to pledge and to bequeath, and to grant as a gift, and to do with these purchases everything that he elects, the said Shim'on, from the day
11. on which this deed is executed and in perpetuity. (I covenant) that (these purchases are) not (affected by) lawsuit, nor by contest, nor by any oath whatsoever and that I, the said 'Abi-'adan will clear these purchases from anyone,
12. anyone at all, distant or near, and I will leave (them) unencumbered for you, you, the said Shim'on, for you and for your sons after you in perpetuity. And as well, you, the said Shim'on, are indemnified . . . by me, I,
13. the said 'Abi-'adan, against all that I may claim, or that may be claimed in my name against you in relation to these purchases, pertaining to houses and courtyards, and (in relation to) requital and specification, and agreements and oath, that may still be claimed
14. concerning thornbushes and . . . ; And there is agreement in relation to exchanges and profits . . . . entirely, (concerning) purchases and clearances, as is customary for purchases and clearances as is written in perpetuity. Accordingly,
15. the said 'Abi-'adan has apportioned our Lord's portion, the leasing-fee for a year, as well, in its (amount of) ten *se'ahs*, until such time as there will be a new edict and this orchard will be registered
16. as a plot of the said Shim'on as in this deed. And everything that is written in a grant, in it, the said son of Lutay, . . . and concerning what the said 'Abi-'adan (has agreed) pertaining to you. And if we,
17. 'Abi-'adan and Ḥaṣmar'il, the said persons, will . . . or will deviate from this (agreement) without consent, we will owe to you, you, the said Shim'on, in the entire price of these purchases and with respect to absolutely everything that
18. we may claim or that may be claimed in our name against you regarding them, and to our Lord, Rabb'el the King as well, and claims without consent. And empowered and clean and . . . is the said Shim'on
19. and his sons after him, and anyone else who may acquire this deed by his assignment (of it) regarding these purchases as (provided) in it in perpetuity.

20. And no one may attach a condition to anything that the witnesses have signed.

Recto

Lower Version

21. On the second of Tebet, in the twenty-eighth year of Rabb'el the King, King of the Nabateans, who (brings) life and salvation to his people,
22. in Maḥoz ʿEglatain. On that day he purchased, he, Shimʿon, son of . . . .
23. of Maḥoz ʿEglatain from me, I, 'Abi-ʿadan, daughter of 'Aptaḥ, son of Manigares an orchard of date-palms that belongs to the said 'Abi-ʿadan
24. (and) that is called Gahadiya which (is) in Galgala, which is in Maḥoz ʿEglatain, together with irrigation ditches and assigned watering periods; half of
25. one hour on the first day of the week, every single week in perpetuity. And these are its boundaries: to the east, the road;
26. and to the west; the houses of Ḥunainu, son of Tayim-'llahi,and the houses of Taha, the daughter of ʿAbad-Ḥaretat; to the south: the orchard of
27. our Lord, Rabb'el, the King, King of the Nabateans, who (brings) life and salvation to his people; and to the north: the swamp. That orchard, in its entirety,
28. within all its boundaries, and everything that belongs to the said 'Abi-ʿadan within it, by entitlement and permission, (by) boundary and portion, and (by) valid document and sound registration and parcelling
29. and entitlement and (including) orchard and spring and . . . . . . and as above; and wood, wet or dry, and arid land such as is in it, and . . . .
30. and . . . and . . . and partnership and testamentary rights, and . . ., courtyards inside it in every place, and everything (whatsoever), small or large,
31. as is fitting for him in relation to these purchases, the sunny areas and (where) shade falls—the said Shimʿon has purchased with silver, (in the sum of) one hundred and sixty
32. eight *sela*ʿs exactly. This silver, the full price of these purchases, has been received by me, I, the said 'Abi-ʿadan, the fixed price of
33. the purchases . . . . . . in full value, mature and non-refundable in perpetuity. (He is entitled) to buy and to sell, and to pledge and to bequeath, and to grant as a gift,
34. and to do with these purchases everything that he elects, the said Shimʿon, from the day on which this deed is executed and in

35. perpetuity. (I covenant) that (these purchases are) not (affected by) lawsuit, nor by contest, nor by any oath whatsoever and that I, the said 'Abi-'adan will clear these purchases from anyone, anyone
36. at all, distant or near, and I will leave (them) unencumbered for you, you, the said Shim'on, for you and for your sons after you in perpetuity.
37. And as well, you, the said Shim'on, are indemnified . . . by me, I, the said 'Abi-'adan, against all that I may claim, or that may be claimed
38. in my name against you in relation to these purchases, pertaining to houses and courtyards, and (in relation to) requital and specification, and agreements and oath, that may still be claimed
39. concerning thornbushes and . . . . ; And (there is) agreement in relation to exchanges and profits . . . . . .
40. . . . . entirely, (concerning) purchases and clearances, as is customary for purchases and clearances as is written in perpetuity. Accordingly,
41. the said 'Abi-'adan has apportioned with respect to this orchard our Lord's portion, the leasing-fee for a year, as well, in its (amount of) ten *se'ahs*,
42. until such time as there will be a new edict and this orchard will be registered as a plot of the said Shim'on as in this deed. And everything that
43. is written in a grant, in it, the said son of Lutay, . . . and (also) concerning what the said 'Abi-'adan (has agreed) pertaining to you. And if we
44. 'Abi-'adan and Ḥaṣmar'il, the said persons, will . . . or will deviate from this (agreement) without consent, we will owe to you, you, the said Shim'on,
45. in the entire price of these purchases and with respect to absolutely everything that we may claim or that may be claimed in our name against you regarding them, and to our Lord,
46. Rabb'el the King as well, and claims without consent. And empowered and clean and . . . is the said Shim'on and his sons
47. after him, and anyone else who may acquire this deed by his assignment (of it) regarding these purchases as (provided) in it in perpetuity. And no one
48. may attach a condition to anything that the witnesses have signed.

49. 'Abi-'adan, on her behalf
50. Ḥaṣmar'il the son of Lutah . . . .
51. Archelaus son of . . . , written in his own hand
52. Wahab-'Ilahi, son of Mushalimu, signed in his own hand
53. Wahab-Dushara, son of Shulay, signed in his own hand
54. Zabad-ba'al, son of Zabadion, signed in his own hand

55. ‘Azur, son of ‘Awatu, the scribe, and he drafted it

Notes to P. Yadin 3

Line 2: For the vocalization Gahadiya, see Chapter 7.

Line 3: The editors (236–237) correctly fill a *vacat* in the papyrus at the start of line 3 with [די לאביעד]ן, by comparison with line 23, and translate ‘belonging to ’Abi-‘adan’ (literally, ‘which [is] to ’Abi-‘adan’). The words ‘half of one hour on the first day of the week, every single week in perpetuity’ represent a notable change from ‘as is fitting’ which appear at the corresponding place in P. Yadin 2. The reason for the change is discussed in Chapter 7.

Line 4: The boundary to the west is changed by the addition of ‘the houses of Ḥunainu, son of Tayim-’llahi’.

Line 15: Missing from the apportionment provision are the words ‘with respect to this orchard’ that are found in P. Yadin 2 at this point in the deed. But this would not affect the sense. In any event, these words do appear in line 41.

Line 16: The words ‘as in this deed’ after ‘as a plot of the said Shim‘on’ are new to this document compared with P. Yadin 2, but do not alter the sense: they make clear that the description of the orchard in the king’s register will match that in this deed. The vital words ‘And everything that is written in the grant, in it, the said son of Lutay, . . . and concerning what the said ’Abi-‘adan (has agreed) pertaining to you’ have been restored here by the editors on the basis of lines 42–43 in the outer text. The Aramaic word translated ‘grant’ here is מתנא, which comes from נתן, meaning, ‘he gave, granted’. The word appears in this sense in lines 2 and 13 of P. Yadin 7 (a deed of gift from 120 CE). The verbal form למתנן (‘to grant as a gift’) is one of the standard rights included in a sale to a purchase (as in P. Yadin 2.9 and 31 and P. Yadin 3.10 and 33). The editors (243) consider that the word here could also represent a variation of נתא, meaning ‘condition, authorization’, but I submit that this view rests on a failure to realize the connection between P. Yadin 3 and 4 as argued above (P. Yadin 4 is the מתנא mentioned here) and overlooks the ample evidence for the meaning ‘grant’ in these papyri. My detailed argument for translating מתנא as ‘a grant’ is set out in Chapters 7 and 8.

Line 17: I have restored ‘Ḥaṣmar’il’ from line 44 (see Chapter 7 for my argument for this reading).

Line 43: After the words ‘the said son of Lutay’ there is an indecipherable word but which must mean something like ‘agrees’. Ḥaṣmar’il the son of Lutay is agreeing both to what is in the grant and to what ’Abi-‘adan has agreed.

Line 52: The scribe spells his father's name 'Lutay' but the man himself 'Lutah' (using a final *he* instead of a final *yod*).
Line 53: 'Wahab-Dushara' means 'gift of Dushara' (*wahaba* being Arabic for 'he gave'). Dushara was the principal god of the Nabateans (see Chapter 2). This is one of the rare links with Nabatean religious beliefs and practices in P. Yadin 1–4.

Line 54: 'Zabad-ba'al' means 'gift of Baal' and is another sign of Nabatean religious beliefs and practices.

P. Yadin 4

Lower Version

Recto

1. On the . . . of Tebet, in the twenty-eighth year of Rabb'el the King, King of the Nabateans, who (brings) life and salvation to his people, in Maḥoz 'Eglatain.
2. On that day I, Ḥaṣmar'il the son Lutay, her husband owe to you, you, 'Abi-'adan, daughter of 'Aptaḥ, son of Manigares, in silver, ... *sela's*
3. . . . .
4. . . . .
5. . . . . an orchard of date-palms, which (belongs) to the son of Lutay, which is called . . . . . . and which (is) in Galgala, which (is) in Maḥoz 'Eglatain, together with irrigation ditches and assigned watering periods, as is fitting.
6. And these are its boundaries: to the east, the orchard of Shim'on which is called . . . . ; and to the west; the houses of Ḥunainu, son of Tayim-'llahi, to the south:
7. the orchard of our Lord, Rabb'el, the King, King of the Nabateans, who (brings) life and deliverance to his people; and to the north: . . . .
8. . . . .
9. . . . . the orchard that (is described) above . . . .
10. . . . . year twenty
11. and eight of our Lord in well-being . . . . . . that any person at all . . . . . . anything, small
12. or large . . . . in the purchases of the said orchard[9] prior to the time that is written above . . . . the said silver[10]
13. . . . .

[9] Literally, 'that orchard'. See Figure 8.1 for the start of line 12.
[10] Literally, 'this silver'.

14. before you from anyone, distant or near, that I will grant to you the real property that (is described) above. Accordingly, (I) acknowledge liability,
15. I, in the (amount of) the said silver, which (is) not (affected by) lawsuit, nor by contest, nor by oath, in any respect, and if . . . . I, the said son of Lutay,
16. I will owe to you, you, the said 'Abi-'adan in the entire price of those purchases and in the entire price of the real property that (is described) above and everything (to) which you will agree
17. in accordance with the desire . . . . and to our Lord,
18. Rabb'el the King as well, and claims without consent . . . . . . (sc. regarding anything) that by this deed shall be done. And no one may attach a condition to anything that the witnesses
19. have signed.

20. Ḥaṣmar'il the son of Lutay had it signed.
21. . . . . by his order.
22.
23.
24.
25.
26.

References

Abdelaziz, Mahdi (2005) 'Notes on the Nabataean Legal System', *Dirasat: Human and Social Sciences*, 32: 189–99.

Almagor, Eran and Skinner, Joseph (eds) (2013) *Ancient Ethnography: New Approaches*. London: Bloomsbury.

Alpass, Peter (2013) *The Religious Life of Nabataea*. Religions in the Graeco-Roman World. Leiden: E. J. Brill.

al-Khraysheh, Fawwaz Hammad (1986) *Die Personennamen in den nabatäischen Inschriften des Corpus Inscriptionum Semiticarum*. (Inaugural-Dissertation zur Erlangung der Doktorwürde des Fachbereichs Aussereuropäische Sprachen und Kulturen der Philipps-Universität). Marburg: Lahn.

al-Qudrah, Hussein and Abdelaziz, Mahdi (2008) 'Kinship Terms in the Nabataean Inscriptions', *Arabian Archaeology and Epigraphy* 19: 192–96. Open text, accessed at: <https://eis.hu.edu.jo/deanshipfiles/pub103812316.pdf>.

Alzoubi (Abdelaziz), Mahdi (2012) *Les formules juridiques dans les inscriptions nabatéennes*. Saarbrücken: Presses Academiques Francophones.

Anderson, B. (2009) 'Double-Crossing Jordan: Strabo's Portrait of Syllaeus and the Imagining of Nabataea', *SHAJ* 10: 391–97.

Anderson, Benedict (2006 [1983]) *Imagined Communities: Reflections on the Origins and Spread of Nationalism*. Revised edition. London and New York: Verso.

Anderson, Siwan (2007) 'The Economics of Dowry and Brideprice', *Journal of Economic Perspectives* 21: 151–74.

Axel, Brian Keith (ed.) (2002a) *From the Margins: Historical Anthropology and Its Futures*. Durham, NC and London: Duke University Press.

Axel, Brian Keith (2002b) 'Introduction: Historical Anthropology and Its Vicissitudes', in Axel 2002a: 1–44.

Baly, Denis (1974) *The Geography of the Bible*. Revised edition. New York: Harper & Row.

Bamyeh, Mohammed A. (2006) 'The Nomads of Pre-Islamic Arabia', in Chatty 2006: 34–48.

Banning, E. B. (1986) 'Peasants, Pastoralists, and "Pax Romana": Mutualism in the Southern Highlands of Jordan', *Bulletin of the American Schools of Oriental Research* 261: 25–50.

Barth, Fredrik (1956) 'Ecologic Relationships of Ethnic Groups in Swat, North Pakistan', *American Anthropologist* 58: 1079–89.

Barth, Fredrik (1964) *Nomads of Southern Persia*. Oslo: Universitetsforlaget.

Barth, Fredrik (ed.) (1969a) *Ethnic Groups and Boundaries: The Social Organization of Culture Difference.* London: George Allen and Unwin.

Barth, Fredrik (1969b) 'Introduction', in Barth 1969a: 9–38.

Barth, Fredrik (1973) 'A General Perspective on Nomad–Sedentary Relations in the Middle East', in Nelson 1973: 11–22.

Bartlett, John R. (2007) 'Nabataean Religion', in Politis 2007: 55–78.

Benoit O. P., P., Milik, J. T., and Vaux, O. P., R. de (eds) with contributions from Crowfoot, G. M., Crowfoot, E., and Grohmann, A. (1961) *Discoveries in the Judaean Desert II: Les Grottes de Murabba'at. Texte.* Oxford: Clarendon Press.

Beyer, Klaus (2004) *Die aramäischen Texte vom Toten Meer. Band II.* Göttingen: Vandenhoeck & Rupprecht.

Bing, Gertrud (1960) 'Aby M. Warburg', *Rivista storica italiana* 72: 100–113.

Boserup, Ester (1970) *Women's Role in Economic Development.* New York: St Martin's Press.

Bourdieu, Pierre (2004) *Science of Science and Reflexivity.* Chicago, IL: University of Chicago Press.

Bowersock, G. W. (1983) *Roman Arabia.* Cambridge, MT: Harvard University Press.

Bowsher, J. (1989) 'The Nabataean Army', in David French and C. S. Lightfoot (eds) *The Eastern Frontier of the Roman Empire: Proceedings of a Colloquium Held at Ankara in September 1988.* BAR International Series 553. Oxford: British Archaeological Reports, 19–30.

Brenner, Athalya (ed.) (1999) *Ruth and Esther: A Feminist Companion to the Bible (Second Series).* Sheffield: Sheffield Academic Press.

Cantineau, J. (1930–1932) *Le Nabatéen.* 2 vols. Paris: Libraire Ernest Leroux.

Chatty, Dawn (ed.) (2006) *Nomadic Societies in the Middle East and North Africa: Entering the 21st Century.* Leiden and Boston: E. J. Brill.

Choi, Jungwha (2013) *Jewish Leadership in Roman Palestine from 70 C.E. to 135 C.E.* Leiden: E. J. Brill.

Chokkakula, Srinivas (2009) 'Interrogating Irrigation Ineqalities: Canal Irrigation Systems in Injil District, Herat', Afghanistan Research and Evaluation Unit, Case Studies Series. Kabul: Afghanistan Research and Evaluation Unit. Accessed at <http://www.areu.org.af/Uploads/EditionPdfs/914E-Irrigation%20Inequities-CS-print.pdf.pdf>.

Clifford, James and Marcus, George E. (eds) (1986) *Writing Culture: The Poetics and Politics of Ethnography.* Berkeley, CA: University of California Press.

Cohen, Anthony P. (1989) *The Symbolic Construction of Community. Key Ideas.* London and New York: Routledge.

Comaroff, John and Comaroff, Jean (1992) *Ethnography and the Historical Imagination.* Studies in the Ethnographic Imagination. Boulder, Co: Westview Press.

Coote, Robert B. and Gottwald, Norman K. (eds) (2007) *To Break Every Yoke: Essays in Honor of Marvin L. Chaney*. Sheffield: Sheffield Phoenix Press.

Cotton, Hannah M. (1994) 'A Cancelled Marriage Contract from the Judaean Desert (XHev/Se Gr. 2)', *JRelS* 84: 64–86, Plates I–II.

Cotton, Hannah M. (1997) 'Land Tenure in the Documents from the Nabataean Kingdom and the Roman Province of Arabia', *ZPE* 119: 255–65.

Cotton, Hannah M. (1998) 'The Rabbis and the Documents', in Goodman 1998: 167–79.

Cotton, Hannah M. (2009) 'The Continuity of Nabataean Law in the Petra Papyri: A Methodological Exercise', in Cotton, H. M., Hoyland, R. G., Price, J. J., and Wasserstein, D. J. (eds), *From Hellenism to Islam: Cultural and Linguistic Change in the Roman Near East*. Cambridge: Cambridge University Press, 154–74.

Cotton, Hannah M. and Greenfield, Jonas C. (1994) 'Babatha's Property and the Law of Succession in the Babatha Archive', *ZPE* 104: 211–24.

Cotton, Hannah M. and Greenfield, Jonas C. (1995) 'Babatha's *Patria*: Mahoza, Maḥoz 'Eglatain, and Zo'ar', *ZPE* 107: 126–34.

Cotton, Hannah M. and Yardeni, Ada (1997) *Discoveries in the Judaean Desert. Volume 27. Aramaic, Hebrew and Greek Documentary Texts from Naḥal Ḥever and Other Sites: With an Appendix Containing Alleged Qumran Texts (The Seiyal Collection II): Desert*. Oxford: Clarendon Press.

Cotton, Hannah M., Cockle, Walter E. H., and Millar, Fergus G. B. (1995) 'The Papyrology of the Roman Near East: A Survey', *JRS* 95: 214–35.

Cowley, A. (1923) *Aramaic Papyri of the Fifth Century B.C., Edited, with Translation and Notes*. Oxford: Clarendon Press.

Cronin, C. (1977) 'Illusion and Reality in Sicily', in A Schlegel (ed.), *Sexual Stratification: A Cross-Cultural View*. New York: Columbia University Press, 67–93.

Czajkowski, Kimberley (2017) *Localized Law: The Babatha and Salome Komaise Archives*. Oxford: Oxford University Press.

Dabrowa, E. (ed.) (1994) *The Roman and Byzantine Army in the East*. Kraków: Uniwersytet Jagiellonski.

Davis, Ellen F. (2009) *Scripture, Culture, and Agriculture: An Agrarian Reading of the Bible*. Cambridge: Cambridge University Press.

Decker, Stephanie (2013) 'The Silence of the Archives: Business History, Post-Colonialism and Archival Ethnography', *Management and Organizational History* 8: 155–73.

Decker, Stephanie (2014) 'Solid Intentions: An Archival Ethnography of Corporate Architecture and Organizational Remembering', *Organization* 21: 514–42.

Denzin, Norman K. (1997) *Interpretive Ethnography: Ethnographic Practices for the 21st Century*. Thousand Oaks, CA: Sage Publications.

De Romanis, Federico and Maiuro, Marco (2015) *Across the Ocean: Nine Essays on Indo-Mediterranean Trade*. Leiden: E. J. Brill.

Dilley, Roy (ed.) (1999) *The Problem of Context*. Methodology and History in Anthropology, Volume 4. New York and Oxford: Berghahn Books.

Dube, Saurabh (2010) 'Lost and Found: Villages between Anthropology and History', in Mines and Yazgi 2010a: 31–50.

Dube, Shyama Charan (1955) *Indian Village*. London: Routledge and Kegan Paul.

Ellis, Frank (1988) *Peasant Economics: Farm Households and Agrarian Development*. Cambridge: Cambridge University Press.

Enzel, Yehouda, Agnon, Amotz, and Stein, Mordechai (eds) (2006) *New Frontiers in Dead Sea Paleoenvironmental Research*. The Geological Society of America, Special Paper 431. Boulder, Co: The Geological Society of America.

Esler, Philip F. (1998) *Galatians*. New Testament Readings. London and New York: Routledge.

Esler, Philip F. (2009) 'Judean Ethnic Identity in Josephus' *Against Apion*', in Zuleika Rodgers with Margaret Daly-Denton and Ann Fitzpatrick McKinley (eds), *A Wandering Galilean: Essays in Honour of Sean Freyne*. Leiden: E. J. Brill, 73–91.

Esler, Philip F. (2011) *Sex, Wives, and Warriors: Reading Biblical Narrative with Its Ancient Audience*. Eugene, OR: Wipf & Stock.

Esler, Philip F. (2014) 'Reading Matthew by the Dead Sea: Matthew 8:5–13 in Light of P. Yadin 11', *HTS Theological Studies* 70.

Evans, Jane DeRose (1992) *The Art of Persuasion: Political Propaganda from Aeneas to Brutus*. Ann Arbor, MI: University of Michigan Press.

Fenske, Michaela (2007) 'Micro, Macro, Agency: Historical Ethnography as Cultural Anthropology Practice', *Journal of Folklore Research* 44: 67–99.

Firth, Raymond (1964) 'Capital, Savings and Credit in Peasant Societies: A Viewpoint from Economic Anthropology', in Firth and Yamey 1964: 15–34.

Firth, Raymond and Yamey, B. S. (eds) (1964) *Capital, Savings and Credit in Peasant Societies: Studies from Asia, Oceania, the Caribbean, and Middle America*. London and New York: Routledge.

Fitzmyer, Joseph A. (2008) *A Guide to the Dead Sea Scrolls and Related Literature. Revised and Expanded Edition*. Grand Rapids, MI: William B. Eerdmans.

Freeman, Philip (1996) 'The Annexation of Arabia and the Grand Imperial Strategy', in Kennedy 1996: 91–118.

Friedl, E. (1967) 'The Position of Women: Appearance and Reality', *Anthropological Quarterly* 40: 97–108.

Friesen, Steven J. (2004) 'Poverty in Pauline Studies: Beyond the So-Called New Consensus', *JSNT* 26: 323–61.

Galloway, Patricia (2006) *Practicing Ethnohistory: Mining Archives, Hearing Testimony, Constructing Narrative.* Lincoln, Nebraska and London: University of Nebraska Press.

Galor, Katharina, Humbert, Jean-Baptiste, and Zangenberg, Jürgen (eds) (2006) *Qumran, The Site of the Dead Sea Scrolls: Archaeological Interpretations and Debates.* Studies on the Texts of the Desert of Judah, Volume 57. Leiden: E. J. Brill, 213–19.

Gay y Blasco, Paloma and Wardle, Huon (2007) *How to Read Ethnography.* London and New York: Routledge.

Geer, Russel M. (1954) *Diodorus of Sicily, with an English Translation by Russel M. Geer.* In Twelve Volumes, Volume 10. Loeb Edition. London and Cambridge: William Heinemann Ltd and Harvard University Press.

Geertz, Clifford (1972) 'The Wet and the Dry: Traditional Irrigation in Bali and Morocco', *Human Ecology* 1: 23–39.

Geertz, Clifford (1973) *The Interpretation of Cultures.* New York: Basic Books.

Georgi, Laura (1982) 'Pollination Ecology of the Date Palm and Fig Tree: Herodotus 1.193.4–5', *Classical Philology* 77: 224–28.

Ginzburg, Carlo (1989) *Clues, Myths, and the Historical Method.* ET of 1986 Italian original by John and Anne C. Tedeschi. Baltimore, IL: Johns Hopkins University Press.

Goodman, M. D. (ed.) (1998) *Jews in a Graeco-Roman World.* Oxford: Clarendon Press.

Goody, Jack (1973) 'Bridewealth and Dowry in Africa and Eurasia', in Goody and Tambiah 1973: 1–58.

Goody, Jack and Tambiah, S. J. (1973) *Bridewealth and Dowry.* Cambridge Studies in Social Anthropology, 7. Cambridge: Cambridge University Press.

Gracy, Karen F. (2004) 'Documenting Communities of Practice: Making the Case for Archival Ethnography', *Archival Science* 4: 335–65.

Graeber, David (2011) *Debt: The First Thousand Years.* New York: Melville House Publishing.

Graf, David F. (1990) 'The Origin of the Nabataeans', *Aram* 2: 45–75.

Graf, David F. (1994) 'The Nabataean Army and the *Cohortes Ulpiae Petraeorum*', in Dabrowa 1994: 265–311; reprinted (with the same pagination) in Graf, David F. (1997) *Rome and the Arabian Frontier: From the Nabataean to the Saracens.* Aldershot: Ashgate.

Graf, David F. (2007) 'Nabataeans Under Roman Rule (After AD 106)', in Politis 2007: 173–86.

Granger-Taylor, H. (2006) 'Textiles from Khirbet Qazone and the Cave of Letters', in Schrenk 2006: 113–34.

Greenbaum, Noam, Ben-Zvi, Arie, Haviv, Itai, and Enzel, Yehouda (2006) 'The Hydrology and Paleohydrology of the Dead Sea Tributaries', in Enzel et al. 2006: 63–93.

Gross, Andrew D. (2008) *Continuity and Innovation in the Aramaic Legal Tradition.* Leiden: E. J. Brill.

Gross, Andrew D. (2013) 'The Aramaic Law of Sale from the Papyrological and Rabbinic Evidence' in Hagedorn and Kratz 2013: 129–64.

Hackl, Ursula, Jenni, Hanna, and Schneider, Christoph, with Keller, Daniel (2003) *Quellen zur Geschichte der Nabatäer. Textsammlung mit Übersetzung und Kommentar.* NTOA 51. Fribourg: Vandenhoeck & Rupprecht.

Hadas, G. (2012) 'Ancient Agricultural Irrigation Systems in the Oasis of Ein Gedi, Dead Sea, Israel', *Journal of Arid Environments* 86: 75–81.

Hadidi, A. A. (ed.) *Studies in the History and Archaeology of Jordan.* Volume 1. Jordan: Department of Antiquities.

Hagedorn, Anselm C. and Kratz, Reinhard G. (eds) (2013) *Law and Religion in the Eastern Mediterranean: From Antiquity to Early Islam.* Oxford: Oxford University Press.

Hall, Edith (1989) *Inventing the Barbarian: Greek Self-Definition Through Tragedy.* Oxford: Clarendon Press.

Hall, Jonathan M. (1997) *Ethnic Identity in Greek Antiquity.* Cambridge: Cambridge University Press.

Hallo, William H. and Younger, K. Lawson (eds) (2003) *Context of Scripture,* 2. Leiden: E. J. Brill.

Hammond, P. (1973) *The Nabataeans: Their History, Culture and Archaeology.* Sweden: Paul Astroms Forlag.

Hanson, Thor (2015) *The Triumph of Seeds: How Grains, Nuts, Kernels, Pulses, and Pips Conquered the Plant Kingdom and Shaped Human History.* New York: Basic Books.

Harlan, Michael (1995) *Roman Republican Moneyers and Their Coins 63 BC–49 BC.* Aspects of Ancient Classical Coins. London: Seaby.

Hartog, Francois (1988) *The Mirror of Herodotus: The Interpretation of the Other in the Writing of History.* ET of *Le miroir d'Hérodote*, translated by Janet Lloyd, 1980. Berkeley, CA: University of California Press.

Healey, John F. (1989) 'Were the Nabataeans Arabs?', *Aram* 1: 38–44.

Healey, John F. (1990–1991) 'Nabataean to Arabic: Calligraphy and Script Development Among the Pre-Islamic Arabs', *Manuscripts of the Middle East* 5: 41–52.

Healey, John F. (1993) *The Nabataean Tomb Inscriptions of Mada'in Salih. Journal of Semitic Studies,* Supp. 1. Oxford: Oxford University Press.

Healey, John F. (2001) *The Religion of the Nabataeans: A Conspectus.* Leiden: E. J. Brill.

Healey, John F. (2003) 'A Nabataean Funerary Inscription from Madaba', in Hallo and Younger 2003: 193.

Healey, John F. (2007) 'Nabataean Inscriptions: Language and Script', in Politis 2007: 45–52.

Healey, John F. (2009) *Aramaic Inscriptions and Documents from the Roman Period*. Textbook of Syrian Semitic Inscriptions, Volume IV. Oxford: Oxford University Press.

Healey, John F. (2013) 'Fines and Curses: Law and Religion among the Nabataeans and their Neighbours', in Hagedorn and Kratz 2013: 165–186.

Hegelund, Allan (2005) 'Objectivity and Subjectivity in Ethnographic Method', *Qualitative Health Research* 15: 647–68.

Helly, Dorothy O. and Reverby, Susan M. (eds) (1992) *Gendered Domains: Rethinking Public and Private in Women's History*. Ithaca, NY: Cornell University Press.

Henrich, J. and Gil-White, F. J. (2001) 'The Evolution of Prestige: Freely Conferred Deference as a Mechanism for Enhancing the Benefits of Cultural Transmission', *Evolution and Human Behavior* 22: 165–96.

Hirschfeld, Yizhar (ed.) (2007a) *En-Gedi Excavations II. Final Report (1996–2002)*. Jerusalem: Israel Exploration Society.

Hirschfeld, Yizhar (2007b) 'Introduction' in Hirschfeld 2007a: 1–22.

Hoftijzer, J. and Jongeling, K. (1995) *Dictionary of the North-West Semitic Inscriptions*. With appendices by R. C. Steiner, A. Mosak Moshavi, and B. Porten. Two volumes. *Handbuch der Orientalistik* 1/21. Leiden: E. J. Brill.

Hohfeld, Wesley Newcomb (1978) *Fundamental Legal Conceptions*, ed. Walter Wheeler Cook. Westport, Conn: Greenwood Press.

Holtz, Shalom E. (2014) *Neo-Babylonian Trial Records. Writings from the Ancient World*. Atlanta, GA: SBL.

Hopkins, David C. (2007) '"All Sorts of Work": Agricultural Labour in Ancient Palestine', in Coote and Gottwald 2007: 149–72.

Hort, Sir Arthur (1916) *Theophrastus: Enquiry into Plants. Volume 1*. Loeb Edition. London and New York: William Heinemann and G. P. Putnam's Sons.

Hutchinson, John and Smith, Anthony (eds) (1996a) *Ethnicity*. Oxford: Oxford University Press.

Hutchinson, John and Smith, Anthony (1996b) 'Introduction', in Hutchinson and Smith 1996a: 3–14.

Ibn Khaldun, 'Abd al-Rahman (1961) *Al-Muqaddima*. Beirut: Darab-Kitâb al-Lubnani.

Ilan, Tal (2002) *Lexicon of Jewish Names in Late Antiquity: Part I: Palestine 330 BCE–200 CE*. Texts and Studies in Ancient Judaism, 91. Tübingen: Mohr Siebeck.

Ingholt, Harald (1976) 'Varia Tadmorea', in *Palmyre, bilan et perspectives (Colloque de Strasbourg [18–20 octobre 1973] à la mémoire de Daniel Schlumberger et Henri Seyrig)*. Travaux du Centre de recherche sur le Proche-Orient et la Grece antiques. Strasbourg: AECR, 101–37.

Ingold, Tim (2008) 'Anthropology is *Not* Ethnography', The Radcliffe-Brown Lecture in Social Anthropology at the British Academy, *Proceedings of the British Academy* 154: 69–92.

Ingold, Tim (2014) 'Forum: That's Enough About Ethnography', *HAU: Journal of Ethnographic Theory* 4: 383–95.

Invernizzi, A. and Salles, J. F. (eds) (1993) *Arabia Antiqua: Hellenistic Centres Around Arabia.* Rome: Is. M. E. O.

Jaussen, A. and Savignac, R. (1909) *Mission archéologique en Arabie.* Volume 1. Paris: E. Leroux.

Jones, Horace Leonard (1930) *Strabo, Geography, Books 15–16, with an English Translation by Horace Leonard Jones.* Loeb Edition. Cambridge, MT and London: Harvard University Press.

Kartzow, Marianne Bjelland (2009) *Gossip and Gender: Othering of Speech in the Pastoral Epistles.* Berlin and New York: Walter de Gruyter.

Katzoff, Ranon and Schaps, David (eds) (2005) *Law in the Documents of the Judaean Desert.* Leiden: E. J. Brill.

Kelly, William W. (1983) 'Concepts in the Anthropological Study of Irrigation', *American Anthropologist* 85: 880–86.

Kennedy, David L. (ed.) (1996) *The Roman Army in the East.* Journal of Roman Archaeology Supp. Series, 18. Ann Arbor, MI.

King, Diane E. (2013) *Kurdistan on the Global Stage: Kinship, Land and Community in Iraq.* New Brunswick: Rutgers University Press.

Kirch, Patrick V. (1992) *The Archaeology of History, Volume Two,* in his work co-written with Marshall Sahlins: *Anahulu: The Anthropology of History in the Kingdom of Hawaii.* Chicago and London: The University of Chicago Press.

Klein, S. (1929) 'לחקר השמות והכינויים', *Leshonenu* 1: 325–50.

Kloppenborg, John S. (2006) *The Tenants in the Vineyard: Ideology, Economics, and Agrarian Conflict in Jewish Palestine.* WUNT 195. Tübingen: Mohr Siebeck.

Koffmahn, Elisabeth (1968) *Die Doppelurkunden aus der Wüste Juda.* Studies on the Texts of the Judean Desert, 5. Leiden: E. J. Brill.

Kolb, Bernhard (2007) 'Nabataean Dwellings: Domestic Architecture and Interior Decoration', in Politis 2007: 145–72.

Kraeling, Emil G. (1953) *The Brooklyn Museum Aramaic Papyri: New Documents of the Fifth Century* B.C. *From the Jewish Colony of Elephantine.* New Haven: Yale University Press.

Latour, Bruno (2004) 'Why Has Critique Run Out of Steam? From Matters of Fact to Matters of Concern', *Critical Inquiry* 30: 225–48.

Lee, R. W. (1956) *The Elements of Roman Law, with a Translation of the Institutes of Justinian.* Fourth edition. London: Sweet & Maxwell.

Lennartsson, Rebecka (2011) 'Notes on "Not Being There": Ethnographic Excursions in Eighteenth-Century Stockholm', *Ethnologia Europaea* 42: 105–14.

Lennartsson, Rebecka (2012) 'Archival Ethnography: Reflections on a Lost Note', *Historische Anthropologie.* Accessed at: <http://edoc.hu-berlin.de/histfor/14/PHP/Beitraege_14-2012.php>.

Le Roy Ladurie, Emmanuel (1980) *Montaillou: Cathars and Catholics in a French Village 1294–1324*. ET of 1978 French original by Barbara Bray. Harmondsworth: Penguin.

Levick, B. (1982) 'Propaganda and the Imperial Coinage', *Antichthon* 16: 104–16.

Levine, Baruch A. (2000) 'The Various Workings of the Aramaic Legal Tradition: Jews and Nabateans in the Naḥal Ḥever Archive', in Schiffman et al. 2000: 836–57.

Lewis, Naphtali (1989) *The Documents from the Bar Kokhba Period in the Cave of Letters: Greek Papyri and Aramaic and Nabatean Signatures and Subscriptions*. Jerusalem: Israel Exploration Society, The Hebrew University of Jerusalem and the Shrine of the Book. (Note that Lewis was alone responsible for the Greek papyri, and Yigael Yadin and Jonas C. Greenfield for the Aramaic signatures and subscriptions.)

Littmann, E. (1913) 'Semitic Inscriptions', in *Syria. Publications of the Princeton Archaeological Expeditions to Syria* (Div. IV, Sect. A, Leyden). Leiden: E. J. Brill, 1–93.

Lofland, John and Lofland, Lyn H. (1995) *Analyzing Social Settings: A Guide to Qualitative Observation and Analysis*. Third edition. Belmont, CA: Wadsworth.

Longenecker, Bruce (2010) *Remember the Poor: Paul, Poverty and the Greco-Roman World*. Grand Rapids, MI: William B. Eerdmans.

Macdonald, M. C. A. (1999) '*Personal Names in the Nabataean Realm*: A Review Article', *Journal of Semitic Studies* 44: 251–89.

Maine, Henry Sumner (1930) *Ancient Law: Its Connection with the Early History of the Family, and Its Relation to Modern Ideas*, ed. Frederick Pollock. London: Oxford University Press.

Malina, Bruce J. (1996) 'Mediterranean Sacrifice: Dimensions of Domestic and Political Religion', *Biblical Theology Bulletin* 26: 26–44.

Malina, Bruce J. (2001) *The New Testament World: Insights from Cultural Anthropology*. Third edition. Louisville, KY: Westminster John Knox Press.

Maresch, K. and Packman, Z. M. (eds) (1990) *Papyri from the Washington University Library Collection, Part 2*. Papyrologica Coloniensia 18. Opladen: Westdeutscher Verlag GmbH.

Meggitt, Justin (1998) *Paul, Poverty and Survival*. Studies of the New Testament and Its World. Edinburgh: T. and T. Clark International.

Meshorer, Yaakov (1975) *Nabataean Coins*. Qedem 3. Monographs of the Institute of Archaeology. Jerusalem: Hebrew University of Jerusalem.

Meyers, Carol (1999) '"Women of the Neighborhood" (Ruth 4.17): Informal Female Networks in Ancient Israel', in Brenner 1999: 110–27.

Meyers, Carol (2013) *Rediscovering Eve: Ancient Israelite Women in Context*. Oxford: Oxford University Press.

Michael, Barbara (1997) 'Female Heads of Patriarchal Households: The Baggara', *Journal of Comparative Family Studies* 28: 170–82.

Milik, J. T. (1982) 'Origines des Nabatéens', in Amman A. Hadidi (ed.) *Studies in the History and Archaeology of Jordan*. Volume 1. Amman, Jordan: Department of Antiquities, 261–65.

Miller, J. Innes (1969) *The Spice Trade of the Roman Empire: 29 B.C. to A.D. 641*. Oxford: Clarendon Press.

Millett, Paul (1991) *Lending and Borrowing in Ancient Athens*. Cambridge: Cambridge University Press.

Mines, Diane P. and Yazgi, Nicolas (eds) (2010a) *Village Matters: Relocating Villages in the Contemporary Anthropology of India*. New Delhi: Oxford University Press.

Mines, Diane P. and Yazgi, Nicolas (2010b) 'Introduction: Do Villages Matter?', in Mines and Yazgi 2010a: 1–28.

Mosse, David (2008) 'Epilogue: The Cultural Politics of Water—A Comparative Study', *Journal of Southern African Studies* 34: 939–48.

Muffs, Y. (1969 [2003]) *Studies in the Aramaic Legal Papyri from Elephantine*. Studia et Documenta ad Iura Orientis Antiqui Pertinentia, 8. Leiden: E. J. Brill.

Naveh, Joseph (1990) 'Nameless People', *Israel Exploration Journal* 40: 108–123.

Negev, Avraham (1991) *Personal Names in the Nabataean Realm*. Qedem 32. Monographs of the Institute of Archaeology. Jerusalem: Hebrew University of Jerusalem.

Nehmé, Laia (2015) '*Strategoi* in the Nabataean Kingdom: A Reflection of Central Places?', *Arabian Epigraphic Notes* 1: 103-22.

Nelson, C. (ed.) (1973) *The Desert and the Sown*. Berkeley, CA: Institute of International Studies.

Nesson, C., Rouvillois-Brigol, M., and Vallet, J. (1973) *Oasis du Sahara algérien*. Paris: Institute Géographique.

Nicholas, Barry (1962) *An Introduction to Roman Law*. Oxford: Clarendon Press.

Nolan, Patrick and Lenski, Gerhard (2014) *Human Societies: An Introduction to Macrosociology*. Twelfth edition. New York: Oxford University Press.

Oakes, Peter (2004) 'Constructing Poverty Scales for Graeco-Roman Society: A Response to Steven Friesen's "Poverty in Pauline Studies"', *JSNT* 26: 367–71.

Oakes, Peter (2009) *Reading Romans in Pompeii. Paul's Letter at Ground Level*. London: SPCK.

Okely, Judith and Callaway, Helen (eds) (1992) *Anthropology and Autobiography*. ASA Monographs 29. London and New York: Routledge.

Oldfather, C. H. (1935) *Diodorus of Sicily, with an English Translation by C. H. Oldfather*. In ten volumes, Volume II. Loeb Edition. London and Cambridge: William Heinemann Ltd and Harvard University Press.

Oleson, John P. (2007) 'Water Supply, Irrigation and Agriculture', in Politis 2007: 217–50.

Oudshoorn, Jacobine G. (2007) *The Relationship between Roman and Local Law in the Babatha and Salome Komaise Archives: General Analysis and Three Case Studies on Law of Succession, Guardianship and Marriage.* Studies on the Texts of the Desert of Judah, 69. Leiden: E. J. Brill.

Parkin, Robert and Stone, Linda (eds) (2004) *Kinship and Family: An Anthropological Reader.* Oxford: Blackwell.

Pilch, John J. (ed.) (2001) *Social Scientific Models for Interpreting the Bible: Essays by the Context Group in Honor of Bruce J. Malina.* Leiden: E. J. Brill.

Politis, Konstantinos D. (2006) 'The Discovery and Excavation of the Khirbet Qazone Cemetery and Its Significance Relative to Qumran', in Galor et al. 2006: 213–22.

Politis, Konstantinos D. (ed.) (2007) *The World of the Nabataeans: Volume 2 of the International Conference The World of the Herods and the Nabataeans held at the British Museum, 17–19 April 2001.* Stuttgart: Franz Steiner Verlag.

Popenoe, Paul B. and Charles L. Bennett (1913) *Date Growing in the Old World and the New.* (Bennett contributed chapter XV on the food value of the date). Los Angeles: George Rice & Sons.

Porten, Bezalel (1968) *Archives from Elephantine: The Life of an Ancient Jewish Military Colony.* Berkeley, CA: University of California Press.

Porten, Bezalel and Yardeni, Ada (1986–1999) *Textbook of Aramaic Documents from Ancient Egypt.* Jerusalem: The Hebrew University.

Premnath, D. N. (2007) 'Loan Practices in the Hebrew Bible', in Coote and Gottwald 2007: 173–85.

Quinn, N. (1977) 'Anthropological Studies on Women's Status', *Annual Review of Anthropology* 6: 181–225.

Radner, Karen (2001) 'Neo-Assyrian Period', in Westbrook and Jasnow 2001: 265–88.

Rogers, Susan Carol (1975) 'Female Forms of Power and the Myth of Male Dominance: A Model of Female/Male Interaction in Peasant Society', *American Ethnologist* 2: 727–56.

Rohrbaugh, Richard L. (2001) 'Gossip in the New Testament', in Pilch 2001: 239–59.

Rosaldo, Michelle Zimbalist (1974) 'Women, Culture, and Society: A Theoretical Overview', in Rosaldo and Lamphere 1974: 17–42.

Rosaldo, Michelle Zimbalist and Lamphere, Louise (eds) (1974) *Women, Culture, and Society.* Stanford, CA: Stanford University Press.

Rosaldo, Renato (1980) *Ilongot Headhunting: 1883–1974: A Study in Society and History.* Stanford, CA: Stanford University Press.

Rosaldo, Renato (1993) *Culture and Truth: The Remaking of Social Analysis: With a New Introduction.* Boston, Mass: Beacon Press.

Rosen, Steven A. (2007) 'The Nabateans as Pastoral Nomads: An Archaeological Perspective', in Politis 2007: 345–72.

Rowlandson, J. (1996) *Landowners and Tenants in Roman Egypt: The Social Relations of Agriculture in the Oxyrhynchite Nome*. Oxford Classical Monographs. Oxford: Clarendon Press.

Sahlins, Marshall (1992) *Historical Ethnography, Volume One* in his work co-written with Patrick V. Kirch: *Anahulu: The Anthropology of History in the Kingdom of Hawaii*. Chicago and London: The University of Chicago Press.

Sangren, P. Steven (1988) 'Rhetoric and the Authority of Ethnography: "Postmodernism" and the Social Reproduction of Texts', *Current Anthropology* 29: 405–35.

Sartre, Maurice (2005) *The Middle East Under Rome*. ET by Catherine Porter and Elizabeth Rawlings. Harvard: Harvard University Press.

Satlow, Michael L. (2001) *Jewish Marriage in Antiquity*. Princeton, NJ: Princeton University Press.

Satlow, Michael L. (2005) 'Marriage Payments and Succession Strategies in the Documents from the Judean Desert', in Katsoff and Shaps 2005: 51–65.

Schams, Christine (1998) *Jewish Scribes in the Second-Temple Period*. JSOT Supp. Series, 291. Sheffield: Sheffield Academic Press.

Scheidel, Walter and Friesen, Steven J. (2009) 'The Size of the Economy and the Distribution of Income in the Roman Empire', *JRS* 99: 61–91.

Schiffmann, Lawrence H., Tov, Emanuel, and VanderKam, James C., (eds) (2000) *The Dead Sea Scrolls Fifty Years After Their Discovery: Proceedings of the Jerusalem Conference, July 20–25, 1997*. Jerusalem: Israel Exploration Society and the Shrine of the Book.

Schmitt-Korte, Karl (1990) 'Nabataean Coinage—Part II. New Coin Types and Variants', *The Numismatic Chronicle* 150: 105–33.

Schrenk, Sabine (ed.) (2006) *Textiles in Situ: Their Find Spots in Egypt and Neighbouring Countries in the First Millennium* CE. Riggisberger Berichte 13. Riggisberg: Abegg-Stiftung.

Schwartz, Daniel R. (2014) *Judeans and Jews: Four Faces of Dichotomy in Ancient Jewish History*. Toronto: University of Toronto Press.

Sharistanian, Janet (ed.) (1987) *Beyond the Public/Domestic Dichotomy: Contemporary Perspectives on Women's Public Lives*. Contributions to Women's Studies, 78. Westport, CT: Greenwood Press.

Sidky, Homayun (2003) *A Critique of Postmodern Anthropology—In Defense of Disciplinary Origins and Traditions*. Lewiston, NY: Edwin Mellen.

Skinner, J. (2012) *The Invention of Greek Ethnography: From Homer to Herodotus*. New York: Oxford University Press.

Smith, William Cantwell (1991 [1962]) *The Meaning and End of Religion*. Minneapolis, MN: Fortress.

Spencer, Jonathan (1989) 'Anthropology as a Kind of Writing', *Man* n.s. 24: 145–64.

Starcky, J. (1954) 'Un contrat nabatéen sur papyrus', *Revue Biblique* 61: 161–81.

Stern, Menaḥem (ed.) (1974, 1980, and 1984) *Greek and Latin Authors on Jews and Judaism*. Three volumes. Jerusalem: The Israel Academy of Sciences and Humanities.

Stoler, Ann Laura (2009) *Along the Archival Grain: Epistemic Anxieties and Colonial Common Sense*. Urbana, IL: University of Illinois Press.

Stoller, Paul (2015) 'In Defence of Ethnography', The Huffington Post, 24 August 2015. Accessed at: <http://www.huffingtonpost.com/paul-stoller/in-defense-of-ethnography_b_8028542.html>.

Stone, Laurence (1979) 'The Revival of Narrative: Reflections on a New Old History', *Past and Present* 85: 3–24.

Studer, Jacqueline (2007) 'Animal Exploitation in the Nabataean World', in Politis 2007: 251–72.

Sydenham, E. A. (1952) *The Coinage of the Roman Republic*. London: Spink.

Tajfel, Henri (ed.) (1978a) *Differentiation between Social Groups: Studies in the Social Psychology of Intergroup Relations*. European Monographs in Social Psychology. London: Academic Press.

Tajfel, Henri (1978b) 'Introduction', in Tajfel 1978a: 1–23.

Tajfel, Henri, Billig, M. G., Bundy, R. P., and Flamment, Claude (1971) 'Social Categorization and Intergroup Behaviour', *European Journal of Social Psychology* 1: 149–78.

Taylor, Jane (2002) *Petra and the Lost Kingdom of the Nabataeans*. London and New York: I. B. Tauris.

Taylor, Joan (2012) *The Essenes, the Scrolls, and the Dead Sea*. Oxford: Oxford University Press.

Tengberg, Margareta (2012) 'Beginnings and Early History of Date Palm Garden Cultivation in the Middle East', *Journal of Arid Environments* 86: 139–47.

Terpstra, Taco (2015) 'Roman Trade with the Far East: Evidence for Nabataean Middlemen in Puteoli', in De Romanis and Maiuro 2015: 73–94.

Thomas, W. I. and F. Znaniecki, F. (1918–1920) *The Polish Peasant in Europe and America: Monograph of an Immigrant Group*. Five volumes. Chicago, IL: University of Chicago Press.

Toren, Christina, and de Pina-Cabral, João (eds) (2011) *The Challenge of Epistemology: Anthropological Perspectives*. New York: Berghahn.

Ul-Hak, Asrar (1998) *Case Study of the Punjab Irrigation Department: Consultancy Report*. Lahore: International Irrigation Management Institute, available at: <http://publications.iwmi.org/pdf/H_30079i.pdf>.

Wade, Andrew, Manley, Ron, Black, Emily, Guest, Joshua, Al Nuimat, Sameeh, and Jamjoum, Khalil (2011) 'Future Projections of Water

Availability In a Semi-Arid Region of the Eastern Mediterranean: A Case Study of Wadi Hasa, Jordan', in Mithren, Steven and Black, Emily (eds) (2011) *Water, Life and Civilization: Climate, Environment and Society in the Jordan Valley*. Cambridge: Cambridge University Press, 175–188.

Walker, Susan (1985) *Memorials to the Roman Dead*. London: British Museum Press.

Walter, Heinrich and Breckle, Siegmar-W. (1986) *Ecological Systems of the Geobiosphere: 2 Tropical and Subtropical Zonobiomes*. Berlin: Springer Verlag.

Wenning, Robert (1987) *Die Nabatäer—Denkmäler und Geschichte: Eine Bestandesaufnahme des archäologischen Befundes*. Novum Testamentum et Orbis Antiquus, 3. Göttingen: Vandenhoeck & Ruprecht.

Wenning, Robert (1993a) 'Eine neuerstellte Liste der nabatäischen Dynastie', *Boreas* 16: 25–38.

Wenning, Robert (1993b) 'Das Ende des nabatäischen Königreichs', in Invernizzi and Salles 1993: 81–103.

Wenning, Robert (2007) 'The Nabataens in History (Before AD 106)', in Politis 2007: 25–44.

Westbrook, Raymond and Jasnow, Richard (eds) (2001) *Security for Debt in Ancient Near Eastern Law*. Culture and History of the Ancient Near East. Leiden: E. J. Brill.

Wolcott, Harry F. (1999) *Ethnography: A Way of Seeing*. Walnut Creek, CA: Alta Mira Press.

Wolf, Eric (1966) *Peasants*. Foundations of Modern Anthropology Series. Englewood Cliffs, NJ: Prentice-Hall Inc.

Woolf, Greg (2013) 'Ethnography and the Gods in Tacitus' *Germania*', in Almagor and Skinner 2013: 133–52.

Wuthnow, H. (1930) *Die semitischen Menschennamen in griechischen Inschriften und Papyri des vorderen Orients*. Leipzig: Dieterich'sche Verlagsbuchhandlung.

Yadin, Yigael (1962) 'The Expedition to the Judean Desert, 1961: Expedition D—The Cave of the Letters', *Israel Exploration Journal* 12: 227–57.

Yadin, Yigael (1963) *The Finds from the Bar Kokhba Period in the Cave of Letters. (Judean Desert Studies)*. Jerusalem: The Israel Exploration Society.

Yadin, Yigael (1971) *Bar-Kokhba: The Rediscovery of the Legendary Hero of the Last Jewish Revolt against Imperial Rome*. London: Weidenfeld and Nicolson.

Yadin, Yigael (2002) *The Documents from the Bar Kokhba Period in the Cave of Letters: Hebrew, Aramaic and Nabatean-Aramaic Papyri* (Plates). Judean Desert Studies. Jerusalem: Israel Exploration Society, Institute of Archaeology, Hebrew University and the Shrine of the Book, Israel Museum.

Yadin, Yigael, Greenfield, Jonas C., Yardeni, Ada, and Levine, Baruch A. (eds) (2002) *The Documents from the Bar Kokhba Period in the Cave of*

Letters: Hebrew, Aramaic and Nabatean-Aramaic Papyri. Judean Desert Studies. Jerusalem: Israel Exploration Society, Institute of Archaeology, Hebrew University and the Shrine of the Book, Israel Museum.

Yardeni, Ada (2000a) *Textbook of Aramaic, Hebrew and Nabataean Texts from the Judaean Desert and Related Material. A: The Documents (in Hebrew)*. Jerusalem: Hebrew University, Ben-Zion Dinur Center of Research in Jewish History.

Yardeni, Ada (2000b) *Textbook of Aramaic, Hebrew and Nabataean Texts from the Judaean Desert and Related Material. B: Translation, Paleography, Concordance (in Hebrew and English)*. Jerusalem: Hebrew University, Ben-Zion Dinur Center of Research in Jewish History.

Yardeni, Ada (2001) 'The Decipherment and Restoration of Legal Texts from the Judaean Desert: A Reexamination of *Papyrus Starcky (P. Yadin 36)*', *Scripta Classica Israelica* 20: 121–37.

Yaron, Reuven (1961) *Introduction to the Law of the Aramaic Papyri*. Oxford: Clarendon Press.

Zulueta, Francis de (1953) *The Institutes of Gaius. Part II. Commentary*. Oxford: Clarendon Press.

Author Index

Subject Index

The manufacturer's authorised representative in the EU for product safety is Oxford University Press España S.A. of el Parque Empresarial San Fernando de Henares, Avenida de Castilla, 2 – 28830 Madrid (www.oup.es/en or product.safety@oup.com). OUP España S.A. also acts as importer into Spain of products made by the manufacturer.

www.ingramcontent.com/pod-product-compliance
Lightning Source LLC
Chambersburg PA
CBHW071250180926
51613CB00001B/2
* 9 7 8 0 1 9 8 7 6 7 1 6 9 *